The Mountain Biker's Guide to
COLORADO

Featuring Over 150 of the State's Best Rides

WARNING:

Mountain biking is a sport with inherent danger, which may result in severe injury or death. Read and understand this warning before using this book. This book is not intended to serve as an instructional manual and should not take the place of proper instruction. Employ a professional guide or instructor if you are unsure of your ability to handle any circumstances that may arise. The information contained within this book is a compilation of opinions and as such, is unverified. These opinions are neither facts nor promises and should not be treated as so. Rely first and foremost upon your skill, experience, conditions, and common sense rather than the opinions expressed in this book including descriptions and difficulty ratings, as they are all entirely subjective. If you are unwilling to assume complete responsibility for your safety, and if you (or your estate) is unwilling to never try to sue Fixed Pin Publishing if you get hurt or killed, do not use this guidebook.

Errors may exist in this book as a result of the author and/or the people with whom they consulted. Because the information was gathered from a multitude of sources, they may not have been independently verified and therefore **the publisher, or the authors, cannot guarantee the correctness of any of the information contained within this guidebook.**

THE AUTHORS AND PUBLISHER EXPRESSLY DISCLAIM ANY REPRESENTATIONS AND WARRANTIES REGARDING THIS GUIDE. THEY MAKE NO REPRESENTATIONS OR WARRANTIES, EXPRESSED OR IMPLIED, OF ANY KIND REGARDING THE ACCURACY OR RELIABILITY OF THE CONTENT OF THIS BOOK. THERE ARE NO WARRANTIES OF MERCHANTABILITY OR FITNESS FOR A PARTICULAR PURPOSE. THE USER ASSUMES ALL RISK ASSOCIATED WITH THE USE OF THIS BOOK AND ALL ACTIVITIES CONTAINED WITHIN IT, ESPECIALLY MOUNTAIN BIKING.

The Mountain Biker's Guide to Colorado

Author: Dan Hickstein
Photography: Dan Hickstein unless otherwise credited.
Cartography: Mike Boruta
Cover photo: Heather McDowell enjoys the beautiful Dyke Trail, p236   photo: Fredrik Marmsater
Opening page photo: Jame Curran rips through the trees at Walker Ranch, p58.   photo: Greg Mionske

International Standard Book Number:
ISBN 978-0-9819016-5-7

Library of Congress Catalog in Publication Data:
Library of Congress Control Number: 2011942935

Fixed Pin Publishing is continually expanding its guidebooks and loves to hear from locals about their home areas. If you have an idea for a book or a manuscript for a guide, or would like to find out more about our company, contact:

Jason Haas
Fixed Pin Publishing
P.O. Box 3481
Boulder, CO 80307
jason@fixedpin.com

Ben Schneider
Fixed Pin Publishing
P.O. Box 3481
Boulder, CO 80307
ben@fixedpin.com

Acknowledgements

I would like to offer my deepest thanks to the following people for their assistance during the writing of this guidebook.

My parents, Dennis and Mary, for their love and support.

Laura Johnson, Katie Johnson, Curt Stevens, and Daisy Johnson for their wonderful company both on and off the trail.

Professors Henry Kapteyn and Margaret Murnane, my incredible PhD advisors who let me take a year of sabbatical to carry out the research for this guidebook.

Jason Haas and Ben Schneider, for making this book a reality.

Mike Boruta, for his incredible maps.

Jason Vogel and the Boulder Mountain Bike Alliance for assistance with the Boulder chapter, Jason Bertolacci and COMBA for assistance with the Denver chapter, and Lisa Shafer and Routt County Riders for assistance with the Steamboat chapter. Huge thanks to them all for building, maintaining, and defending our trails.

Stefan Griebel, Kristin Butcher, and Joel Gratz for their wonderful essays.

Brandon Turman, Fred Marmsater, Greg Mionske, Brandon J. Doza, Yann Ropars, Greg Younger, Scott Morris, Curt Stevens, Dan Steuer, Xavier Torrents, Chris Nowak, Mike Barrow, Mitchell Sprinsky, Theodore B. Van Orman, Steve Zdawczynski, Paula Jo Jaconetta, and Nathan Pulley for their fantastic photographs.

Jordan "Captain Guidebook" Hill for sharing his expertise.

Ben Beezly for his assistance editing the text.

Finally, "big ups" to Jordan Kunz, Josh Stahl, Thayne Dickey, Ely Porter, Cole Fennel, Craig Belgard, and Andrew McDavid.

UNITED STATES

COLORADO

Area of Detail

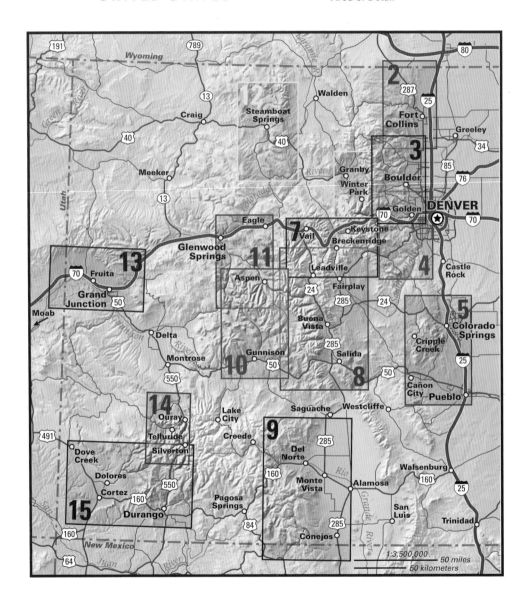

Colorado – The Mountain Biker's Paradise

Nothing compares to the simple pleasure of a bike ride. — *John F. Kennedy*

Colorado puts the "mountain" back in mountain biking, offering routes up towering peaks, singletrack traverses along ridgelines at 12,000 feet, and glimpses of elk, moose, and bear. There are plenty of civilized trails as well, providing riders the opportunity to cruise alongside turquoise lakes (see page 198), romp through alpine meadows (see chapters 6 though 12), and glide through picturesque prairie grasslands (see chapters 2 through 4). There is a trail for every season and every rider.

This introduction contains tips on where to ride, when to ride, and what kind of bike to sit on while doing so. Most importantly, there is the "How to Use This Book" section, which explains how the rides are rated for quality, as well as physical and technical difficulty. Riders should be sure to read this section before setting out on an adventure in order to ensure that their idea of a "black diamond trail" is the same that is used in this book.

Disclaimer

Mountains are not fair or unfair, they are just dangerous. — *Reinhold Messner*

Those who have ridden a mountain bike know this: mountain biking is inherently dangerous. Hitting a tree, flipping over the handlebars, and smashing a pedal into a shin are all part of a good day on the trail. Additionally, rockfall, flash floods, binge consumption of granola bars, and heat stroke all pose serious risks to the wellbeing of a mountain biker. This book will not keep you safe on the trail. In fact, by providing gripping descriptions that encourage you to explore new and unfamiliar trails, it might indirectly lead to your untimely demise. Use your judgment, ride with friends, walk your bike through dangerous sections, and live to ride another day.

The author suddenly realizes he had more speed than this corner would allow.

When to Ride

May your trails be crooked, winding, lonesome, dangerous, leading to the most amazing view. May your mountains rise into and above the clouds. — *Edward Abbey*

Colorado is a land for all seasons, and there are almost always rideable trails somewhere in the state, no matter the season. During the middle of summer, riders flock to the high country for incredible alpine singletrack near Crested Butte, Steamboat Springs, Winter Park, Durango, Summit County, Vail, Aspen, and Telluride. When the high elevation trails become covered in snow in the autumn, the excellent lower-elevation riding in Fruita, Grand Junction, Durango, Boulder, Denver, Colorado Springs, and Fort Collins is in it's prime. During the coldest part of the winter, in January and February, most people trade bikes for skis. However, there are many trails along the Front Range – most notably Lake Pueblo State Park – that can be ridden during sunny periods in the winter. Low elevation trails start to melt out in late March, and by late June most of the high elevation riding is dry.

Colorado weather changes rapidly and it's possible to encounter muddy conditions during any month of the year. Riding on muddy trails damages them, as well as trashing bike components. Avoid riding when the trails are wet. In the winter, it is often possible to get an early start and ride when the trails are still frozen – an experience that is sometimes closer to skiing than to biking.

Choosing what time of day to ride is also an important consideration. The temperature in Colorado routinely changes 30°F between day and night. So, by riding early in the morning or near sunset, it is possible to ride comfortably even when the mid-day temperatures soar into the 90s. For high alpine rides, the threat of thunderstorms dictates an early start. It is standard practice to avoid peaks and ridges above treeline after twelve-noon and to descend at the first sight of large clouds.

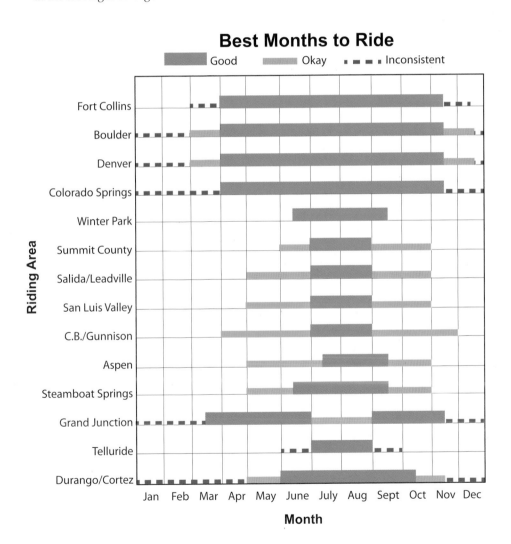

Introduction

Weather Secrets for Colorado Mountain Bikers   *by Joel Gratz*

The best way to approach backcountry weather is to be like the TV character MacGyver: have a plan, but be ready to change it up on the fly if the Russians unexpectedly show up. Here's your crash course on Colorado weather, and a step-by-step checklist to help you quickly plan your ride.

The Seasons

The months of April and May can be very muddy in the mountains, and alternate between dry and wet conditions at the lower elevations.

- June begins to dry out in the mountains, but heavier rain can occur any day along the front range foothills and urban areas.
- July and August is the "monsoon" season, when juicy air invades Colorado from the south and causes many thunderstorms over the mountains.
- In September, temperatures begin to cool, and the skies are sunny most days. Until the snow starts flying (anytime from late September through early November), the autumn months feature some of the sunniest, driest, most comfortable riding conditions of the entire year.

Watch Out

The four most important weather conditions to consider when planning your ride are lightning, rain (and snow, which falls even in the summer), temperatures, and winds. While the other conditions can make riding unpleasant, lightning can end your life in a nanosecond, so this is the most important consideration.

Lightning is to be avoided, period. While some people might brag about being out in a lightning storm many times without incident, it only takes one random strike to change that story for the worst. If I sound like I'm trying to make you paranoid of lightning – good, that's the point. In 2009, myself and another friend made some bad decisions and were caught in the middle of a large, flat, treeless field with continuous lightning striking within one quarter of a mile. The strikes were so close that the lightning flash and the thunder seemed to happen simultaneously. I dreaded the possible headline in the following day's newspaper: "Local meteorologist struck and killed by lightning." We were lucky and weren't struck, but I'll emphasize the word "lucky." Here are some tips to stay safe:

- The only safe place from lightning is in a solid, enclosed structure such as a house or car. So plan your ride before thunderstorms pop up and get back to your car or house before the first strike. An open-walled pavilion or other out-building does not provide a safe shelter from lightning.

- If you are caught on the trail above treeline or in an open field and can't get into a forest of trees, find the lowest spot, get off your bike, move well away from it, and crouch down so only the balls of your feet are touching the ground. If you are riding with other people, make sure to move 100–200 feet away from each other. If lightning does strike a member of your group, at least the others will be far enough away to avoid being struck. If the entire group is together and gets struck, everyone might be knocked out and there will be nobody to provide medical attention.

- If you are in a forest, find a low area among dense but small trees and wait for the lightning to pass.

- When should you seek shelter? Find a safe place when lightning is within six miles (less than 30 seconds between seeing lightning and hearing thunder). For each 5 seconds you count between seeing lightning and hearing thunder, the lightning strike is about one mile away.

- Technically you should wait 30 minutes after your hear the last clap of thunder to leave your "safe" area, but if you can tell the storm is quickly moving away, you can get back after it a little sooner than this conservative guideline.

Step-by-step plan

1. **A day or two before your ride, look at the weather forecast.** While many times individual days will be similar (i.e. both Saturday and Sunday have a 30% chance of thunderstorms), sometimes you'll find one day to be far better than another, and can plan your ride accordingly.

   Use the National Weather Service "point" forecast. A chance of storms from 10-20% is rather low – don't worry about it too much. Chances from 30-50% are substantial, so definitely have an alternate plan just in case. Greater than a 50% chance of storms is basically saying, "we're pretty sure there will be a storm," so perhaps you should attempt a shorter ride or get out early in the morning before storms pop up.

   Go here for the government forecast: http://www.nws.noaa.gov. Enter the closest city and state in the upper-left corner, and get the forecast. *Hint: when you're on the forecast page, there is a terrain map in the lower right. Use the map to click on the "point" that you're actually going to ride, like a hillside a few miles out of the town you entered. This will give you a more detailed forecast for your elevation.*

   FInally, check out my website: www.chanceofweather.com. I try to make the weather simple by giving you more usable information, like "What time will the first lightning strike hit?"

2. **Just before your ride, look at the weather forecast again, and check the radar.** By looking at current radar, you might be able to tell if there is a big thunderstorm (i.e., a red blob on radar) heading toward the trail.

   Access the radar image from the same National Weather Service forecast page I talked about in Step #1. The radar link is just above the "point-and-click" map.

3. **Evaluate the weather as you ride.** Flat clouds are good – it's likely that they won't form into thunderstorms. Tall, hard-edged puffy clouds with dark bottoms are bad – they are likely to form a thunderstorm.

Flat clouds (right) are fine. Tall clouds with dark bottoms (left) are more likely to form a thunderstorm!

Have fun out there, MacGyver. For the best ride, remember to check the forecast ahead of time, look at current radar before you ride, evaluate the clouds through the day, and be ready to find a safe spot if the Russians – er, I mean if lightning becomes an issue.

Restaurants, Bike Shops, and Accommodations

I am easily satisfied with the very best. — *Winston Churchill*

The introduction to each chapter lists of some recommendations for restaurants, bike shops, hotels, and campgrounds. These are not comprehensive listings. Despite numerous broken bike parts, the author failed to visit every bike shop in the state. Additionally, his taste in restaurants is questionable at best. Thus, the recommendations in this book should serve merely as a starting point. Readers looking for more comprehensive restaurant and hotel reviews should pick up one of the many travel guides to the region (the Moon Handbook to Colorado is among the best) or consult the internet (yelp.com has excellent restaurant reviews for Colorado).

Driving

Everything in life is somewhere else, and you get there in a car. — *E.B. White*

Inspite of the popularity of commuting by bicycle in many cities in Colorado, it is probably best to use a car for a mountain biking trip in the state. Many towns are not simple to reach with public transportation and the trailheads are often many miles from the center of town. Additionally, the weather in Colorado is difficult to forecast, changes quickly, and can vary substantially from place to place – a car provides the option to quickly retreat to warmer climes should the weather turn sour. Rental cars are readily available at any major airport, and some internet sleuthing usually yields a good price.

That said, it is entirely possible to reach almost any town using some combination of local airports, buses, and shuttles. Several of the skiing resort-towns are especially well equipped for the carless traveller, offering shuttle services and a variety of bike rentals. Crested Butte, Aspen, Vail, and Breckenridge all boast trail networks that start within riding distance of town. The ridiculously motivated will note that it is – at least theoretically – possible to ride from Denver Airport to any trailhead in the state.

Camping

Camping: nature's way of promoting the motel industry. — *Dave Barry*

When the weather gods cooperate, camping in Colorado is a delightful experience. Most mountain towns are surrounded with a plethora of developed campgrounds that provide picnic tables, restrooms, and (sometimes) showers for approximately $20 to $30 per site per night. For those looking to save money and escape the din of huge camper trailers, there is usually free camping available along dirt roads in most National Forests. These primitive camping options generally provide no amenities, and it is necessary to pack out your own trash. It is difficult to find definitive information on which lands allow undeveloped camping and the best strategy is to ask at a local Forest Service office – they usually know the best spots.

Trail Access and Mountain Biking Etiquette

My father considered a walk among the mountains as the equivalent of churchgoing. — *Aldous Huxley*

During the late 1980s mountain biking exploded in popularity and the local mountain bikers swarmed the trails around Boulder, Colorado. Within a few years, all of the trails near town were completely closed to mountain biking. The story of Boulder shows just how quickly trails can be closed to biking and that mountain bikers should tread carefully in order to maintain access to the excellent riding in Colorado.

Being a good citizen on the trail is easy. Here are a few simple tips that will make other trail users happy and help keep trails open to mountain bikes.

- **Ride in control.** This is really important. Hikers hate to have their pets or children run over by bikes. Riders should make every effort not to startle people on the trail.
- **Stay on the trail.** Nobody likes hillsides crisscrossed with unofficial mountain bike trails – stick with the designated trails.
- **Ride when it's dry.** Biking and hiking on muddy trails destroys them as well as destroying your bike.
- **Help maintain the trails.** Many trails are built

Springtime mud on the South Boulder Trails.

and maintained by volunteers. Get involved with your local mountain biking club and spend at least one day per summer building or maintaining trail. It's lots of fun!
- **Dismount near horses.** For some reason many horses freak out when they see people riding bikes and can toss their rider as well as stomp on the cyclist. So always walk your bike when encountering a horse.

Bikes

The bicycle is just as good company as most husbands and, when it gets old and shabby, a woman can dispose of it and get a new one without shocking the entire community. — *Ann Strong*

Mountain bikers love to talk about bikes, but the truth is that the bike doesn't really matter. Sure, some bikes will go a little faster than others or be able to land bigger jumps, but the trails in this book will be fun on any bike. That said, if money is no object, a full-suspension bike with three to six inches of travel is ideal for most Colorado riders. If constrained by a budget, consider a front-suspension bike; they offer quality components at a significantly reduced price.

Most of the classic rides in Colorado involve prolonged steep climbing. Thus, it's a good idea to have very easy gears available. It is only the strongest riders that can live without the 22-tooth chainring, aka, the "granny-gear". Singlespeed riders should consider bringing a larger cog for their trip to Colorado – 32x20 is recommended for the more technical trails, and 29er riders frequently use 32x22.

Trails in Colorado are often rocky, loose, and littered with thorns, making flat tires a frequent annoyance. Tubeless tires are much more resistant to flats and most savvy mountain bikers in the state now roll without tubes. Wheels that are compatible with tubeless tires are more expensive, but they are worth it. Tubeless tires run at lower pressure (providing better grip) and they can be filled with a goopy sealant that can auto-magically plug small holes. When the author switched to tubeless tires, he went from one flat per week to one flat per year.

Riders visiting Colorado should consider bringing flat pedals. The trails here are generally technical, and small crashes and "dabs" are very common. Clipless pedals offer an increase in pedaling efficiency and bike handling, but can make it difficult to step away from the bike. A good pair of flat pedals combined with sticky rubber bike shoes offers a similar level of control and allows the rider to bail when things go wrong. Additionally, stream crossings and hike-a-bikes are common on alpine trails and are much easier with rubber-soled shoes.

Gear

Life is like riding a bicycle – in order to keep your balance, you must keep moving. — *Albert Einstein*

Bikes break, but with the right tools, they can often be fixed on the trail. These basic items should always be in the repair kit:

- Multi-tool – Make sure it has all of the sizes of hex-wrenches to fit your bike. The big 8 mm can be difficult to find on a small tool, but is vital for tightening loose cranks.
- Chain tool and extra links – Without a chain tool, broken chains are impossible to fix. Some multi-tools have chain tools built in.
- Pump – Flat tires happen: always bring the pump.
- Tire leavers – To get the tires off the wheel without damaging the rim, it's best to have the proper tools.
- Extra tubes – Colorado has lots of spikey plants, so bring lots of extra tubes.
- Patch kit – When the tubes run out, it's time to start patching them.
- Extra tire – On long rides it's a good idea for someone in the group to carry an extra tire.

Even if the bike survives, it's likely that bad weather will strike. The following gear usually helps prevent hypothermia.

- Rain jacket – The weather in Colorado is completely unpredictable. A good-quality waterproof jacket is mandatory for all rides.
- Warm gloves – If it's cold enough for a jacket, gloves will also be necessary.
- Several liters of water – Colorado can be hot and dry, so bring plenty of water.
- Three headlamps – You never know when you'll taco a wheel and have to walk out in the dark. Three headlamps are necessary: the first will be out of batteries, your buddy will need the second, and you can use the third.
- Extra food – Keep a few granola bars in the bottom of the pack. Make sure they're a terrible flavor so that they aren't consumed before an emergency.
- Iodine tablets – In most regions of Colorado, streams are plentiful and can serve as a source of water in a pinch. Occasionally, they are contaminated with giardia or cryptosporidium, so it is a good idea to use iodine to kill the germs.
- A few dollars and a credit card – The bills can be used as a temporary sidewall repair, and when you are riding back through town at the end of the day exhausted, the candy bar you buy will be worth its weight in gold.

Fitness

The secret to mountain biking is pretty simple. The slower you go the more likely it is you'll crash. — *Julie Furtado*

When planning a trip to Colorado, it is easy to get caught up in decisions about which bike to ride and what gear to bring, but the most important factor might be physical fitness. There are lots of good trails in Colorado for every fitness level, but many of the classics are really tough. For example, the famous rides in Crested Butte (like Doctor Park and Reno–Flag–Bear–Deadman) involve steep climbing on dirt roads for several hours before providing the great singletrack. In Colorado, more climbing usually leads to better trails and fewer crowds. Thus, when planning a trip, be sure to practice riding up some long, steep hills.

Ride	Technical Difficulty	Physical Difficulty	Stars	Distance (miles)	Dogs	Location	Page Number
2 - FORT COLLINS							**20**
Bobcat Ridge	◆◆	Very Strenuous	4	9.7	🐾	15 mi SW of Ft Collins	22
Devil's Backbone	◼	Moderate	3.5	11.6	🐾	15 mi SW of Ft Collins	24
Blue Sky Trail	◼	Moderate	3	9.6	🐾	7 mi W of Ft Collins	26
Horsetooth Mtn Park	◼	Strenuous	3.5	9.2	🐾	8 mi W of Ft Collins	28
Lory State Park	◆	Strenuous	3.5	9.2	🐾	10 mi NW of Ft Collins	30
Foothills Trail	◆	Moderate	3.5	up to 11.0	🐾	3 mi W of Ft Collins	32
Youngs Gulch	◼	Moderate	3	9.4	🚫	20 mi NW of Ft Collins	34
Soapstone Prairie	◼	Moderate	3.5	21.6	🐾	30 mi N of Ft Collins	36
3 - BOULDER							**40**
S. Boulder Trails	◼	Moderate	2.5	up to 20.0	🚫	3 mi S of Boulder	44
Dirty Bismark	●	Easy	2	14.9	🐾	4 mi S of Boulder	46
E. Boulder Trail	●	Easy	1.5	12.0	🐾	5 mi E of Boulder	48
Foothills Trail	●	Easy	2	5.2	🚫	Starts in Boulder	50
Boulder Valley Ranch	○	Easy	2	up to 8.5	🚫	4 mi N of Boulder	52
Betasso Preserve	◼	Moderate	3	3.1	🐾	6 mi W of Boulder	54
Switzerland Trail	●	Moderate	2	17.6	🚫	10 mi W of Boulder	56
Walker Ranch	◼	Strenuous	3.5	7.1	🐾	8 mi SW of Boulder	58
Heil Ranch	◼	Moderate	2.5	9.3	🐾	10 mi N of Boulder	60
Picture Rock Trail	◼	Moderate	3	10.0	🐾	1 mi SW of Lyons	63
Hall Ranch	◆	Strenuous	3.5	9.6	🐾	2 mi SW of Lyons	64

Check Out the Table of Rides!

Colorado is huge and the riding possibilities are nearly endless. To make the process of planning the perfect trip and picking the perfect ride easier, this book contains a handy Table of Rides that summarizes the key data for each ride including the length, technical difficulty, phyiscal difficulty, quality, distance, location, and if dogs are allowed. We've hidden it at the back of the book in the Appendix starting on page 358. Be sure to check it out!

How to use this book

Each ride is described by a bunch of different ratings, symbols, numbers, etc. Below is an explanation of what it all means.

Letter
To the left of the title for each ride, there is a big capital letter in a circle. In each chapter, every ride is assigned a letter and these letters correspond to the turn-by-turn directions that are shown on the map. So, if you see "B2" written on the map, this corresponds to a turn on ride B. The rides are listed in order based on their location.

Quality
When I see an adult on a bicycle, I do not despair for the future of the human race. — *H.G. Wells*

The quality or "fun factor" of each ride is described by a number of stars up to a maximum of five. Rides that offer interesting technical challenges, nice views, and quality singletrack receive more stars. Here is what each star rating means:

★	A forgetable ride. Not unpleasant, but unremarkable.
★★	A fun trail, but nothing to write home about.
★★★	A local favorite!
★★★★	Among the best in the state.
★★★★★	A worldwide classic.

Most of the rides in this book get at least two stars. This isn't because the author has low standards, but because he picked only the best rides in each region to go into this book. Colorado is chock full of excellent mountain biking and the rides that earn five stars in this book are truly world class.

Trailhead Location

The location of the trailhead is shown in parentheses below the title of each ride. It describes how far riders will need to drive to get to the start of the ride from the nearest major town.

Summary

For readers with short attention spans, the essence of each ride is condensed into a one-sentence summary. Those seeking to maximize adventure should simply read the summary and leave this book in the car.

Technical Difficulty

Get a bicycle. You will not regret it if you live. — *Mark Twain*

The technical difficulty rating provides a recommendation of the bike handling skills required to have fun on a trail. This book uses a "ski-trail" rating system that is based on the rating system created by the International Mountain Biking Association (IMBA). The rating assumes that riders are willing to walk their bikes through a few difficult sections along the trail. So, a trail that consists of mostly blue-square terrain, but contains a few short sections of black diamond, will still be rated blue square because it is still fun for intermediate riders – they will simply walk their bike around a few difficulties.

White Circle – Dirt road. This rating is reserved for dirt roads and gravel bike paths. Riders should not encounter any obstacles on these trails. However, keep in mind that conditions may change. For example, a smooth dirt road could become rutted and dangerous after a big rainstorm.

Green Circle – Beginner. This terrain is generally suitable for novice riders. It typically contains some small rocks and drops, but they will only be a few inches high.

Green/Blue – Beginner/Intermediate. This rating refers to trails that are mostly green-circle riding but have a number of blue square sections that might frustrate the novice.

Blue Square – Intermediate. Terrain that receives this rating is very common in Colorado. A blue square trail will typically have loose rock, roots, small stream crossings, and drops up to 12 inches. Riders should be able to ride up and down sidewalk curbs to enjoy a blue square trail.

Blue/Black – Intermediate/Advanced. This rating is for rides that fall somewhere between blue square and black diamond. Often this rating refers to trails that are littered with loose rock – they do not require advanced bike handling skills, just lots of concentration. The rating may also refer to trails that consist of blue square riding with an occasional dangerous section that should be walked by intermediate riders.

Black Diamond – Advanced. Black diamond trails require advanced bike handling skills. They can have drops of two feet, large rocks, and very steep riding. Loose rock abounds. Novice riders will not enjoy these trails and will likely shower their wrath upon the friend who suggested that the trail is "easy enough."

Double Diamond – Expert. These trails are recommended for expert riders only. They are generally steep, loose, and filled with technical features. Most riders will be walking their bikes frequently. Hospitalization is likely.

Extreme (EX) – Professional. These trails require professional-level riding skills. Expect huge jumps, massive drops, and crazy rock gardens. Survival is unlikely.

Physical Difficulty

You never have the wind with you – either it is against you or you're having a good day.
—Daniel Behrman

The physical difficulty provides an estimate of the average athletic challenge of each ride. This rating answers the question "how fast will my heart be beating as I ride this trail?" This rating is the average physical difficulty, so a fifty-mile long ride will still be rated "Easy" if it is flat. So, remember to take a look at the distance of the ride when determining the overall athletic challenge.

Easy – The trail is mostly flat. Riders can generally carry on a conversation.

Moderate – There is some real hill-climbing involved, but nothing too insane (by Colorado standards).

Strenuous – There are lots of steep hills, and/or very technical riding. Expect to take frequent breaks.

Very Strenuous – If the author frequently felt like he was going to vomit while riding the trail, it gets this rating.

Insanely Strenuous – If the author actually did vomit while riding the trail, then it gets this rating.

Distance

The distance is the length of the ride as described in the Riding Directions. Frequently, it is possible to create a longer ride using the trails shown on the map or mentioned as options in the text. The distance is the round-trip distance, so a seven-mile trail that is described as an out-and-back will be listed as fourteen miles. If the distance is described as "Up to 30 miles," this implies that the route is an out-and-back or an extensive trail system and that turning around early is recommended.

The distances are calculated from the GPS tracks that the author recorded for each ride. In most cases, the GPS track is slightly shorter than the true distance (i.e., that measured using a well-calibrated bike-wheel odometer) by about five to twenty percent. Thus, riders using a bike-wheel odometer to track distance should expect to arrive at mile 10.0 when their bike computer reads between 10.5 and 12.0 miles. Riders using GPS units may also notice a discrepancy between their distance measurements and the distances in this book. The mileage recorded with a GPS unit depends on the manufacturer of the GPS unit, the frequency of track-point recording, the strength of the GPS signal, and the speed of the rider. Even distances listed on trail signs and maps are frequently imprecise. Thus, some error can be expected regardless of the method used to reckon distance. Treat all measurements of distance in the backcountry as rough estimates.

Time

The time listed for each ride is a guess of how long it will take an "average" rider to complete each ride. Obviously, these should be taken with a big grain of salt. The time that it will take to complete a ride depends on the weather, fitness, and countless other factors. The range of times given should cover most riders who attempt the ride, but it is entirely possible that riders will go faster or slower than the given times.

Type

The type refers to whether a ride is a loop, an out-and-back, a lollipop loop, or a shuttle ride. A lollipop loop is a ride that has a section of out-and-back and a section that is a loop. If the ride is listed as "shuttle," this means that the ride starts and ends in different places and that it's necessary to set up a car shuttle.

Trail Surface

This indicates the type of trails and/or roads that compose the ride. The options are singletrack, doubletrack, dirt road, gravel road, paved road, and bike path. Singletrack is used to refer to most trails regardless of width. Doubletrack is relatively rare and occurs when an old dirt road turns into two parallel trails. The trail surfaces are listed in order of distance. So, a listing of "paved road, singletrack" means that there is more paved road than singletrack. If a ride consists of less than 10% of one type of surface, then that surface is generally not listed.

Climbing/Descending

The climbing is the total elevation gained by the trail, while the descending is the total elevation loss. The elevation is listed in feet. Loop rides, since they start and end in the same place, have the same amount of descending as climbing so only one number is given. For out-and-back rides, both the climbing and descending are listed. In this case, the numbers refer to just the "out" portion of the ride and not the "back." Obviously, on the way back, riders will climb the hills that they descended on the way out. So, to find the total climbing for an out-and-back ride, it is necessary to sum the climbing and descending. Climbing and descending information should always be treated as rough estimates since they are highly dependent on the technique used to calculate them.

Season

This section lists the season or seasons when the ride is best completed – it is only a recommendation. For example, many of the rides in the Front Range are listed as being good in the spring and the fall. However, they are fine to ride in the summer if you avoid riding during the heat of the day, and can be ridden during dry periods in the winter.

Crowds

Sometimes it's nice to go mountain biking on a trail where there are not many other people. The trails are rated in terms of how many other trail users might be encountered. Keep in mind that the crowds are hugely dependent on the time of day, the day of the week, and the weather. For example, most trails offer solitude when ridden at sunrise. There are three ratings for the "crowdedness" of each trail:

Few – There are not many people on this trail, even during popular times.

Some – During peak season and peak times, there will likely be enough people on the trail to make mountain biking somewhat tedious. However, during other times the trail should be peaceful.

Crowded – This trail is not recommended on sunny weekend afternoons or other popular times. Riders should expect to encounter other users at all times.

Dogs

Since many people like to bring the pooch along for a mountain bike ride, each ride is rated for its suitability for our floppy-eared friends. Biking is nearly impossible while holding a leash, so if there is a leash law, the trail is listed as being "no dogs." As dog owners already know, leash laws are subject to change. So, even though this book might claim that a trail is suitable for canines, don't forget to read the signs at the trailhead. There are three ratings for the dog-compatibility for each trail.

 Yes – Dogs are allowed.

 Maybe – Dogs are allowed, but the trail is not well suited for dogs. For example, if a trail is very crowded, it is probably a bad idea to bring Fido.

 No – Dogs are not allowed.

Ride Description

The ride description tells you what to expect when riding the trail. The prose has a subtle charm that has been favorably compared to Hemmingway and Steinbeck.

Driving Directions

The driving directions explain how to reach the trailhead. The following abbreviations are used for roads:

I – Interstate (e.g., I-70)
US – US Highway (e.g., US-285)
CO – Colorado Highway, State Highway, or State Route (e.g., CO-119)
County – County Road, County Highway, or County Route (e.g., County-72)
FS – Forest Service Road (e.g., FS-440a)

Riding Directions

The Riding Directions consist of descriptions of each turn necessary to complete the ride. The letters (A1, A2) refer to the same labels on the map. The decimal numbers (for example "5.6") give the distance (in miles) from the start of the ride to that point.

Map

The incredible maps in this book were crafted by Mike Boruta. He has included many helpful features. First, the elevation coloring-scheme is consistent throughout the book. So, a map that is mostly brown is showing terrain that is at lower elevation than a map that is colored green and white. Second, the color scheme of the map is consistent with the elevation profile, making it easy to compare the map to the elevation profile. Third, the trails are shown in black and the roads in red, so it is a simple matter to plan your own ride.

The recommended rides (highlighted in yellow) are drawn on the maps using GPS data collected by the author. So, the positions for the highlighted trails are likely to be very accurate. However, the maps contain many other trails, roads, and features that come from a variety of different sources such as National Forest and local government databases. The accuracy of this data is variable and it is likely that some of the roads and trails shown on these maps no longer exist. Though the maps attempt to distinguish which roads are four-wheel-drive jeep roads and which are passable by two-wheel-drive passenger car, most of this information has not been vetted by the author, the cartographer, or likely anyone else in the past twenty years. Readers who wish to explore Colorado's mountain roads (while maintaining the resale value of their vehicle) are advised to invest in one of the many excellent books on the subject.

In order to show as much detail as possible, the maps use different scales. So, an inch on one map may represent 0.25 miles while on another map it may represent 10 miles.

The maps in this book do not always display private property or wilderness boundaries, nor do they always indicate which trails are closed to cycling. Please do not use these maps as an excuse to trespass. The prevailing attitude among many Colorado property owners is to "Shoot first and ask questions later."

Each maps display one or several trails. The letters on the maps (e.g., A1, A2) refer to the Riding Directions for a specific ride. A1 and A2 are the first two waypoints for ride A, and B1 and B2 are the first two waypoints for ride B. The ride letters begin anew for each chapter.

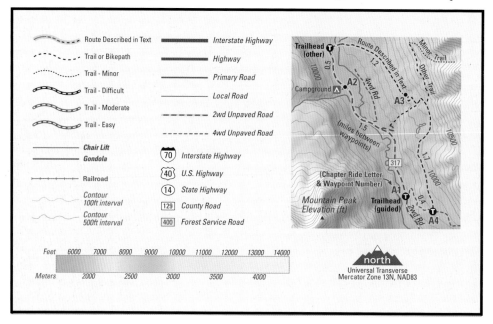

Elevation Profile

The elevation profile displays the elevation of the ride verses the distance from the trailhead. For loop rides, the entire ride is displayed. For out-and-back rides, both the "out" and the "back" portion of the ride are shown on the elevation profile. Since each profile is scaled to be the same size, the steepness of the lines does not directly indicate the steepness of the hills on the ride. However, since the same color scheme has been used on all of the elevation profiles, it is possible to compare elevation profiles for different rides. An elevation profile that has several different colors means that a ride has a lot of elevation gain, while a profile that is only one color indicates a ride that doesn't have as much elevation gain.

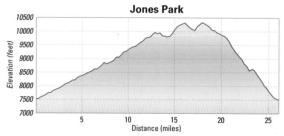

This elevation profile shows that the Jones Park ride requires an alarming amount of climbing. Luckily, a car shuttle can be used to eliminate most of the uphill!

Dylan Younger walks the plank at Winter Park Resort.   photo: Greg Younger

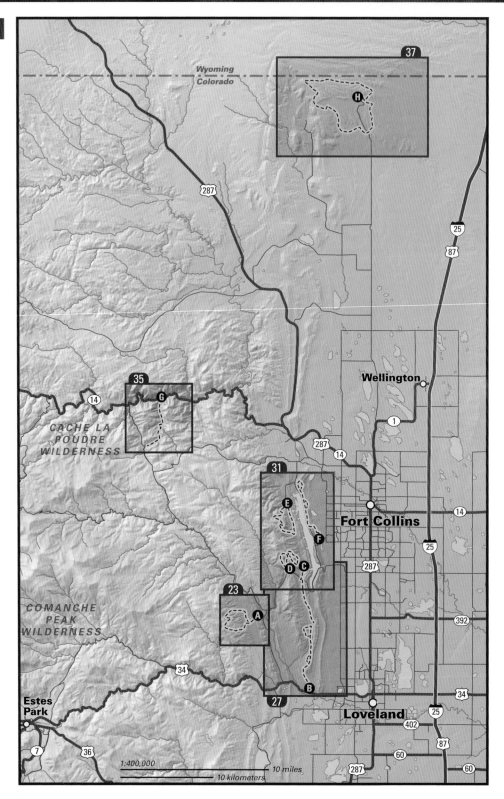

Fort Collins

With a plethora of excellent singletrack within biking distance, and a downtown area packed with good restaurants and bars, Fort Collins should not be overlooked as a mountain biking destination. It is located less than two hours north of Denver and boasts a long mountain biking season, making it perfect for an impromptu weekend mountain biking trip. Additionally (though this is hotly contested) the presence of the New Belgium, Odell's, and the Fort Collins Brewery is enough to win Fort Collins the title of "Best Beer in Colorado."

Fort Collins offers a variety of mountain biking options, with trails to satisfy nearly every whim. From endless miles of butter-smooth singletrack at Soapstone Prairie to steep climbing at Bobcat Ridge, Fort Collins has you covered. However, what sets this region apart from other Front Range mountain biking centers is the abundance of fantastic technical riding. The Foothills Trail, Bobcat Ridge, and Horsetooth Mountain Park all feature great challenging riding on rocky trails.

Accommodations

Fort Collins is home to Colorado State University and has enough hotels and motels to accommodate big events like graduation and football games. So, it is generally easy to find a hotel room in Fort Collins. There is also excellent camping nearby. The southern end of Horsetooth Reservoir (see Ride D) offers pay camping and cabins, but these sites are usually booked in advance on summer weekends. Poudre Canyon (see Ride G) is also very popular for camping and offers a number of options. West of Loveland, there is camping at Carter Lake, Pinewood Lake, and Flatirons Reservoir.

Bike Shops

Full Cycle
2101 South College Avenue. 970-484-1800
A broad selection of bikes and parts, with stores in Boulder as well.

Lee's Cyclery (two locations)
202 W. Laurel and 931 E. Harmony. 970-482-6006
Bikes, gear, and service.

Eats and Drinks

Odell's Brewery
800 East Lincoln Avenue. 970-498-9070
Home to the best beer in Colorado (90 Shilling), Odell's offers daily tours and has a taproom bar where you can sample their fine products.

Old Town Fort Collins
College Avenue (US-287), between Mulberry Street & Laporte Avenue
The Old Town area is home to dozens of restaurants and bars so hungry bikers are sure to find something appealing.

Rasta Pasta
200 Walnut Street. 970-224-4323
Crazy-delicious fusion of Caribbean and Italian cuisine. Try the Chicken Montego Bay!

A Bobcat Ridge ★★★★☆

(15 miles southwest of Fort Collins)

Technical Difficulty:	
Physical Difficulty:	**Very Strenuous**
Distance:	9.7 miles
Time:	2 – 4 hours
Type:	Lollipop loop
Surface:	Singletrack, doubletrack
Climbing:	2,000'
Season:	Spring, Fall
Crowds:	Some
Dogs:	Dogs are prohibited

Fun technical features linked by great singletrack

Ride Description

It's time to let the bobcat out of the bag and inform you that the Ginny Trail is one of the best trails in the Front Range for the skilled rider looking for drops, rocks, and the occasional log-ride. The ride is described as a loop using the Valley Loop Trail and doing most of the climbing on the steep, loose Power Line Trail. This method avoids the technical challenge of climbing the Ginny Trail, but many people prefer to simply ride the Ginny Trail out-and-back. Note that the Power Line Trail is only open to uphill riding.

There are several other trails at Bobcat Ridge Natural Area that are conducive to mountain biking. The Valley Loop Trail is a 4-mile loop of mostly-flat singletrack and gravel trail. The Eden Valley Spur is a 1.3-mile out-and-back that can be ridden as part of a tour of the Ginny Trail.

Driving Directions

From downtown Fort Collins, head south on US-287. Turn right on Harmony Road (County-38). Continue on County-38 for about 10 miles as it wraps around the southern end of Horsetooth Reservoir. At the small town of Masonville, turn left on County-27 and go 0.6 miles. Turn right onto County-32C and arrive at the trailhead in 0.7 miles. (If driving from the south, it is quicker to take US-34 west from Loveland and then head north on County-27.)

Riding Directions

A1 - 0.0 From the parking lot, begin riding on the wide gravel trail towards the large picnic shelter. At the shelter, turn left on the Valley Loop Trail towards the Ginny Trail.

A2 - 0.8 Bear right on the Valley Loop Trail as the Ginny Trail goes left. (Or, turn left if you wish to ride the Ginny Trail as an out-and-back.) Enjoy a mile of nice singletrack before beginning the arduous climb.

A3 - 1.8 Turn left on the Valley Loop Trail as the Tipi Ring Trail goes right. Go about 0.2 miles and turn right on the Power Line Trail, an old dirt road. Climb steeply.

A4 - 2.8 At a Y-intersection, take either path: the trail rejoins in 0.2 miles.

A5 - 3.5 Turn left on the Ginny Trail. Enjoy some great riding!

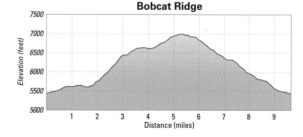

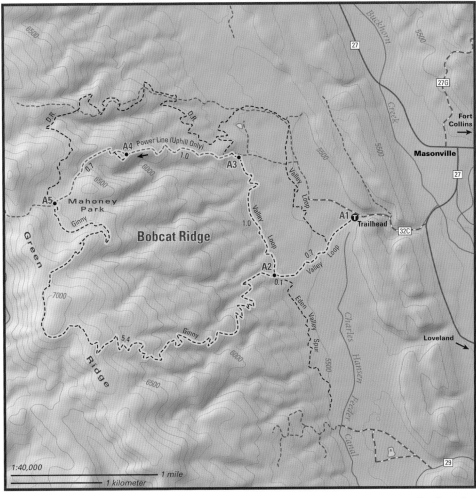

A2 - 8.9 Arrive back at the Valley Loop Trail. Turn right and retrace your route back to the parking lot.

Greg Christensen stays in balance on one of the many log rides on the Ginny Trail.   photo: Yann Ropars

Fort Collins

(B) Devil's Backbone ★★★★☆

(3 miles west of Loveland, 15 miles southwest of Fort Collins)

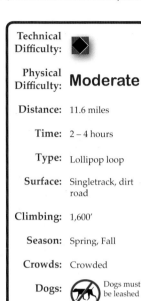

Technical Difficulty:	◆◆
Physical Difficulty:	**Moderate**
Distance:	11.6 miles
Time:	2 – 4 hours
Type:	Lollipop loop
Surface:	Singletrack, dirt road
Climbing:	1,600′
Season:	Spring, Fall
Crowds:	Crowded
Dogs:	Dogs must be leashed

Sometimes smooth, sometimes rocky, but always fun

Ride Description

The trails near the Devil's Backbone Trailhead feature wonderful singletrack through beautiful fields of prairie grass and along rocky ridgelines. Many of the trails are butter-smooth and are great fun on the singlespeed. However, there are several rocky sections that are much more pleasant on a full-suspension bike. There are no trees along this ride, so it bakes in the sun on hot days.

It is possible to ride from the Devil's Backbone Trailhead near Lovelend all the way to Horsetooth Reservoir near Fort Collins. To reach Horsetooth Reservoir, simply continue north on the Blue Sky Trail to the Inlet Bay Trail, reaching the Soderberg Trailhead at Horsetooth Reservoir in 4.5 miles (see Ride C).

Driving Directions

From Fort Collins, head south on US-287 for about 10 miles until you reach downtown Loveland. Follow signs for US-34 and head west on Eisenhower Boulevard (US-34). After 4.1 miles, turn right on Hidden Valley Drive and go 0.3 miles. Turn right into the Devil's Backbone Trailhead parking area. (From Denver, take I-25 north to reach US-34.)

Riding Directions - see map on page 27

B1 - 0.0 From the Devil's Backbone Trailhead, start riding northwest on the Wild Loop Trail. Bear right at the intersection with Hunter Loop.

B2 - 2.5 Reach the southern end of the Laughing Horse Loop. Turn right (on the way back, ride the other side of the loop).

B3 - 3.0 Reach the north end of the Laughing Horse Loop. Turn right on the Blue Sky Trail.

B4 - 3.3 Come to a nice vista, and then blast down some technical switchbacks.

B5 - 4.1 Follow the Blue Sky Trail as it hits a dirt road and turns right.

B6 - 4.3 When a wooden gate blocks the road, turn left onto the Blue Sky singletrack.

B7 - 4.5 Continue straight as the Indian Summer Trail goes left.

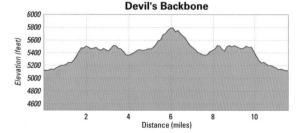

B8 - 5.2 Make a left on Indian Summer Trail. *(If you want to ride to Horsetooth Reservoir, continue straight on Blue Sky.)*

B7 - 7.1 Turn right, back onto the Blue Sky Trail. Retrace your tracks, but this time ride the other side of the Laughing Horse Loop.

Josh Stahl picks up speed on a wide-open section of the Devil's Backbone Trail.

©Blue Sky Trail ★★★☆☆

(7 miles west of Fort Collins)

Fort Collins

Technical Difficulty:	◯
Physical Difficulty:	**Moderate**
Distance:	9.6 miles
Time:	2 – 3 hours
Type:	Out-and-back
Surface:	Singletrack
Climbing/ Descending:	600'/400' (one-way)
Season:	Spring, Fall
Crowds:	Crowded
Dogs:	🚫 Dogs must be leashed

Great smooth cruising with options for longer rides

Ride Description

The Blue Sky Trail is a beautiful stretch of red-dirt singletrack without too much climbing or technical riding. This ride is described as an out-and-back, which is perfect for riders sneaking out for a quick evening ride. However, those looking for a longer ride can take the Blue Sky Trail all the way to the Devil's Backbone Trailhead near Loveland (see Ride B). Alternatively, those who would rather add some exciting technical riding should turn left on the Rimrock Trail at mile 4.8; the "staircase" section is very exciting!

Driving Directions

Though it is possible to park at the Blue Sky Trailhead near County-38, parking at the Soderberg Trailhead provides a nice warm-up on a bike path. Parking at any of the trailheads near Horsetooth Reservoir (including the Soderberg Trailhead) costs about $6. To reach the Soderberg Trailhead from downtown Fort Collins, head south on US-287. Turn right on Harmony Road (County-38) and go 8.0 miles. Turn right on Shoreline Drive and travel 1.3 miles. Turn left into the Soderberg Trailhead.

Riding Directions

C1 - 0.0 From the Soderberg Trailhead, start riding south on the Inlet Bay Trail (a bike path).

C2 - 1.1 Bear left onto the Blue Sky Trail.

C3 - 1.8 Pass under Country-38E at an underpass and enjoy some great singletrack on the Blue Sky Trail.

C4 - 4.8 Arrive at an intersection where the Rimrock Trail goes left. This is a good turnaround point. *(Strong riders can continue south for another 6 miles to the Devil's Backbone Trailhead.)*

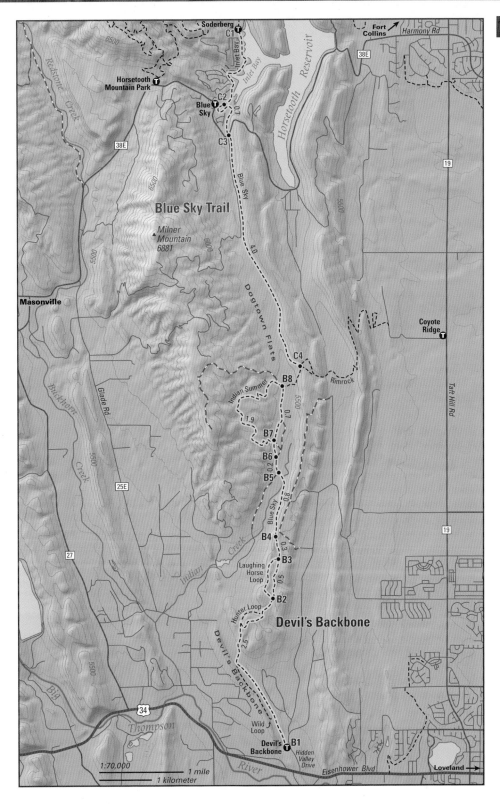

Soderberg
C1
Inlet Bay
Fort Collins
Harmony Rd
38E
38E
19

Horsetooth
Mountain Park
C2
Blue
Sky
0.7
C3

Blue Sky

6600

Blue Sky Trail

▲ Milner
Mountain
6881

6600

Masonville

Buckhorn

Glade Rd

Creek

5500

Dogtown Flats

4.0

5500

Coyote
Ridge

Taft Hill Rd

C4

B8

Rimrock

Indian Summer

1.9

0.7

5500

B7

B6

0.2

B5

0.8

Blue Sky

25E

Creek

19

B4

0.3

B3

Laughing
Horse
Loop

0.5

B2

Hunter Loop

Devil's Backbone

27

2.5

Devil's Backbone

5500

Indian

Big

34

Thompson

Wild
Loop

B1

Devil's
Backbone

Hidden
Valley
Drive

Loveland →

1:70,000

1 mile

1 kilometer

Eisenhower Blvd

River

Horsetooth Mountain
Park ★★★★☆☆

(8 miles west of Fort Collins)

Technical Difficulty:	◆
Physical Difficulty:	**Strenuous**
Distance:	9.2 miles
Time:	2 – 3 hours
Type:	Loop
Surface:	Singletrack, closed dirt road
Climbing:	2,400′
Season:	Spring, Summer, Fall
Crowds:	Crowded
Dogs:	Dogs must be leashed

This ride is just one of many excellent loops at Horsetooth

Ride Description

With its sublime views of Horsetooth Reservoir and challenging rocky trails, Horsetooth Mountain Park is a popular destination for Front Range mountain bikers. Most of the single-track trails are blue square and black diamond, but there are a few options for the novice rider as well. Additionally, several of the trails are actually dirt roads and offer great views combined with little technical challenge. However, most of the trails and roads are reasonably steep, so a solid workout is guaranteed.

This recommended loop is a good option for those wishing to spend several hours at Horsetooth Reservoir. It includes two of the best technical trails in the park (Wathen and Spring Creek Trails) and one of the best easier trails (the Stout Trail). Shorter rides are certainly possible, and there's enough single-track at Horsetooth for an exhausting day of riding.

Driving Directions

From downtown Fort Collins, head south on College Avenue (US-287). Turn right (west) on Harmony Road (which becomes County-38) and go 8.8 miles, passing near the southern end of Horsetooth Reservoir. Shortly after the reservoir, turn into the Horsetooth Mountain Park Trailhead. It costs about $6 to park at Horsetooth.

Riding Directions - see map on page 31

D1 - 0.0 From the trailhead, start riding on the South Ridge Trail (a wide gravel trail). The trail becomes an old dirt road and climbs steeply.

D2 - 0.8 Continue on the South Ridge Trail as the Soderberg Trail goes right.

D3 - 2.2 Go right on the Wathen Trail. Continue right on Wathen as West Ridge goes left. Enjoy a great downhill!

D4 - 3.4 Turn left on the Spring Creek Trail. Go about 0.1 miles and turn right on Herrington Trail.

D5 - 3.8 Make a right on the Stout Trail.

D6 - 5.9 Turn left on the Towers Trail (a wide dirt road) and climb steeply.

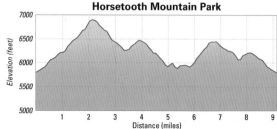

D7 - 6.6 Pass a turn for the Herrington Trail on the right, go about 0.1 miles further, and turn left on Herrington Trail.

D5 - 6.9 Bang a right on Herrington as Stout goes left. Blast down a short hill and turn left onto Spring Creek Trail.

D4 - 7.3 Continue on Spring Creek as Wathen goes right.

D8 - 7.7 Turn right on Soderberg Trail.

D2 - 8.4 Go left on the South Ridge Trail and rocket back to the trailhead.

Doug Cutter, Jim Kanter, and Angelo Forero on the Valley Trail at Lory State Park.   photo: Yann Ropars

Fort Collins

(E) Lory State Park - Timber Trail ★★★★☆

(10 miles northwest of Fort Collins)

Technical Difficulty:	◆
Physical Difficulty:	**Strenuous**
Distance:	9.2 miles
Time:	2 – 3 hours
Type:	Loop
Surface:	singletrack
Climbing:	2,300'
Season:	Spring, Fall
Crowds:	Some
Dogs:	Dogs must be leashed

One of the most technical trails at Lory, the Timber Trail is steep and rocky

Ride Description

Like the neighboring Horsetooth Mountain Park, Lory State Park offers miles of great singletrack, ranging from easy cruises to tough, technical climbs. If this isn't enough, cyclists can ride from Lory into Horsetooth and create an epic ride. This suggested loop scrambles up the rugged Timber Trail and down the exciting Howard Trail, but merely scratches the surface of the riding at Lory. The trails are well signed, and there are maps available at the visitor center. Riders searching for smoother trails should check out the West Valley and East Valley trails that run near the edge of the reservoir and offer plenty of smooth riding through a beautiful prairie. Being a Colorado State Park, it costs about $6 per car to enter Lory.

Driving Directions

From Fort Collins, head north on US-287 and bear left to stay on US-287. Go straight on County-54 (as US-287 turns right) and drive 2.7 miles. Turn left on County-52E and go 0.9 miles. Turn left on County-23E and travel 1.4 miles. Make a right on County-25G and go 1.6 miles. Turn left into Lory State Park. After paying the fee at the visitor center, continue about 0.1 mile and turn right into the Timber Trailhead.

Riding Directions

E1 - 0.0 From the Timber Trailhead, start riding on the Timber Trail.

E2 - 1.9 Continue straight on the Timber Trail as the Kimmons Trail goes left. Shortly after, continue straight on Timber as the Well Gulch Trail goes left.

E3 - 3.5 Come to an old dirt road and turn left. This is still the Timber Trail.

E4 - 4.3 Turn right on the Howard Trail as the Arthurs Rock Trail goes left.

E5 - 6.2 Continue straight on the Mill Creek Link as the Arthur's Rock Trail goes left.

E6 - 6.5 Turn left on the Mill Creek Trail. (*Right leads to Horsetooth Mtn Park.*)

E7 - 6.8 Turn left at a sign for "Authur's Rock Parking Lot 0.1 Mi." Pass the parking area and start riding on the West Valley Trail.

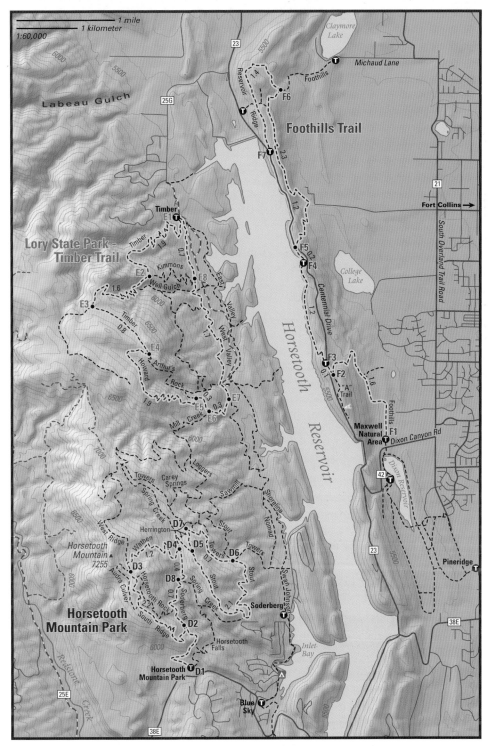

E8 - 8.5   Continue on West Valley as Kimmons goes left.

E1 - 9.2   Arrive back at the Timber Trailhead!

Fort Collins

(F)Foothills Trail ★★★★☆

(3 miles west of Fort Collins)

Technical Difficulty:	◆
Physical Difficulty:	**Moderate**
Distance:	up to 11.0 miles
Time:	1 – 4 hours
Type:	Lollipop loop
Surface:	singletrack, paved road
Climbing:	1,800′
Season:	Spring, Fall
Crowds:	Crowded
Dogs:	Dogs must be leashed

Excellent, technical riding with great views of Horsetooth Reservoir

Ride Description

Located just west of Fort Collins, Horsetooth Reservoir is surrounded by fantastic mountain biking. Lory State Park and Horsetooth Mountain Park offer great trails on the western shore of the Reservoir, and the Foothills Trail traces the eastern shore. Everyone has their own opinion of the best way to ride the Foothills Trail, with different names given based on the starting point: Michaud Lane, Maxwell, Shoreline, and Pineridge. This ride covers most of the Foothills Trail, omitting just a short section to the south and another to the north. There are a number of very technical sections and steep climbs, and this ride feels like an epic adventure, despite being only a few miles from downtown.

Driving Directions

From downtown Fort Collins, head south on US-287. Turn right on Prospect Road and go 3.0 miles. Bust a left on Overland Trail Road and go 0.7 miles. Make a right on Dixon Canyon Road (County-42), and go 0.5 miles before turning right into the Maxwell Natural Area Trailhead.

Riding Directions - see map on previous page

F1 - 0.0 From the trailhead at the Maxwell Natural Area, start riding north on the Foothills Trail. Continue on the Foothills Trail through several intersections with smaller trails.

F2 - 1.6 Go right on the Foothills Trail as the A-Trail goes left. *(The A-Trail takes you to a nice vista atop the large white "A". The "A" stands for "Aggies," the previous name of the CSU football team.)*

F3 - 1.7 Cross Centennial Drive (there is a large trailhead here) and continue on singletrack on the other side. The trail immediately splits: go left on the less technical option.

F4 - 2.9 Arrive at a dirt lot. Continue straight and find the singletrack on the other side.

F5 - 3.1 Cross Centennial Drive again. Descend steeply to the base of the dam and then climb arduously back up to the ridge.

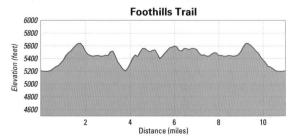

Fort Collins

F6 - 5.4   Come to an unsigned T-intersection and turn left (this is the Reservoir Ridge Trail). *(Going right takes you to a trailhead at the end of Michaud Lane, an optional start/end point for the ride.)*

F7 - 6.8   The trail crosses back to the west side of Centennial Drive, but soon ends and you must ride on the road for a short distance. Mercifully, this avoids the climb near the dam.

F5 - 8.0   Turn right onto the Foothills Trail. Follow your tracks back to the start of the ride.

Sore for a week
The 10 best epic rides

10. Steamboat Springs – Rabbit Ears Pass

9. Boulder – Boulder Valley Ranch to Heil to Hall

8. Durango – Hermosa Creek (out-and-back!)

7. Denver – Buffalo Creek – The New Classic

6. Fruita – The Edge Loop

5. Fort Collins – Blue Sky to Horsetooth to Lory

4. Denver – Kenosha Pass to Georgia Pass

3. Summit County – The Tenmile Traverse

2. Summit County – The Copper Triangle

1. The Colorado Trail (see page 358)

Young's Gulch ★★★☆☆

(20 miles northwest of Fort Collins)

Technical Difficulty:	
Physical Difficulty:	**Strenuous**
Distance:	9.4 miles
Time:	2 – 3 hours
Type:	Out-and-back
Surface:	Singletrack
Climbing/ Descending:	1,500' / 200' (one-way)
Season:	Spring, Summer, Fall
Crowds:	Crowded
Dogs:	

A classic Front Range hill climb. Best ridden on a hot day due to the "refreshing" stream crossings

Ride Description

With a strenuous climb followed by a fun, rocky descent, Young's Gulch is a great workout for the summer evening. The frequent stream crossings and rocky sections provide enough technical challenge to keep things interesting. The riding is great, but this trail is disappointingly short and fades away into private property just when you were hoping that it would go on forever. Those looking for more riding nearby should check out Hewlett Gulch, which is located just a few miles east on CO-14 on the north side of the road. There are a number of camping options in Poudre Canyon, including a campground across the highway from the Young's Gulch Trailhead.

Driving Directions

From Fort Collins, head north on US-287 for about 10 miles. Turn left onto CO-14 (Poudre Canyon Highway) and drive 12.9 miles. Turn left into the Young's Gulch Trailhead.

Riding Directions

G1 - 0.0 From the parking lot, find the Young's Gulch Trail and take it uphill. Cross many streams.

G2 - 4.7 Eventually the trail fades away a few hundred yards from Stove Prairie Road. There are numerous "No Trespassing" signs, and it does not appear possible to reach the road without trespassing.

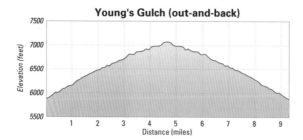

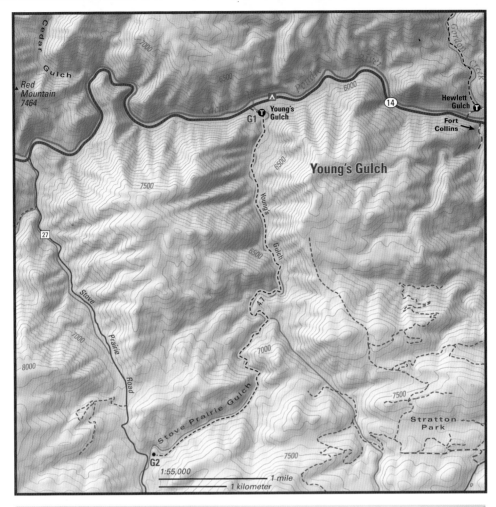

Doug Cutter glides along the gorgeous singletrack at Horsetooth Mountain Park   photo: Yann Ropars

Fort Collins

(H) Soapstone Prairie ★★★★★

(30 miles north of Fort Collins)

Technical Difficulty:	
Physical Difficulty:	**Moderate**
Distance:	21.6 miles
Time:	3 – 5 hours
Type:	Loop
Surface:	Singletrack, doubletrack, dirt road
Climbing:	2,000'
Season:	Spring, Fall
Crowds:	Few
Dogs:	Not even in cars!

A long, beautiful cruise through rolling hills and prairie grasses

Ride Description

Soapstone Prarie and the adjoining Red Mountain Open Space are home to a vast network of smooth singletrack and dirt roads. Portions of this ride are less than one mile from the Wyoming border and the setting reflects this – this is cowboy country! Gorgeous fields of prairie grasses dance in the wind, and a number of old windmills make this trail seem like a journey back to the early days of the American West.

The riding at Soapstone Prairie is generally smooth and mild. It's a refreshing change from the typical rock-strewn hill-climbs of the Front Range. The lack of trees mean that Soapstone Prairie soaks up the sunshine and it is probably possible to ride this loop during dry periods in the winter. However, Soapstone Prairie Natural Area is only open from dawn to dusk, March 1 to November 30. Those who dislike heat stroke should avoid this ride on hot summer days.

There are several more trails in the Soapstone Prairie Natural Area and at the neighboring Red Mountain Open Space. For more information, consult the Natural Areas Map available from the City of Fort Collins. For a shorter ride, consider riding just the Mahogany Loop, which consists of 7 miles of delightful singletrack.

Driving Directions

From downtown Fort Collins, drive north on College Avenue (US-287). Make a right on Terry Lake Road (CO-1) and drive 3.8 miles. Turn left on CO-15 (still called Terry Lake Road). Turn right on Rawhide Flats Road and go 6 miles to the entrance station. Drive an additional 3 miles to the northern trailhead.

Riding Directions

H1 - 0.0 From the parking area, start riding on the Mahogany Trail. Continue straight as the Towhee Trail goes left.

H2 - 0.4 Turn left on the Mahogany Loop.

H3 - 2.2 Turn right on the east branch of the Mahogany Loop.

H4 - 3.2 Turn right towards the Canyon Trail, go about 200 feet, then make a left onto the Canyon Trail (doubletrack).

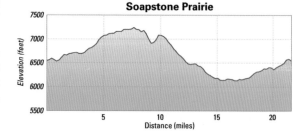

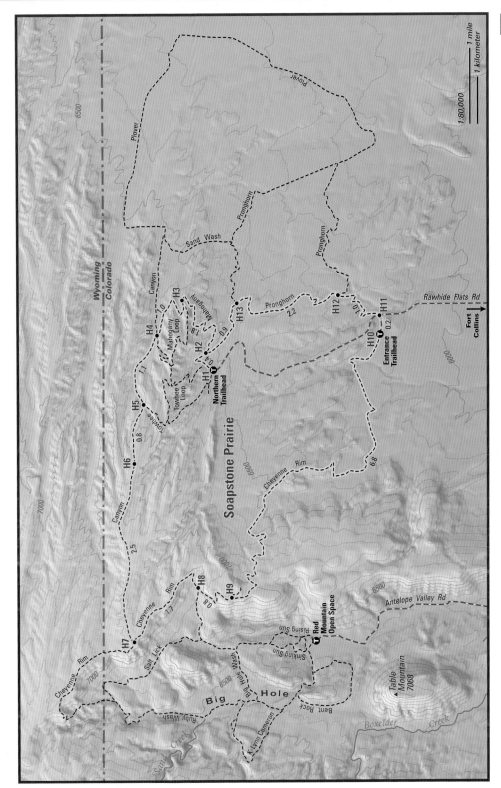

1:80,000

1 mile
1 kilometer

Wyoming
Colorado

Plover

Plover

Pronghorn

Sand Wash

Pronghorn

Pronghorn

Rawhide Flats Rd

Canyon

7.0

Mahogany

H3

Mahogany
Loop

H4

1.8

0.9

H13

Pronghorn

2.2

H12

0.7

H11

0.2

H2

0.4

H1

**Northern
Trailhead**

H10

**Entrance
Trailhead**

Fort
Collins

6000

1.1

Towhee
Loop

Towhee

H5

0.8

Soapstone Prairie

6500

Cheyenne   Rim

6.8

H6

Canyon

2.5

7000

6500

6000

H8

H9

Cheyenne   Rim

1.7

0.8

Big   Hole   Wash

Rising Sun

**Red
Mountain
Open Space**

Antelope Valley Rd

6500

H7

Salt Lick

Rising Sun

Sinking Sun

▲ Table
Mountain
7068

Cheyenne   Rim

7000

Ruby Wash

Big Hole Wash

Bent Rock

K Lynn Cameron

Big   Hole

Boxelder   Creek

6500

6500

H5 - 4.3 Continue straight as the Towhee Trail goes left.

H6 - 5.1 As you pass an old windmill, the singletrack turns into faint doubletrack.

H7 - 7.6 Turn left on the Cheyenne Rim Trail. *(If you turn right, you can ride into Wyoming in less than a mile!)*

H8 - 9.3 Continue straight on the Cheyenne Rim Trail as a trail goes right towards Red Mountain Open Space.

H9 - 10.1 Continue straight on the Cheyenne Rim Trail as Overlook Spur goes left.

H10 - 16.9 Arrive at a trailhead. Ride east along the road towards the entrance station.

H11 - 17.1 At the entrance station, turn left, ride up the road about 100 feet, then turn right on the Pronghorn Trail.

H12 - 18.1 Turn left on the Pronghorn Loop.

H13 - 20.3 Make another left and go through a gate on a trail signed "To Mahogany Loop."

H2 - 21.2 Turn left on Mahogony and quickly arrive back at the parking lot.

Miles of smooth singletrack await at Soapstone Prairie.

Laura Johnson picks her way through the rocks on the Bobcat Ridge Trail.

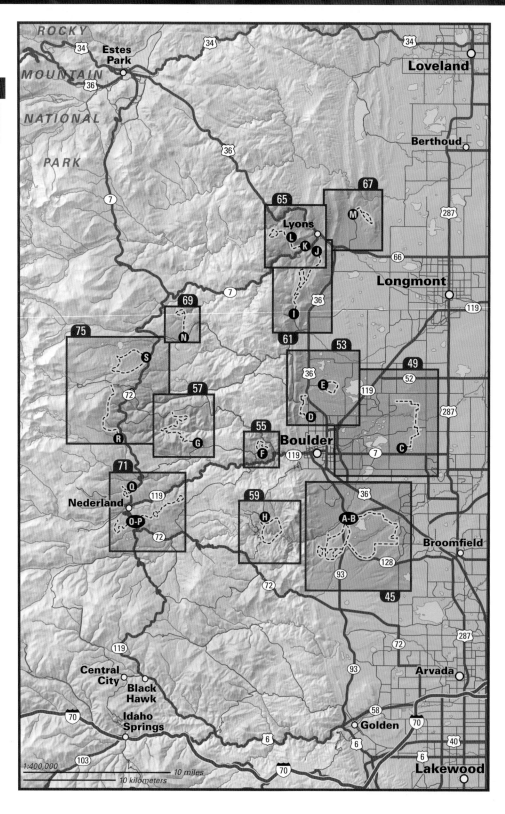

Boulder, Nederland, & Lyons

Home to the University of Colorado, Boulder is nestled against the eastern toe of the Rocky Mountains and offers a multitude of possibilities for mountain biking, rock climbing, and organic dining. The mountain biking trails run the gamut from technical mountain epics to smooth cruises. The old classics like Walker Ranch (near Boulder) and Hall Ranch (Lyons) still draw crowds, but are facing stiff competition from excellent, newly developed trail systems like West Magnolia (Nederland) and the South Boulder Trails.

Many of the trails near Boulder were closed to bikes during the early days of mountain biking, but the situation has improved substantially through the efforts of local advocacy groups and polite mountain bikers. Currently, there are a number of mountain biking options close to Boulder with more trails planned. Trail use is still a very contentious issue here, so remember to be friendly and courteous to other trail users and don't ride when the trails are muddy.

Accommodations

Boulder is a great place to find a nice hotel, motel, or cute bed-and-breakfast, but it's a miserable place to find a campsite. Your best bet for camping is to head about thirty minutes west to the mountain town of Nederland where there are several pay-campgrounds as well as an assortment of free camping options.

If you are looking to stay in town, there are several options in addition to the traditional motel room. Many people have good luck renting a house from homeowners who are on vacation – try Craigslist (craigslist.org). Also, Boulder is home to one of the few Chautaquas still in operation – most of these adult summer camps died out after their heyday in the 1920s – and you can rent a cabin right next to the Flatirons (chautauqua.com, 303-442-3282).

Boulder International Hostel
1107 12th Street, Boulder. 303-442-0523
Located close to the University of Colorado, this hostel offers inexpensive dorm beds and private rooms.

Boulder

Bike Shops

There are many excellent bike shops in Boulder. The following are the author's personal favorites.

Sports Garage
2705 Spruce Street, Boulder. 303-473-0033
High-end shop selling Yeti, Spot, and other quality brands. Excellent demo bikes available.

University Bicycles
839 Pearl Street, Boulder. 303-444-4196
Massive selection of road and mountain bikes – also offers rentals.

The Fix
3015 Sterling Circle, Unit 100, Boulder. 303-939-8349
Located near the new Valmont Bike Park, The Fix specializes in dirt jumping, downhill, and free-ride bikes. This is the best place to go for flat pedals and sticky-rubber shoes.

Full Cycle (Two locations)
1211 13th Street & 1795 Pearl Street, Boulder. 303-440-1002
Good selection of bikes and parts.

Boulder Cycle Sport (Two locations)
4580 N. Broadway & 629 S. Broadway. 303-444-2453
Plenty of good bikes for all budgets.

Redstone Cyclery
138 Main Street, Lyons. 202-823-5810
A small shop packed with excellent bikes.

Eats and Drinks

Boulder

Brewpub: Mountain Sun and Southern Sun (Two locations) - **1535 Pearl Street and 627 South Broadway, Boulder. 303-546-0886**
The Mountain Sun and the Southern Sun are Boulder staples and have been serving microbrews, burgers, and wings to hungry bikers, climbers, and skiers for as long as anyone can remember.

Brewpub: Walnut Brewery
1123 Walnut Street, Boulder. 303-447-1345
Located right in the middle of Downtown Boulder, the Walnut Brewery serves good pub food and excellent beer.

Breakfast: Walnut Café (Two locations)
3073 Walnut Street and 673 South Broadway, Boulder. 303-447-2315
Quick, inexpensive, and delicious.

Tapas: The Mediterranean Restaurant
3073 Walnut Street, Boulder. 303-447-2315
"The Med" has the best happy hour in Boulder: from 4 to 6:30 you can stuff yourself with amazing tapas, pizzas, and sangria for reasonable prices.

Fine dining: Pearl Street between 9th Street and 11th Street in Boulder
The west end of Pearl Street is loaded with great restaurants and is a great place to go for a classy dinner. The West End Tavern, The Kitchen, Centro, Salt, and Jax all offer award-winning food and drink.

Lyons

Brewpub: Oskar Blues
303 Main Street, Lyons. 303-823-6685
The source of Dale's Pale Ale (the best beer in the world that comes in a can), Oskar Blues is conveniently located in Lyons, near the trailheads for Hall Ranch and Picture Rock. They serve excellent pub-food with a Cajun flair. Fried pickles anyone?

Nederland

Coffee: Happy Trails
98 Highway 119 South, Nederland. 303-258-3435
This small coffee shop looks like an abandoned shack from the outside, but on the inside you'll find some of the best coffee you've ever tasted as well as some delicious pastries.

Coffee: Buffalo Bill's Coffee & Confections
101 Highway 119 South, Nederland.
303-258-2455
Operating out of a few historic railroad cars, Buffalo Bill's serves homemade mini-doughnuts, ice cream, candy, and excellent coffee.

Pizza and Beer: Backcountry Pizza
20 East Lakeview Drive #212, Nederland.
303-258-0176
Located next to the supermarket, this tiny restaurant and bar offers fantastic pizza and well-chosen beers.

Kathmandu Restaurant
110 North Jefferson Street, Nederland
303-285-1169
Serving up delicious Indian and Nepali food at appetizing prices, Kathmandu is a fantastic après ride destination. Great for vegetarians.

BONUS RIDE

Left Hand OHV - The Left Hand Canyon OHV area is generally known as a place to drive jeeps and shoot guns. However, it is also a good place to mountain bike on steep, rocky trails. The riding isn't good by most people's standards, but if you're looking to test your downhill skills on some gnarly hills, this might be the best place in Boulder County to do so.

Once again, Josh Stahl fails to make it home before sunset

(A) South Boulder Trails ★★★★★

Marshall Mesa, Spring Brook, Flatirons Vista, & Doudy Draw

(3 miles south of Boulder)

Boulder

Technical Difficulty:	◐
Physical Difficulty:	**Moderate**
Distance:	3 – 20 miles
Time:	30 minutes – 4 hours
Type:	Riding Area
Surface:	Mostly wide singletrack
Elevation (low/high):	5,500'/6,200'
Season:	Spring, Summer, Fall
Crowds:	Crowded
Dogs:	Boulder County Voice and Sight Tag required

A network of fun, easy singletrack within biking distance of Boulder

Ride Description

Until recently, the riding in South Boulder was largely ignored by mountain bikers in favor of longer, more technical trails. However, in the last few years, several new trails have been constructed in the area, and the riding has improved substantially. The trails are well marked and easy to follow, so just read the descriptions, have a look at the map, and go ride.

One of the greatest loops is the "Tour de South Boulder," a linkup of all the best trails. Start at the Marshall Mesa Trailhead, ride Marshall Mesa to Community Ditch. Then cross CO-93 and follow Community Ditch to Doudy Draw. Take Doudy Draw to Spring Brook, ride the loop, and then ride Flatirons Vista. Ride back the way you came, or take the Greenbelt Trail.

Driving Directions

Though all of the trails are interconnected, there are three main trailheads that provide convenient access to specific trails. If cycling from Boulder (highly recommended), the Marshall Mesa Trailhead is the easiest to reach.

Trailhead Directions and Recommended Rides:

Marshall Mesa Trailhead - From Boulder, head south on Broadway (CO-93).
Turn left on Eldorado Springs Drive and make an immediate right into the trailhead.

"Marshall Mesa Loop" — ● Distance: 3.3 miles
This was one of the first mountain biking trails in the area and is still a good, quick loop. Take Marshall Valley to Community Ditch to Coal Seam.

Doudy Draw Trailhead - From Boulder, head south on Broadway (CO-93). Turn right on Eldorado Springs Drive, go 1.7 miles, and turn left into the trailhead.

Spring Brook Loop — ◐ Distance: 5.0 miles
The Spring Brook Loop contains some of the best singletrack within easy cycling distance from Boulder. Take the Doudy Draw Trail until you reach the Spring Brook Loop. Ride either direction around the Spring Brook Loop (most prefer counterclockwise) and then head back.

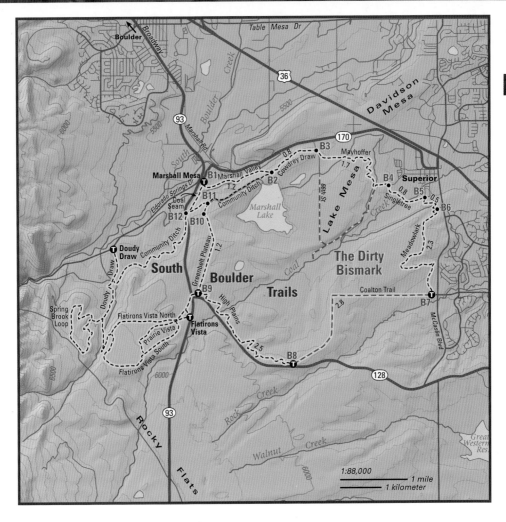

Flatirons Vista Trailhead - From Boulder, head south on Broadway (CO-93). Continue past Eldorado Springs Drive. About 0.2 miles past the junction with CO-128, carefully turn right into the Flatirons Vista Trailhead.

Flatirons Vista — ⬤ Distance: 3.7 miles

This nice beginner's loop lives up to its name, providing great views of the Flatirons. Take the Prairie Vista Trail to the Flatirons Vista Loop and ride clockwise.

Ⓑ The Dirty Bismark ★★☆☆☆

(3 miles south of Boulder)

Technical Difficulty:	●
Physical Difficulty:	**Easy**
Distance:	15.0 miles
Time:	2 – 3 hours
Type:	Loop
Surface:	Singletrack, dirt road, paved road
Climbing:	1,200'
Season:	Year-round *
Crowds:	Some
Dogs:	Some trails have leash laws

A long workout on gentle trails, all within biking distance of Boulder

Ride Description

Back in the 1980s, the Coors Classic was the premier road biking race in America and the Morgul-Bismark was one of the most famous stages, connecting Marshall Road, McCaslin Boulevard, CO-128 and CO-93. The mountain biker's version, the Dirty Bismark, is a combination of trails and dirt roads that run just inside the Morgul–Bismark. The Dirty Bismark is suitable for the beginning mountain biker, but is long enough to be a solid workout for the expert. For an even longer ride, consider riding to the trailhead from Boulder.

*During warm periods in the winter, the Dirty Bismark can be one of the first rides near Boulder to be snow-free. However, avoid riding the South Boulder Trails when they are muddy – they are easily damaged.

Driving Directions

From Boulder, head south on Broadway (CO-93) for 2 to 3 miles. Turn left on Eldorado Springs Drive and make an immediate right into the Marshall Mesa Trailhead parking lot. The Marshall Mesa Trailhead is easy to reach by bicycle from Boulder via the "Broadway Boogie" bike path (which runs along Broadway Street) and connects to Marshall Road.

Garrett Wilson on South Boulder Trails   photo: Theodore B Van Orman

Riding Directions

B1 - 0.0   From the Marshall Mesa Trailhead, pass through the gate and bear left at the junction, following the Marshall Valley Trail east.

B2 - 1.2   Turn left on the Cowdrey Draw Trail as the Community Ditch Trail goes right.

B3 - 2.0   Cross a paved road (66th St) start riding on the on the Mayhoffer-Singletree Trail.

B4 - 3.8   Continue straight on the Singletree Trail, a gravel bike path that is signed "Rock-Creek Coal-Creek Trail System."

B5 - 4.5   Turn right on the Meadowlark Trail, passing through a green gate.

B6 - 5.0   Cross a bridge and turn right to continue on the Meadowlark Trail

B7 - 7.3   Arrive at a trailhead and turn right on the Coalton Trail (an old dirt road).

B8 - 10.0   Reach a parking lot on CO-128. Make a right, pass through a gate, and take the High Plains Trail east.

B9 - 12.6   Reach a trailhead and turn right onto the Greenbelt Plateau Trail.

B10 - 13.8   Turn right and ride down a few wooden stairs.

B11 - 14.0   Turn left on the wide Community Ditch Trail.

B12 - 14.4   Just before Community Ditch Trail hits CO-93, turn right onto the Coal Seam Trail and follow this back to the Marshall Mesa Trailhead.

South Boulder Trails at sunset

C East Boulder Trail ★★★★★

(5 miles east of Boulder)

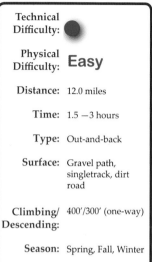

Technical
Difficulty: ●

Physical
Difficulty: **Easy**

Distance: 12.0 miles

Time: 1.5 – 3 hours

Type: Out-and-back

Surface: Gravel path,
singletrack, dirt
road

Climbing/ 400'/300' (one-way)
Descending:

Season: Spring, Fall, Winter

Crowds: Some

Dogs: (no dogs symbol)

A gentle beginner's ride or a good winter workout

Ride Description

The East Boulder Trail (which consists of Teller Farm Trail, White Rocks Trail, and the Gunbarrel Farm Trail), is mostly wide, flat, and boring. However, this makes it a great place to introduce friends to mountain biking. Additionally, its position away from the mountains and its lack of trees make it one of the first trails to melt out after a snowstorm. Riders looking for a longer workout should consider riding to this trail from Boulder. It is possible to incorporate the East Boulder Trail as part of a larger loop involving many of Boulder's fine bike paths.

*Dogs are allowed off-leash on the Teller Farm Trail with a Boulder County "Voice-and-sight" tag. No dogs are allowed on White Rocks.

Driving Directions

From 28th Street (US-36) in Boulder, head east on Arapahoe Road and go 5.2 miles. About one mile past 75th Street, turn left at a sign for "Teller Farm South Trailhead." Reach the trailhead parking lot in about 0.2 miles.

Riding Directions

C1 - 0.0   From the trailhead, start riding on the Teller Farm Trail. This trail is wide, flat, and easy. Follow it past Teller Lake.

C2 - 2.1   Arrive at the Teller Farm North Trailhead. Turn left into the parking lot and ride on a bike path that parallels Valmont road for 0.2 miles.

C3 - 2.3   Cross Valmont Road and arrive at the White Rocks Trailhead. Start riding on the White Rocks Trail. The trail is a combination of gravel path, singletrack, and old dirt roads.

C4 - 6.0   Arrive at the East Boulder Trail – Gunbarrel Trailhead. Turn around and head back the way you came.

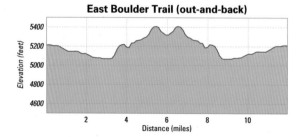

East Boulder Trail (out-and-back)

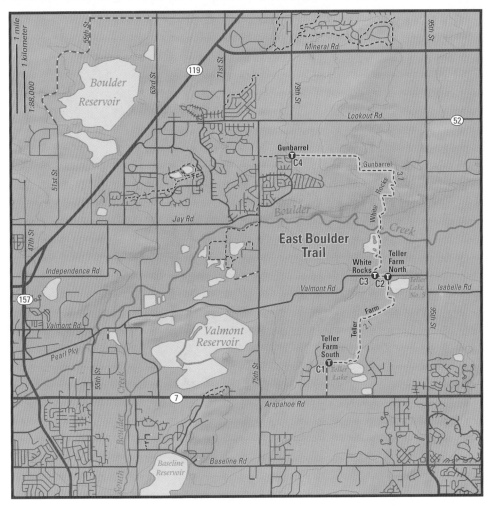

Spectacular, smooth singletrack on the Dirty Bismark.

Boulder

(D) Foothills Trail ★★☆☆☆

(Starts from Boulder)

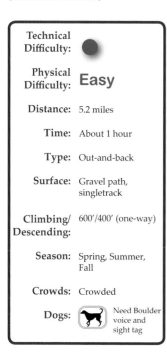

Technical Difficulty:	●
Physical Difficulty:	**Easy**
Distance:	5.2 miles
Time:	About 1 hour
Type:	Out-and-back
Surface:	Gravel path, singletrack
Climbing/ Descending:	600'/400' (one-way)
Season:	Spring, Summer, Fall
Crowds:	Crowded
Dogs:	Need Boulder voice and sight tag

An easy cruise connecting to Boulder Valley Ranch

Ride Description

The Foothills Trail provides a nice, smooth pathway along the base of the hills. The first two miles of the Foothills Trail are very smooth and can probably be ridden with a road bike. About half a mile after crossing Lee Hill Road, the trail becomes rockier and more challenging with some short sections of blue-square riding. The Foothills Trail can be used to connect Boulder with the trails at Boulder Valley Ranch, which can, in turn, be ridden up to Left Hand Canyon and the start of Heil Ranch.

Driving Directions

From downtown Boulder, head north on Broadway and turn left into the Wonderland Lake Trailhead parking lot. The trailhead is 2.3 miles north of the intersection of Broadway and Pearl Street.

Riding Directions

D1 - 0.0 From the Wonderland Lake Trailhead, start riding on the Wonderland Lake Trail.

D2 - 0.3 Turn left on a paved road (Utica Avenue). Follow this for a few hundred feet, and then turn left on the Wonderland Lake Trail.

D3 - 0.6 Turn right at a T-intersection.

D4 - 1.5 Arrive at a parking lot. Cross Lee Hill Road and continue on the Foothills Trail.

D5 - 1.7 Follow the trail as it makes a sharp left.

D6 - 2.6 Arrive at the underpass under US-36. Either follow this to Boulder Valley Ranch, or turn around.

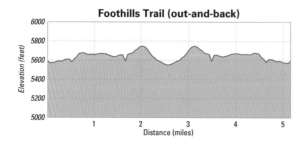

David Weber leads the pack through the narrow trees at West Magnolia Trails   photo: Fredrik Marmsater

(E) Boulder Valley Ranch ★★★★★

(4 miles north of Boulder)

Technical Difficulty:	○
Physical Difficulty:	**Easy**
Distance:	2.8 – 8.5 miles
Time:	20 minutes or more
Type:	Loop with options
Surface:	Dirt road, wide trail
Climbing:	200'
Season:	Fall, Winter, Spring
Crowds:	Crowded
Dogs:	Need Boulder voice and sight tag

These traffic-free dirt roads are great for easy cruising

Ride Description

Most of the trails at Boulder Valley Ranch are non-technical and consist of old ranch roads that have been turned into hiking and biking trails. They melt out quickly after a snowstorm and are a great place to take the neophyte mountain biker. Be sure to read the trail signs – some of the trails at Boulder Valley Ranch are closed to bikes.

The ride highlighted on the map is a quick loop composed of the Eagle Trail and the Sage Trail. To add more miles, there are several out-and-back trails that connect with this central loop. Those looking for an even longer ride should consider linking the Foothills Trail with the Eagle Trail, to the Left Hand Trail, and then connecting this to Heil Ranch (Ride I).

Driving Directions

From Boulder, head north on either Broadway or 28th Street until they merge and become US-36. From this intersection, continue north on US-36 for 1.1 miles. Turn right on Longhorn Road at a sign for "Boulder Valley Ranch" and proceed 1.0 miles until you see the trailhead parking on the right.

Riding Directions

E1 - 0.0 From the trailhead, ride south on the Sage Trail.

E2 - 0.7 Turn left on the Eagle Trail. *(OPTION: make a sharp right, climb a very steep hill, and ride the western section of the Eagle Trail. It's 1.9 miles to an underpass beneath US-36 that connects with the Foothills Trail.)*

E3 - 1.6 Turn left on the Sage Trail. *(OPTION: Turn right to stay on the Eagle Trail. It's 0.5 miles to the Eagle Trailhead where dirt roads connect to trails at Boulder Reservoir Recreation Area.)*

E1 - 2.6 Arrive back at the trailhead. *(OPTION: Ride north on the Left Hand Trail. This trail is a nice tour past the Left Hand Valley Reservoir and reaches the Left Hand Trailhead in 2.8 miles.)*

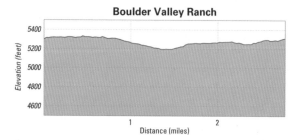

Boulder Valley Ranch

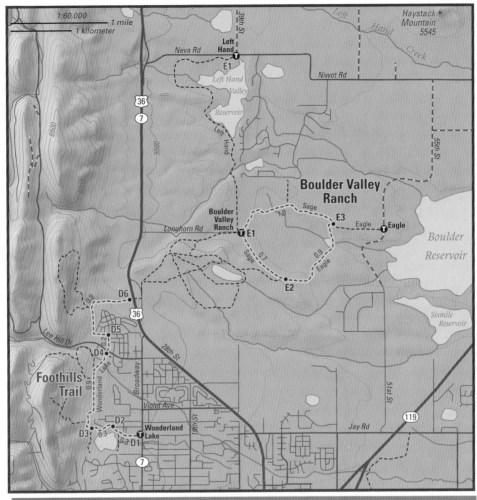

Boulder

The author's mom, Mary Musselman enjoys the singletrack on the Left Hand Trail at Boulder Valley Ranch.

Boulder

(F) Betasso Preserve ★★★☆☆

(6 miles west of Boulder)

Technical Difficulty:	
Physical Difficulty:	**Moderate**
Distance:	3.1 miles
Time:	30 minutes per lap
Type:	Loop
Surface:	Singletrack
Climbing:	700'
Season:	Spring, Summer, Fall
Crowds:	Crowded
Dogs:	Dogs must be leashed

A delightful, quick loop in the hills above Boulder

Ride Description

The loop at Betasso Preserve is a favorite after-work ride for Boulder mountain bikers. Not too technical, yet not too easy, Betasso is adored by novices and experts alike for its great riding and beautiful vistas. This trail is so popular – and has so many blind corners – that special restrictions have been enacted. *Mountain bikes are NOT allowed on Wednesdays and Saturdays* and riders are required to travel in only one direction (either clockwise or counterclockwise). The required direction of travel changes every month and is indicated by a sign near the parking lot. Hikers are encouraged to walk in the opposite direction.

In the summer of 2011, The Benjamin Trail opened, adding four more miles of great singletrack to Betasso Preserve.

It is possible to ride to the trailhead from Boulder, though this involves about a mile of frightening riding along Boulder Canyon Road. From Eben G. Fine Park (at the west end of Arapahoe Avenue), take the bike path up Boulder Canyon. When the bike path ends, continue riding up Boulder Canyon Road. Just before a tunnel, turn right on the Canyon Connector Trail, which climbs steeply and connects to the Betasso Loop Trail in about a mile.

Driving Directions

From Boulder, head west on Canyon Boulevard. About 4 miles from Boulder, turn right onto Sugarloaf Road and go 0.9 miles. Bear right onto Betasso Road and go 0.5 miles. Turn left into the trailhead and park near the picnic shelter.

Riding Directions

F1 - 0.0   From the parking lot, ride down the short path that leads to the loop trail. Read the sign and determine which direction you are required to ride this month.

F2 - 2.9
(clockwise)
0.2
(counterclockwise)

At a picnic table, continue riding on the loop trail as the Canyon Connector Trail leaves to the outside of the loop.

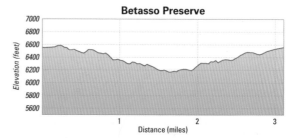

Betasso Preserve

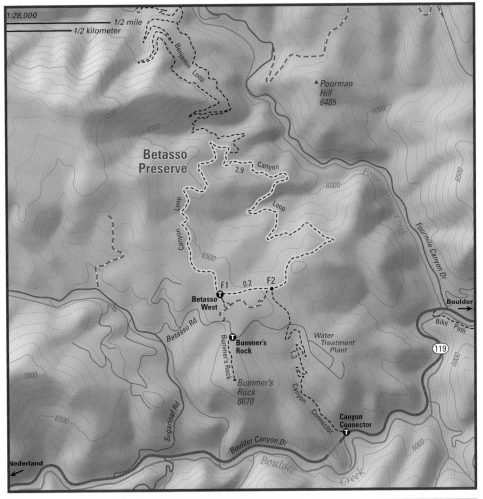

1:28,000

1/2 mile
1/2 kilometer

Benjamin Loop

▲ Poorman
Hill
6485

Betasso
Preserve

2.9 Canyon

Loop

Canyon Loop

Four Mile Creek

Fourmile Canyon Dr

F1 0.2 F2

Betasso
West

Boulder

Bike Path

119

Betasso Rd

Bummer's
Rock

Bummer's Rock

Water
Treatment
Plant

1.3

Bummer's
Rock
6670

Canyon Connector

Sugarloaf Rd

Canyon
Connector

Boulder Canyon Dr

Nederland

Boulder

Creek

Josh Stahl speeds along Walker Ranch.

G Switzerland Trail ★★☆☆☆

(10 miles west of Boulder)

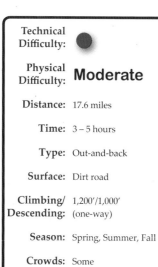

Technical Difficulty:	●
Physical Difficulty:	**Moderate**
Distance:	17.6 miles
Time:	3 – 5 hours
Type:	Out-and-back
Surface:	Dirt road
Climbing/ Descending:	1,200'/1,000' (one-way)
Season:	Spring, Summer, Fall
Crowds:	Some
Dogs:	Consider traffic and length of ride

A gentle tour along an old railroad grade

Ride Description

Following an old narrow-gauge railroad bed, the Switzerland Trail makes broad turns and never climbs too steeply. The road is open to vehicles but most of the traffic consists of slow-moving jeeps. Though the grades are never extreme, this ride is moderately challenging due to long sections of climbing. The road doesn't receive much shade so bring plenty of water. Those looking for an added challenge can continue on the Switzerland Trail past Gold Hill Road for several additional miles.

Driving Directions

From Boulder, head west on Canyon Boulevard and go 4.3 miles past 9th Street. Turn right on Sugarloaf Road and go 4.7 miles. Turn right on Switzerland Trail Road (Sugarloaf Mountain Road) and go 0.8 miles to the parking lot. If you are biking to the trailhead, consider riding the Canyon Link Trail (see Ride F) to reach Sugarloaf Road, or taking Fourmile Canyon Drive to mile 4.2 of the Riding Directions.

Riding Directions

G1 - 0.0 Head towards the back of the Sugarloaf Mountain Trailhead and turn left on the wide dirt road (open to vehicle traffic).

G2 - 3.0 Continue straight on the Switzerland Trail as FS-240 goes left.

G3 - 4.2 After riding into the small village of Sunset, make a soft left onto an unmarked road that goes uphill (still the Switzerland Trail).

G4 - 7.6 Pass by the Mount Alto Picnic Grounds, a lovely place to stop for lunch.

G5 - 8.8 Arrive at a trailhead on Gold Hill Road. Turn around and return the way you came. *(OPTION: The Switzerland Trail continues for several more miles – ride as long as you like!)*

Switzerland Trail (out-and-back)

Boulder

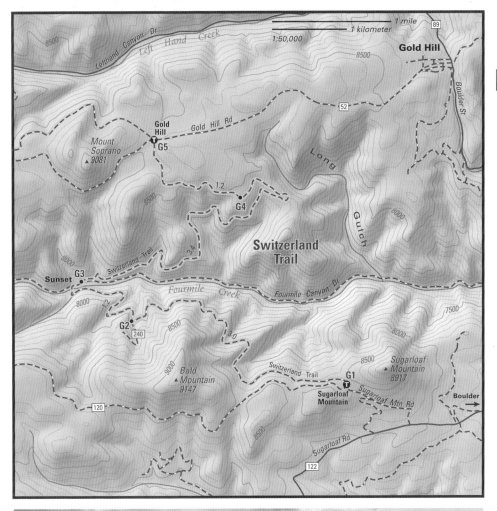

Laura Johnson and Katie Johnson out for a leisurely sunset ride on the South Boulder Trails.

(H)Walker Ranch ★★★★☆

(8 miles southwest of Boulder)

Technical Difficulty:	◆
Physical Difficulty:	**Strenuous**
Distance:	7.1 miles
Time:	1 – 2 hours
Type:	Loop
Surface:	Singletrack,
Climbing:	1,600'
Season:	Spring, Summer, Fall
Crowds:	Crowded
Dogs:	Dogs must be leashed

A tough ride with plenty of steep climbs and technical sections

Ride Description

Walker Ranch is Boulder's favorite after-work bike ride; it's quick enough to finish before sunset but still offers technical and physical challenge. It is a great ride for intermediate riders to push themselves or for advanced riders in need of a good workout. There is a huge, unrideable flight of stairs in the middle of the loop, so prepare for a few minutes of carrying your bike. The loop can be completed in either direction, and it is traditional to argue endlessly about which is the best way to ride Walker. However, clockwise is clearly superior.

Driving Directions

From Broadway Street and Baseline Road in Boulder, head west for 1.3 miles until Baseline turns into Flagstaff Road. Continue onto Flagstaff Road for 7.3 miles as it winds up into the foothills. As the road bends sharply right, turn left on a dirt road into the trailhead. If you get to Gross Reservoir, you've gone a bit too far.

Riding Directions

H1 - 0.0 From the parking lot, find the start of the Walker Ranch Loop (near the big sign) and turn left at the first junction. Traverse across the slope for about a mile and then blast down some fun switchbacks.

H2 - 1.6 The singletrack ends at an old dirt road. Turn right, head down a few loose downhill sections, and eventually cross South Boulder Creek on a large bridge.

H3 - 2.6 Arrive at the stairs and hike your bike for five minutes.

H4 - 2.8 The trail splits and the less technical option goes right. The trails rejoin in 0.1 miles, so go either way.

H5 - 4.7 Pass the Crescent Meadows parking area. Continue on the Walker Ranch Loop. Enjoy an excellent downhill section.

H6 - 6.2 Ford a stream and climb back up a long hill.

H1 - 7.1 Arrive back at the parking lot. Go for another lap!

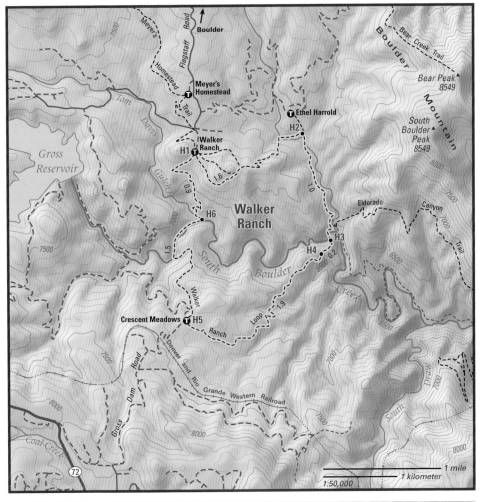

Courtney Grimm doesn't stop to smell the flowers at Walker Ranch

Boulder

(I) Heil Ranch ★★★★★

(10 miles north of Boulder)

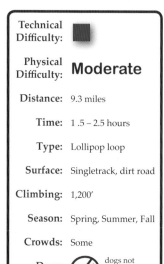

Technical Difficulty:	■
Physical Difficulty:	**Moderate**
Distance:	9.3 miles
Time:	1.5 – 2.5 hours
Type:	Lollipop loop
Surface:	Singletrack, dirt road
Climbing:	1,200′
Season:	Spring, Summer, Fall
Crowds:	Some
Dogs:	dogs not allowed

These quiet trails through the woods are frequented by deer and wild turkeys

Ride Description

Heil Ranch is a wonderful piece of wilderness tucked away just a few miles from Boulder. The trails at Heil don't have many huge rocks or overly steep climbs. However, the singletrack is studded with many small rocks, making the riding strenuous. The newly constructed (2009) Picture Rock Trail allows ambitious cyclists to ride from Heil Ranch to Hall Ranch near Lyons – a great link-up! The truly hard-core will ride to the trailhead from Boulder via the Foothills Trail and Boulder Valley Ranch (see rides D and E).

The author originally assumed that the Wild Turkey Trail was named for a trail-builder's predilection for fine bourbon. However, one cold day in December, he rode around a corner and came face-to-face with one dozen prehistoric-looking birds – a flock of wild turkeys!

Driving Directions

From the intersection of US-36 and Broadway in north Boulder, head north on US-36 for 4.8 miles. Turn left on Lefthand Canyon Drive and go 0.7 miles. At a sign for "Heil Ranch," turn right onto Geer Canyon Drive and go 1.2 miles. Turn right into the Heil Ranch Trailhead. The trail starts at the far end of the parking lot.

Riding Directions

I1 - 0.0   Leave the parking lot near the map kiosk. Ride up a wide dirt road, following signs that read, "To Wapiti Trail."

I2 - 0.5   Make a left on the Wapiti Trail as the dirt road continues straight.

I3 - 2.6   Turn right on the Ponderosa Loop as the other branch of Ponderosa Loop goes left.

I4 - 2.7   Turn right on the Wild Turkey Loop. (Watch out for wild turkeys!)

I5 - 3.8   Continue straight on Wild Turkey as the Picture Rock Trail goes right.

I6 - 5.5   Head left on the Ponderosa Loop.

I4 - 6.6   Arrive back at the intersection with Wild Turkey. Bear right to stay on Ponderosa and follow your tracks back to the parking lot.

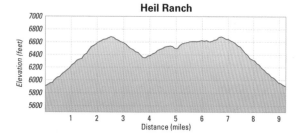

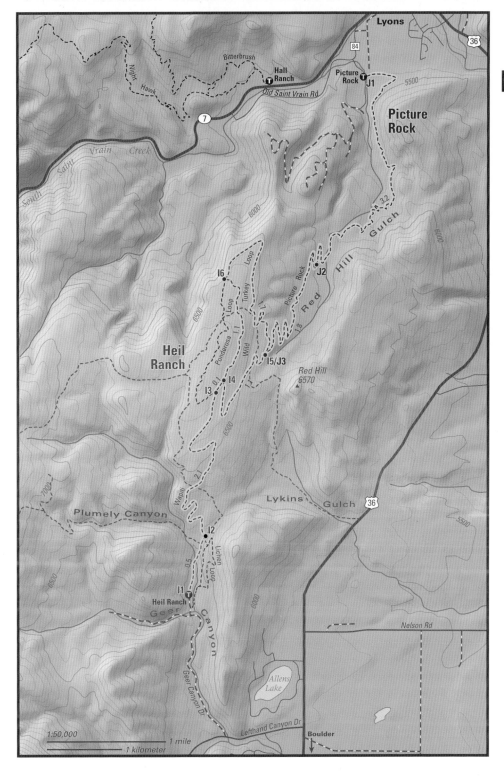

Boulder

Lyons

Hall
Ranch

Picture
Rock

J1

Picture
Rock

Bitterbrush

Old Saint Vrain Rd

Night Hawk

South Saint Vrain Creek

6000

5500

6000

Loop

I6

Picture Rock

J2

Red Hill Gulch

3.2

Turkey

Loop

1.7

1.8

6500

Ponderosa

Wild

1.1

**Heil
Ranch**

I3

I4

0.1

1.3

I5/J3

Red Hill
6570 ▲

6500

Wapiti

2

Lykins Gulch

36

5500

Plumely Canyon

7000

6500

I2

0.5

Lichen Loop

6000

I1

Heil Ranch

Geer Canyon

Nelson Rd

Allens
Lake

Geer Canyon Dr

Lefthand Canyon Dr

Boulder

1:50,000

1 mile

1 kilometer

Ely Porter encounters autumn's first snow at Heil Ranc

(J) Picture Rock Trail ★★★☆☆

(1 mile southwest of Lyons)

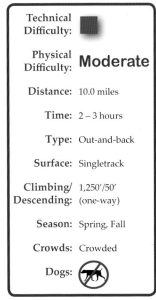

Technical Difficulty:	■
Physical Difficulty:	**Moderate**
Distance:	10.0 miles
Time:	2 – 3 hours
Type:	Out-and-back
Surface:	Singletrack
Climbing/ Descending:	1,250'/50' (one-way)
Season:	Spring, Fall
Crowds:	Crowded
Dogs:	🚫

Fun singletrack leads to a tough climb up the "Wall of Heil"

Boulder

Ride Description

The Picture Rock Trail is named for a type of beautiful sandstone that was historically quarried here. The trail has two distinct sections. The first three miles, up to the old quarry, climb gently and are suitable for beginner riders. The final two miles become much steeper and require some tenacity. The Picture Rock Trail is very popular with wildlife and it is common to see large herds of deer. Those looking for an epic ride should use the Picture Rock Trail to connect Heil Ranch with Hall Ranch for one of the best link-ups in the Boulder region. Keep an eye out for the stone picnic table a few miles up the trail; not only is it a great place to take a break, but the top of the table is made of a huge slab of "picture rock" sandstone from a local quarry.

Driving Directions

From Boulder, drive north on US-36 for about 15 miles. Turn left at the T-intersection to stay on US-36 and reach Lyons. After passing through downtown, turn left on CO-7 and go 0.5 miles. Turn left on Old Saint Vrain Road (County-84) and go 0.3 miles. Turn left on Red Gulch Road and go 0.4 miles. Turn right into the trailhead parking lot.

Riding Directions - see map on page 61

J1 - 0.0   From the trailhead, cross Red Gulch Road and start riding on the Picture Rock Trail.

J2 - 3.2   Arrive at the old quarry with the remains of an antique car. As you leave the quarry, turn right on singletrack. Climb the steep "Wall of Heil."

J3 - 5.0   Arrive at the end of the Picture Rock Trail and a junction with the Wild Turkey Loop. Turn around and go back the way you came, or do a lap on Wild Turkey and Ponderosa first (see Ride I).

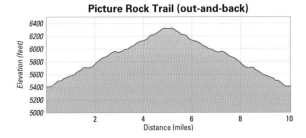

Picture Rock Trail (out-and-back)

Ⓚ Hall Ranch ★★★★☆

(2 miles southwest of Lyons)

Technical Difficulty:	◆
Physical Difficulty:	**Strenuous**
Distance:	9.6 miles
Time:	1.5 – 2.5 hours
Type:	Lollipop Loop
Surface:	Singletrack
Climbing:	1,600'
Season:	Spring, Fall
Crowds:	Crowded
Dogs:	

A Front Range classic, Hall Ranch draws crowds to enjoy its fast singletrack and technical rock-crawling

Ride Description

Fast downhills, technical climbing, and glimpses of high peaks combine to make Hall Ranch one of the best rides in the Front Range. Most of the trail is reasonably smooth, but successfully making it up the steep rock-garden requires serious skills. There are not many trees along the trail, so be prepared to cook in the sun on hot days. Some parts of the trail (notably the north side of the Nelson Loop) stay muddy for several days after a heavy rain.

Driving Directions

From Boulder, head north on US-36 for about 15 miles. At a T-intersection, turn left onto CO-7/CO-66. Drive through Lyons and come to another T-intersection: turn left on CO-7, and drive 1.5 miles. Turn right into the Hall Ranch Trailhead.

Riding Directions

K1 - 0.0 Start riding on the singletrack that leaves the lower parking lot near the large information sign.

K2 - 0.2 Continue on the Bitterbush Trail as the Nighthawk Trail goes left.

K3 - 0.7 Continue on the Bitterbush Trail at another junction with the Nighthawk Trail.

K4 - 2.2 A bench marks the end of the technical rock garden and serves as a nice place to rest before heading down some water-bars.

K5 - 2.5 At a junction, continue straight on the Bitterbush Trail as the Antelope Trail goes right.

K6 - 3.8 Come to a Y-junction with the Nelson Loop. You can go either way around this loop, but most people prefer to go left.

K6 - 6.0 Return to the Nelson/Bitterbush junction. Retrace your tracks down the Bitterbush Trail and back to the parking lot.

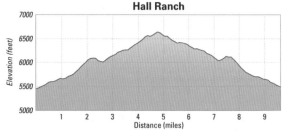

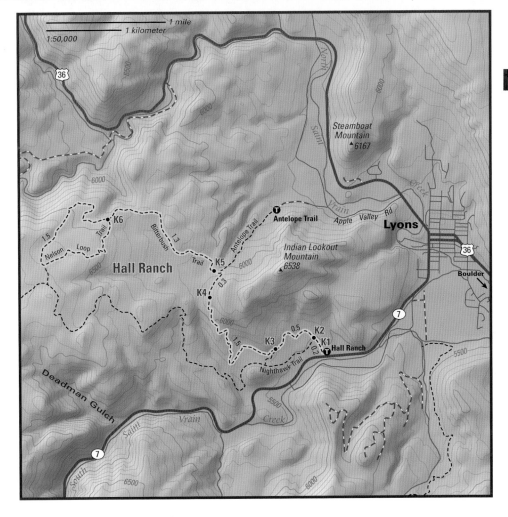

Boulder

ⓛ Hall Ranch via the Antelope Trail ★★★☆☆

Distance: **7.6 miles**

To avoid the difficult rock-garden section, you can start the ride on the Antelope Trail, which intersects the ride description at mile 2.5. To reach the start of the Antelope Trail, head northwest from Lyons on US-36, turn left on Apple Valley Road, and then turn left again onto Antelope Drive. The Antelope Trail climbs steeply for 1.0 miles before joining the ride description at mile 2.5. The parking lot at the Antelope Trailhead is often full on sunny weekends.

Ⓜ Rabbit Mountain ★★★★★

(6 miles northeast of Lyons)

Technical Difficulty:	
Physical Difficulty:	**Moderate**
Distance:	5.9 miles
Time:	1 – 2 hours
Type:	Out-and-back
Surface:	Singletrack
Climbing:	900′
Season:	Spring, Fall
Crowds:	Crowded
Dogs:	Dogs must be leashed

Several miles of enjoyable riding over many rabbit-sized rocks

Ride Description

Neither much of a mountain nor particularly full of rabbits, Rabbit Mountain does offer enough miles of trail for a pleasant evening ride. The trail features some great views of the Continental Divide as well as some sections of bumpy singletrack. Rabbit Mountain is very popular with hikers, so be prepared to go slowly during peak times

The suggested ride completes both the Eagle Wind lollipop loop as well as the Little Thompson Overlook Trail. It is, of course, possible to ride only one of the trails, thereby shortening the ride.

Driving Directions

From Boulder, take US-36 north for about 10 miles. At the T-intersection, turn right onto CO-66 and go 1.1 miles. Turn left onto 53rd Street (which turns into 55th Street) and drive 3.0 miles until you can make a right into the Rabbit Mountain Trailhead.

Riding Directions

M1 - 0.0 From the parking lot, take the main trail up the hill.

M2 - 0.5 Turn right towards the Eagle Wind Trail as the Little Thompson Overlook Trail goes left.

M3 - 0.6 Make a right onto the Eagle Wind Trail as the Indian Mesa Trail (a dirt road) goes left.

M4 - 1.0 Come to the loop of the Eagle Wind Trail. Go left, ride the loop, and head back the way you came.

M2 - 3.5 Turn right on the Little Thompson Overlook Trail, ride it out and back (roughly one mile each way), and then head back to trailhead.

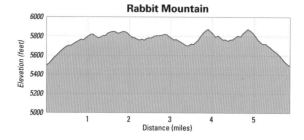

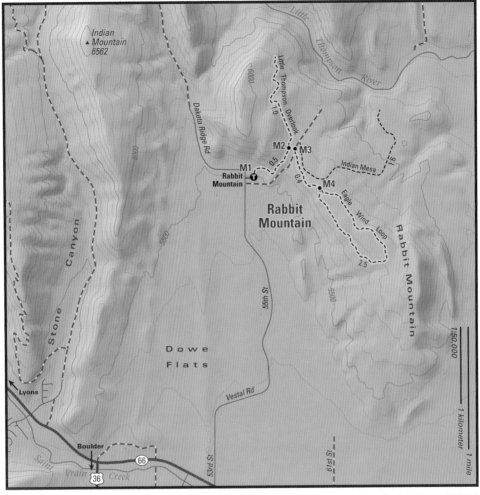

Another glorious sunset at Hall Ranch.

(N) Ceran Saint Vrain ★★★☆☆

(20 miles north of Boulder)

Technical Difficulty:	
Physical Difficulty:	**Moderate**
Distance:	6.1 miles
Time:	1 – 2 hours
Type:	Lollipop loop
Surface:	Singletrack, jeep road
Climbing:	1,200′
Season:	Summer, Fall
Crowds:	Some
Dogs:	🐕

The first 2 miles are absolutely fantastic!

Ride Description

The first few miles of the Ceran Saint Vrain Trail are some of the best singletrack in the Front Range. However, the full ride involves a tough climb on a loose jeep road followed by a descent on tough, loose singletrack. This ride is in a dense forest, so it stays fairly cool, even during hot summer days. This is also a popular spot for camping and trout fishing.

Driving Directions

From Boulder, head north on US-36. Turn left on Lefthand Canyon Drive and go 5.2 miles. Turn right on James Canyon Drive and follow this through Jamestown as it turns into Overland Road. Shortly after the road turns to dirt, turn right into the Ceran Saint Vrain Trailhead. If you get to the Peak-to-Peak Highway, you've gone about a mile too far.

Riding Directions

N1 - 0.0   From the parking lot, start riding on the Ceran Saint Vrain Trail and cross a bridge.

N2 - 1.9   Turn left on an old road (FS-252) and climb steeply.

N3 - 2.1   Continue straight on the road as an unmarked trail goes left.

N4 - 2.5   At a signpost with a broken sign, turn left on an old dirt road (FS-252A).

N5 - 2.8   Continue straight on the road as unmarked singletrack goes left. *(To the left is a nice variation that avoids some of the climbing on the road.)*

N6 - 3.2   Make a left on wide singletrack signed as "252C."

N7 - 3.7   The singletrack mentioned at mile 2.8 comes in on the left; continue straight.

N3 - 4.0   Arrive back at the dirt road, turn right and ride back to the parking lot.

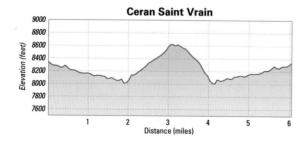

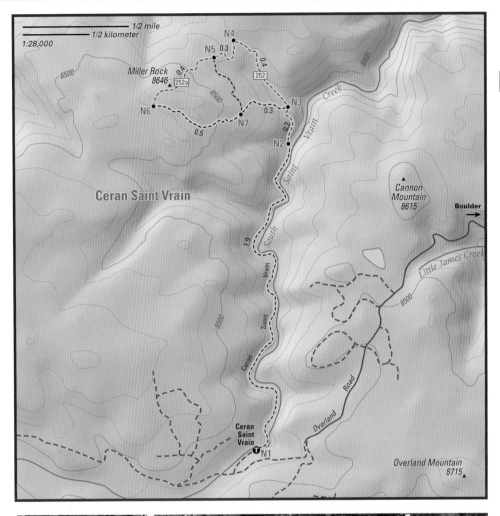

Craig Belgard takes a corner a little too fast on the Ceran Saint Vrain Trail.

◎West Magnolia - The Hobbit Trails ★★★★☆

(2 miles south of Nederland)

Technical Difficulty:	▪
Physical Difficulty:	**Easy**
Distance:	6.0 miles
Time:	1 – 2 hours
Type:	Loop
Surface:	Singletrack, dirt road
Climbing:	600'
Season:	Summer, Fall
Crowds:	Some
Dogs:	🐕

These gentle trails through the woods offer relief from Front Range hill climbing

Ride Description

West Magnolia is a wonderful, complex network of winding singletrack and dirt roads. There are posted maps and signs to help you navigate the trails, but the trail system is confusing and many trails are not marked. However, since most of the trails here are gentle, rolling singletrack, it's a great place to wander around and explore. This loop is one of the easiest to find and offers excellent riding.

Driving Directions

From the traffic circle in Nederland, head south on the Peak-to-Peak Highway (CO-119/CO-72) and go 2.0 miles. At Magnolia Road, turn right and park at the Magnolia Trailhead.

Riding Directions

O1 - 0.0 From the parking area, start riding south along Magnolia Road.

O2 - 0.5 Turn left on Root Canal (Trail #927), go 50 feet, and bear right at the T-intersection. In the next mile, you will come to several intersections where the trail splits and quickly re-joins – go either way.

O3 - 1.4 Come to a dirt road, turn left, go about 100 feet, and turn left again onto singletrack.

O4 - 1.5 Cross a dirt road and continue riding on singletrack (Hobbit 1, Trail #927).

O5 - 2.3 Make a right on a dirt road, go about 50 feet, and turn left onto singletrack (the Hobbit 2 Trail).

O6 - 3.0 Arrive at a dirt parking lot. Continue straight across and find the start of the Hobbit 3 singletrack on the other side.

O7 - 3.9 Turn right on a dirt road, go about 200 feet, and turn left on singletrack (Trail 355I).

O8 - 4.1 Go left on a dirt road. Quickly make another left, pass around a gate, and turn right on single-track labeled "926F."

West Magnolia - The Hobbit Trails

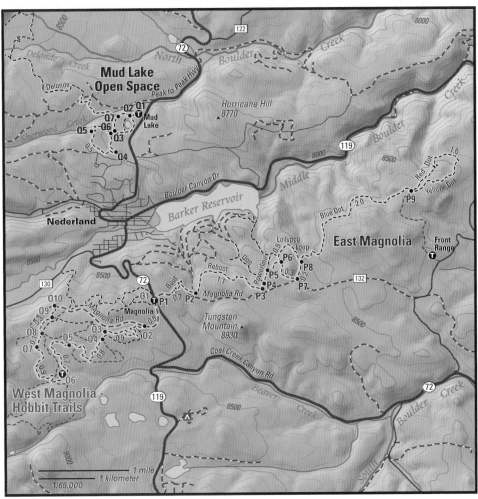

O9 - 4.4   Come to a campsite and turn right on a dirt road. Go about 400 feet and turn left on trail 926F.

O10 - 4.5   Arrive at Magnolia Road. Turn right and ride back to the parking lot. Alternatively, you can turn left on one of the trails and find a more adventurous way back to the trailhead.

Laura Johnson explores the beautiful singletrack at West Magnolia.

(P) East Magnolia ★★★★☆

(2 miles south of Nederland)

Technical Difficulty:	
Physical Difficulty:	**Strenuous**
Distance:	11.1 miles
Time:	2 – 3 hours
Type:	Lollipop loop
Surface:	Singletrack
Climbing:	1,500'
Season:	Summer, Fall
Crowds:	Some
Dogs:	

Beautiful singletrack through forests, meadows, and aspens

Ride Description

Too darn hot to ride in Boulder? The East Magnolia trails offer beautiful singletrack through a cool forest. The trails on the east side of Magnolia Road are somewhat rockier and more difficult than those on the west side, but still feature some butter-smooth sections that glide through aspen groves and meadows. The trails here can be confusing and are seldom signed. So, be sure to pack some extra food, plenty of water, and your lust for adventure.

Driving Directions

From the traffic circle in Nederland, head south on the Peak-to-Peak Highway (CO-119/CO-72) for 2.0 miles. At Magnolia Road, turn right and park at the Magnolia Trailhead.

Riding Directions - see map on page 71

P1 - 0.0 From the trailhead, cross CO-119 and start riding east on Magnolia Road. In 0.1 miles, turn left on the singletrack (Boot Trail) that leaves the road to the north.

P2 - 0.7 Reach a small road and continue on the singletrack that bends back into the woods. (This is the Reboot Trail.)

P3 - 1.8 Turn left and follow the powerlines (called "Powerline Trail").

P4 - 1.9 Continue straight as the Doe Trail goes left.

P5 - 2.0 Bear right on a wide trail as the Powerlines Trail goes straight.

P6 - 2.2 Arrive at the west end of "The Lollypop Loop." Take the right fork.

P7 - 2.5 Continue on the trail as it passes near a small parking area on Magnolia Road.

P8 - 2.7 Continue straight as the other branch of the Lollypop Loop comes in from the left. You are now on the Blue Dot Trail.

P9 - 4.7 Come to a Y-intersection and turn right on the Yellow Dot Trail, which turns into the Red Dot Trail and loops back around.

P9 - 6.3 Arrive back at the Blue Dot Trail. Retrace your path to the Lollypop Loop.

P8 - 8.3 Turn right on the north side of the Lollypop Loop, a narrow trail through the pines.

P6 - 8.8 Back at the west junction of the Lollypop Loop, go right. Head back to the parking lot the way you came.

ⓠ Mud Lake Open Space ★★★★★

(2 miles north of Nederland)

Technical Difficulty:	●
Physical Difficulty:	**Easy**
Distance:	2.1 miles
Time:	20 minutes per lap
Type:	Loop
Surface:	Singletrack
Climbing:	250′
Season:	Spring, Summer, Fall
Crowds:	Some
Dogs:	Dogs must be leashed

A gentle loop around Mud Lake makes a perfect date ride.

Ride Description

Need a ride for that "special someone" who doesn't know how to mountain bike? The smooth, mostly-flat trails at Mud Lake provide the perfect venue. Additionally, should a nicely chilled bottle of champagne magically appear, there are a number of picnic tables near the lake where you could sit and "admire the view."

Despite the lack of technical features, the riding at Mud Lake is actually really fun. The only problem is that there are only about three miles of trail available for mountain biking. Try doing a few laps!

Driving Directions

From the traffic circle in Nederland, head west on CO-72 (the Peak-to-Peak Highway), and go about 1.5 miles. Turn left at a sign for the Mud Lake Open Space and arrive at the large gravel parking area.

Riding Directions - see map on page 71

Q1 - 0.0 Start riding on the main trail that is located near a large sign.

Q2 - 0.1 Turn left on the Tungsten Loop.

Q3 - 0.5 Turn left towards the Kinnickinnick Loop. In a few hundred feet, make a left on the Kinnickinnick Loop itself.

Q4 - 0.8 Continue right on the Kinnickinnick Loop as a spur trail goes left.

Q5 - 1.3 Pass a wooden bench with a great view of the Indian Peaks.

Q6 - 1.6 Turn left towards the Tungsten Loop. Then, in a few hundred feet, make a left on the Tungsten Loop itself.

Q7 - 1.8 Continue straight as a trail to Caribou Ranch Open Space goes left. (This trail is fun and continues for 0.7 miles to Caribou Ranch; beyond that, bikes are not allowed.)

Q2 - 2.0 Arrive back at the first intersection; head back to the parking lot or do another lap!

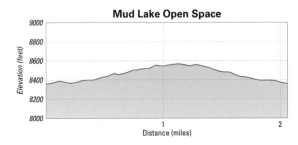

(R) Sourdough Trail ★★★☆☆

(7 miles north of Nederland)

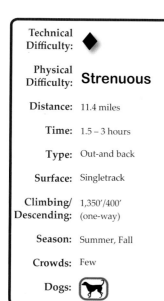

Technical Difficulty:	◆
Physical Difficulty:	**Strenuous**
Distance:	11.4 miles
Time:	1.5 – 3 hours
Type:	Out-and back
Surface:	Singletrack
Climbing/ Descending:	1,350'/400' (one-way)
Season:	Summer, Fall
Crowds:	Few
Dogs:	🐕

Rough riding on a rocky trail through a dense pine forest.

Ride Description

Much like sourdough bread, opinions are divided on the Sourdough Trail. Some people (the author included) love the challenging riding and secluded setting, but others loathe the loose, rocky singletrack. Perched near 10,000 feet, and winding through a shady forest, the Sourdough Trail is a great place to beat the summer heat. Be sure to bring the repair kit and the first aid supplies; this rocky trail has a reputation for bending wheels and inflicting blood loss.

Driving Directions

From the traffic circle in Nederland, head north on the Peak-to-Peak Hwy (CO-72) for 6.8 miles. Turn left on County-116 at a sign for the University of Colorado Research Station. After about 0.5 miles, turn left into a large parking area. Those looking for some nice dirt road riding can continue riding up County-166, turn left on Rainbow Lakes Road, and then left on FS505.

Riding Directions

R1 - 0.0   From the parking lot, cross the road and find the signed Sourdough Trail on the other side. There are a few intersections with other trails, but they are always well signed. Just follow the Sourdough Trail.

R2 - 5.7   Arrive at a paved road (Brainard Lake Road). Turn around and ride back to your car.

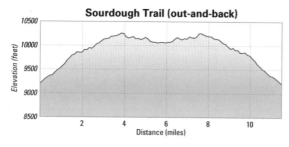

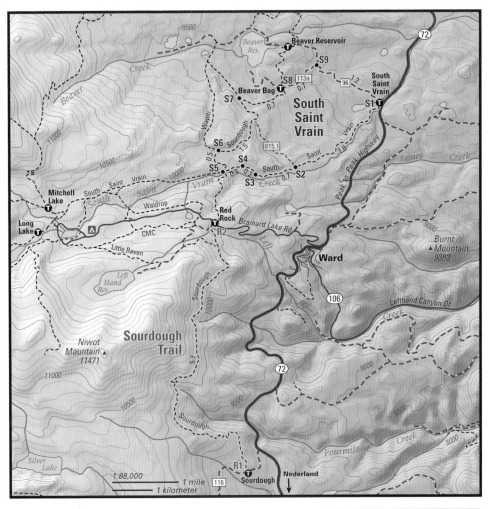

The view of the Indian Peaks Wilderness from the end of Brainard Lake Road.

Boulder

 South Saint Vrain ★★★★★

(14 miles north of Nederland)

Technical Difficulty:	◆
Physical Difficulty:	**Very Strenuous**
Distance:	7.6 miles
Time:	1.5 – 3 hours
Type:	Loop
Surface:	Singletrack
Climbing:	1,200'
Season:	Summer, Fall
Crowds:	Few
Dogs:	

A tough, rocky ride through the woods

Ride Description

Like many of the trails north of Nederland, the South Saint Vrain Trail isn't a "mountain biking" trail; it's a rough hiking trail that makes a decent bike ride for riders who don't mind dismounting and walking some steep, rocky sections. On the plus side, it's a great place to beat the summer heat and avoid the cycling crowds.

The western portion of the South Saint Vrain Trail previously entered the Indian Peaks Wilderness Area. However, in the summer of 2010, the trail was re-routed to stay outside of the wilderness boundary. This creates the possibility of many awesome loop rides in the Brainard Lake area.

Driving Directions

From the traffic circle in Nederland, head north on the Peak-to-Peak Highway (CO-72) and go 14.0 miles. Turn left on Beaver Reservoir Road (County-96) and park at the small trailhead on the left (a pull-out on the side of the road).

Riding Directions

S1 - 0.0   From the small trailhead on County-96, head south on the South Saint Vrain Trail, climbing steadily on rocky trail.

S2 - 1.8   Cross a dirt road (FS-815.1).

S3 - 2.5   At a small "Trail" sign, turn right on singletrack and pedal up a steep hill.

S4 - 2.7   At a confusing pair of junctions, follow signs for "Brainard Lake" and "Trail 909".

S5 - 3.0   Come to a well-signed junction and turn right on the Sourdough Trail.

S6 - 3.5   Go right on the Sourdough Trail as the Wapiti Trail goes left.

S7 - 5.0   Turn right on the Sourdough Trail as the Wapiti Trail comes back in on the left.

S8 - 5.7   Arrive at the Beaver Bog Trailhead. Turn right on the dirt road (FS-113A).

S9 - 6.4   Turn right onto County-96.

S1 - 7.6   Arrive back at the trailhead!

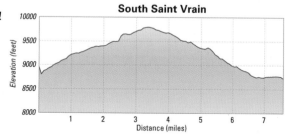

We've Come a Long Way, Baby:
A short history of the Boulder Mountainbike Alliance

By Kristin Butcher

Things were a lot different twenty years ago: bar-ends were essential, suspension-stems seemed like a stroke of genius, and Boulder, Colorado became the first city in the United States to ban mountain biking.

What defines us as mountain bikers isn't our willingness to fall, but our drive to get back up again (and, for us klutzes, again and again). When Boulder's bike community was dealt the crushing blow of a bike ban in 1987, they didn't get even; they got organized. Forming what is now the 20-year-old Boulder Mountainbike Alliance, the fledgling members of BMA swapped their bike gloves for work gloves and began demonstrating their commitment to the trails through volunteerism.

"The agencies didn't know what the hell to do with us," chuckled former BMA President Mike Barrow. By 1994, BMA racked up over 1,200 volunteer hours rerouting a large section of Walker Ranch Loop. "Up until that point, we'd been given simple trail maintenance projects," Barrow continued, "After this project put us on the map, the local land managers realized that there was an opportunity to make use of volunteers to build entirely new trails."

With an energized base and an eye for the future, BMA adopted trails that remain mountain bike favorites, such as the Sourdough Trail and parts of the South Boulder Trails. BMA's trail projects soon resembled a greatest hits album of the area's best trails, including Hall Ranch, Heil Ranch, Betasso Preserve, West Magnolia and the coup de grace of Boulder-area riding—the swoopy trailgasm called Picture Rock, designed and built by BMA in cooperation with Boulder County.

One volunteer at a time, BMA grew into a bike-fueled powerhouse, racking up over 30,000 volunteer hours and receiving several accolades, including the Boulder County Land Conservation Partnership Award. With several hundred members and a history of service that dates back to 1991, BMA has proved that we're not just here, but we're here for the long haul. Oh, and mountain biking is no longer banned in Boulder, so that's neat.

BMA volunteers building the Doudy Draw Trail
photo: Mike Barrow

The tale of the BMA shows that good bike trails don't come for free; they are earned by the hard work of the mountain biking community. To make changes in your own community, contact your local advocacy group and become a member. Even better, turn a shovel, write a letter, throw a party—or just bring cookies and a smile to a trailwork day.

To learn more about Boulder-area trails, ongoing trail projects, and social rides, visit www.bouldermountainbike.org.

After leaving a job in software engineering, Kristin Butcher sold nearly all of her worldly possessions and spent two years living on the road as part of the Subaru/ IMBA Trail Care Crew, riding bikes in 44 states. She is now a freelance writer and columnist for Bike Magazine based in Boulder, Colorado.

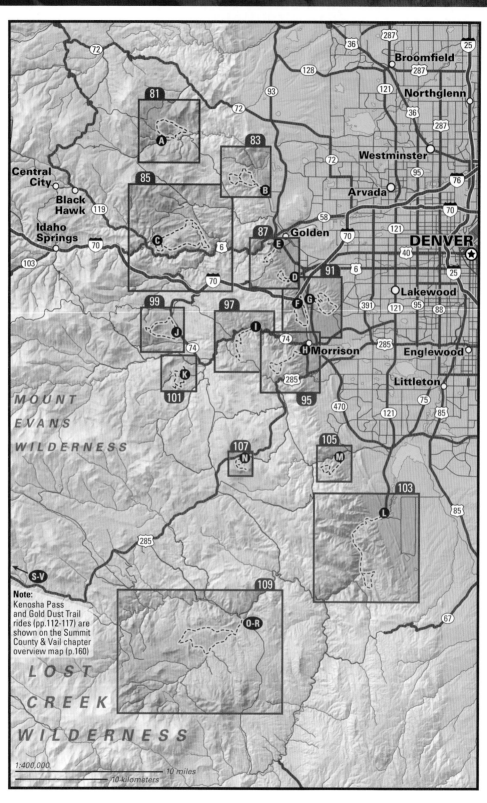

Broomfield

Northglenn

Central City

Black Hawk

Westminster

Idaho Springs

Arvada

Golden

DENVER

Lakewood

Morrison

Englewood

Littleton

M O U N T

E V A N S

W I L D E R N E S S

Note:
Kenosha Pass and Gold Dust Trail rides (pp.112-117) are shown on the Summit County & Vail chapter overview map (p.160)

L O S T

C R E E K

W I L D E R N E S S

1:400,000

10 miles

10-kilometers

Denver & Golden

Who says that the big city isn't a great place to be a mountain biker? Not only is Denver a convenient location for day trips to Winter Park, Summit County, and Vail, but it also boasts a variety of great local rides along the foothills that can be reached in 30 minutes or less. The town of Golden, on the west edge of the Denver Metropolis, is surrounded by a high concentration of quality riding, and great rides like White Ranch, Golden Gate State Park, and Centennial Cone draw crowds. This chapter also includes several spectacular rides near Kenosha Pass, which is located about one hour southwest of Denver down US-285.

The riding around Denver typically involves steep climbing, rocky trails, and plenty of technical challenge. This is great for advanced riders trying to get ready for race season, but can be tedious for the rest of us. Thankfully, there are several trails that break the "steep-n-rocky" monotony. Buffalo Creek, Centennial Cone, Green Mountain, Lair o' the Bear, and Meyers Ranch still have a few tough sections, but are much smoother and are more suitable for beginners.

Accommodations

Denver has a population of nearly one million people and offers countless hotel, motel, and hostel options. There are several campgrounds near Buffalo Creek (see ride O), as well as some near Kenosha Pass (see rides S and T).

Bike Shops

Denver is the largest town in Colorado and has an overwhelming number of bike shops; here are a few favorites.

Wheat Ridge Cyclery
7085 38th Avenue, Wheat Ridge (Denver). 303-424-3221
A huge shop with a large selection.

Mojo Wheels
5790 Dartmouth Avenue, Denver. 303-986-8216
A cool shop that focuses on downhill, freeride, and dirt-jumping.

Golden Bike Shop
722 Washington Avenue, Golden. 303-278-6545
This small shop has a well-chosen selection of bikes, especially 29ers.

Eats and Drinks

Brewpub: Vine Street Pub
1700 Vine Street, Denver. 303-388-2337
The third pub in the famous Boulder-born "Mountain Sun" trilogy. Tasty burgers 'n' beer.

Breakfast: Hotcakes
Corner of 18th Avenue and Humbolt Street, Denver. 303-832-4351
The name says it all: killer pancakes.

Coffee: Windy Saddle Coffee
1110 Washington Avenue, Golden. 303-279-1905
Great coffee and pastries, right in downtown Golden.

Ⓐ Golden Gate Canyon State Park - Mountain Lion Trail ★★★★☆

(16 miles northwest of Golden)

Technical Difficulty:	◆
Physical Difficulty:	**Strenuous**
Distance:	8.9 miles
Time:	2 – 4 hours
Type:	Loop
Surface:	Singletrack, doubletrack
Climbing:	2,400′
Season:	Summer, Fall
Crowds:	Some
Dogs:	Horses are allowed on trail.

A grueling climb then a wild downhill along a riverbed

Ride Description

The Mountain Lion Trail is a step up in difficulty from other Front Range classics like Walker Ranch, Hall Ranch, or Mt. Falcon. The first 2.5 miles test a rider's endurance with 1,000 vertical feet of climbing, and the rocky riding in the streambed requires solid technical skills. Wait until late spring to do this ride, as the "dry" streambed is often flowing with water in the early season! Golden Gate Canyon State Park has a number of additional trails open to mountain biking; consult a park map for more information. There are a number of nice backcountry campsites along the trail, so consider packing camping gear on the bike and spending the night!

Driving Directions

From the intersection of CO-93 and US-6 in Golden, head north on CO-93 for 1.4 miles and turn left on Golden Gate Canyon Road. Follow this for 3.8 miles, and turn left to stay on Golden Gate Canyon Road for another 9.0 miles. Stop at the self-service fee station (on the right) or the ranger station and buy a daily park pass (about $6). Turn right on Crawford Gulch Road and reach the Bridge Creek Trailhead parking lot on the left in 2.2 miles.

Riding Directions

A1 - 0.0 Leave the Bridge Creek Trailhead on the signed Burro Trail heading towards the Mountain Lion Trail.

A2 - 0.8 Turn left on the Mountain Lion Trail, go a short distance, and turn left again to stay on Mountain Lion.

A3 - 1.0 Continue straight on the Mountain Lion Trail as a trail to City Lights Ridge goes left.

A4 - 1.5 Arrive at a beautiful little lake. Continue on the Mountain Lion Trail.

A5 - 1.7 Continue straight on the Mountain Lion Trail as the Buffalo Trail goes left. Prepare for some tough climbing.

A6 - 2.7 Reach the top of the hill, and get ready for some crazy, technical downhill fun!

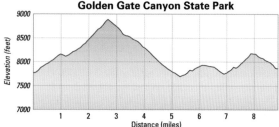

Golden Gate Canyon State Park

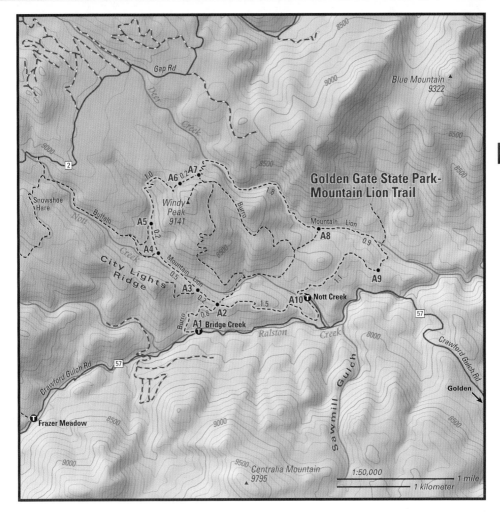

Golden Gate State Park-
Mountain Lion Trail

A7 - 2.9 Continue left on the Mountain Lion Trail as the Windy Peak Trail goes right.

A8 - 4.7 Continue straight on the Mountain Lion Trail as the Burro Connector Trail goes right.

A9 - 5.6 Turn left to stay on the Mountain Lion Trail (watch for the sign!).

A10 - 6.7 Arrive at the Nott Creek Trailhead parking lot. The Mountain Lion Trail continues just to the left of the red-brick toilet building.

A2 - 8.2 Arrive back at the junction with the Burro Trail. Turn left and follow the Burro Trail back to the Bridge Creek Trailhead.

A1 - 8.9 Arrive back at the car!

(B) White Ranch ★★★★☆

(3 miles northwest of Golden)

Technical Difficulty:	◆
Physical Difficulty:	**Very Strenuous**
Distance:	10.3 miles
Time:	2 – 4 hours
Type:	Lollipop loop
Surface:	Singletrack
Climbing:	2,600'
Season:	Spring, Summer, Fall
Crowds:	Some
Dogs:	Dogs must be leashed

Tough, technical riding provides the best total-body workout in the Front Range

Ride Description

There are many options for mountain biking on the trails at White Ranch, with some of them being only moderately difficult. With that said, this ride is one of the most difficult in the Front Range: it is guaranteed to leave you exhausted, bloodied, and defeated. The climbing on the Belcher Gulch Trail is heinously steep and the descent on Mustang is technical and intimidating. However, if you can manage to survive until the Longhorn Trail, the fast descent (with exciting drops!) is pure bliss for the skilled rider.

There are not many trees along the steep climb up the Belcher Hill Trail, and this section of the ride bakes in the sun. Even so, riding on a hot day is highly recommended – dripping sweat and passing out from heatstroke at White Ranch is a time-honored Front Range mountain biking tradition!

Driving Directions

From Golden, head north on CO-93 for about 3 miles. Turn left on W 56th Avenue and go 1.1 miles. At a T-intersection, turn right on Pine Ridge Road and immediately arrive at the White Ranch Trailhead.

Riding Directions

B1 - 0.0   Leave the parking lot on the Belcher Hill Trail and enjoy the easy cruising before things get difficult.

B2 - 1.2   Continue straight on Belcher Hill Trail as Whippletree Trail goes right. Climb steeply.

B3 - 1.8   Continue straight on Belcher Hill as Longhorn goes right.

B4 - 2.4   Continue straight on Belcher Hill as Mustang goes left. Continue past two intersections with Round Up Loop on the right.

B5 - 2.9   Continue straight on Belcher Hill as Maverick loop goes right. Cross Sawmill Trail and climb past difficult water-bars on Belcher Hill.

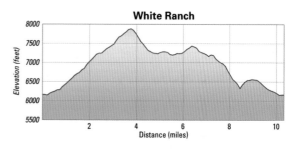

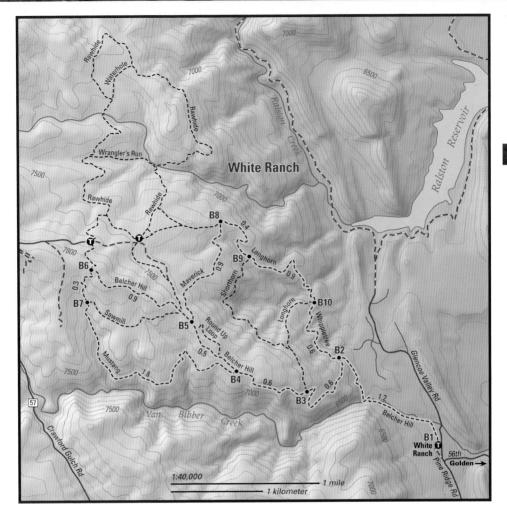

B6 - 3.8   Arrive at the top of the hill! Go left on Mustang as Belcher Hill goes right. Ride down the cool wooden ramps!

B7 - 4.1   Go right on Mustang as Sawmill goes left.

B4 - 5.9   Turn left on Belcher Hill and climb up this section again.

B5 - 6.4   Turn right on Maverick.

B8 - 7.3   Bear right on Longhorn.

B9 - 7.7   Continue straight on Longhorn as Shorthorn goes right.

B10 - 8.6 Continue straight on Whippletree.

B2 - 9.2   Turn left on Belcher Hill. Head back to the parking lot.

Ⓒ Centennial Cone ★★★★☆

(14 miles west of Golden)

Technical Difficulty:	
Physical Difficulty:	**Moderate**
Distance:	13.4 miles
Time:	2 – 3 hours
Type:	Loop
Surface:	Singletrack, dirt road
Climbing:	3,000'
Season:	Spring *, Summer, Fall
Crowds:	Crowded
Dogs:	

A long loop of smooth, fast singletrack

Ride Description

Centennial Cone is a Front Range gem, sporting smooth single-track and fine views. Due to the popularity of the trail with both mountain bikers and hikers, an interesting truce has been declared: on the weekends, mountain bikers are allowed to bike only on even-numbered days, while the odd-numbered days belong to the hikers. Both biking and hiking are allowed on the weekdays. This trail is mostly smooth, but novices should be aware that there are a few sections perched on steep hillsides where riders could take a nasty tumble.

*Centennial Cone is closed annually from December 1 to January 31 for Elk Hunting. Additionally, the Elk Range Trail is sometimes closed in the spring for elk calving (check the park webpage). If the Elk Range Trail is closed, the Travois Trail can still be ridden as an out-and-back.

Driving Directions

From the intersection of CO-93 and US-6 in Golden, head west on US-6 for 11.4 miles. Turn right on CO-119 and go 0.3 miles. Turn right onto Douglas Mountain Drive (County-60) and go 1.0 mile. Turn right on Centennial Cone Road and reach the trailhead parking lot in less than 1 mile.

Riding Directions

C1 - 0.0 From the parking lot, start riding on the Elk Range Trail for a short distance. Turn right on the Travois Trail.

C2 - 0.4 Turn right on the Juniper Trail. (You can continue on the Travois Trail to shorten the ride.)

C3 - 1.2 Continue straight on the Juniper Trail as the Mayhem Gulch Trail goes downhill to the right.

C4 - 2.0 Turn right on the Travois Trail.

C5 - 6.0 Cross a bridge over a ravine.

C6 - 9.0 Turn left on the Evening Sun Loop as the Travois Trail goes right.

C7 - 10.2 Turn left on the Elk Range Trail and follow this all the way back to the parking lot.

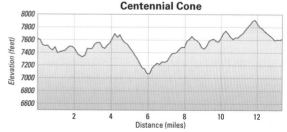

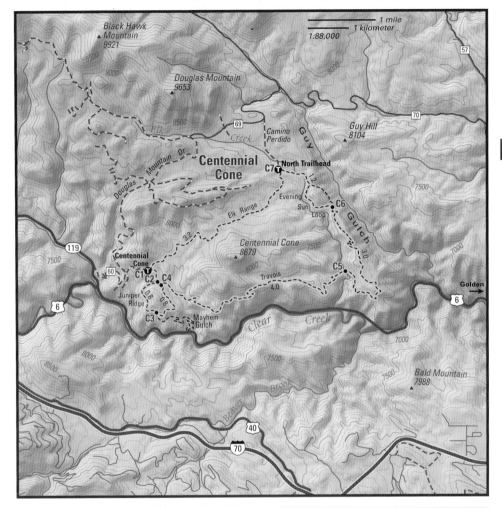

Black Hawk
▲ Mountain
9921

Douglas Mountain
9653

1 mile
1 kilometer
1:88,000

57

70

69
Camino
Perdido

Guy Hill
8104 ▲

**Centennial
Cone**

C7 ⊤ **North Trailhead**

Evening

Sun

C6

Loop

Elk Range

Centennial Cone
8679 ▲

Travois
4.0

C5

Golden →

6

119

60

**Centennial
Cone**

C1 ⊤

C2 C4

Juniper
Ridge

0.8 0.8

6

C3

Mayhem
Gulch

Clear   Creek

Bald Mountain
7988 ▲

40

70

Denver & Golden

Thayne Dickey enjoys an early springtime ride at Green Mountain.

(D) Apex Park ★★★★☆

(3 miles south of Golden)

Technical Difficulty:	◆
Physical Difficulty:	**Moderate**
Distance:	5.5 miles
Time:	1 hour
Type:	Loop
Surface:	Singletrack
Climbing:	1,400'
Season:	Spring, Fall
Crowds:	Crowded
Dogs:	Dogs must be leashed

Classic Front Range riding; plenty of rocks and steep climbing

Ride Description

Apex is a small park packed with great mountain biking trails. They are in the usual style of the Denver region, which involves lots of steep climbing and loose rocks. This isn't everyone's cup of tea, but it's a great way to get a quick workout and to improve your mountain biking skills. There are a number of trails at Apex and they are all fun on the mountain bike. This suggested route is a good, quick ride and it is legal to ride on both even and odd days (see below).

Due to conflicts between hikers and mountain bikers, a complicated system of trail closures has been implemented at Apex. When this book was published, mountain bikers could ride wherever they pleased on even numbered days (like the 4th and the 12th of September, for instance) but were restricted to riding uphill-only on certain sections of trail on odd numbered days (like the 5th and 13th of September). Argos, Enchanted Forest, and part of Apex Trail are affected by the closure. Check the signs at the trailhead, since these regulations may change.

Driving Directions

From Golden, head south on US-6 for roughly 2 miles. Turn right on CO-93 (Heritage Road). Go 0.9 miles and turn right into a large paved parking lot.

Riding Directions

D1 - 0.0 From the parking lot, ride uphill on the wide trail. After the trail turns right, turn left on the signed Apex Trail.

D2 - 0.3 Turn right on the Argos Trail and climb steadily.

D3 - 1.0 Turn right on Pick N' Sledge.

D4 - 1.8 Arrive back at the intersection with Pick N' Sledge. Bear left.

D5 - 2.4 Make a sharp right onto Grubstake and climb steeply.

D4 - 3.9 Arrive back at the intersection with Pick N' Sledge. Turn left on Pick N' Sledge.

D3 - 4.7 Arrive back at the intersection with Argos. This time, turn right on Pick N' Sledge.

D6 - 4.8 Turn left on Apex Trail and ride back to the trailhead.

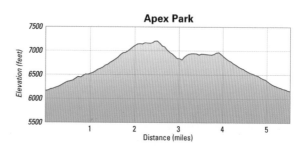

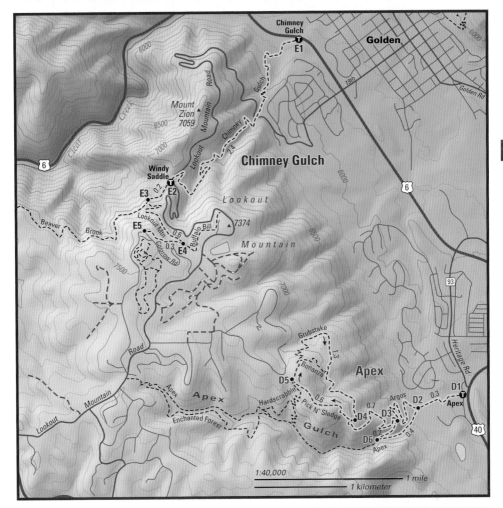

Kevin Dean treads carefully on a narrow section of the Dakota Ridge Trail.

Chimney Gulch ★★★☆☆

(1 mile west of Golden)

Technical Difficulty:	◆
Physical Difficulty:	**Strenuous**
Distance:	7.0 miles
Time:	1.5 – 3 hours
Type:	Out-and-back
Surface:	Singletrack
Climbing/ Descending:	1,800' / 100' (one-way)
Season:	Spring, Summer, Fall
Crowds:	Crowded
Dogs:	Dogs must be leashed

A classic after-work hill climb

Ride Description

Chimney Gulch is a great place to get in shape for the savage hill climbs that are typical of rides in the Front Range. Some sections are quite steep and loose, and it is common to see people walking their bikes. Fortunately, the tough parts are usually followed by easy sections that allow riders to recover before tackling the next crux. The first section of the climb is exposed to the sun and, on hot days, it will feel like you are baking in an oven.

The ride back down is seriously fun, but remember to ride in control. On the trails around Golden, you will frequently encounter grandmothers, babies, and cute puppies, all of which strongly dislike being run over by mountain bikes.

Driving Directions

From central Denver, reach Golden by taking I-70 west and merging onto CO-58. Just after passing through Golden, turn left on US-6 and go 0.6 miles until you see a large dirt parking area of the right. The trailhead is not signed, but it is usually full of mountain bikers and paragliders.

Riding Directions - see map on previous page

E1 - 0.0 From the trailhead, start riding up the Chimney Gulch Trail.

E2 - 2.4 Cross Lookout Mountain Road at a large parking lot (the Windy Saddle Trailhead) and continue on the Lookout Mountain Trail.

E3 - 2.6 Turn left on the Lookout Mountain Trail as the Beaver Brook Trail goes right.

E4 - 3.2 Turn right on the Lookout Mountain Trail as the Buffalo Bill Trail goes left.

E5 - 3.5 Arrive at the top of the Lookout Mountain Trail as it intersects Colorow Road. Turn around and head back down! *(It is also possible to cross Colorow Road and follow singletrack that parallels the road to eventually reach the top of the Apex Trail.)*

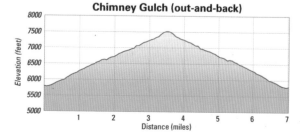

Laura Johnson admires the old homestead on the Elk Range Trail at Centennial Cone.

(F) Mathews/Winters - Dakota Ridge ★★★★☆

(5 miles south of Golden)

Technical Difficulty:	◆
Physical Difficulty:	**Strenuous**
Distance:	6.1 miles
Time:	1 – 2 hours
Type:	Loop
Surface:	Singletrack
Climbing:	1,100′
Season:	Spring, Fall
Crowds:	Crowded
Dogs:	Dogs must be leashed

Great technical riding along Dakota Ridge combined with fun cruising at Red Rocks

Ride Description

The Dakota Ridge Trail runs along a formation called Dinosaur Ridge. Though the ridge was named after the many dinosaur fossils found here, the title serves as a good description of the mountain biking as well: traversing the ridge is like riding along the back of a humongous stegosaurus! Those looking for challenging, technical riding will love this ride. Riders who prefer fewer rocks should simply ride the second half of this loop as an out-and-back – it is much smoother.

Driving Directions

From Golden, head south on US-6 for about 2 miles. Turn right at Heritage Road (CO-93) and go 1 mile. Turn right onto US-40 and follow this for 1.3 miles as it passes under I-70 and turns into CO-26. Just after the I-70 overpass, turn right into the Matthews/Winters parking lot.

Riding Directions

F1 - 0.0 From the Matthews/Winters Trailhead parking lot, ride back out the trailhead road, cross CO-26, and ride uphill on an old dirt road.

F2 - 0.4 The dirt road ends at a gate, turn right on singletrack.

F3 - 1.1 Continue straight as you pass the Zorro Trail on the left. (The Zorro Trail can be used to connect this ride with the trails at Green Mountain.)

F4 - 2.3 Turn right on the paved road (Alameda Parkway).

F5 - 2.4 Bear left on the Dakota Ridge Trail as Alameda Parkway makes a sharp turn right.

F6 - 2.8 Turn right on the paved road (CO-26), ride 0.1 miles, and take the first left on Red Rocks Park Road.

F7 - 3.0 Turn right onto an unmarked trail (Red Rocks Trail). Cross a few roads, following signs for the Red Rocks Trail.

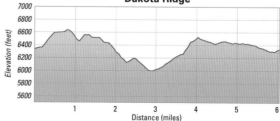

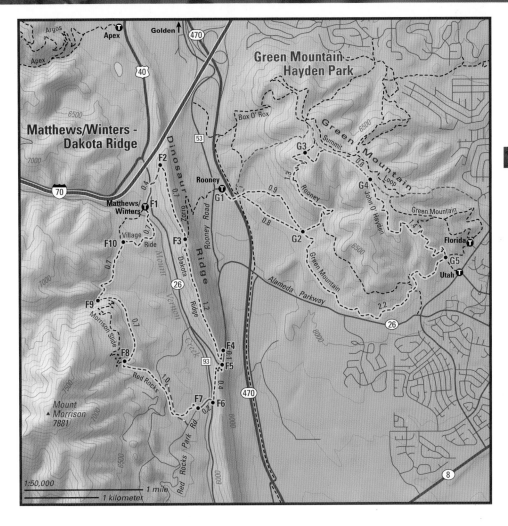

F8 - 4.8 Turn right to stay on the Red Rocks Trail as the Morrison Slide Trail goes left. (The Morrison Slide Trail is also a fun ride, but it climbs very steeply and is best ridden in the other direction.)

F9 - 4.7 Continue straight on the Red Rocks Trail as the Morrison Slide Trail rejoins.

F10 - 5.4 Go right on the Village Ride Trail.

F1 - 6.1 Arrive back at the Matthews/Winters Trailhead!

Ⓖ Green Mountain - Hayden Park ★★⯨☆☆

(5 miles south of Golden)

Technical Difficulty:	
Physical Difficulty:	**Moderate**
Distance:	6.9 miles
Time:	1.5 – 2.5 hours
Type:	Loop
Surface:	Singletrack, dirt road
Climbing:	1,300′
Season:	Spring, Fall
Crowds:	Some
Dogs:	Dogs must be leashed

Smooth trails and manageable grades make for great singlespeeding

Ride Description

Green Mountain (6,800′) is an oasis of adventure within the big city. It is located in William Frederick Hayden Park, a large piece of land owned by the City of Lakewood. The mountain biking is delightful, with most of the trails being smooth and the climbs gradual. The summit of Green Mountain rises about 1,000 vertical feet above the trailhead, but the well-maintained trails make the climbing feel easy. Upon reaching the top of Green Mountain, riders are treated to a commanding view of the Denver metro area as well as glimpses of snowcapped peaks.

Driving Directions

From Golden, head southeast on US-6 for 1.9 miles. Bear right onto CO-470 and go about 2.5 miles. Take the exit for Alameda Parkway and turn right. Take the first right on Rooney Road. Turn right into the trailhead parking lot.

Riding Directions - see map on previous page

G1 - 0.0 From the trailhead, ride over CO-470 on the pedestrian bridge. On the other side, bear right onto singletrack.

G2 - 0.9 Come to a four-way intersection. Turn left on the Rooney Trail. Bear left at the next intersection.

G3 - 2.2 Near the top of Green Mountain, come to a Y-intersection and turn right. Quickly turn right again onto a dirt road (the Green Mountain Trail).

G4 - 3.0 Bear right onto the John O. Hayden Trail. Enjoy a sweet descent!

G5 - 4.4 At a T-intersection with the Green Mountain Trail, turn right.

G2 - 6.6 Back at the four-way intersection. This time, continue straight, taking the other option back towards the trailhead.

G1 - 7.4 Turn left onto a road, cross the bridge over CO-470, and coast back into the parking lot.

Green Mountain

John Worthen delicately balances over a creek crossing on the Gold Dust Trail.

(H) Mount Falcon ★★★☆☆

(10 miles southwest of Denver)

Technical Difficulty:	
Physical Difficulty:	**Strenuous**
Distance:	9.2 miles
Time:	2 – 3 hours
Type:	Lollipop loop
Surface:	Singletrack, doubletrack
Climbing:	2,300'
Season:	Spring, Summer, Fall
Crowds:	Crowded
Dogs:	Dogs must be leashed

Merciless Front Range hill climbing at its best

Ride Description

Mount Falcon is a classic Front Range gut-buster. The tough climbing starts right out of the parking lot – the first three miles ascend 1,600 feet! The riding isn't too technical or scary, just consistently steep. After reaching the top, the ride back down is great fun thanks to the abundance of water bars and other features. The trails at Mount Falcon take longer to dry out than other trails in the area. Don't ride when the trails are muddy.

Those looking for epic rides should note that Mount Falcon can easily be linked with trails at Green Mountain, Dakota Ridge (Matthews/Winters), Lair o' the Bear, and/or Bear Creek Lake State Park.

Driving Directions

Reach Morrison by taking CO-470 to the exit for CO-8/Morrison Road and heading west. From Morrison, head south on CO-8 (turn left if coming from CO-470) for 0.9 miles. Turn right on Forest Ave and go 0.2 miles. Turn right on Vine Street and take this for 0.3 miles until it ends at the Mount Falcon Trailhead parking lot.

Riding Directions

H1 - 0.0 From the parking lot, start riding on the Castle Trail.

H2 - 0.1 Continue straight on the Castle Trail as the Turkey Trot Trail (closed to bikes) goes right. Climb steeply up switchbacks.

H3 - 1.4 Continue straight on the Castle Trail as the Turkey Trot Trail rejoins.

H4 - 2.5 Continue straight on the Castle Trail as the Walkers Dream Trail goes right.

H5 - 2.6 Continue straight on the Castle Trail as the Two Dog Trail goes left.

H6 - 3.0 Continue straight on the Castle Trail as the Meadow Trail goes left and a trail to the ruins of the Walker Home goes right.

H7 - 3.4 Turn right to stay on the Castle Trail as the Meadow Trail goes left.

H8 - 3.7 At the restrooms, turn left on the Parmalee Trail.

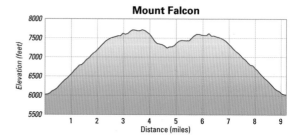

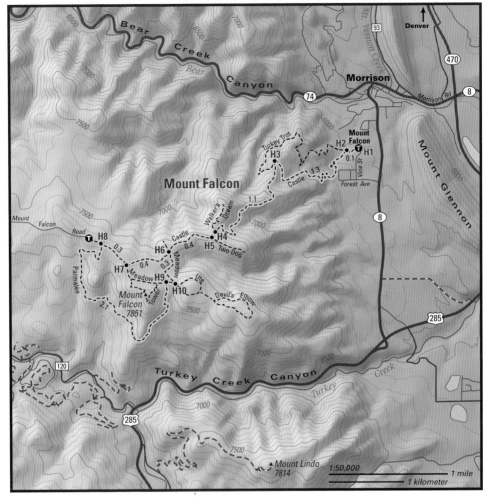

Denver & Golden

H9 - 5.8   Turn right on the Meadow Trail.

H10 - 5.9   Turn left on the Meadow Trail as the Ute Trail goes right.

H6 - 6.2   Turn right on the Castle Trail and follow your tracks back to the parking lot!

(I) Lair o' the Bear ★★☆☆☆

(10 miles southwest of Denver)

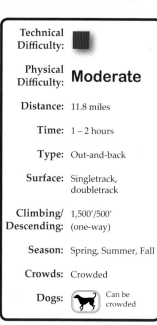

Technical Difficulty:	■
Physical Difficulty:	**Moderate**
Distance:	11.8 miles
Time:	1 – 2 hours
Type:	Out-and-back
Surface:	Singletrack, doubletrack
Climbing/ Descending:	1,500'/500' (one-way)
Season:	Spring, Summer, Fall
Crowds:	Crowded
Dogs:	Can be crowded

Flowing singletrack through the forest

Ride Description

The Bear Creek Trail starts out flat and easy as it meanders near its namesake creek in Lair 'o the Bear Park and then becomes more technical as it passes through Corwina, O'Fallon, and Pence Parks. There are some great sections of curvy riding through the woods. Most of the ride passes through dense pine forest, making it a good way to stay out of the sun on a hot day. Strong riders should consider making a giant loop by riding Dakota Ridge to Mount Falcon to Lair o' the Bear.

Driving Directions

From I-70, take I-470 south to the Morrison Road Exit and head west on Morrison Road. Pass through Morrison and continue straight on Morrison Road as it becomes CO-74. 5.2 miles past Morrison, turn left into the Lair 'o the Bear Trailhead.

Riding Directions

I1 - 0.0   From the Lair o' the Bear Trailhead, find the start of the Bear Creek Trail at the west end of the parking lot. The first section of the trail is a gentle gravel path.

I2 - 1.3   Turn left on the Bear Creek Trail as it becomes singletrack.

I3 - 3.1   Continue on the Bear Creek Trail past an intersection with the Panorama Point Trail.

I4 - 4.3   Continue on the Bear Creek Trail as the Meadow View Trail goes right.

I5 - 4.8   Arrive at a kiosk with a map. Continue on the Bear Creek Trail through several junctions.

I6 - 5.9   Reach Meyers Gulch Road. Turn around and go back the way you came.

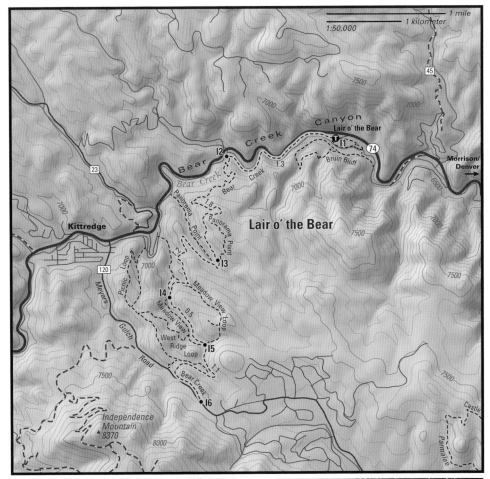

1 mile
1 kilometer
1:50,000

Bear Creek Canyon

Lair o' the Bear

45

74

Morrison/
Denver

Kittredge

23

Bear Creek

Bear Creek

Bruin Bluff

1.3

12

1.8

Panorama Point

Panorama Point

Lair o' the Bear

13

120

Meyers Gulch Road

Picnic Loop

Meadow View Loop

14

0.5

Meadow View

West Ridge Loop

15

Bear Creek

16

Independence
Mountain
▲ 8370

Castle

Parmalee

David Simon sneaks in a late-afternoon ride at Alderfer   photo: Theodore B Van Orman - tbvophoto.com

Denver & Golden

(J) Elk Meadow - Bergen Peak ★★★☆☆

(15 miles west of Denver)

Technical Difficulty:	◆
Physical Difficulty:	**Strenuous**
Distance:	10.0 miles
Time:	2 – 3 hours
Type:	Loop
Surface:	Singletrack
Climbing:	2,400′
Season:	Spring, Summer, Fall
Crowds:	Crowded
Dogs:	Dogs must be leashed

A tough climb up Bergen Peak on a well-worn trail

Ride Description

Elk Meadow Park offers several miles of mellow trails, but the best ride here is a tough one that crosses into the Bergen Peak Wildlife Area and ascends Bergen Peak (9,700′). This loop can be ridden in either direction, as both the Bergen Peak Trail and the Too Long Trail are strenuous on the way up and great fun on the way down. Those looking for an easier ride can simply skip the trek up Bergen Peak and make a loop using the Meadow View Trail.

Driving Directions

From Denver, take I-70 west to Exit 252. Head south on CO-74 (Evergreen Parkway) and go 5.1 miles. Turn right on Lewis Ridge Road, go about 500 feet, and turn right into the trailhead parking lot.

Riding Directions

J1 - 0.0   From the Elk Meadow parking lot, start riding north on the Painter's Pause Trail.

J2 - 0.1   Turn left on the Sleepy S Trail.

J3 - 0.6   Continue on the Sleepy S Trail as the Elk Ridge Trail goes right.

J4 - 1.2   Go right on the Meadow View Trail.

J5 - 1.8   Turn left on the Bergen Peak Trail and begin a tough climb towards the top of Bergen Peak. If you're looking for a challenge, try to ride all the way to the top without dismounting!

J6 - 4.3   Turn left to stay on the Bergen Peak Trail as the Too Long Trail goes right.

J7 - 5.1   The trail ends a few hundred feet before the summit: leave your bike and scamper up the rocks to reach the top. Turn around and get ready for the downhill!

J6 - 6.0   Turn left on the Too Long Trail and enjoy the downhill.

J8 - 8.0   Go left on the Meadow View Trail.

J9 - 8.5   Continue straight on the Meadow View Trail as the Founders Trail goes right.

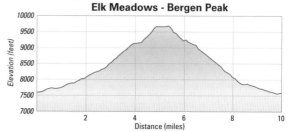

Elk Meadows - Bergen Peak

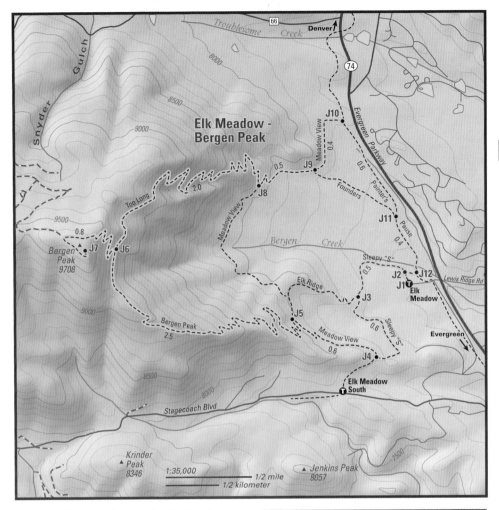

J10 - 8.9   Turn right on the Painter's Pause Trail.

J11 - 9.5   Continue on Painter's Pause as the Founder's goes right.

J12 - 9.9   Turn right on the Sleepy S Trail.

J2 - 10.0   Turn left and arrive at the parking lot.

Jason Haas mixes a little mountain biking with rock climbing at Buffalo Creek.

(K) Alderfer/Three Sisters Park ★★★☆☆

(10 miles southwest of Denver)

Technical Difficulty:	
Physical Difficulty:	**Strenuous**
Distance:	7.1 miles
Time:	1.5 – 3 hours
Type:	Loop
Surface:	Singletrack
Climbing:	1,300′
Season:	Spring, Summer, Fall
Crowds:	Crowded
Dogs:	Dogs must be leashed

A tough climb to the top of Evergreen Mountain

Ride Description

Alderfer/Three Sisters Park has miles of great trails ranging from blue-square to black diamond. The trails north of Buffalo Park Road tend to be less strenuous than those on the south side. The loop described below is a tough ride to the top of Evergreen Mountain followed by the technical Sisters Trail. Those looking for an easier ride can construct a loop from the other trails shown on the map, which are generally less technical than the highlighted ride. The trails are well-signed.

Alderfer/Three Sisters Park is very popular with hikers. In fact, it was voted the best after-work hike in the Denver area by the readers of Westworld. So, watch your speed and be courteous to other trail users.

Driving Directions

To reach the small town of Evergreen, take I-70 to Exit 252 and follow CO-74 south for 7.6 miles. From Evergreen, head southwest on CO-73 for 0.5 miles (a right turn if you are coming form I-70). Turn right onto Buffalo Park Road (County-89) and go 1.3 miles. Turn right into a dirt parking lot (the East Trailhead of Alderfer Park).

Riding Directions

K1 - 0.0 From the east parking lot, head west on Buffalo Park Road for about 50 feet and turn left onto the East Evergreen Mountain Trail.

K2 - 0.3 Continue left on the Evergreen Mountain Trail as the Ranch View Trail goes right.

K3 - 0.8 Continue to the right on the Evergreen Mountain Trail as a neighborhood access trail goes left.

K4 - 2.2 Arrive at the junction with the Summit Trail. Turn left on the Summit Trail and prepare for some tough climbing.

K5 - 2.8 Arrive at the loop at the top of the Summit Trail. Ride this short loop in either direction.

K5 - 3.2 Finish the loop and ride back down the Summit Trail. Wheee!

K4 - 3.9 Turn left on the West Evergreen Mountain Trail.

K6 - 4.8 Turn left on the Wild Iris Loop.

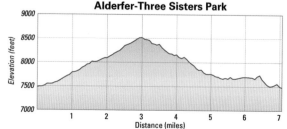

Alderfer-Three Sisters Park

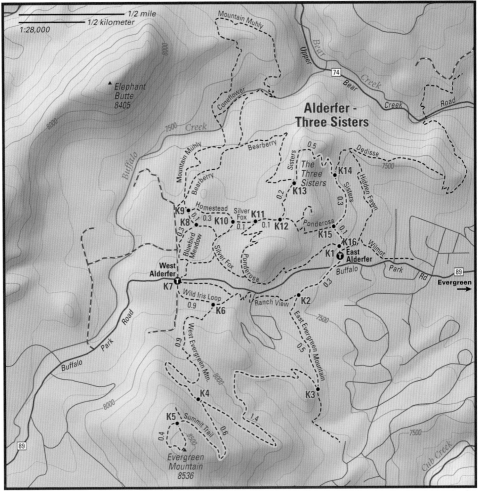

K7 - 5.1   Turn left on the boardwalk, cross Buffalo Park Road, and arrive at the west trailhead of Alderfer Park. Go left on the Bluebird Meadows Trail.

K8 - 5.4   Turn left on Homestead Trail.

K9 - 5.5   Make a right on Homestead as Bearberry goes left.

K10 - 5.8   Go left on the Silver Fox Trail.

K11 - 5.9   Turn left on Ponderosa.

K12 - 6.0   Turn left on the Sisters Trail and prepare for some more technical riding. *(To shorten the ride and avoid the technical riding, continue on Ponderosa Trail.)*

K13 - 6.2   Continue straight on Sisters Trail as Bearberry Trail goes left.

K14 - 6.7   Go straight on the Sisters Trail as the Hidden Fawn Trail goes left.

K15 - 6.9   Go left on the Sisters Trail.

K16 - 7.0   Continue straight at a junction and arrive back at the east parking area.

Denver & Golden

(L) Waterton Canyon ★★★☆☆

(About 10 miles southwest of Denver)

Technical Difficulty:	
Physical Difficulty:	**Strenuous**
Distance:	17.3 miles
Time:	2 – 4 hours
Type:	Lollipop loop
Surface:	Singletrack, dirt road
Climbing:	3,500'
Season:	Spring, Summer, Fall
Crowds:	Crowded
Dogs:	

Warm-up on a dirt road and then enjoy fast singletrack through the woods

Ride Description

The singletrack riding on this loop is simply excellent: not too difficult, just fast and fun. However, there are about 7 miles of dirt road between the trailhead and the singletrack! In the words of the late, great Kurt Vonnegut: *so it goes.* At least the dirt road up Waterton Canyon is reasonably scenic and free from vehicle traffic. Those looking for more single-track can continue on the Colorado trail for as long as they like; it's gorgeous singletrack for the next 35 miles until the Wilderness Boundary!

Waterton Canyon was closed for all of 2011 for removal of sediment from the Strontia Springs Reservoir. It is possible that it might be closed in the future for various dam-mainte-nance operations.

Driving Directions

From the southwest side of I-470, take the exit for Wadsworth Blvd (CO-121). Continue south on CO-121 (quickly becomes South Platte Canyon Road) for 4.3 miles. Turn left on Waterton Canyon Road and quickly make another left into the Waterton Canyon Trailhead parking lot.

Riding Directions

L1 - 0.0 From the huge parking lot, cross the road and find the start of the Colorado Trail, which soon becomes a wide gravel road.

L2 - 6.3 Pass a huge dam on the right and a ranger station on the left.

L3 - 6.7 Turn left on the Colorado Trail (#1776) and climb on singletrack.

L4 - 7.9 Turn left at a sign for "Roxborough State Park".

L5 - 8.2 Go left on a trail that is signed "Indian Creek Trail #800" as a trail to "Indian Creek Trailhead" goes right.

L6 - 10.1 Turn left at a sign for "Waterton Canyon". Watch out for a few tricky technical sections!

L2 - 10.9 Arrive back at the rang-er station. Turn right and ride the dirt road back to the trailhead!

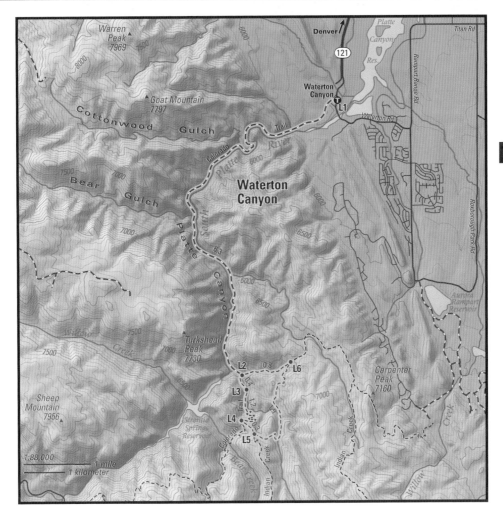

Katie Johnson on the Colorado Trail from Kenosha Pass to Georgia Pass.   photo: Xavier Torrents

Deer Creek Canyon ★★★★☆

(15 miles southwest of Denver)

Technical Difficulty:	
Physical Difficulty:	**Strenuous**
Distance:	7.3 miles
Time:	2 – 3 hours
Type:	Lollipop loop
Surface:	Singletrack
Climbing:	1,900'
Season:	Spring, Summer, Fall
Crowds:	Crowded
Dogs:	Dogs must be leashed

A grueling, rocky climb leads to smooth singletrack and fantastic views of Denver

Ride Description

Deer Creek is two trails for the price of one: the first is smooth and the second is rocky. Unfortunately, the grueling climb on the Plymouth Creek Trail comes *before* the nice, smooth riding on the Red Mesa Trail. There are a few sections of the Plymouth Creek Trail (like the infamous "wall of shame") that will require riders to walk their bikes. Luckily, the great views of Denver make all of the suffering worthwhile. An optional loop on the Plymouth Mountain Trail adds an extra 2 miles to the ride.

Driving Directions

From Golden, head south on CO-470 for about 9 miles. Take the exit for Ken Caryl Avenue and turn right on Ken Caryl. Take the first left on South Valley Road and go 2.0 miles. Turn left on Valley Road and then right on Deer Creek Canyon Road (County-124) and go 0.7 miles. Turn left on Grizzly Drive and go 0.4 miles. Turn right into the Deer Creek Canyon parking area.

Riding Directions

M1 - 0.0 From the trailhead, start riding on the Plymouth Creek Trail.

M2 - 1.2 Continue straight on the Plymouth Creek Trail as the Meadowlark Trail (hiking only) goes right.

M3 - 1.7 Continue straight on the Plymouth Creek Trail as the Plymouth Mountain Trail goes left. Go a short distance and turn right on Plymouth Creek Trail at a second intersection with the Plymouth Mountain Trail.

M4 - 1.9 Continue straight on Plymouth Creek as Homesteader (hiking only) goes left.

M5 - 2.4 Turn right on the Red Mesa Loop.

M6 - 2.5 Continue straight on the Red Mesa Loop as Golden Eagle (hiking only) goes right.

M5 - 4.8 Arrive back at the start of the Red Mesa Loop. Turn right on the Plymouth Creek Trail and follow your tracks back to the trailhead. (*Riders looking for more mileage should turn right on the Plymouth Mountain Trail and complete the loop, adding 2.2 miles to the ride.*)

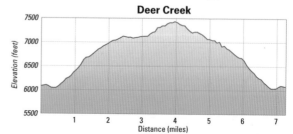

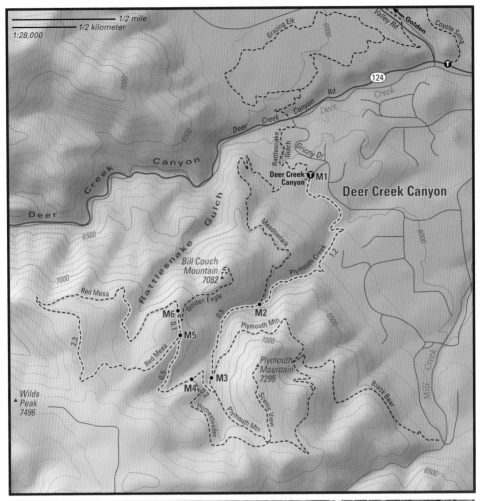

Katie Johnson on the Colorado Trail near Kenosha Pass.

# (N)Meyer Ranch ★★★★★

(15 miles west of Denver)

Technical Difficulty:	
Physical Difficulty:	**Moderate**
Distance:	4.0 miles
Time:	1 hour
Type:	Loop
Surface:	Singletrack
Climbing:	900′
Season:	Spring, Summer, Fall
Crowds:	Crowded
Dogs:	Dogs must be leashed

Generally relaxing riding on wide trails through the woods.

Ride Description

This loop at Meyer Ranch connects several easy trails with the more technical Old Ski Run Trail for a quick 4-mile ride. For an easier loop, consider skipping the Old Ski Run Trail and riding Lodgepole instead. The trails at Meyer Ranch are popular with hikers and dog walkers, so ride slowly around the blind corners. And yes, as the presence of the "Old Ski Run" Trail suggests, there really was skiing at Meyer Ranch. Back in the 1940s, skiers were transported from the road to the base of the single rope tow in horse-drawn sleighs. Meyer Ranch is still popular with cross country and backcountry skiers when the Front Range gets enough snow.

Driving Directions

From CO-470 in Denver, head southwest on US-285 for 11 miles. Exit at South Turkey Creek Road, turn left, and find the trailhead on the south side of US-285.

Riding Directions

N1 - 0.0   Leave the parking lot and start riding up the wide dirt road.

N2 - 0.2   At the toilets, turn right on the Owl's Perch Trail.

N3 - 0.4   Turn right onto the Lodgepole Loop Trail.

N4 - 1.0   Turn right on the Sunny Aspen Loop.

N5 - 1.3   Make a right on the Old Ski Run Trail.

N6 - 2.0   Arrive at the small lollipop loop at the end of the Old Ski Run Trail, turn left, ride the loop, and head back down Old Ski Run.

N5 - 3.1   Arrive back at the junction with the Sunny Aspen Loop; turn right.

N7 - 3.5   Continue on the Sunny Aspen Loop as the Lodgepole Loop goes left.

N3 - 3.7   Back at the intersection with Owl's Perch. Retrace your path back to the parking lot.

N1 - 4.0   Arrive back at the parking lot.

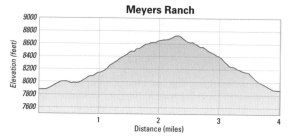

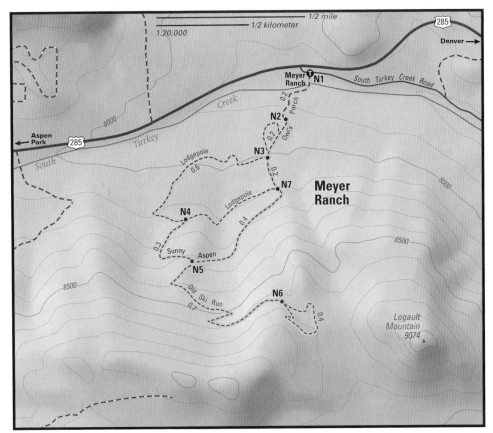

Sabrina Forrest tackles a steep section of the Blackjack Trail.

◎ Buffalo Creek - The Classic Loop ★★★★✦

(40 miles southwest of Denver)

Technical Difficulty:	
Physical Difficulty:	**Moderate**
Distance:	14.8 miles
Time:	2 – 4 hours
Type:	Loop
Surface:	Singletrack
Climbing:	2,100'
Season:	Spring, Summer, Fall
Crowds:	Some
Dogs:	🐕

Spectacular! Smooth rolling on Buffalo Creek's trademark sandy trails

Ride Description

Buffalo Creek is a fantastic escape from life in the big city. Located about one hour from Denver, "Buff Creek" offers lots of camping options (both free and pay) and enough great singletrack to keep a rider occupied for years. The region is also famous for its rock climbing – climbers call it "The South Platte" – and is notorious for its coarse-grained rock that tends to leave hands and knees bloodied. The rock makes the mountain biking painful as well, leaving the trails covered with pea-sized gravel that makes cornering very "exciting." It takes most riders a few crashes before they learn to go slowly around the gravel-strewn turns.

This loop is perhaps the most famous ride at Buffalo Creek. It doesn't take nearly as long as its 15-mile length would lead you to believe: the trails are smooth and some of the riding is on a dirt road. The decent down Sandy Wash is one of the best sections of singletrack in the Front Range!

Driving Directions

There are several trailheads in the Buffalo Creek area. Most people park at the Forest Service Work Center in the town of Buffalo Creek, or at the Little Scraggy Trailhead. If you are camping, just start riding from the campsite – how convenient!

To reach the Buffalo Creek Trailhead from Denver, drive southwest on US-285 and go about 20 miles. When you come to Pine Junction, turn left on Pine Valley Road (County-126) and go 10 miles. In the town of Buffalo Creek, turn left into the Forest Service Work Center parking area.

To reach the Little Scraggy Trailhead, follow the above directions, but continue approximately 4 miles past the town of Buffalo Creek. Turn right on FS-550 and take the first right into the Little Scraggy Trailhead.

Riding Directions

O1 - 0.0 From the town of Buffalo Creek, head back northwest on CO-126 and turn left on Buffalo Creek Road.

O2 - 4.5 Turn right onto the Baldy Trail. Bear right onto Baldy as Gashouse goes left.

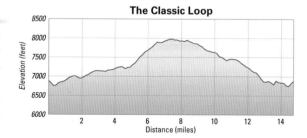

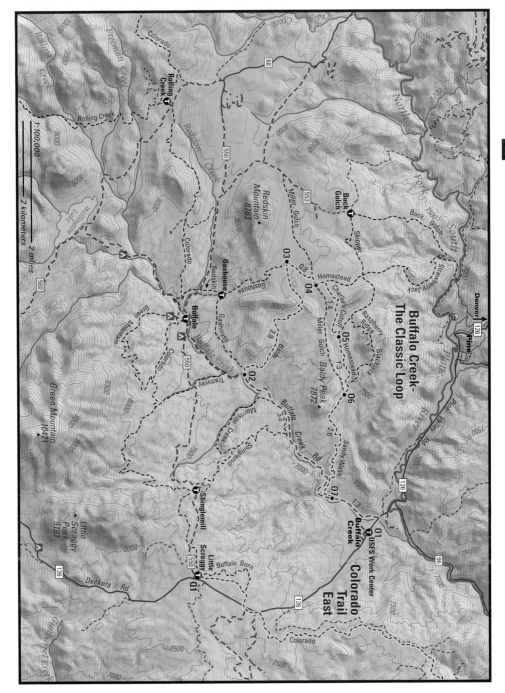

Buffalo Creek-
The Classic Loop

Colorado
Trail
East

O3 - 7.4   Bear right as Baldy merges with Gashouse. Go 0.5 miles and then turn right on the Miller Gulch Trail.

O4 - 8.2   Turn left on the Homestead Trail and go 0.2 miles. Turn right onto the Charlie's Cutoff Trail.

O5 - 9.6   Turn right onto the Homestead Trail.

O6 - 10.9   Continue straight onto the Sandy Wash Trail. As the name implies, you should prepare for a wild, sandy descent!

O7 - 13.5   Arrive back at Buffalo Creek Road. Turn left and ride back to your car.

(P) The New Classic: Shinglemill, Colorado Trail, Redskin, Gashouse, Sandy Wash ★★★★⯪ ■   Distance: 25 miles

If you liked the previous ride, then you'll love this one: it's longer and a little more technical. Take Buffalo Creek Road to the Shinglemill Trail. Sweat your way up Shinglemill, cross FS-550, and turn right onto the Colorado Trail. Enjoy some great riding and then turn right on the Redskin Trail. Turn left onto Gashouse, and climb up to Miller Gulch. Finish as for The Classic Loop. Epic!

(Q) Colorado Trail East ★★★★⯪ ■   Distance: 14 miles

The Colorado Trail offers excellent (albeit rather sandy) riding. Starting from the Little Scraggy Trailhead, you can ride the Colorado Trail all the way to Waterton Canyon. The first 6 miles are nice, rolling singletrack without much elevation gain or loss. At mile 7, the trail begins descending steeply, dropping over 1,500 vertical feet down to the South Platte River. Unless you are prepared for an epic adventure, it's best to turn around before this descent.

(R) The "Black Diamond Loop"
★★★★★ ◆◆   Distance: 2.4 miles

Just when it seemed that the riding that Buffalo Creek couldn't get any better, the summer of 2011 saw the opening of one of the best technical challenge loops in the Front Range. The new loop consists of two trails: the climb on Raspberry Ridge and the descent on Blackjack. Riders looking for some great single-diamond riding can ride Raspberry Ridge out-and-back, while those looking for the full double-diamond rock-rolling experience can head down Blackjack and complete the loop. Volunteers from the Colorado Mountain Biking Association completed much of the construction of these trails, and they did an amazing job. The trail flows from beautiful singletrack to exhilarating descents down steep granite slabs and offers alternate lines for hard-core riders to practice drops. Many of the most exciting features are signed with the name and the difficulty of the obstacle. Be especially fearful of "The Slot Machine." The loop is designed to be ridden in the clockwise direction – up Raspberry Ridge and down Blackjack. Find the start of the Raspberry Ridge trail on the Homestead Trail, about 0.3 miles northwest of the intersection with Charlie's Cutoff.

Craig Belgard blazes along the Sandy Wash Trail, Buffalo Creek.

(S) Kenosha Pass to Lost Creek Wilderness ★★★★☆

(50 miles southwest of Denver)

Technical Difficulty:	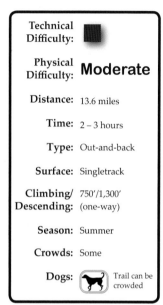
Physical Difficulty:	**Moderate**
Distance:	13.6 miles
Time:	2 – 3 hours
Type:	Out-and-back
Surface:	Singletrack
Climbing/ Descending:	750'/1,300' (one-way)
Season:	Summer
Crowds:	Some
Dogs:	Trail can be crowded

Savor incredible views while swooping through aspen groves

Ride Description

This section of the Colorado Trail is a celebration of high-alpine singletrack. Flowing through meadows and aspen groves, the smooth singletrack begs to be ridden at high speeds. But don't go too fast, the amazing views of the South Park basin and the golden aspens (in the fall) are not to be missed! There are a few tough climbs on this ride, but overall it should serve as a good trail to get novice riders hooked on mountain biking. The beautiful scenery at Kenosha Pass is no secret and these trails can be packed during sunny weekends, especially during the peak "aspen-hunting" season in September. If you're riding when the aspens are changing, watch out for other riders who are looking at the brilliant trees instead of the trail.

Driving Directions

From Denver drive southwest on US-285 to Kenosha Pass (46.6 miles from the intersection of CO-470 and US-285). Turn left onto a dirt road (FS-126) and drive about 0.2 miles to the East Kenosha Pass Trailhead parking lot and park near the toilets.

Riding Directions

S1 - 0.0 Take the Colorado Trail, which leaves the road near the East Kenosha Pass Trailhead parking lot.

S2 - 5.8 Cross a small bridge over a creek.

S3 - 6.2 Cross a dirt road.

S4 - 6.8 All too soon you come to the boundary of the Lost Creek Wilderness where bicycles are not permitted. So, turn around and ride back to Kenosha Pass.

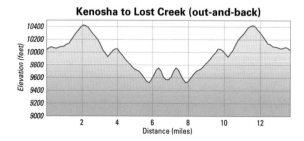
Kenosha to Lost Creek (out-and-back)

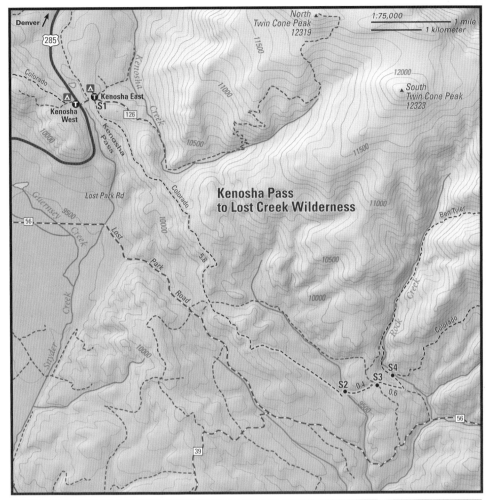

Kenosha Pass to Lost Creek Wilderness

(T) Kenosha Pass to Georgia Pass ★★★★★

(50 miles southwest of Denver)

Technical Difficulty:	◆
Physical Difficulty:	**Strenuous**
Distance:	22.5 miles
Time:	4 – 7 hours
Type:	Out-and-back
Surface:	100% singletrack!
Climbing/ Descending:	3,000'/1,000' (one way)
Season:	Summer, Fall
Crowds:	Some
Dogs:	🐕

A glorious ride! Best in the early fall, when the aspens are changing

Ride Description

This excellent section of the Colorado Trail is THE classic "September aspens ride". Be sure to bring several cameras to capture the views and the fall colors. The Colorado Trail is well marked and the riding is a nice blend of technical riding and smooth, fast trail. The tough climbing isn't encountered until after mile 6, so those looking for a more moderate ride can simply turn around before the big climb.

Driving Directions

From Denver, drive southwest on US-285. Kenosha Pass is 46.4 miles from the junction of US-285 and I-470.

Riding Directions

T1 - 0.0 Start riding on the Colorado Trail on the west side of Kenosha Pass (the right side of the road as you are driving from Denver).

T2 - 1.0 Come to a nice bench. Take a photo of the fantastic view.

T3 - 5.1 Pass through a red gate.

T4 - 5.7 Cross a dirt road and continue on the Colorado Trail.

T5 - 5.9 Turn right on the Colorado Trail as it merges with the West Jefferson Trail. Go 0.1 miles, and then turn left to stay on the Colorado Trail as the Jefferson Creek Trail continues straight. *(See OPTION below.)*

T6 - 7.5 Continue on the Colorado Trail as a trail goes left (signed as "Michigan Creek Road").

T7 - 10.7 Continue straight as the Jefferson Creek Trail goes right.

T8 - 11.3 Arrive at Georgia Pass! Turn around and go back the way you came. *(Those with legs of steel can follow the Colorado Trail to the Gold Hill Trailhead near Breckenridge, which is about 18 miles from Georgia Pass.)*

Kenosha to Georgia Pass (out-and-back)

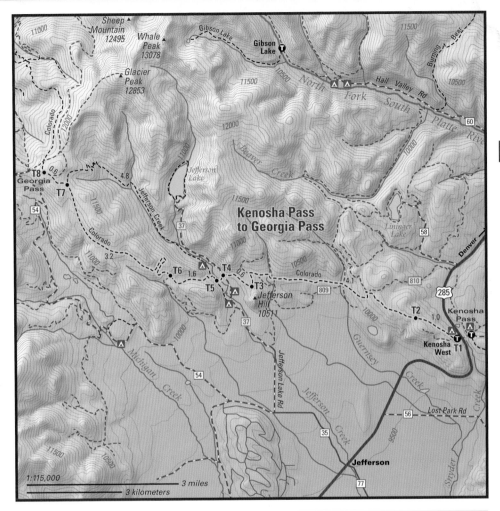

Ⓤ The Jefferson Creek Trail ★★★★☆ ◆

Jefferson Creek is an option encountered at mile 6.0 of the previous ride. It is much less popular than the Colorado Trail and offers some nice riding through a forest. There are some sections of very tough climbing, but it is not much worse than that found on the Colorado Trail.

Riding Directions

T5- 5.9   Stay straight on the Jefferson Creek Trail and pass through a campground. Climb some steep, technical hills.

T7 - 10.7   Turn right on the Colorado Trail and rejoin the Kenosha Pass to Georgia Pass Riding Directions at mile 10.7.

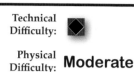

Gold Dust Trail ★★★★★

(70 miles southwest of Denver)

Technical Difficulty:	
Physical Difficulty:	**Moderate**
Distance:	9.0 miles
Time:	2 – 3 hours
Type:	Shuttle
Surface:	Singletrack
Climbing/ Descending:	500'/2,000' (one-way)
Season:	Summer
Crowds:	Few
Dogs:	🐕

Fantastic singletrack beginning at the top of Boreas Pass and plunging into the South Park basin

Ride Description

The Gold Dust Trail consists of 9 miles of delightful alpine singletrack. There is one section of climbing along the flank of Little Baldy Mountain, but otherwise the entire trail has a nice downhill grade. Here, the ride is described using a shuttle from Como to the top of Boreas Pass. The ride can also be completed as a loop by adding 11.2 miles of gradual climbing along Boreas Pass Road (for a total of 20.4 miles).

Driving Directions

To set up the shuttle, first leave a car at the lower trailhead in Como. To reach Como from Denver, head west of US-285, cross Kenosha Pass, and turn right into the town of Como. Meander through city streets and head northwest on CR-838, reaching the trailhead in about 0.75 miles. Leave a car here and drive the bikes/ riders up to Boreas Pass.

To reach Boreas Pass, head back into Como on CR-838. Make two left turns to head north on Boreas Pass Road (CR-33) and go about 3.5 miles. Make a sharp right to remain on Boreas Pass Road and reach Boreas Pass is about 7.5 miles. Start the ride at Boreas Pass.

Riding Directions

V1 - 0.0   From Boreas Pass, start riding south on Boreas Pass Road.

V2 - 0.4   Turn right onto the Gold Dust Trail singletrack.

V3 - 2.1   Cross a dirt road (CR-801) and continue on the Gold Dust Trail (Trail #698).

V4 - 4.1   Cross another dirt road (CR-50) and continue on the Gold Dust Trail.

V5 - 8.3   The trail hits a dirt road. Bear left.

V6 - 8.5   Turn right, riding off the dirt road and onto more singletrack.

V7 - 9.0   The trail ends at CR-838. Drive (or bike!) back up to Boreas Pass.

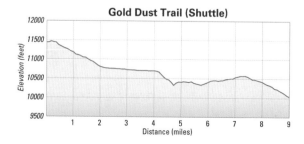

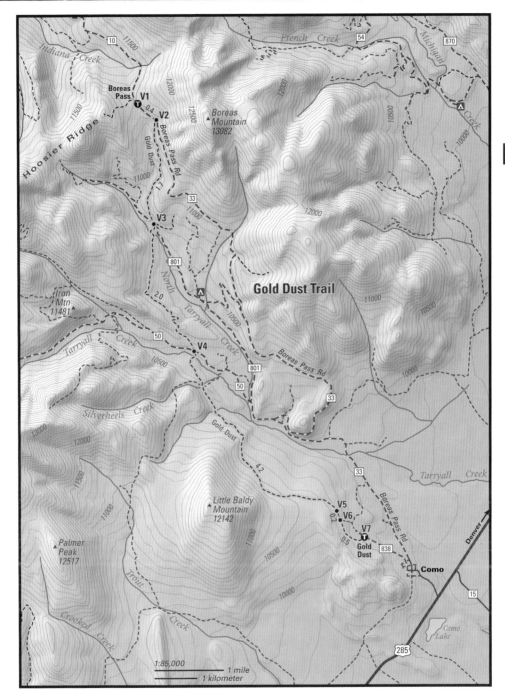

Gold Dust Trail

Boreas Pass
V1
0.4
V2
Boreas
Mountain
13082
Indiana Creek
10
11500
12000
12500
Hoosier Ridge
11500
11000
Gold Dust
Boreas Pass Rd.
1.7
33
V3
801
11000
North
Iron
Mtn
11481
12000
2.0
Tarryall Creek
10500
50
Tarryall Creek
V4
801
10500
50
33
Silverheels Creek
13000
12000
11500
11000
Gold Dust
4.2
Little Baldy
Mountain
12142
V5
0.2
V6
33
V7
838
Gold Dust
0.5
Palmer
Peak
12517
Trout Creek
11000
10500
10000
Tarryall Creek
Boreas Pass Rd
Denver
15
Como
Como
Lake
285
Crooked Creek
French Creek
54
870
Michigan Creek
10500
10000
12000
11000
10500
10000
12000

1:85,000
1 mile
1 kilometer

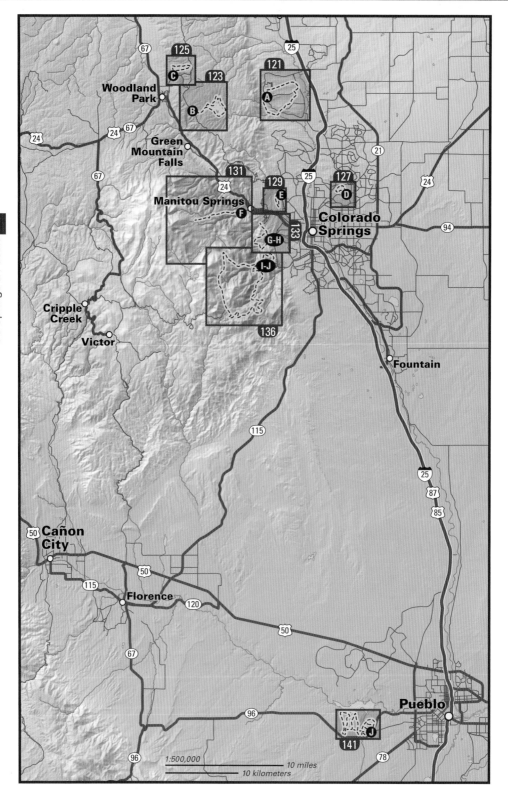

Colorado Springs & Pueblo

Colorado Springs does its best to portray itself as the politically conservative home of the Air Force Academy, but this is just an elaborate ruse to conceal some of the best mountain biking in the Front Range. "The Springs" offers nearly year-round riding on trails that run the gamut from easy cruising to insane technical challenges. Palmer Park, a tiny city park packed with incredible singletrack, is located right in the middle of town. Colorado Springs basks in the sun, and sandy trails like Captain Jacks and Section 16 are frequently rideable during dry periods in the winter.

Not to be outdone, Pueblo (40 miles south of Colorado Springs) boasts the best winter singletrack in the Front Range: Lake Pueblo State Park. Also known as Pueblo Reservoir, Lake Pueblo offers a winning combination of smooth, scenic singletrack, technical trails down canyons, and glorious views of Pikes Peak in the distance.

Accommodations

Colorado Springs is one of Colorado's largest cities and offers hotel and motel options for all budgets. The camping is also excellent, with numerous pay campgrounds located to the west of town. It is even possible to find free camping on some of the dirt roads near Woodland Park and points further west. For those making a trip to Lake Pueblo State Park, things couldn't get much more convenient: there is a pay campground located right at the trailhead. This campground is packed in the summer, but is relatively empty during the winter.

Bike Shops

Old Town Bike Shop
426 S Tejon Street, CO Springs. 719-475-8589
This well-stocked shop saved the day when the author was searching for a replacement crank bolt.

Great Divide Ski Bike & Hike
400 N Santa Fe Avenue, Pueblo. 719-546-2453
This large shop is located right in downtown Pueblo.

Vance's Bicycle World
2220 S Prairie Avenue, Pueblo. 719-566-6925
Vance held the record for the highest bunny-hop for several years in the 1980s.

Eats and Drinks

Phantom Canyon Brewing Co
2 East Pikes Peak Avenue, Colorado Springs. 719-635-2800
Serves microbrew beer and pub-food in a historic building in downtown Colorado Springs.

Shamrock Brewing Co
108 West 3rd Street, Pueblo. 719-542-9974
Another of Colorado's many delightful brewpubs, this time with an Irish theme.

CO Springs & Pueblo

Ⓐ Air Force Academy - Falcon Trail ★★★★☆

(15 miles north of Colorado Springs)

Technical Difficulty:	
Physical Difficulty:	**Moderate**
Distance:	12.4 miles
Time:	2 – 3 hours
Type:	Loop
Surface:	Singletrack
Climbing:	1,500'
Season:	Spring, Summer, Fall
Crowds:	Some
Dogs:	🚫

A fast, fun trail without prolonged climbs

Ride Description

It's rare in the Front Range to find an exciting trail that doesn't involve a lung-busting hill-climb. Thus, the lack of giant hills makes the Falcon Trail quite a treat! This trail does climb a respectable 1,500 feet, but this is spread out over a number of small hills and over 13 miles. Despite the absence of painful climbing, the Falcon Trail is far from boring, offering numerous fast sections that slalom through the trees. Additionally, the Falcon Trail has played host to several endurance races, including the 2010 edition of the 24 Hours of Colorado Springs race. How many laps can you do in 24 hours?

This ride is located on the grounds of the US Air Force Academy and may be closed depending on the national security alert level. Visitors will need to show ID and (likely) have their vehicles searched when passing through the gate. So, be sure to leave the hunting knife and drug paraphernalia at home.

Driving Directions

From Colorado Springs, head north on I-25 for about 5 miles. Take Exit 150 (North Academy Boulevard) and turn left, heading northwest on S Gate Boulevard. Pass through the gate and continue for about 2 miles. Turn right on Stadium Boulevard and go 2.0 miles. Turn left on Academy Drive and go 3 miles. Turn right into the Falcon Trail parking area on the right.

Riding Directions

A1 - 0.0   From the parking area, start riding west (clockwise) on the Falcon Trail. The trail crosses several roads, but continues directly on the other side. There are mile markers and many signs along the trail, so it is easy to follow.

A2 - 7.8   Cross Community Center Drive and continue on singletrack on the other side.

A1 - 12.4   Arrive back at the trailhead. Do another lap!

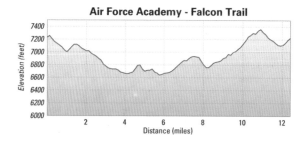

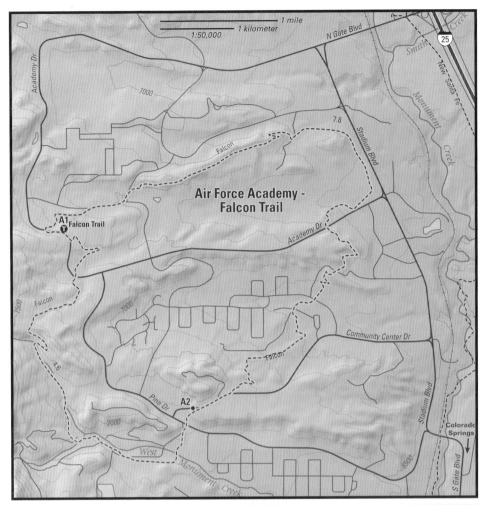

Air Force Academy -
Falcon Trail

ⒷRampart Reservoir ★★★★☆

(30 miles NW of Colorado Springs)

CO Springs & Pueblo

Technical Difficulty:	⬤
Physical Difficulty:	**Easy**
Distance:	14.4 miles
Time:	2 – 3 hours
Type:	Lollipop loop
Surface:	Singletrack
Climbing:	1,900'
Season:	Spring, Summer, Fall
Crowds:	Some
Dogs:	🐕 *

Delightful, smooth singletrack along the shores of beautiful Rampart Reservoir

Ride Description

Great views and classic singletrack make Rampart Reservoir fun for everybody. There are several technical sections that will force most riders to walk their bikes, but generally Rampart Reservoir involves nice cruising up and down small hills. The trail is popular with picnickers and hikers, so be careful to avoid these obstacles. It is possible to eliminate the dirt road riding by parking at the main Rampart Reservoir Trailhead (B4), but this requires paying the $5 entrance fee. The directions below recommend starting at the Rainbow Gulch Trailhead, where there is no fee.

* Dogs are allowed, but the trails can be crowded with people, pets, and bikes.

Driving Directions

From Colorado Springs, head northwest on US-24. Just as you reach the town of Woodland Park, turn right on Baldwin Street (County-22) and follow this for 2.9 miles. Turn right on Loy Creek Road (Rampart Range Road) and go 1.5 miles. Turn right again to stay on Rampart Range Road and go 2.4 miles. Turn left into the Rainbow Gulch Trailhead parking area.

Riding Directions

B1 - 0.0   From the Rainbow Gulch Trailhead, ride downhill on the Rainbow Gulch Trail (an old dirt road).

B2 - 1.4   Turn right on the Rampart Reservoir Trail. (You will follow this trail around the reservoir and arrive back to this point at mile 12.9.)

B3 - 4.7   Turn left on the paved road and cross the dam.

B4 - 5.5   After crossing the dam, continue on the road until it ends at a parking lot. Continue on the trail that leaves from the far side of the parking lot.

B5 - 9.8   Continue straight on the Rampart Reservoir Trail as an unmarked trail (Trail #700a) goes right.

B2 - 12.9   Turn right on the dirt road (Rainbow Gulch Trail) and ride back uphill to the parking lot.

B1 - 14.4   Arrive back at the trailhead!

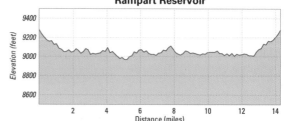

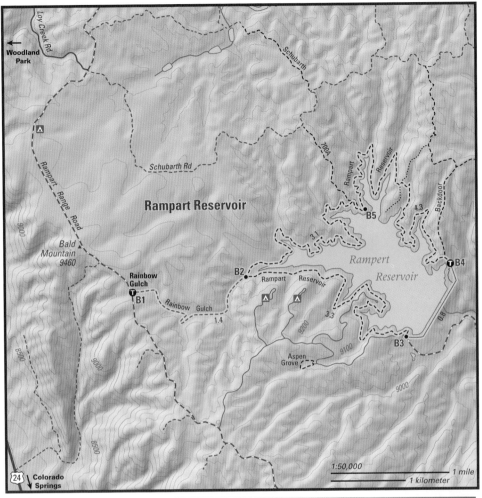

©Lovell Gulch ★★★☆☆

(20 miles northwest of Colorado Springs)

Technical Difficulty:	
Physical Difficulty:	**Moderate**
Distance:	5.5 miles
Time:	about an hour
Type:	Loop
Surface:	Singletrack, doubletrack
Climbing:	1,000'
Season:	Summer, Fall
Crowds:	Some
Dogs:	

A network of smooth trails through the woods

Ride Description

Lovell Gulch is home to many interlaced trails tucked into the woods above Woodland Park. This loop links some of the most obvious trails, but the more adventurous riders will find plenty of side trails to keep them entertained. These trails can be very popular with hikers, runners, and dog walkers, so be sure to ride in control and be courteous.

Driving Directions

From Colorado Springs, head northwest on US-24. Just as you are entering the town of Woodland Park, turn right at the "Team Telecycle" bike shop on Baldwin Street (County-22) and go 2.1 miles. Turn left into the trailhead. The trailhead is small and is hidden next to a road maintenance facility.

Riding Directions

C1 - 0.0   From the trailhead, start riding north on the main trail.

C2 - 0.2   Bear right through a series of Y-intersections.

C3 - 0.7   Arrive at a sign that reads "Lovell Gulch Loop" and turn right.

C4 - 1.4   Continue straight as a trail goes right.

C5 - 2.3   After climbing a hill, come to a small dirt parking lot on Rampart Range Road and turn left on Trail #706.

C3 - 4.4   Arrive back at the start of the loop. Turn right and head back to the trailhead.

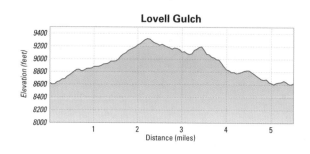

Lovell Gulch sports beautiful flowers in the springtime.

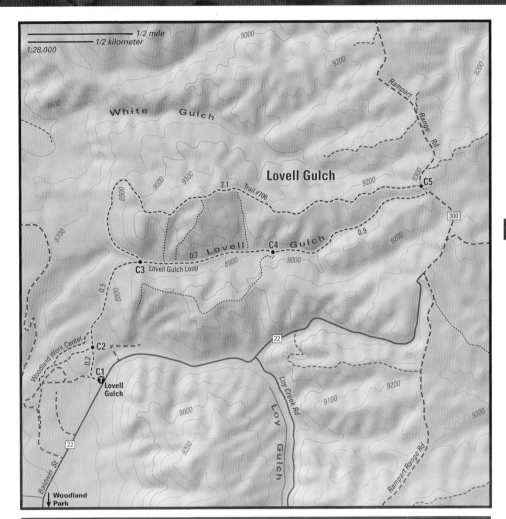

The author riding the rocks at Palmer Park.

(D) Palmer Park - Templeton Trail ★★★⯨☆

(Starts in Colorado Springs)

Technical Difficulty:	◆◆
Physical Difficulty:	**Strenuous**
Distance:	3.5 miles
Time:	1 – 2 hours
Type:	Loop
Surface:	Singletrack
Climbing:	700′
Season:	Spring, Fall
Crowds:	Some
Dogs:	Leash law may apply.

Sustained black diamond riding, conveniently located in town!

Ride Description

Palmer Park is simply incredible - it offers miles and miles of great mountain biking trails packed into a tiny city park. The trails range from easy to difficult, but as far as the author is concerned, the Templeton Trail is the best. Don't underestimate this 3.5-mile loop: it's really tough! There are dozens of tricky black diamond downhill sections and some uphill sections that require serious trials skills. The trails at Palmer park are well signed and the park is small, so it is difficult to get badly lost. Go explore!

Driving Directions

Take Exit 145 from I-25 and head east on Fillmore Street (which eventually turns into N Circle Drive). After 2.6 miles, turn left on Paseo Road and go 1.4 miles. Turn left on a dirt road and quickly make another left. Reach the Yucca Flats parking area in a few hundred feet.

Riding Directions

D1 - 0.0   From the parking lot, head north and follow signs for the Templeton Trail, riding it counterclockwise. You will eventually arrive back at the parking area. Ride another lap or explore some of the other great trails at Palmer Park!

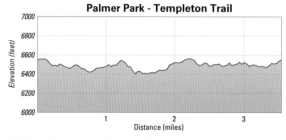

Pikes Peak from Rampart Reservoir.

Palmer Park - Templeton Trail

Forrest Noble at Palmer Park.   photo: Fredrik Marmsater

Ⓔ Garden of the Gods ★★✦✦✦

(5 miles northwest of Colorado Springs)

Technical Difficulty:	
Physical Difficulty:	**Easy**
Distance:	3.2 miles
Time:	about 30 minutes
Type:	Lollipop loop
Surface:	Singletrack, bike path
Climbing:	200'
Season:	Spring, Fall
Crowds:	Crowded
Dogs:	Must be on a leash

A relaxing trail with great views of sandstone spires and Pikes Peak

Ride Description

The Garden of the Gods is a beautiful place, but it only offers a few trails for mountain biking: the rest are hiking-only. This quick loop is flat and easy except for one tricky hill. It would serve as a good introduction to mountain biking for a first time rider. The visitors center near the parking area provides maps of the park that show all of the mountain biking and hiking trails.

Driving Directions

From I-25, take Exit 146 and head west on Garden of the Gods Road for 2.3 miles. Turn left on 30th Street. After 1.3 miles, turn left into the large visitor center parking lot.

Riding Directions

E1 - 0.0 From the visitors center, head to the north side of the parking lot and take the underpass under 30th Street. Turn left onto the bike path that soon parallels Gateway Road.

E2 - 0.6 When the bike path ends at an intersection, cross Gateway Road and find the signed start of the Chambers Trail. Most of the trails in this region are open to mountain biking, so you can wander around or follow this recommended route:

E3 - 0.8 Continue straight on the Ute Trail as another trail goes left.

E4 - 1.4 Turn left on the Niobrara Trail. Go 0.1 miles and turn left again to stay on the Niobrara Trail.

E5 - 1.9 Continue straight on the Niobrara Trail as the Ute Connector Trail goes left.

E6 - 2.1 Turn right on to the Valley Reservoir Trail.

E7 - 2.2 Bear left on Chambers Trail as Galloway Homestead Trail goes right.

E2 - 2.5 Arrive back at Gateway Road. Follow the bike path back to the visitor center.

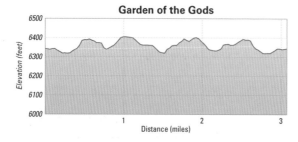

Garden of the Gods

CO Springs & Pueblo

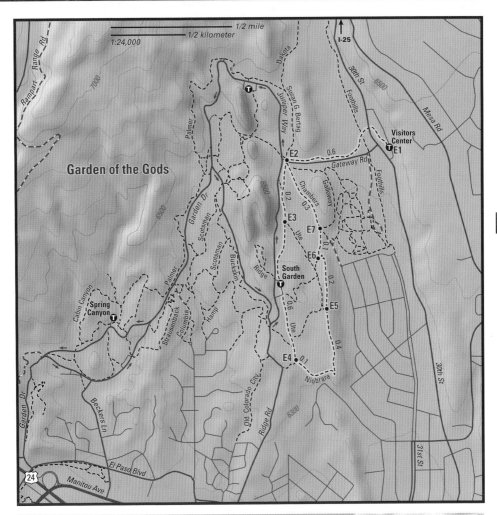

Garden of the Gods

Sandstone formations at the Garden of the Gods.   Photo: Nathan Pulley

(F) The Barr Trail on Pikes Peak ★★★☆☆

(Starts in Manitou Springs, 7 miles west of Colorado Springs)

Technical Difficulty:	◆◆
Physical Difficulty:	**Insanely Strenuous**
Distance:	12.6 miles
Time:	3 – 5 hours
Type:	Out-and-back
Surface:	Singletrack
Climbing/ Descending:	3,800'/300' (to Barr Camp)
Season:	Sumer, Fall
Crowds:	Very Crowded
Dogs:	see below

A massive hill climb from Hades!

Ride Description

The Barr Trail is the main footpath to the top of Pikes Peak and is consequently very crowded. From the parking lot, the trail climbs steeply up stairs and sandy switchbacks. Eventually it has mercy and climbs more gently, through forests, reaching Barr Camp in six miles. This is the traditional turn-around point for mountain bikes since the trail beyond Barr Camp is very rough, viciously steep, and bikes will mostly be pushed rather than ridden.

Intrepid alpine cyclists will note that bikes are also allowed on many of the trails that intersect the Barr Trail. Those who enjoy the lung-crushing feeling of riding at 11,000 feet might like these trails. The Elk Park Trail is a popular ride and the Bottomless Pit Trail entices the adventurer to pay a visit based on the name alone.

Barr Camp offers cabins and tent camping, as well as hot meals, so consider reserving a spot and making your ride an overnight adventure! The Barr Trail is one of the most crowded trails in the state, so be sure to stay in control and to yield to other trail users. Dogs are not specifically prohibited, but the narrow, crowded trail makes bringing a pooch a bad idea.

Driving Directions

Take I-25 Exit 141 and head west on US-24 for 4.0 miles. Turn left on Manitou Avenue towards Manitou Springs and go 1.5 miles. Turn left on Ruxton Avenue, following signs for the Cog Railway. As you pass the railway station, turn right at a sign for the Barr Trailhead. Drive up a very steep hill, and arrive at the parking lot.

Riding Directions

F1 - 0.0   From the trailhead, carry your bike up a flight of stairs and start "riding" up the Barr Trail.

F2 - 0.5   Turn right to stay on the Barr Trail as another trail goes left.

F3 - 2.9   Continue straight on the Barr Trail as the Incline Trail goes right.

F4 - 3.0   Go left to stay on the Barr Trail as a trail goes right to the Fremont Experimental Forest.

F5 - 4.6   Continue straight on the Barr Trail as an unmarked trail (Manitou Reservoir Trail) goes right. A sign reads, "PIKES PEAK SUMMIT 7.8"

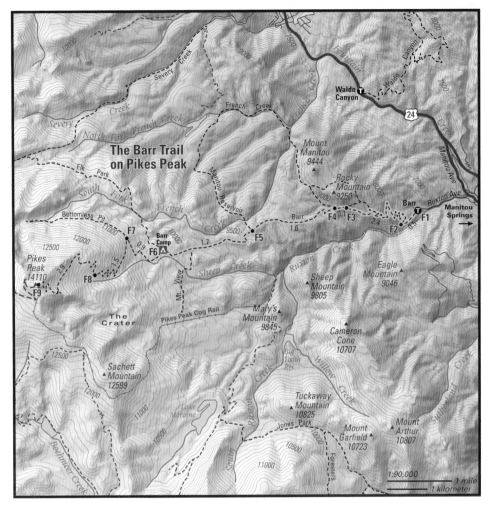

The Barr Trail on Pikes Peak

F6 - 6.3 Arrive at Barr Camp! Turn around and head back to the trailhead, or "push" onwards to the summit.

OPTION: (to the summit of Pikes Peak)

F7 - 7.2 Continue on Barr Trail as Bottomless Pit Trail goes right.

F8 - 8.7 Pass the Timberline Shelter A-Frame on the left.

F9 - 11.6 Arrive at the top of the Barr Trail near the cog railway station. Make your way to the tippy-top! Then, ride back down the Barr Trail, being sure to preserve your own life in addition to those of other trail users.

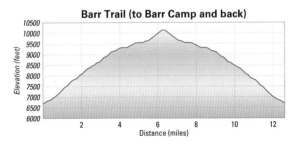

Ⓖ Section 16 ★★★★☆

(4 miles west of Colorado Springs)

Technical Difficulty:	◆
Physical Difficulty:	**Moderate**
Distance:	5.8 miles
Time:	1 – 2 hours
Type:	Loop
Surface:	Singletrack, dirt road
Climbing:	1,800′
Season:	Spring, Summer, Fall
Crowds:	Some
Dogs:	Must be on a leash

A butter-smooth climb leads to a technical rocky downhill

Ride Description

Starting from the Section 16 Trailhead, this loop of the Palmer Trail is a popular after-work ride among advanced riders. Most of the climb is completed on dirt roads and very smooth singletrack, so the great downhill comes with very little suffering compared to typical Front Range rides. The Paul Intemann Trail leaves the Palmer Trail at mile 5.0 and can be ridden to add extra mileage. Those looking for a less technical ride can simply turn around at the top of the climb and enjoy smooth riding on the way back down.

Driving Directions

From downtown Colorado Springs, head west on Colorado Avenue. Turn left on 21st Street and go 1.1 miles. Turn right on Lower Gold Camp Road and go 2.0 miles until you come to the Section 16 Trailhead on the right.

Riding Directions

G1 - 0.0 Start riding southwest (uphill) on Gold Camp Road.

G2 - 0.3 Turn right on High Drive (a dirt road).

G3 - 1.1 Turn right on the Palmer Trail and climb steadily on smooth singletrack.

G4 - 4.6 Turn left to stay on the Palmer Trail. A spur trail goes straight.

G5 - 4.8 Continue straight as a trail goes left. (This trail is signed as "To Intemann Trail" and reaches Intemann Trail via a very steep and technical descent. Going left at G6 is the better, less technical way of reaching Intermann Trail.)

G6 - 5.0 Continue straight as the Intemann Trail goes left. (This is the better, less technical way of reaching Intemann Trail.)

G1 - 5.8 Arrive back at the Section 16 Trailhead!

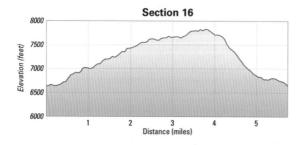

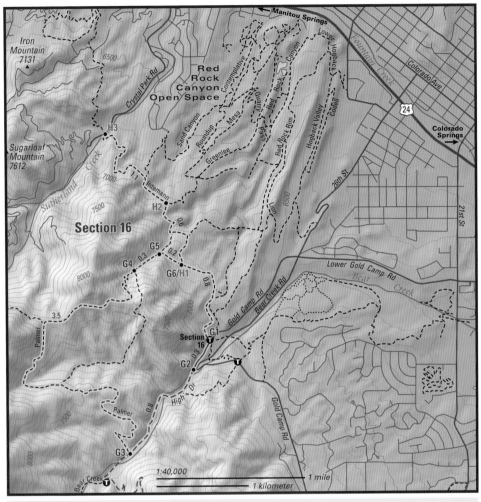

(H) The Paul Intemann Memorial Nature Trail

◆ **Distance: 1.7 miles (one-way)** ★★★☆☆

The Intemann Trail offers challenging riding that traverses the slope heading towards Manitou Springs. It was originally intended as a singletrack connector between Colorado Springs and Pikes Peak. Unfortunately, due to some sort of property conflict, the trail is not open to public use past Crystal Park Road. Nevertheless, the section that connects to the Section 16 Loop is a great piece of singletrack. It can be used to reach the trails at Red Rock Canyon Open Space or simply ridden as an out-and-back.

Riding Directions

H1 - 0.0   Follow the Section 16 directions to mile 5.0. Turn left on the Intemann Trail.

H2 - 0.6   Continue straight on the Intemann Trail as a connector trail to Red Rock Canyon Open Space goes right.

H3 - 1.7   Arrive at Crystal Park Road. Turn around and go back the way you came.

Laura Johnson enjoys smooth singletrack and beautiful scenery at Garden of the Gods.

ⓘ Captain Jack's ★★★★☆

(6 miles from Colorado Springs)

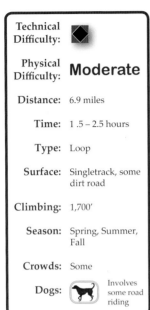

Technical Difficulty:	◆
Physical Difficulty:	**Moderate**
Distance:	6.9 miles
Time:	1.5 – 2.5 hours
Type:	Loop
Surface:	Singletrack, some dirt road
Climbing:	1,700'
Season:	Spring, Summer, Fall
Crowds:	Some
Dogs:	Involves some road riding

It's like riding down a giant waterslide!

Ride Description

Captain Jack's Trail (or, "CAP'N JACKS" as it is sometimes signed) is a famous singletrack loop that is covered with pea-sized rocks. These little rocks act like ball bearings, making the climbs difficult and the downhills somewhat out-of-control and very, very fun. As if to compensate for the lack of traction, sections of the trail have been carved out into large troughs, making it seem like a bobsled course for bicycles. Don't be dismayed if the huge parking lot at High Drive and Gold Camp Road is packed, most of these people are just taking the dog for a walk on the initial dirt road section and you will be free of them once you turn onto the singletrack. If the parking is completely full, you can also park further down Gold Camp Road at the Captain Jack's Trailhead.

Driving Directions

At I-25 Exit 140, take S Nevada Road south and go 0.5 miles. Turn right on E Cheyenne Road and take it for 5.6 miles until you reach the Gold Camp Trailhead at the intersection of Cheyenne Canyon Road, High Drive, and Gold Camp Road.

Riding Directions - see map on next page

I1 - 0.0 Ride past the large metal barricade at the far end of the parking lot and pedal up the old dirt road (Gold Camp Trail).

I2 - 0.7 About 200 feet before you reach North Cheyenne Creek, turn right onto unmarked singletrack. At a switchback, continue to the right as the Seven Bridges Trail (unsigned) goes left.

I3 - 1.9 Turn right at a three-way junction.

I4 - 2.7 Cross a dirt road (High Drive) and continue on singletrack.

I5 - 4.9 Continue on the main trail as two small trails go right.

I6 - 5.2 Arrive at the Captain Jack's Trailhead. Turn right on Gold Camp Road.

I1 - 6.9 Arrive back at the car. Too easy? Try the extremely technical Seven Bridges Trail!

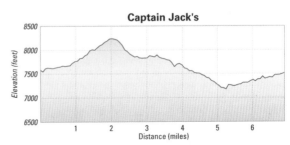

CO Springs & Pueblo

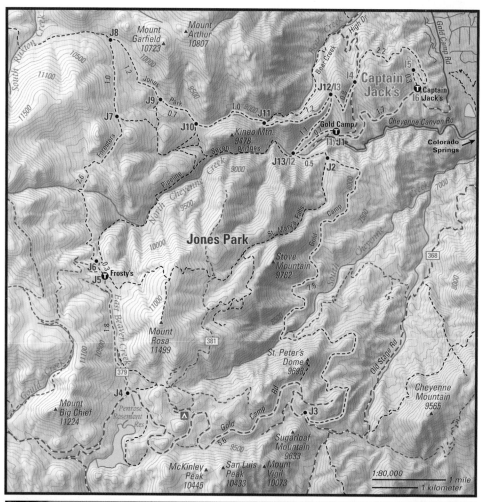

The author holds on tight through one of Captain Jack's trademark sandy corners.

J Jones Park ★★★★☆

(5 miles west of Colorado Springs)

CO Springs & Pueblo

Technical Difficulty:	◆
Physical Difficulty:	**Strenuous**
Distance:	9.9 or 26.1 miles
Time:	1.5 – 5 hours
Type:	Shuttle or loop
Surface:	Singletrack, dirt road
Climbing:	4,500' (without a shuttle)
Season:	Spring, Summer, Fall
Crowds:	Some
Dogs:	

A wild downhill on sandy motorcycle trails

Ride Description

Those who like the fun, waterslide-like downhills on Captain Jack's will love Jones Park. The singletrack descends about 2,500 feet of elevation; so many people ride Jones Park as a shuttle. Shuttling is recommended especially for riders with high-clearance trucks that can make it all the way up FS-379, to the start of the singletrack. Riding Jones Park as a loop (without a shuttle) involves about 14 miles of sandy dirt road. However, since a large section of Gold Hill Road is closed to vehicle traffic, the climb is more pleasant than might be expected and offers a chance to relax and admire the scenery.

The classic Jones Park ride reaches the Jones Park Trail via the Foresters Trail, which is excellent, but does involve several steep climbs. Shuttlers who would like to avoid uphill riding can take the Pipeline Trail instead. However, Pipeline is very sandy, intersects Jones Park lower down, and misses some good riding. Several years ago, there were a number of wooden features and jumps on the Pipeline Trail, but they have been removed (possibly by the Forest Service, since such construction is illegal). The author recommends Foresters over Pipeline, but do a few laps and decide for yourself!

If you are riding Jones Park as a loop, you might consider eliminating much of the road riding by climbing the St Mary's Falls Trail (see ride description). St Mary's is very steep and has plenty of loose gravel, but some argue that this is preferable to riding on Gold Camp Trail.

There is free camping at Wye Campground, located on FS-381, just east of FS-379.

Driving Directions

If you're not shuttling, simply park at the Gold Camp Trailhead. For the shuttle, leave a car at the Gold Camp Trailhead and take the riders and bikes up to Frosty's Trailhead at the end of FS-379. Reaching Frosty's Trailhead requires a high-clearance vehicle, but a typical car will be able to make it most of the way.

To reach Gold Camp Trailhead: Leave I-25 at Exit 140 and take S Nevada Road south for 0.5 miles. Turn right on E Cheyenne Road and take it for 5.6 miles until you reach the trailhead at the intersection of Cheyenne Canyon Road, High Drive, and Gold Camp Road.

To reach Frosty's Trailhead from Gold Camp TH: Head east on Cheyenne Canyon Road for about 3 miles. Go right on Evans, and go 0.2 miles. Turn left on Mesa, and go 0.1 miles. Make a right on Penrose, and go 0.9 miles. Turn right on Old Stage Road (FS-368) and go 6.2 miles. Go right on Gold Camp Road and go 4.7 miles. Make a right on FS-379 and go 1.4 miles or as far as your car's clearance will allow.

Riding Directions - see map on page 136

J1 - 0.0   From the Gold Camp Trailhead, ride past the large metal gate at the far end on the parking lot and start riding west on Gold Camp Trail.

J2 - 1.3   Encounter a closed tunnel and climb the steep singletrack that goes around it. Come to an intersection with the St Mary's Falls Trail and go left to stay on Gold Camp Trail.

J3 - 8.8   Come to an intersection with Old Stage Road. Turn right to continue on Gold Camp Road, which is now open to vehicle traffic.

J4 - 14.4   Turn right on FS-379.

J5 - 16.2   **Shuttle ride starts here.** Arrive at a large parking area (Frosty's Trailhead). Take Trail #701 (Foresters Trail).

J6 - 16.5   Continue straight on Trail #701 (Foresters Trail) as Trail #668 (Pipeline Trail) goes right. (OPTION: Pipeline Trail reaches the Jones Park Trail in 3.5 miles of very steep, sandy descending.)

J7 - 19.1   Continue straight as an unmarked trail goes right. (This unmarked trail is Trail #720 and can be used as a more direct way to reach the Seven Bridges Trail, an extremely rocky technical test.)

J8 - 20.1   Turn right on the Jones Park Trail (Trail #667) and get ready for more downhill fun!

J9 - 21.3   Go straight as an unmarked trail goes uphill to the right.

J10 - 22.0   Continue straight on the Jones Park Trail as the Pipeline Trail goes right. (You can take the Pipeline Trail and then turn left to ride the crazy "triple-diamond" descent of the Seven Bridges Trail.)

J11 - 23.0   Continue right on the Jones Park Trail (crossing a stream) as the Bear Creek Trail goes left. (OPTION: If you turn left on the Bear Creek Trail you will end up on High Drive, where you can turn left and reach the Palmer/Section 16 Trail in 0.3 miles. Can you handle that much great riding?)

J12 - 24.2   Turn right on an unmarked but very obvious trail. (If you continue straight, you can join the Captain Jack's ride at mile 1.9 and continue to the lower parking lot on Gold Camp Road.)

J13 - 25.4   Turn left on Gold Camp Trail.

J1 - 26.1   Arrive back at the Gold Camp Trailhead.

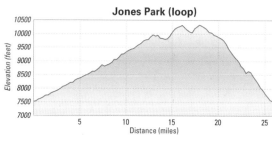

Old railroad tunnel on Gold Camp Trail.

Graeson Lewis high above Palmer Park.   photo: Fredrik Marmsater

Ⓚ South Shore of Pueblo Reservoir ★★★★★

(8 miles west of Pueblo)

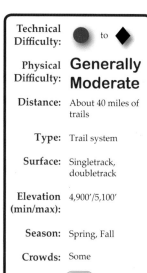

Technical Difficulty:	● to ◆
Physical Difficulty:	**Generally Moderate**
Distance:	About 40 miles of trails
Type:	Trail system
Surface:	Singletrack, doubletrack
Elevation (min/max):	4,900'/5,100'
Season:	Spring, Fall
Crowds:	Some
Dogs:	🐕

A fantastic, extensive trail system

Ride Description

The south shore of Lake Pueblo is jam-packed with excellent, recently constructed singletrack. With a beautiful setting, excellent views of Pikes Peak in the distance, a warm climate, and on-site camping, Lake Pueblo is the premier cool-weather mountain biking destination in the Front Range. The low elevation and lack of shade make riding in the summer almost out of the question, but the abundance of sunshine does allow the trails to dry quickly during sunny periods in the winter.

There are two distinct styles of trail at Lake Pueblo. Most of the mileage here consists of smooth, meandering singletrack with only short hills – a singlespeeder's paradise! In contrast, there are "the canyons." These short steep trails are loaded with rocks, wooden ladders, and plenty of technical riding. Trails names like Broken Hip, Skull Canyon, Pinball, and Freeride convey the appropriate sense of excitement and danger found on the canyon trails.

Driving Directions

From I-25, take Exit 99B and head west on 6th Street and go 0.2 miles. Turn left on Santa Fe Avenue and go 0.1 miles. Turn right on 4th Street (which eventually turns into CO-96) and go about 7 miles. Turn right on S Marina Road and enter the state park. After about 0.5 miles, stop at the tollbooth and pay the entrance fee. Shortly after the tollbooth, turn left towards the Arkansas Point Campground. Park near the campground office and find the start of the South Shore Trail.

Riding Directions

Use the map and wander around! Those looking for technical challenges should check out the short-but-sweet canyon drops near Skull Canyon. Riders looking for lots of mileage on fast, smooth singletrack can take the South Shore Trail west to Outer Limits and Voodoo Loop. Have fun!

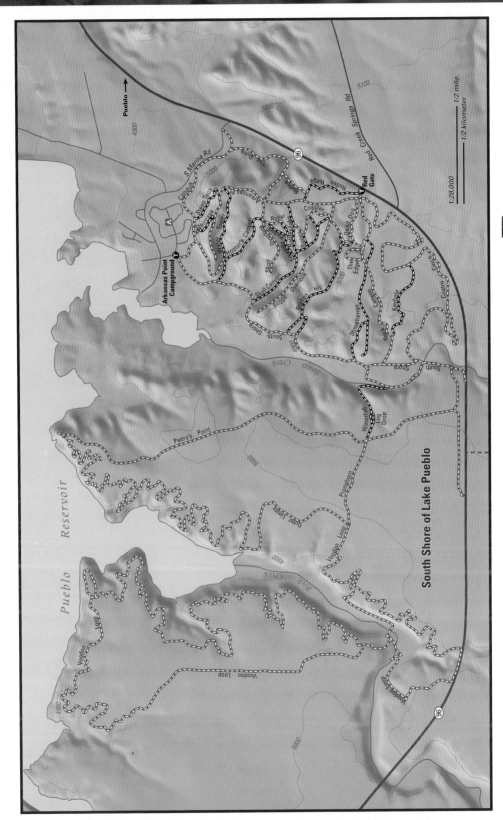

CO Springs & Pueblo

Pueblo →

Red Creek Springs Rd

5100

5000

4900

1/2 mile

1/2 kilometer

1:28,000

96

S Marina Rd

5000

True Dukes

Conduit

Steep Tech

Arkansas Rd

Rodeo

Ridge

Red Gate

Marmoset

Inner Tube

Hunter's Canyon

Roller Coaster

Digger

Dead Dog

Arkansas Point Campground

Skull Canyon

Skull

Broken Hip

The Edger

Cuchara

Boggs

Overlook

Stonehenge

Canyon

Keyhole

Cuatro

South Shore

Logs

Rock

Boggs Creek

South Shore

Waterfall

Log Drop

Pedro's Point

5000

Pronghorn

Voodoo Loop

Otter Tail

South Shore of Lake Pueblo

Pueblo Reservoir

Rock Creek

4900

Voodoo Loop

Voodoo Loop

4900

5000

96

5000

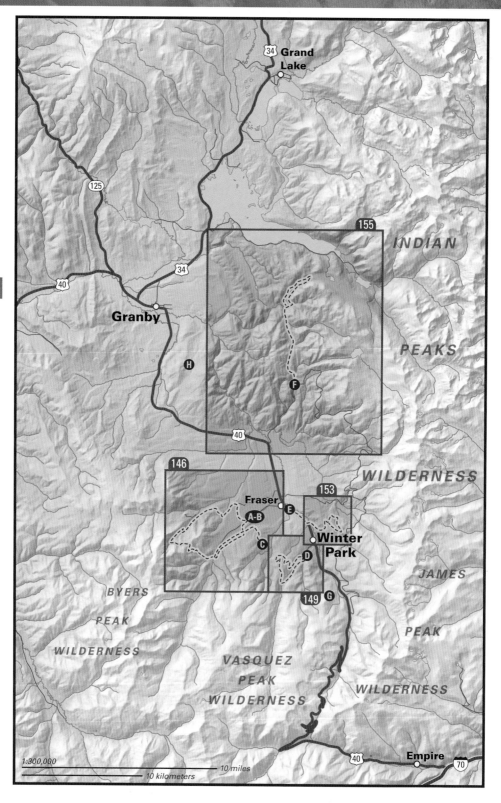

Grand
Lake

INDIAN

Granby

PEAKS

H

F

WILDERNESS

Fraser

A-B

E

Winter
Park

C

D

JAMES

G

BYERS

PEAK

PEAK

WILDERNESS

VASQUEZ

WILDERNESS

PEAK

WILDERNESS

Empire

1:300,000

10 miles

10 kilometers

Winter Park

Located just over one hour from Denver, Winter Park is the perfect getaway when summer temperatures climb above 90 degrees and Front Range trails become saunas. Winter Park is located in Middle Park, one of the three high mountain basins of northern Colorado (the other two being North Park and South Park). Since it is located in a flat valley, Winter Park offers some relief from the massive hill-climbs typical of rides in the Front Range. Many of the trails in this chapter, such as the Chainsaw-Flume Loop and the Idlewild Trails, feature minimal climbing that is spread throughout the ride instead of being condensed into one giant, lung-busting hill.

The Fraser Valley is Denver's winter playground and is home to the downhill ski areas of Winter Park, Sol Vista, and several cross country skiing destinations. Even during the summer, the place can be chilly, and in the winter, it's down-right frigid. Fraser has an annual mean temperature of about 32 degrees and narrowly lost a legal battle with International Falls, Minnesota about which city can use the title of "The Icebox of the Nation."

High above Winter Park Resort   photo: Xavier Torrents

Accommodations

Despite being so close to Denver, the Winter Park experience is surprisingly casual. There is an abundance of free camping, as well as several pay campgrounds, located west of Fraser. Those looking for more civilized lodging will find that Winter Park is home to many hotels and motels, which often offer discounted rates during the summer season.

Bike Shops

Totally Wired Cyclery
543 Zerex Street (US-40), Fraser. 970-726-6923
Located in the Alco shopping center on the north side of Fraser, Totally Wired might take its name from the fact that it shares space with one of the best coffee shops in Colorado: Rocky Mountain Roastery. Totally Wired has great mechanics and has been known to rent a few high-end bikes.

Epic Mountain Sports
74815 US-40, Fraser. 970-726-2868
Located in downtown Winter Park in the Park Place Shopping Center, Epic offers parts, service, and Giant rental bikes.

Eats and Drinks

Rocky Mountain Roastery
543 Zerex Street (US-40), Fraser. 970-726-4400
Located next to Totally Wired Cyclery and serving some of the best coffee in town, this is convienence at it's best. There is also a location on US-40 in Winter Park.

Tabernash Tavern
72287 US-40, Tabernash. 970-726-4430
Fantastic upscale dining in a rustic old building.

Carver's Cafe
93 Cooper Creek Way, Winter Park. 970-726-8202
Located in Cooper Creek Square, a pedestrian mall on the west side of US-40 in downtown Winter Park, Carver's serves the best breakfasts in town.

Love in the mountains:
Top 10 rides to do with your significant other

10. Boulder – Nederland – West Magnolia

9. Fruita – Bookcliffs

8. Summit County – Baker's Tank

7. Winter Park – Chainsaw-Flume

6. Crested Butte – Lower Loop

5. Leadville – Turquoise Lake

4. Fruita – Highline Lake State Park

3. Leadville – Twin Lakes

2. Steamboat – South Fork of the Elk

1. Telluride – Gondola – Village Trail

Liz Wall and Ben Schneider.

Winter Park

Tipperary Creek Loop ★★★★☆

(5 miles northwest of Winter Park)

Technical Difficulty:	
Physical Difficulty:	**Moderate**
Distance:	13.2 miles
Time:	2 – 3 hours
Type:	Loop
Surface:	Singletrack, dirt road
Climbing:	1,500'
Season:	Summer, Fall
Crowds:	Some
Dogs:	🐕

Plenty of fast-'n-fun singletrack makes this the classic Winter Park ride

Ride Description

The Tipperary Creek Trail itself is a little boring, but when combined with the Northwest Passage Trail and the Flume Trail, it makes an excellent loop ride. The trails are smooth and fast, so the 13 miles go by quickly. Those looking for more mileage should check out Creekside, Chainsaw, and the secret trails the locals have stashed here. Those riding from Fraser can take the Givelo Trail singletrack, which parallels County-73 for 1.1 miles, running from the Rodeo Grounds in Fraser to the Northwest Passage Trailhead.

Driving Directions

From Winter Park, drive north to Fraser on US-40. Turn left on Eisenhower Drive and go two blocks. Turn left on Leonard Lane and go 4 blocks. Turn right on Mill Avenue, which turns into County-73 (St Louis Creek Road). Go about 2 miles until you come to a small, dirt parking area on the right.

Riding Directions

A1 - 0.0   From the trailhead, find the Northwest Passage singletrack and head northwest.

A2 - 1.5   Turn left on County-50, a dirt road.

A3 - 4.5   Turn left on the Tipperary Creek Trail.

A4 - 6.7   Continue straight on Tipperary Creek as Backscratch goes right.

A5 - 7.8   Reach the top of the hill and continue down the other side. Yee haw!

A6 - 8.2   Continue left on the Spruce Creek Trail as the Dead Horse Loop Trail goes right.

A7 - 10.1   Come to the end of the Spruce Creek Trail and turn right on a dirt road (FS-160). Go a short distance and turn left onto FS-159 (Aqueduct Road). Turn left on the Flume Trail.

A8 - 12.3   Go left on Chainsaw. Cross a bridge and continue straight. At a T-intersection, turn right on the Creekside Trail.

A1 - 13.2   Arrive back at the trailhead on County-73.

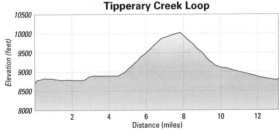

Ⓑ Creekside Loop ★★★⯪☆

🔴 **Distance: 3.4 miles**

The Creekside Loop is a great beginner loop with sections of excellent singletrack, and begins at the same trailhead as Tipperary Creek. The directions are a little confusing because there are two trails named Creekside: Creekside Trail and the Creekside Loop Trail. From the road, head south on the Creekside Trail and bear right at the first intersection. Stay on the Creekside Trail for 2.0 miles until you can make a sharp left on the Creekside Loop Trail. At 2.7 miles, turn left on Chainsaw and then turn right onto the Creekside Trail.

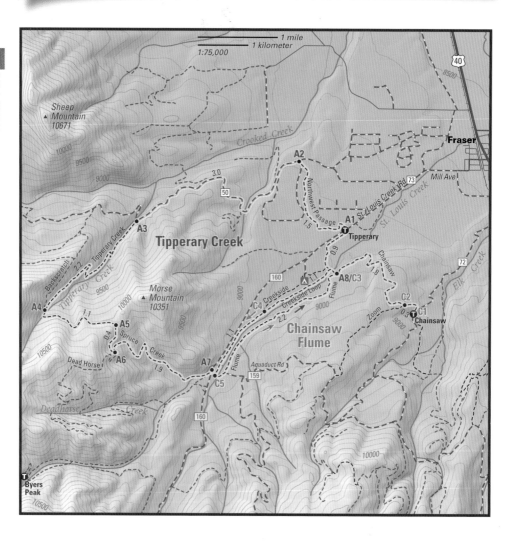

Chainsaw-Flume ★★★★☆

(4 miles northwest of Winter Park)

Technical Difficulty:	
Physical Difficulty:	**Moderate**
Distance:	8.6 miles
Time:	1.5 – 2.5 hours
Type:	Lollipop loop
Surface:	Singletrack
Climbing:	900'
Season:	Summer, Fall
Crowds:	Some
Dogs:	

Sample some delightful singletrack on chainsaw, then enjoy the famous descent on Flume

Ride Description

Tired of slogging up dirt roads to get to the classic singletrack? Try this loop! The great singletrack starts right from the parking lot and flows through beautiful forests and meadows. Those looking or a longer ride could easily combine these trails with the Tipperary Creek Loop. And these are just the tip of the iceberg – there are miles and miles of good trails hidden in the woods west of Fraser. The trees in this area have been hit hard by the invasive pine beetle and it's likely that significant logging will take place to remove the dead trees. It's possible that the exact locations of the trails in this area (especially chainsaw) will change slightly in the coming years.

Winter Park

Driving Directions

From Winter Park, head north on US-40 for about 2 miles. Turn left on County-72 and go 2.5 miles until you come to a large dirt parking area on the left. You will see a small sign on the right indicating the start of the Chainsaw Trail.

Riding Directions

C1 - 0.0   From the trailhead, start riding on the Chainsaw Trail singletrack.

C2 - 0.3   Go right on Chainsaw as Zoom goes left.

C3 - 2.1   Head right on Chainsaw as Flume goes left. Cross a bridge and turn left on the Creekside Loop Trail.

C4 - 3.2   Continue straight onto the Creekside Trail.

C5 - 4.3   Turn left on the Aqueduct Road, go about 0.15 miles, and turn left on the Flume Trail at a sign.

C3 - 6.5   Arrive back at the Chainsaw Trail. Turn right and head back to the trailhead.

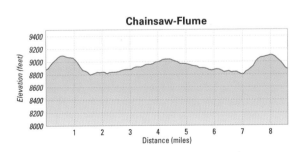

Chainsaw-Flume

ⒹWTB Loop ★★★☆☆

(Starts in Winter Park)

Technical Difficulty:	
Physical Difficulty:	**Moderate**
Distance:	7.2 miles
Time:	1 – 2 hours
Type:	Lollipop Loop
Surface:	Singletrack, dirt road
Climbing:	1,000'
Season:	Summer, Fall
Crowds:	Some
Dogs:	

A short loop, sampling a few of the many trails in the area

Ride Description

The Vasquez Road area west of Winter Park is a complicated network of dirt roads, trails made from old dirt roads, and singletrack trails. Expect to get lost, but to eventually find some great singletrack. Many of these trails have been here for a long time, but there are also a number of newly constructed trails that complicate navigation. This loop connects a few sections of singletrack with some dirt roads to form a very enjoyable loop.

Driving Directions

There is very limited parking at the start of the trail, so it is advisable to park in town and ride to the start of the trail. From Winter Park, head west on Vasquez Road (it's on the south side of town) for about 0.5 miles. Turn left on Arapaho Road and go for 0.4 miles until you reach a small, dirt parking area.

Riding Directions

D1 - 0.0 From the "trailhead," start riding up Little Vasquez Trail (a dirt road).

D2 - 0.2 Turn right on the Blue Sky Trail singletrack. Continue straight as the Twin Bridges Trail goes right.

D3 - 1.6 Come to a clearing where you have the choice of two dirt roads. Bear left and ride along the smoother dirt road.

D4 - 1.9 At a T-intersection, turn right on another dirt road. Go about 500 feet and turn right on Vasquez Road. After a short distance, turn left on FS-159.

D5 - 2.9 Continue straight past a dirt road on the right. Go about 500 feet and turn right on the next dirt road (D2) and go past a gate.

D6 - 3.7 Turn right (downhill) as D2-Green goes left. Go about 0.2 miles and turn right on the WTB Trail singletrack.

D7 - 5.0 Turn left on D4, an old dirt road. Continue straight through two intersections with D3.

Curt Stevens enjoys the evening light on the WTB Loop

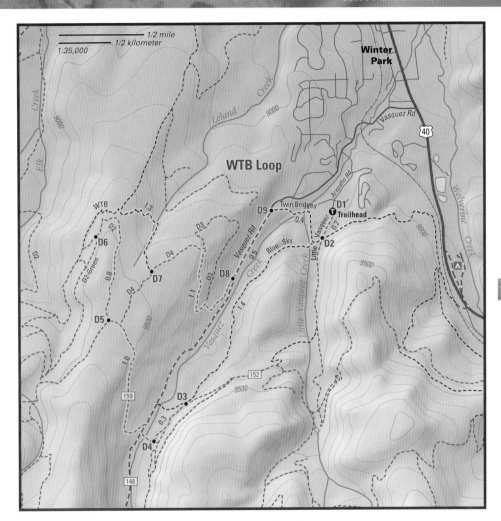

D8 - 6.1 Turn left on a smooth dirt road (Vasquez Road).

D9 - 6.6 Turn right on the Twin Bridges Trail. (This is an easy turn to miss. Look for the trail on the right just past a large dumpster.)

D2 - 7.0 Make a left onto the Blue Sky Trail and retrace your tracks back to town.

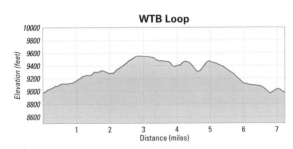

(E) Idlewild Loop ★★★★☆

(Starts in Fraser, 4 miles northwest of Winter Park)

Technical Difficulty:	
Physical Difficulty:	**Easy**
Distance:	9.3 miles
Time:	1.5 – 2.5 hours
Type:	Lollipop loop
Surface:	Singletrack, bike path
Climbing:	1,100'
Season:	Summer, Fall
Crowds:	Some
Dogs:	🐕

A network of smooth singletrack tucked behind a neighborhood

Ride Description

The Idlewild Trails are a great example of the Fraser Valley's smooth, meandering singletrack: they cruise through the forest with only the occasional technical section or major hill-climb. Also, like most trail systems in the area, they are composed of a number of interlaced and often unmarked trails that will cause many riders to get lost. However, with so many great trails to discover, getting lost isn't so bad!

The Idlewild trails start from the Rendezvous housing development and the all the roads are signed "No Parking." Thus, it is recommended to park in Fraser and take the bike path to the trails. Many people park at the Totally Wired bike shop since the mall offers food, bike parts, and incredible coffee. What else does a mountain biker need? (Recent trail construction has made it possible to access the Idyllwild Trails from the town of Winter Park. See map.)

Driving Directions

From Winter Park, head north on US-40 for about 2 miles. On the south end of Fraser, turn left into the strip mall with the "Alco" discount store, the Totally Wired Cyclery, and the Rocky Mountain Roastery.

Riding Directions

E1 - 0.0 From the Totally Wired bike shop, start riding southeast along the Fraser River bike path that parallels US-40.

E2 - 1.4 Turn left on Rendezvous Road, crossing US-40.

E3 - 2.5 Turn right on Friendship Drive.

E4 - 2.8 Turn right on the Meadow Trail.

E5 - 3.0 Head right on the Crosstrails Trail. Continue past intersections with the Serendipity Trail and the Winterwoods Trail.

E6 - 3.5 Turn left onto the Whoops Trail.

E7 - 3.7 Turn right on the Southfork Loop.

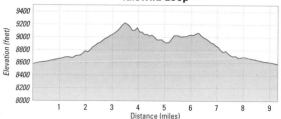

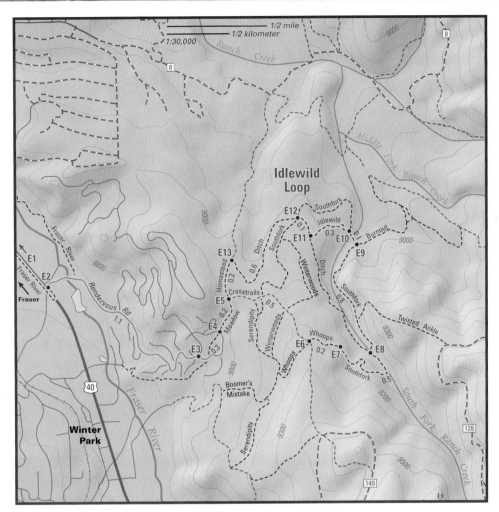

E8 - 4.2   Cross the South Fork of Ranch Creek and continue on the Southfork Loop. (Ditch Trail goes left.)

E9 - 5.0   Continue on the Southfork Loop as the Burnout Loop goes right.

E10 - 5.1 Shortly after crossing a bridge over the South Fork of Ranch Creek, turn left on unmarked singletrack (Idlewild Trail).

E11 - 5.4 Turn right on the Ditch Trail.

E12 - 5.5 Continue straight on the Ditch Trail as it crosses the Southfork Loop Trail.

E13 - 6.1 Turn left on the Homestead Trail.

E5 - 6.3   Arrive back at the intersection of Crosstrails and Meadow. Head back towards US-40 on the Meadow Trail. Retrace your path along the roads and bike path to Fraser.

(F) Strawberry ★★★★☆

(10 miles north of Winter Park)

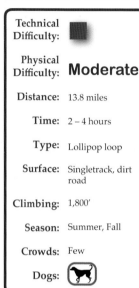

Technical Difficulty:	■
Physical Difficulty:	**Moderate**
Distance:	13.8 miles
Time:	2 – 4 hours
Type:	Lollipop loop
Surface:	Singletrack, dirt road
Climbing:	1,800'
Season:	Summer, Fall
Crowds:	Few
Dogs:	🐕

Lots of good cruising through the woods with occasional deadfall

Ride Description

The forests around Winter Park have been hit hard by the recent pine beetle infestation and many hillsides have turned from lush green to an eerie brown. The beetles are not only an aesthetic concern, but have also caused many trees to fall across the trails. In the summer of 2010, portions of the Strawberry Trail were littered with deadfall, turning this normally gentle loop into an all-day epic. Since most of the forests near these trails have been reduced to standing deadwood, falling trees will likely be a problem for years to come. So, it's a good idea to inquire about the trail status at a local bike shop or Forest Service office before embarking.

Driving Directions

From Winter Park, head north on US-40 for about 5 miles, passing through Fraser. Just before reaching the tiny town of Tabernash, turn right on County-83 (FS-129) and go 0.4 miles. Turn left on County-84 (FS-129) and drive 4.0 miles. As the road makes a sharp right, park in a large dirt pullout on the left. The Strawberry Trail (a dirt road at this point) starts behind a large metal gate.

Riding Directions

F1 - 0.0   From the trailhead, pass around the gate and begin riding on the Strawberry Trail (an old dirt road).

F2 - 2.1   At a Y-intersection, turn left, following the sign that says "Trail".

F3 - 3.7   Continue on the Strawberry Trail as the Caribou Trail goes right.

F4 - 4.4   Turn right on the Caribou Trail towards the Strawberry Creek Trail.

F5 - 4.7   Go left on the Strawberry Creek Trail.

F6 - 6.9   Turn left onto the West Strawberry Trail. (*You can add miles by going right and doing a short out-and-back of the Strawberry Bench Trail.*)

F7 - 8.3   Continue on the West Strawberry Trail as the Doe Creek Trail goes right. (*The Doe Creek Trail leads down to Lake Granby and is a great descent.*)

F4 - 9.4   Arrive back at the intersection with the Strawberry Trail. Make a right and follow the trail back to where you started.

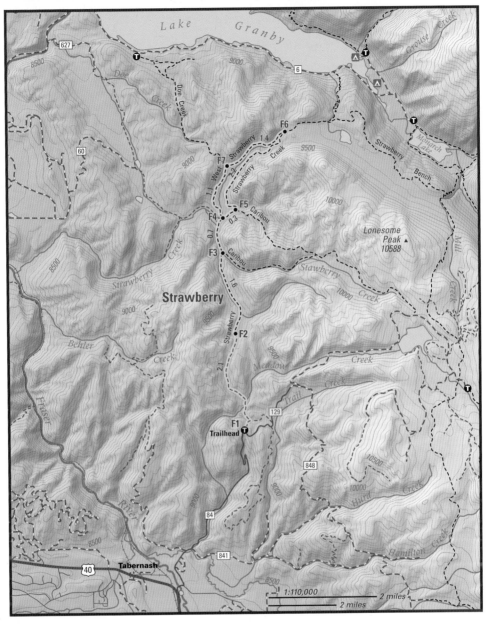

Winter Park

Lake Granby

627

8500

Doe Creek

9000

6

60

9000

F6

1.4

Strawberry Creek

9500

F7

2.1

West Strawberry

1.1

Strawberry

10000

Strawberry Lake

Monarch Lake

Bench

F5

Caribou

F4

0.3

0.7

Lonesome Peak 10588

F3

Caribou

1.6

Strawberry Creek

10000

Strawberry

8500

9000

Strawberry Creek

Behler

9500

Strawberry

F2

9000

Meadow

Creek

Mill Creek

9000

2.1

Trail

Fraser River

129

F1 **Trailhead**

848

10500

10000

Hurd Creek

84

8500

841

9000

40 **Tabernash**

8500

Hamilton Creek

1:110,000

2 miles

2 miles

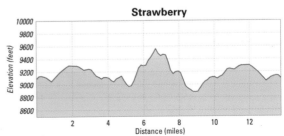

Strawberry

Elevation (feet)	Distance (miles)

10000
9800
9600
9400
9200
9000
8800
8600

2   4   6   8   10   12

Steve Wentz goes big at Sol Vista

Ⓖ Trestle Bike Park at Winter Park Resort ★★★★★

(2 miles south of Winter Park)

Hours:	9:00 - 5:30, early June to late September
Price:	$34 full day as of 2010
Vertical Relief:	1,700'

Description

For riders who dream of hitting hundreds of jumps on the way down to the base of a chairlift, then Trestle Bike Park is heaven on earth. The resort has one traditional downhill trail with steep, rocky terrain (Trestle Downhill), but the bike park is best known for its butter-smooth trails with huge berms, lots of jumps, and numerous wooden features. Almost all of the jumps can be rolled, so beginners and those without proper downhill bikes can still have a great time. There's also an assortment of delightful cross country and green-circle downhill trails, so even novices will enjoy riding here.

Driving Directions

From the town of Winter Park, head south for about 2 miles and turn right into Winter Park Resort.

You'll flip for the incredible jumps and features at Trestle Bike Park!   Photo: Xavier Torrents

Winter Park

(H) Sol Vista Resort ★★★★★

(20 miles north of Winter Park)

Hours:	noon-7:00 (Fri), 10-7 (Sat), 10-5 (Sun), early June to late September
Price:	$25 all day as of 2010
Vertical Relief:	1,000'

Description

Tucked away in a beautiful valley near Granby (about 15 miles north of Winter Park), Sol Vista is a hidden mountain biking paradise. The Sol Vista Bike Park has something for everyone, offering everything from gentle, family-friendly cross country singletrack to lift-served downhill trails with berms and jumps. From the top of the lift, the trails are simple to navigate: turn left for the easy trails, turn right for the difficult ones. The lift-served trails are designed to be ridden with a downhill bike and can be fairly rocky. Those who don't own such burly bikes should consider renting one of the bikes available in the shop at Sol Vista. If you'd rather ride uphill than take the lift, there are many miles of excellent cross country singletrack that start from the base area.

Driving Directions

From Winter Park, head north on US-40 for about 15 miles, passing through Fraser and Tabernash. Turn right on Village Road, following signs for the Sol Vista Ski Resort. Go about 2 miles until you come to the ski area parking lot.

Steve Wentz doesn't bother slowing down for the rocks at Sol Vista Resort.

Mihai Moga cruises the smooth singletrack at Sol Vista Resort.

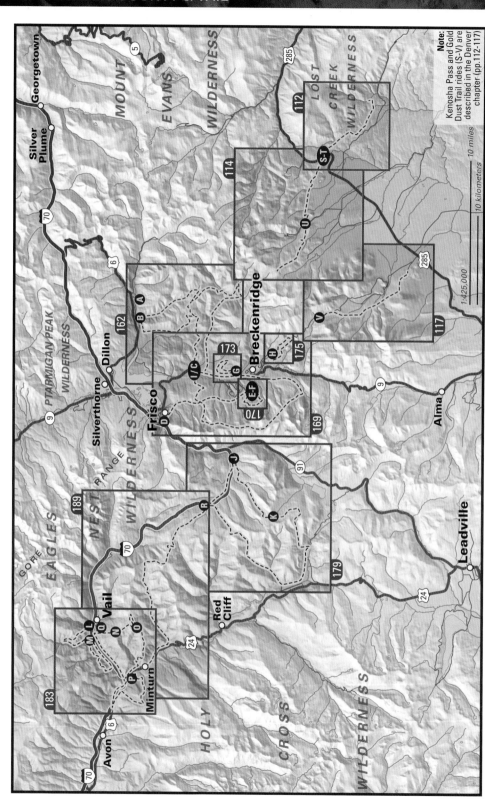

Note:
Kenosha Pass and Gold Dust Trail rides (S–V) are described in the Denver chapter (pp.112–117)

1:425,000

10 miles

10 kilometers

Summit County & Vail

Summit County & Vail

During the winter, Summit County and Vail are home to some of the most popular ski resorts in Colorado. When summer arrives, the snow melts and reveals some of the best alpine mountain biking trails in the state. Foolishly, the mountain biking here is often overlooked in favor of "big name" mountain biking areas like Fruita, Crested Butte, and Steamboat Springs. Many people likely steer clear of Summit County in the summer, fearing the many vexations that accompany I-70 skiing in the winter: stop-and-go traffic, parking fees, expensive hotels, and long lift lines. However, the region is entirely different in the summer: traffic is (generally) tolerable, parking is free, camping is plentiful, and the trails are not crowded. With a great mixture of trails that includes scenic bike paths, gnarly lift-served trails, and plenty of perfect alpine singletrack, Summit County and Vail have trails for all ability levels. Best of all, most of these trailheads are less than two hours from Denver.

Accommodations

Summit County and Vail are major skiing destinations, and hotels, motels, and condos are plentiful. Breckenridge has a range of hotel options and many rides start right from town. Frisco, Silverthorne, and Dillon are conveniently located near the interstate and often feature a lower price tag than Breckenridge or Vail. There are several pay campgrounds around Dillon Reservoir that cost about $20 per site. Free camping is generally allowed on National Forest land in the area and many of the dirt roads leading into the mountains offer nice sites. Try Boreas Pass Road near Breck or Red Sandstone Road near Vail.

Bike Shops

Many of the ski shops convert into bike shops during the summer season, so Summit County is packed with quality bike shops.

Alpine Sports
610 S Ridge Street, Breckenridge. 970-453-8100
Located in downtown Breckenridge, this shop rents full-suspension mountain bikes.

Pioneer Sports
842 N Summit Boulevard, Frisco. 970-668-3668
This shop is conveniently located next to Walmart.

Wilderness Sports
400 Main Street, Frisco. 970-668-8804
Bikes, service, and rentals.

Mountain Pedaler
161 Main Street, Minturn. 970-827-5522
Located in the middle of Minturn, this small shop is packed with excellent mountain bikes.

Summit County & Vail

Eats and Drinks

Breckenridge Brewery
600 S Main Street, Breckenridge. 970-435-1550
A classic Colorado brewpub, the Breckenridge Brewery offers about a dozen delicious microbrews in addition to tasty dinners. Their Oatmeal Stout and Vanilla Porter are perfect for cold mountain nights.

Clint's Bakery & Coffee House
131 S Main Street, Breckenridge. 970-453-2990
Best coffee-and-a-muffin in Colorado.

Blue Moose
540 S Main Street, Breckenridge. 970-453-4859
A good place for the pre-ride bacon-and-eggs breakfast.

Dillon Dam Brewery
100 Little Dam Street, Dillon. 970-262-7777
A great place to go après-ride as the portions are enormous. Their Sweet George's Brown ale is excellent.

Vail Village
Vail offers countless dining establishments, some in the main Vail Village and the rest in Lionshead Village (the base of the gondola). Being one of the classier ski-towns, many are quite up-scale and expensive, but there are moderately priced restaurants too.

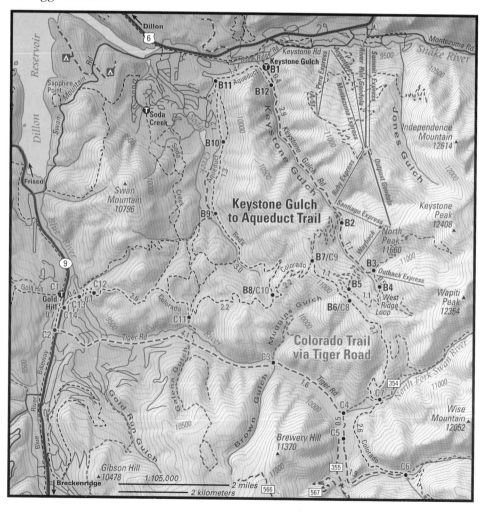

Ⓐ Keystone Resort ★★★★⯪

(6 miles southeast of Dillon)

Hours:	10:00 - 7:00 on weekends, mid-May to mid-September
Price:	$36 full day or $22 one run as of 2010
Vertical Relief:	2,300'

Description

The ride up the River Run Gondola at Keystone seems to take forever, but it's not because the gondola is slow. It carries riders and bikes up a whopping 2,300 vertical feet. Once at the top (11,600'), riders can admire views of Lake Dillon before deciding which trail to take down to the base. Keystone offers trails for riders of all abilities, from gentle green circle cruises to gnarly adventures complete with 20-foot drops. They also have some of the most creative and interesting "North Shore" features to appear at a Colorado Resort, including huge elevated wooden bridges and a giant corkscrew feature that wraps around over 360 degrees. Keystone is similar in size and quality to its main competitor, Winter Park. However, the two resorts offer different styles of riding. The trails at Winter Park tend to be smooth and filled with jumps, while Keystone boasts more rocks, steeps, and features. Those who would rather earn their descent with sweat will be glad to know that several of the easier trails at Keystone are open to uphill riding.

Driving Directions

From I-70, take Exit 205 and head south of US-6. Go about 7.6 miles and turn right on Keystone Road into Keystone Ski Resort. Make your first left and park in the free parking lot.

The author samples some of the log drops at Keystone Resort

Summit County & Vail

Keystone Gulch to Aqueduct Loop ★★★★★

(Starts in Keystone)

Technical Difficulty:	
Physical Difficulty:	**Moderate**
Distance:	17.5 miles
Time:	3 – 5 hours
Type:	Loop
Surface:	Singletrack, dirt road
Climbing:	3,000'
Season:	Summer
Crowds:	Some
Dogs:	

A long dirt road brings you to some of the best singletrack in Summit County

Ride Description

The West Ridge section of the Colorado Trail is the highlight of the famous Tiger Road Loop (see Ride C). This ride includes the West Ridge section and adds a great descent on Red's Trail and a beautiful cruise on the Aqueduct Trail. The initial climb on Keystone Gulch Road is mostly gentle except for the last mile, which, though it is steep and horrible, is a small price to pay for such good riding.

Driving Directions

From I-70, take Exit 205 and head south on US-6 for about 6 miles. Turn right on Keystone Road and take the first right on Soda Ridge Road. Turn left on Keystone Gulch Road and go a few hundred feet to the Keystone Gulch Trailhead parking area.

Riding Directions - see map on page 162

B1 - 0.0 From the Keystone Gulch Trailhead, ride up Keystone Gulch Road for a long time.

B2 - 3.4 Continue straight as a dirt road goes right. (This road can also be used to access the Colorado Trail, but will shorten the ride.)

B3 - 4.5 Bear left on the main gravel road, passing the base of the Outback Express chairlift. Go a few hundred feet and turn right on a gated dirt road that is signed, "West Ridge Loop."

B4 - 5.0 Go right (downhill) on a dirt road. Cross a creek and climb steeply.

B5 - 6.1 Continue slightly left as another dirt road goes right (downhill).

B6 - 6.9 Turn right on the Colorado Trail singletrack.

B7 - 8.0 Continue straight on the Colorado Trail as a trail goes right. (This trail leads back to Keystone Gulch Road.)

B8 - 10.2 Go right on unmarked (but well-worn) singletrack. This is called Red's Trail and it's fantastic!

B9 - 13.2 At a dirt road, turn right and climb uphill on singletrack (the Aqueduct Trail).

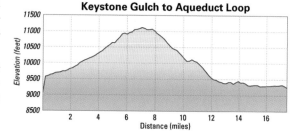

B10 - 14.5 At a Y-intersection, turn left on the main trail.

B11 - 15.7 Turn right on singletrack to stay on the Aqueduct Trail.

B12 - 17.1 Cross the creek on a small bridge and turn left on Keystone Gulch Road.

B1 - 17.5 Arrive back at the Keystone Gulch Trailhead.

Curt Stevens cruises the perfect singletrack on the Aqueduct Trail.

©Colorado Trail via Tiger Road ★★★★★

(4 miles north of Breckenridge)

Technical Difficulty:	
Physical Difficulty:	**Moderate**
Distance:	23.8 miles
Time:	3 – 6 hours
Type:	Loop
Surface:	Singletrack, dirt road
Climbing:	3,500'
Season:	Summer
Crowds:	Few
Dogs:	

Great riding on the Colorado Trail makes this loop a summer tradition

Ride Description

With mile upon mile of beautiful alpine riding, this section of the Colorado Trail is a great introduction to longer rides at high elevation. Though this loop is long (almost 24 miles), much of the climbing is done on dirt roads and the riding along the Colorado Trail is smooth and fast. Those looking for more of a challenge should consider riding the Colorado Trail as an out-and-back. Heck, if you're feeling really masochistic, continue riding all the way to Georgia Pass!

Driving Directions

From I-70, take Exit 203 and head south on CO-9 towards Breckenridge. Drive for 6.2 miles and turn right on Gateway Road. Immediately turn right again into the Gold Hill Trailhead. (If you are starting from Breckenridge, drive north on CO-9 for about 4 miles and turn left into the Gold Hill Trailhead.)

Riding Directions - see map on page 162

C1 - 0.0   From the Gold Hill Trailhead, take the bike path south, towards Breckenridge.

C2 - 0.7   Turn left on Tiger Road. (Do NOT take Tiger Run Road).

C3 - 4.8   Bear right to stay on Tiger Road as a dirt road goes left up Muggins Gulch.

C4 - 6.4   Go right to stay on Middle Fork Road as North Fork Road (County-354) goes left.

C5 - 6.9   Continue straight on Middle Fork Road as South Fork Rd (County-355) goes right.

C6 - 8.8   Just before a fork in the road, turn left onto the signed Colorado Trail (CT). You will take the CT for the next 12 miles, so follow the twin-peaked "Colorado Trail" signs whenever you encounter a junction.

C7 - 11.4   Cross North Fork Road and continue on the CT.

C8 - 14.3   Continue straight on the CT as the West Ridge Loop (unsigned) goes right.

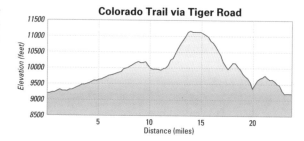

C9 - 15.5   Continue straight on the CT as the West Ridge Loop (signed) goes right. Blast down some fun switchbacks.

C10 - 17.4   Bear left on the CT as Red's Trail (unsigned) goes right.

C11 - 19.9   Pass beneath powerlines and continue on singletrack as doubletrack goes left.

C12 - 22.5   Encounter "The Switchbacks of Doom." Try not to fall down the steep hillside.

C13 - 23.2   After passing a small lake, cross Tiger Run Road and continue on singletrack on the other side.

C14 - 23.6   Cross CO-9 and turn right on the bike path on the other side.

C1 - 23.8   Arrive back at the Gold Hill Trailhead.

Katie Johnson enjoys the wildflowers near Breckenridge.

Summit County & Vail

(D) Peaks Trail ★★★★☆

(Starts in Frisco)

Technical Difficulty:	◆
Physical Difficulty:	**Moderate**
Distance:	17.6 miles
Time:	3 – 5 hours
Type:	Out-and-back
Surface:	Singletrack, bike path
Climbing/ Descending:	1,600'/550' (one way)
Season:	Summer, Fall
Crowds:	Some
Dogs:	🐕 Trail is crowded

Classic singletrack through the woods from Frisco to Breckenridge

Ride Description

The Peaks Trail consists of nine miles of glorious wooded singletrack running between Frisco and Breckenridge. Never too difficult, but not too easy, the trail provides fast downhills to challenge experts but is also suitable for less experienced riders. For the full experience, start in Frisco and ride the Peaks Trail as an out-and-back. Those looking for an easier day can use the Blue River Bike Path to make a loop.

Driving Directions

Take I-70 Exit 201 and head south. Immediately turn right into the large parking area. (Alternatively, if you are in Frisco, simply head west on Main Street and turn left into the parking lot just before you reach I-70.)

Riding Directions

D1 - 0.0 From the car, start riding east on the bike path (follow signs to Breckenridge).

D2 - 0.8 Make a right on 2nd Avenue and arrive at "Zack's Stop", a dirt parking lot. Turn left on the signed Peaks Trail.

D3 - 1.7 After passing a lake, stay left on the blue-blazed Peaks Trail as a wide trail goes right.

D4 - 1.9 Cross a dirt road and continue on the Peaks Trail.

D5 - 3.8 Stay on the Peaks Trail as the Gold Hill Trail goes left.

D6 - 4.1 Continue straight on the Peaks Trail as the Miners Creek Trail goes right.

D7 - 8.8 Arrive at Ski Hill Road in Breckenridge. Turn around and ride back on the Peaks Trail. (*Or, to make a loop on the bike path, turn right on Ski Hill Road and ride into downtown Breckenridge. Just after Park Avenue, turn left on the Blue River Bikeway and take it all the way back to Frisco.*)

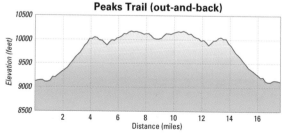

Peaks Trail (out-and-back)

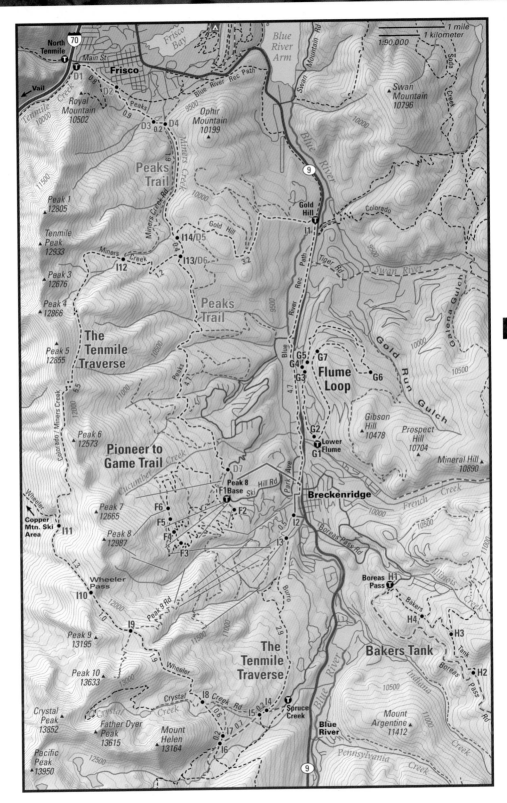

North
Tenmile
70

Vail

Frisco Bay

Blue
River
Arm

Swan Mountain Rd

1 mile
1 kilometer
1:90,000

Main St

Frisco

D1 0.8

Blue River Rec Path

Swan
Mountain
10796

Soda Creek

Vail

D2

Peaks

0.9

Royal
Mountain
10502

D3 0.2 D4

9500

Ophir
Mountain
10199

10000

Miners Creek Rd

Miners Creek

9

Colorado

**Peaks
Trail**

10000

Gold
Hill

Gold Hill

L1

Tenmile

Peak 1
12805

I14/D5

0.4

Tiger Rd

Tenmile
Peak
12933

11500

Miners   Creek

I12

I13/D6

3.2

Swan River

9500

2

Peak 3
12676

9500

**Peaks
Trail**

River Rec Path

Galena Gulch

Peak 4
12866

**The
Tenmile
Traverse**

10500

Blue

G5
G4
G3

G7

**Flume
Loop**

G6

10000

10500

Peak 5
12855

12000

Peaks

4.7

4.7

Gold Run Gulch

Colorado / Miners Creek

5.5

11000

G2

Gibson
Hill
10478

Prospect
Hill
10704

Peak 6
12573

**Pioneer to
Game Trail**

Cucumber Creek

D7

G1

Lower
Flume

Mineral Hill
10890

Wheeler

Copper
Mtn. Ski
Area   I11

Peak 7
12665

F6

F5

F1 Peak 8
Base Ski
Hill Rd

F2

Park Ave

Breckenridge

French Creek

10000

10500

Peak 8
12987

F4

F3

I2

I3

Boreas Pass Rd

0.5

1.3

Wheeler
Pass

I10

12000

Peak 9 Rd

1.0

I9

Burro

2.9

Boreas
Pass

H1

Bakers

Illinois Creek

Peak 9
13195

11500

H4

H3

Tank

Peak 10
13633

1.9

Wheeler

13000

**The
Tenmile
Traverse**

Boreas

Bakers Tank

H2

Pass Rd

Crystal
Peak
13852

Crystal Creek

Crystal

I8 Creek Rd

I5 0.2 0.14

Spruce
Creek

10500

Mount
Argentine
11412

Father Dyer
Peak
13615

Mount
Helen
13164

0.6

I7 0.7

**Blue
River**

11000

Pacific
Peak
13950

12500

0.2

I6

Pennsylvania   Creek

9

Summit County & Vail

(E) Breckenridge Resort ★★★☆☆

(Starts in Breckenridge)

Hours:	9:00 - 5:00 every day, late-June to early-September
Price:	$30 full day or $15 one run (As of 2010)
Vertical Relief:	1,200′

Description

Breckenridge resort doesn't have the crazy wooden features and bermed turns that have now become common on ski resort mountain biking trails. However, they do have a handful of nice singletrack trails and a nice high-speed lift. The resort is in the process of building more mountain biking trails, so within a few years they may have excellent downhill trails similar to Keystone or Winter Park. In the meantime, enjoy the excellent Pioneer to Game Trail loop (Ride F).

Driving Directions

There isn't parking near the base of the chairlift, so it is necessary to park in Breckenridge and either pedal up Ski Hill Road or take the gondola. To reach the gondola from Main Street, head west on Ski Hill Road and turn right on North Park Avenue. There are two free parking lots on the right.

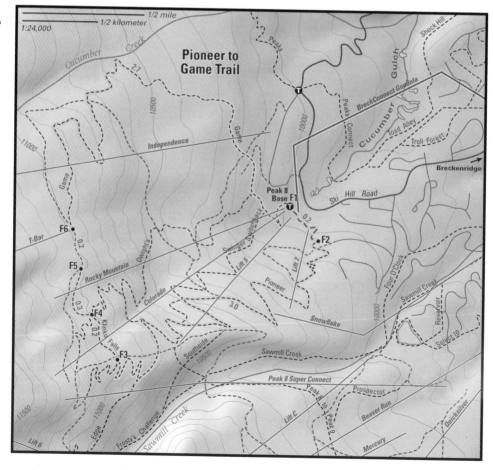

(F) Breckenridge Resort - Pioneer to Game Trail ★★★★☆

(Starts in Breckenridge)

Technical Difficulty:	■
Physical Difficulty:	**Moderate**
Distance:	6.6 miles
Time:	1 – 2 hours
Type:	Loop
Surface:	Singletrack, dirt road
Climbing:	1,800'
Season:	Summer
Crowds:	Some
Dogs:	🐕

A cruise up Pioneer and a fast descent on Game Trail

Ride Description

Though Breckenridge Resort doesn't have many downhill trails, it does offer some nice cross country riding possibilities. This ride combines two of the best trails into a quick, enjoyable loop. The Game Trail features nice downhill riding through forests and Pioneer, with its many switchbacks and gentle grades, is an ideal warm-up.

Driving Directions

This ride starts from the Peak 8 base area. There is no parking at the Peak 8 base, so the best thing to do is to park in the town of Breckenridge and either take the gondola or ride up Ski Hill Road.

Riding Directions - see map on previous page

F1 - 0.0 From the Peak 8 base area, start riding up the gravel road near Chair 5.

F2 - 0.2 Turn right on singletrack (Pioneer Trail). Follow signs for the Pioneer Trail; it's a combination of dirt roads and singletrack.

F3 - 3.2 Turn right on the Klinko Trail. *(You can continue up to Vista Haus and connect to Game Trail, but Klinko gets you there faster.)*

F4 - 3.4 Cross Dwight's Trail and bear slightly left on the Game Trail.

F5 - 3.7 Continue straight on a dirt road.

F6 - 3.9 Near the T-bar lift, find the Game Trail singletrack. Enjoy a sweet downhill!

F1 - 6.6 Arrive back at the Peak 8 base area.

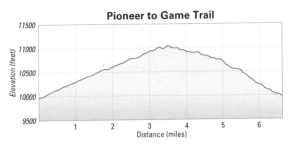

Pioneer to Game Trail

Elevation (feet) / Distance (miles)

Flume Loop ★★★★☆

(1 mile north of Breckenridge)

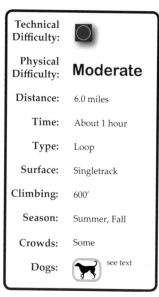

Technical Difficulty:	●
Physical Difficulty:	**Moderate**
Distance:	6.0 miles
Time:	About 1 hour
Type:	Loop
Surface:	Singletrack
Climbing:	600'
Season:	Summer, Fall
Crowds:	Some
Dogs:	🐕 see text

A great cruise along historic mining flumes

Ride Description

Breckenridge is blessed with a number of incredible trails that start right from town. One of the best trails for beginners is the Flume Loop. Most of the trails follow old mining canals (they call them flumes for some reason), and therefore they are smooth and flat. It's not all smooth sailing; there are several short, steep climbs that must be conquered. Dogs are allowed, but the trails can be crowded with hikers and other dogs.

Driving Directions

Unfortunately, there is not an established trailhead for the Flume Trails. However, since the trails are located just north of Breckrenridge, simply find parking in Breck and take the bike path to the start of the Lower Flume Trail. To reach the start of the ride, head north from Breckenridge on either the bike path or CO-9. At Huron Road, turn right and go 0.2 miles. The ride starts on the left, just after the recycling center.

Riding Directions

G1 - 0.0 Find the signed start of the Lower Flume Trail near the east end of the recycling center. Ride uphill.

G2 - 0.1 Continue on Lower Flume as Upper Flume goes right.

G3 - 1.2 Arrive at a paved road. Continue straight.

G4 - 1.3 Turn right on the Lower Flume singletrack. Immediately make another right on Mike's Trail and climb steeply.

G5 - 1.4 Turn left on Middle Flume.

G6 - 3.3 Turn right on Upper Flume.

G7 - 4.4 Continue on Upper Flume as Mike's Trail goes right.

G2 - 5.9 Go left on Lower Flume and ride back to Huron Road.

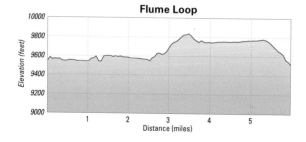

Frisco

Blue River Bikeway

9

Blue River

Middle Flume

1.9

1.1

Mike's

G7

G5

0.1

G4

0.1

G3

Flume Loop

Upper Flume

1.5

Upper Flume

Stalom Singletrack

1.1

Jumbo Mine

G6

Toxic Forest

Gold Run

Gibson Hill 10478

Lower Flume

G2

0.1

Huron Rd

G1 T

Breckenridge

1:50,000

1/2 mile

1/2 kilometer

Michelle Doza cruises the boardwalk on the Peaks Trail. Photo: Brandon J. Doza, brandonjdoza.com

(H) Bakers Tank ★★★★☆

(3 miles southeast of Breckenridge)

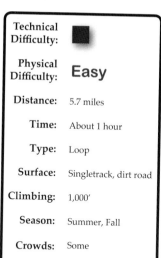

Technical Difficulty:	■
Physical Difficulty:	**Easy**
Distance:	5.7 miles
Time:	About 1 hour
Type:	Loop
Surface:	Singletrack, dirt road
Climbing:	1,000'
Season:	Summer, Fall
Crowds:	Some
Dogs:	🐕

A fast, fun frolic through the forest

Ride Description

This quick loop near Breckenridge consists of a smooth climb on Boreas Pass Road, followed by a great descent on the excellent Bakers Tank singletrack. The trail has a few rough spots, but is generally wide, smooth, and fast. Boreas Pass Road, since it was built on an old railroad grade, climbs gently. There is generally not much vehicle traffic on the road, but a number of blind corners (combined with tourists admiring the views) warrant caution.

Driving Directions

From Breckenridge, head south on CO-9 (Main Street). Turn left on Boreas Pass Road (opposite "Broken Lance Road") and go about 2.5 miles until you arrive at the Boreas Winter Gate Trailhead, a dirt parking area.

Riding Directions

H1 - 0.0 From the Winter Trailhead, start riding up Boreas Pass Road.

H2 - 3.1 Arrive at Bakers Tank: a giant wooden water tank that was used to fill locomotives on the old railroad. Turn left, ride up doubletrack for a few hundred feet, and turn left on singletrack.

H3 - 3.9 Come to a Y-intersection with an arrow pointing left. Turn left.

H4 - 4.7 Continue roughly straight on the main Bakers Tank Trail as another trail goes sharply right and a dirt road goes left.

H1 - 5.7 Arrive back at the trailhead!

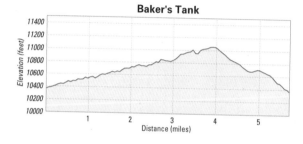

Baker's Tank

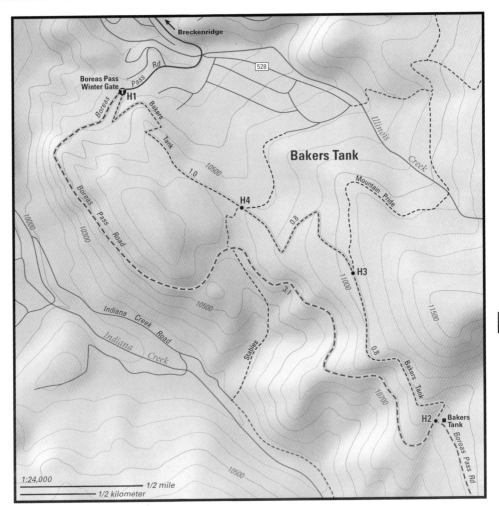

Brandon Doza takes the high road on the B-Line Trail near Breckenridge. Photo: Brandon J. Doza, brandonjdoza.com

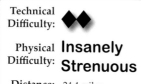

I The Tenmile Traverse ★★★★⯪

(4 miles north of Breckenridge)

Technical Difficulty:	◆◆
Physical Difficulty:	**Insanely Strenuous**
Distance:	24.4 miles
Time:	5 – 9 hours
Type:	Loop
Surface:	singletrack, bike path
Climbing:	5,400′ (!)
Season:	Summer
Crowds:	Few
Dogs:	*

This viciously difficult loop rewards the brave with glorious views and unforgettable descents

Ride Description

This loop is a true alpine epic, passing within a mile of all ten towering peaks in the Tenmile Range, from Peak 10 (13,633′) to Peak 1 (12,805′). The ride starts on the enjoyable Burro Trail, climbs steeply on the Wheeler Trail, and then traverses a spectacular ridgeline on the Miners Creek Trail. A quick cruise on the bike path completes the loop back to Breckenridge.

Most of the singletrack on this loop lies above 11,000 feet and the views are stellar. But all of this alpine glory comes at a high price. Much of the Wheeler Trail consists of hike-a-bike and the descent on the Miners Creek Trail is frighteningly rocky. Bring plenty of food, water, and rain gear and notify your next-of-kin.

Get an early start to avoid thunderstorms. The Miners Creek Trail traverses the crest of the Tenmile Range, and it is an extremely bad place to be during an electrical storm. Due to the high elevation of this ride, it is advisable to wait until mid-July to ensure that all of the snow has melted.

*Dogs must be on a leash on the bike path. Consider using a car shuttle to avoid the bike path section

Driving Directions

You can start this ride from anywhere in Breckenridge, but if you want to ride the paved bike path first (it's a nice warm-up), then park at the Gold Hill Trailhead. To reach the Gold Hill Trailhead, head north from Breckenridge on CO-9. About 4 miles from downtown, turn left at Gateway Road and turn immediately right into the dirt parking lot.

Riding Directions - see map on page 169

I1 - 0.0 From the Gold Hill Trailhead, start riding south along the bike path towards Breck.

I2 - 4.7 The bike path becomes somewhat confusing downtown, so escape by making a right on Ski Hill Road and your first left on S Park Avenue. In a few blocks, make a right on Village Road.

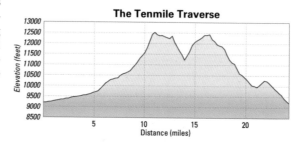

The Tenmile Traverse

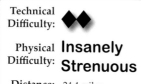

Summit County & Vail

I3 - 5.2   Arrive at the Beaver Run Resort. Make a left into the parking lot, find a dirt road, and follow this for a short distance to the start of the Burro Trail singletrack. (*If you get lost, simply find the bottom of the Beaver Run Chairlift. The Burro Trail begins just a few hundred feet downhill of the lift.*)

I4 - 8.1   Cross a dirt road (Crystal Creek Road) and continue on the Burro Trail.

I5 - 8.3   The Burro Trail ends at a dirt road. Turn right on this road (FS-800/Spruce Creek Road).

I6 - 9.0   Turn right on a dirt road that is signed as "The Wheeler Trail."

I5 - 9.2   About 200 feet past a gate, turn left on the Wheeler Trail singletrack. Get ready for some tough riding!

I6 - 9.8   Cross a dirt road (Crystal Creek Road) and continue on the Wheeler Trail.

I7 - 11.7   Cross another dirt road (Peak 9 Road) and continue on the Wheeler Trail. (*Turning right will quickly take you back to the base of Peak 9 and the start of the Burro Trail. This is your last chance to easily escape back to Breckenridge.*)

I8 - 12.7   Arrive at the summit of Wheeler Pass. Continue on the Wheeler Trail.

I9 - 14.0   Turn right on the Colorado Trail (Miners Creek Trail). (*The Wheeler Trail continues left, downhill, and leads to Copper Mountain Ski Area and CO-91 in about 3 miles. If a thunderstorm is looming, escape to Copper and take the bike path back to Breckenridge via Frisco. The next section of the Tenmile Traverse is an extreme lightning hazard.*)

I10 - 19.5   Arrive at Miners Creek Road. Turn right to remain on the singletrack.

I11 - 20.7   Turn left on the Peaks Trail.

I12 - 21.1   Turn right on the Gold Hill Trail and climb for a mile before enjoying a final downhill section.

I1 - 24.3   Arrive back at the Gold Hill Trailhead!

Summit County & Vail

(J) Colorado Trail to Searle Pass ★★★★⯪

(Starts in Copper Mountain)

Summit County & Vail

Technical Difficulty:	◆
Physical Difficulty:	**Strenuous**
Distance:	15.8 miles
Time:	3 – 5 hours
Type:	Out-and-back
Surface:	Singletrack
Climbing/ Descending:	2,600'/400' (one-way)
Season:	Summer
Crowds:	Some
Dogs:	🐕

A fantastic journey from pine forest into the alpine tundra

Ride Description

Following the Colorado Trail from Copper Mountain to Searle Pass and back, this ride is an excellent introduction to Colorado's beautiful high-alpine sufferfests. Riding at 12,000' is never easy, and most Colorado trails that reach this elevation are littered with boulders. This ride is certainly rough, and even the best riders will be pushing their bikes at times. However, in comparison to other high-elevation trails in the region (see Ride I), this trail offers easy passage to high-altitudes and stunning views. The trail begins from the Copper Mountain ski area, passes through a dense pine forest, them emerges into the high-alpine tundra, complete with tumbling creeks and chirping marmots.

Those who would rather complete this ride in two days will be glad to know that there is lodging available near 11,600'. That's right, shortly before Searle Pass this ride passes Janet's Cabin, one of the 10th Mountain Division Huts. These huts are very popular with backcountry skiers in the winter, and they are available for rent in the summer as well. Book in advance at www.huts.org.

Driving Directions

To reach Copper Mountain, take I-70 to Exit 195 and head south on CO-91. At the traffic light, turn right on Copper Road and go about 0.5 mile. Park in the free parking area on the left. Hop on your bike and make your way to the base of the American Eagle Lift.

Riding Directions

J1 - 0.0 From the bottom of the American Eagle Lift, start climbing on a dirt road and make your first right onto another dirt road. You are now on the Colorado Trail.

J2 - 0.6 As the road turns left, continue straight onto the Colorado Trail singletrack. Follow signs for the Colorado Trail past several intersections with unmarked trails.

J3 - 7.9 Arrive at Searle Pass! Admire the view, then turn around and enjoy an epic descent. *(The Colorado Trail continues to Kokomo Pass in 3.1 miles and Camp Hale in 8.8 miles. See Ride K.)*

Colorado Trail to Searle Pass (out-and-back)

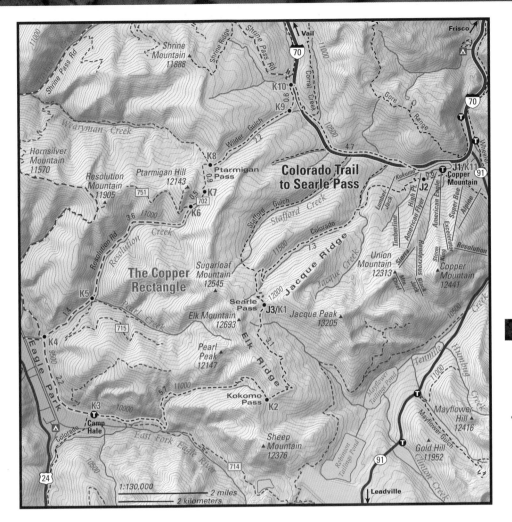

The Copper Rectangle

Colorado Trail to Searle Pass

Daisy-dog leads the way as Laura Johson approaches Searle Pass.

ⓀThe Copper Rectangle ★★★★★

◆ **Distance: 32.8 miles**

The Copper Triangle is a famous road-biking ride (and race) that starts at Copper Mountain, crosses Fremont Pass to Leadville, cruises over Tennessee Pass to Minturn, and then finishes back at Copper. The mountain-bike version of this loop is also a monster, featuring technical singletrack and 6,000' of climbing. From Searle Pass, the route continues through beautiful alpine tundra over Kokomo Pass and down to Camp Hale. The suffering begins as the loop follows Resolution Road, climbing 2,500' to Ptarmigan Pass. From here it's all downhill back to Copper! The author has dubbed the mountain-biking version of the Copper Triangle as "The Copper Rectangle" to distinguish it from the road biking version, but many mountain bikers use "Copper Triangle" to refer to both the road and the mountain version.

Riding Directions

K1 - 7.9 From Searle Pass, continue riding on the Colorado Trail.

K2 - 11.0 Arrive at Kokomo Pass. Get ready for a fast descent.

K3 - 16.7 Arrive at the Colorado Trail Trailhead at Camp Hale. Turn right and ride along the dirt road.

K4 - 18.9 Turn right on Resolution Road.

K5 - 20.3 Continue straight on Resolution Road as FS-715 goes right.

K6 - 23.9 At a T-intersection, turn right on FS-702.

K7 - 24.4 Arrive at Ptarmigan Pass and continue on the road.

K8 - 25.3 As the road makes a sweeping left turn, find the unmarked Wilder Gulch singletrack on the right.

K9 - 27.5 At a Y-intersection, turn left following the sign for the "Vail Pass Rest Area."

K10 - 28.1 Arrive at the Vail Pass Rest Area and find the bike path. Take it downhill, back to Copper.

K11 - 32.8 Arrive back in at Copper Mountain. Make your way back to the parking lot. What an epic ride!

(L)Son of Middle Creek ★★★★☆

(Starts in Vail)

Technical Difficulty:	
Physical Difficulty:	**Moderate**
Distance:	8.6 miles
Time:	2 – 3 hours
Type:	Loop
Surface:	Singletrack, dirt road
Climbing:	2,100'
Season:	Summer
Crowds:	Some
Dogs:	

This short ride contains 100 percent of your recommended daily allowance of mountain-biking fun!

Ride Description

Warning: this ride may be habit-forming! After riding this serving of delicious singletrack, riders often find themselves unable to stop themselves from riding it every time they drive past Vail. Fortunately, the loop is reasonably quick and starts right next to I-70.

This ride begins with a warm-up climb on a dirt road and then continues to climb on singletrack. After some rippin' descent through the woods on the Son of Middle Creek Trail, riders come to an intersection with the North Trail. There are two options: the right fork is easier and makes a shorter loop, while the left fork (described below) descends all the way to the North Frontage Road and is much more technical.

Driving Directions

Follow I-70 to Vail and take Exit 176. If you are coming from the east, simply make a right at the first traffic circle on Spraddle Creek Road and immediately turn left into the trailhead. (Those coming from the west should turn left at the first traffic circle, make a soft right at the second traffic circle on Spraddle Creek Road, and turn left into the trailhead.)

Riding Directions - see map on page 183

L1 - 0.0 From the trailhead, head west along the North Frontage Road.

L2 - 1.1 Turn right on Red Sandstone Road.

L3 - 1.8 Bear left on Red Sandstone Road as it turns to dirt.

L4 - 4.4 Come to a Y-intersection and go right on a dirt road. Go about 0.1 miles and turn right onto the Son of Middle Creek singletrack.

L5 - 6.5 Arrive at a T-intersection with the North Trail. Go left. (Going right takes you back to Red Sandstone Road and shortens the ride.)

L1 - 8.6 Arrive back at the trailhead.

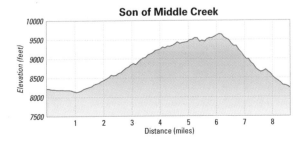

Son of Middle Creek

(M) North Trail ★★★★☆

(Starts in Vail)

Technical Difficulty:	
Physical Difficulty:	**Moderate**
Distance:	10.0 miles
Time:	2 – 3 hours
Type:	Loop
Surface:	Singletrack, bike path
Climbing:	2,000′
Season:	Summer
Crowds:	Some
Dogs:	Dogs must be leashed on bike path

Impeccable singletrack located right next to Interstate-70

Ride Description

The North Trail has all the perks of a remote alpine trail – fantastic views, aspen groves, and narrow singletrack – all while never straying more than a mile from I-70! The climbs have some tight switchbacks, but the trail is surprisingly easy for the rugged landscape it traverses.

Driving Directions

From I-70, take Exit 176. Head west on the North Frontage Road and go about a mile. Turn right on Red Sandstone Road and go 0.3 miles. Turn left into the North Trail parking lot. This lot is signed for three-hour parking, which should be enough for most people to complete this ride. Those who expect to take longer can find parking somewhere along the north frontage road.

The North Trail is *closed from April 15 to June 15* each year for elk calving.

Riding Directions

M1 - 0.0   From the trailhead, follow the North Trail singletrack to the southwest, climbing switchbacks.

M2 - 2.2   Continue straight on the North Trail as the Buffehr Creek Trail goes right.

M3 - 3.0   At a Y-intersection, go right, uphill. (The left fork goes downhill to the Buffehr Creek Trailhead and can be used to shorten the ride.)

M4 - 5.8   Turn left, following the North Trail, as a faint trail goes right. (This trail leads to Red and White Mountain Road.)

M5 - 6.4   The singletrack ends at a dirt road. Turn right.

M6 - 6.8   Turn left on the continuation of the North Trail, passing through a gate.

M7 - 7.5   The trail ends at the paved frontage road. Continue straight, following the road.

M8 - 7.9   At the traffic circle, start riding on the bike path that runs along the left side of the frontage road.

M9 - 9.6   Turn left on Red Sandstone Road.

M1 - 10.0   Arrive back at the trailhead.

North Trail

Summit County & Vail

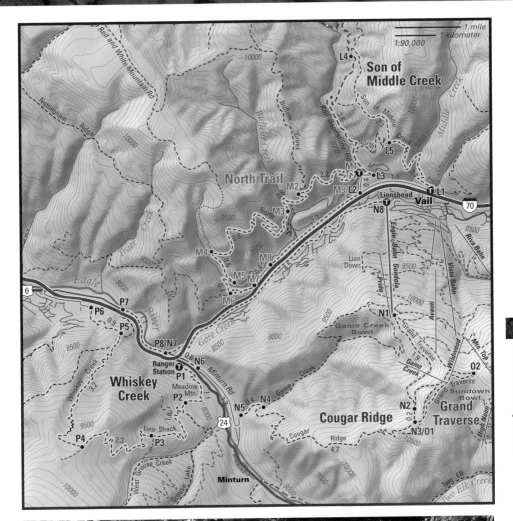

Summit County & Vail

Katie Johnson rides through the lush foliage on the Whiskey Creek Trail.

(N) Cougar Ridge ★★★★☆

(Starts in Vail)

Technical Difficulty: ◆◆

Physical Difficulty: **Moderate**

Distance: 13.6 miles (from the gondola)

Time: 2 – 5 hours

Type: Loop

Surface: Singletrack, bike path, dirt road

Climbing/ Descending: 1,100'/3,200' (from top of gondola)

Season: Summer

Crowds: Some

Dogs: 🚫🐕

Beautiful alpine singletrack followed by a long ride back to Vail on the bike path

Ride Description

The Cougar Ridge trail is an exciting downhill adventure that runs from the top of Vail Resort all the way back down to the Eagle River – a decent of over 2,500 feet! Unfortunately, the singletrack ends in Minturn, which is about 6 miles from the bottom of the gondola in Vail. Luckily, the ride back is mostly on paved bike paths and is reasonable pleasant. It is possible to skip almost all of the climbing on this ride by purchasing a lift ticket and riding the gondola to the top of Vail Resort. Of course, it is also possible to pedal to the top of the gondola on easy trails.

Cougar Ridge, like many of the trails in the area, is *closed May 6 through July 1* each year to allow the local elk to raise their adorable elk-babies.

Driving Directions

The most convenient place to park is in the free parking garage in Lionshead. To reach this, take I-70 to Exit 176 and head west on the *South* Frontage Road. Turn left into the parking lot.

Riding Directions - see map on page 183

To reach the start of this ride, it is easiest to take the Eagle Bahn Gondola. Alternatively, you can just ride one of the easy trails from the base of the gondola to the top. The Lion Down Trail consists mostly of dirt roads, making it an easy, but boring way to reach the top. Simply follow signs from the base area.

N1 - 0.0 From the top of the Eagle Bahn Gondola, wander south and locate the Grand Traverse Trail. Enjoy the sweet singletrack.

N2 - 1.9 Bear right on the Grand Traverse as the other branch of the Grand Traverse loop goes left.

N3 - 2.1 Turn right on the unmarked (but well-worn) Cougar Ridge Trail. There is often a sign here, which reads, "No lift access beyond this point." Get ready for a great descent!

N4 - 6.8 Arrive at the Game Creek Trail. Turn left and continue downhill.

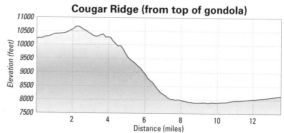

N5 - 7.2 The trail ends at a road. Head downhill. Turn right on 4th Avenue and then turn right to head northwest on Minturn Road.

N6 - 8.5 As Minturn Road crosses the Eagle River, turn right onto a bike path. When the bike path ends, continue on US-24, passing under I-70.

N7 - 9.1 Just past I-70, turn right onto the Gore Valley Bike Path and take this back to Vail, following signs to Lionshead Village.

N8 - 13.6 Arrive back in Lionshead Village.

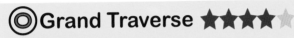 **Grand Traverse** ★★★★☆

 Distance: 6.9 miles

Hidden atop the gondola is the spectacular Grand Traverse Trail. Part of the Grand Traverse forms the start of the Cougar Ridge ride described above, but there is an additional section of the Grand Traverse that is also excellent. Follow the riding directions for Cougar Ridge to mile 2.1.

Riding Directions

O1 - 2.1 Continue straight on Grand Traverse as Cougar Ridge (unmarked) goes right. Enjoy rolling singletrack and beautiful views.

O2 - 3.5 Arrive at a dirt road. It is best to turn around here, since completing the loop is confusing and the singletrack is not as good. However, if you want to complete the loop, turn left on the dirt road and do your best to follow signs for the Grand Traverse Trail.

Erik Holmstrom savors the view from Boreas Pass Road.

Whiskey Creek ★★★★☆

(6 miles west of Vail)

Technical Difficulty:	◆
Physical Difficulty:	**Strenuous**
Distance:	12.7 miles
Time:	2 – 3 hours
Type:	Loop
Surface:	Singletrack, doubletrack, road
Climbing:	2,400′
Season:	Summer
Crowds:	Some
Dogs:	*

Narrow singletrack through fields of wildflowers & aspen groves

Ride Description

After one hour, this ride seems like hell: the first few miles climb steeply on a dirt road that offers little shade from the hot sun. After an hour and a half, this ride is heaven, offering steep trail through aspen groves and narrow singletrack through meadows with up-to-the-handlebar wildflowers.

The last mile of the Whiskey Creek Trail is closed for wildlife protection from March 1 through Aug 31. This ride description avoids the wildlife closure by adding 2 additional miles of road riding. Those riding this trail after Aug 31 can turn right at mile 8.2, and avoid most of the road riding.

*If the dog wants to come along, use a car shuttle to avoid the section of highway riding.

Driving Directions

Take I-70 Exit 171 and head south on US-24. Go a short distance, and then turn right into a ranger station and trailhead parking area.

Riding Directions - see map on page 183

P1 - 0.0 From the ranger station, start riding on the Meadow Mountain Trail, which leaves from the southwest corner of the parking lot.

P2 - 1.1 Continue straight on the doubletrack as a trail to Grouse Creek goes left.

P3 - 2.7 Continue straight on the doubletrack as an unmarked dirt road goes left.

P4 - 5.0 Pass by a small cabin and continue on the Whiskey Creek singletrack. Here comes the fun part!

P5 - 8.2 At an unmarked Y-intersection, turn left. (*The right fork is actually more convenient, but it is closed March 1 through Aug 31. If it's after August 31, turn right.*)

P6 - 9.1 The trail ends at a school. Turn left and find your way out of the school parking lot. Turn left on a paved road and head west, paralleling I-70. Eventually come to US-6, turn right to ride east along US-6.

P7 - 11.2 Go left on the bike path that parallels US-6.

P8 - 12.3 Leave the bike path and ride along US-6, under I-70, and back to the trailhead.

ⓠVail Resort ★★★★★

(Starts in Vail)

Hours:	10:00 - 4:00 every day, late-June to mid-September
Price:	$27 (As of 2010)
Vertical Relief:	2,000'

Description

For their lift-served riding, Vail Resort uses the Eagle Bahn Gondola, which provides over 2000' of elevation gain. The double-diamond downhill riding at Vail is limited in comparison to Winter Park or nearby Keystone, but there are a few trails that will challenge expert riders. Intermediate riders will enjoy excellent singletrack through aspen groves, and there are a couple nice beginner trails as well.

A ride up the gondola can be used to eliminate all or most of the climbing on three classic cross-country trails: Game Creek, Cougar Ridge, and the Two Elk Trail. These trails can be accessed near the top of the gondola and drop all the way to Minturn. Riding any of these trails requires a few miles of pedaling back to Vail on the bike path, but it is a great way to end a day of lift-served riding at Vail.

Driving Directions

Park in the free parking garage in Lionshead. To reach this garage, take I-70 to Exit 176 and head west on the South Frontage Road towards Lionshead. Turn left into the parking lot.

Summit County & Vail

Jumps, Drops, Hucks and Gnar
The Top Eight Freeride Destinations

8. Gunnison – Hartmann Rocks

7. Crested Butte – Crested Butte Resort

6. Fruita – Kokopelli's – Moore Fun

5. Grand Junction – Tabeguache

4. Summit County – Keystone Resort

3. Denver – Buffalo Creek – Blackjack Trail

2. Winter Park – Trestle Bike Park

1. Winter Park – Sol Vista Resort

ⓡ Two Elk Trail ★★★★★

(Starts at Vail Pass, 15 miles southeast of Vail)

Technical Difficulty:	◆
Physical Difficulty:	**Moderate**
Distance:	18.6 miles
Time:	3 – 5 hours
Type:	Shuttle
Surface:	Singletrack, dirt road
Climbing/ Descending:	2,300'/5,000' (one-way)
Season:	Summer
Crowds:	Few
Dogs:	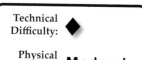

A long picturesque ride through vast fields of wildflowers

Ride Description

The Two Elk Trail features mile-after-mile of stunning alpine scenery and fantastic singletrack riding. The trail intersects the Ten Mile Canyon Bike Path a few miles northwest of Vail pass, but this section is rarely ridden since it is very steep and rough. One option is to start from Vail Resort and either take the gondola, or ride up one of the trails at the resort. For the full experience, it is best to start at Vail Pass and take Shrine Pass Road to reach the singletrack. This option either requires car shuttle (described below) or a massive slog on the bike path up to Vail Pass.

Driving Directions

Take I-70 to Exit 171 and head south on US-24 for a few miles to the town on Minturn. Leave a car in town and shuttle bikes and riders to Vail Pass. To reach the pass, head back to I-70 and go east for 19 miles. Take Exit 190 and immediately turn right into a large pullout on the side of the frontage road

Riding Directions

R1 - 0.0   From Vail Pass, start riding west, up Shrine Pass Road.

R2 - 2.2   Arrive at Shrine Pass; continue straight on Shrine Pass Road.

R3 - 3.9   Make a right on FS-728, towards the Bowman Shortcut Trail.

R4 - 4.4   Continue straight on FS-728 as FS-712 goes right.

R5 - 4.5   Go right on the Bowman's Cutoff Trail singletrack.

R6 - 8.7   Continue straight through a four-way intersection.

R7 - 8.9   Continue straight on the Two-Elk Trail as a trail goes right to Vail Ski Resort.

R8 - 11.5   Arrive at a dirt road near the Orient Express Chairlift. Turn right, go about 100 feet, and turn left on singletrack.

R9 - 12.2   Pass the base of the Skyline Express lift.

R10 - 16.3   Arrive at a trailhead and continue straight, riding along the dirt road.

R11 - 17.9   Come to a paved road and follow this across the railroad tracks and into Minturn.

R12 - 18.6   Arrive in Minturn!

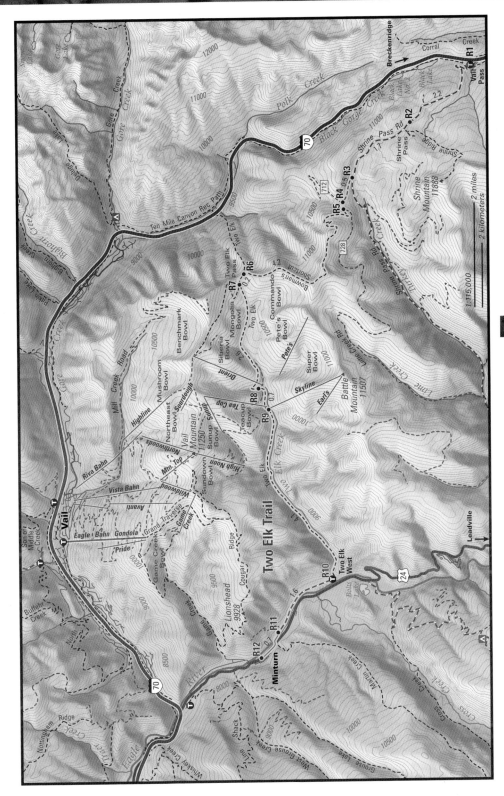

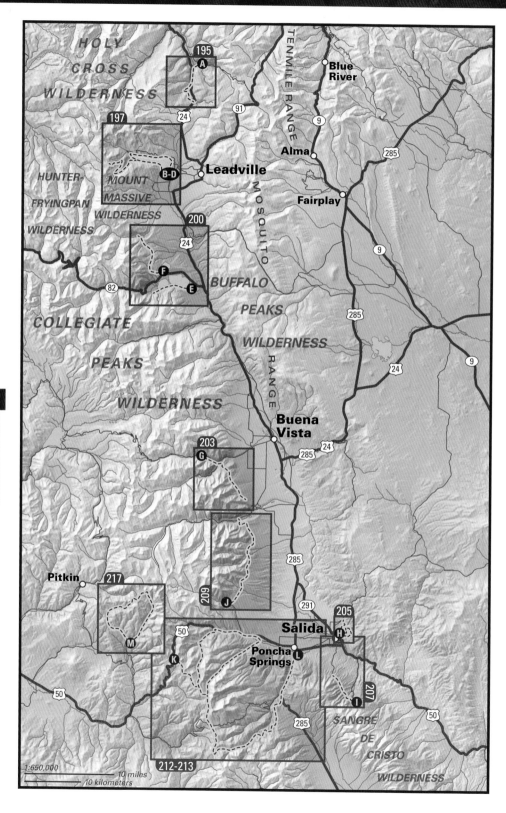

HOLY

CROSS

WILDERNESS

195
A

Blue
River

TENMILE RANGE

24

91

9

197

Alma

285

HUNTER-

FRYINGPAN

B-D
MOUNT
MASSIVE

Leadville

WILDERNESS

Fairplay

MOSQUITO

WILDERNESS

200

24

9

F

E

BUFFALO

82

PEAKS

COLLEGIATE

WILDERNESS

285

PEAKS

RANGE

285

WILDERNESS

24

9

Buena
Vista

203

24

G

285

Pitkin

217

209

285

M

J

291

205

Salida

H

50

L

Poncha
Springs

K

207

50

I

50

285

SANGRE

DE

1:650,000

CRISTO

10 miles
10 kilometers

212-213

WILDERNESS

Leadville & Salida

The Arkansas Valley is one of the finest outdoor destinations in Colorado. The towns are easy going, the singletrack is superb, and the views are sublime. The valley is named for the Arkansas River, which begins near the mining town of Leadville and heads south, admiring the scenery near Buena Vista. By the time the river passes through downtown Salida, it has grown large enough for rafting and kayaking.

The Valley offers a diversity of mountain biking trails, ranging from easy to difficult, but it is most famous for its excellent alpine riding. The Monarch Crest ride is internationally famous for top-notch singletrack and hundred-mile views. However, it is just the tip of the iceberg and mountain bikers will find a lifetime of incredible alpine singletrack. In addition to mountain biking, the region is a mecca for kayaking, hiking, rock climbing, and mountaineering.

The Arkansas Valley is home to many 14,000-foot peaks and many of the best rides are perched above 10,000 feet. Consequently, many trails hold snow until the early summer. Luckily, there are several trails at lower elevations (like the Salida Mountain Trails) that bask in the sun and can be ridden in the spring and fall. Additionally, if bad weather rolls in, the "always dry" trails at Hartman Rocks near Gunnison are just over one hour away.

Leadville: a Colorado mining town

Leadville was founded in 1877 after silver was discovered nearby. By 1880 it had a population of about 40,000 and was the second largest city of Colorado. In 1893, the federal government repealed the Sherman Silver Purchase Act, the price of silver dropped dramatically, and Leadville fell on hard times. Luckily, new mineral riches were soon discovered nearby. The Climax Mine, north of Leadville on CO-91, is one of the largest molybdenum mines in the world and began operation in 1915. Molybdenum is one of the ingredients in many high-strength steel alloys, like the steel used for bicycle frames. The molybdenum business boomed for many decades as the world built cities, tanks, and battleships. Demand eventually slowed and Climax stopped operations during the 1980s. Since then, Leadville has reinvented itself as the home to several grueling running and mountain biking races, such as the famous Leadville Trail 100.

Leadville & Salida

Accommodations

There are many accommodation options in the Arkansas Valley. All of the major towns offer an assortment of motels. In addition, Leadville and Salida are home to two of the few hostels in Colorado. Camping is also plentiful. Near Leadville, there is pay-camping at Turquoise Lake, Twin Lakes, Camp Hale, and near the Mount Elbert Trailhead. Free camping is available at Camp Hale and along Halfmoon Road near the Mount Elbert Trailhead. Near Buena Vista and Salida, most of the major roads heading west into the mountains offer both free and pay camping.

Leadville Hostel & Inn
500 E 7th Street, Leadville. 719-486-9334
Four blocks east of US-24, the Leadville Hostel offers dormitory beds for about $20, as well as inexpensive private rooms. Dogs welcome.

Simple Lodge and Hostel of Salida
224 E 1st Street, Salida. 719-650-7381
Offers bunks for about $20 and private rooms for slightly more. Dogs welcome.

Bike Shops

Cycles of Life
309 Harrison Avenue (US-24), Leadville.
719-486-5533
A great shop located on the main strip in Leadville. Closed Tuesdays.

The Trailhead
707 US-24 N, Buena Vista. 719-395-8002
A big shop with all kinds of outdoor gear, including plenty of bikes.

Absolute Bikes
330 W Sackett Avenue, Salida. 719-539-9295
Located two blocks northeast of 1st Street, Absolute Bikes boasts a good selection of bikes and a great repair shop. Offers rentals.

SubCulture Cyclery
265 ½ E 1st Street, Salida. 719-539-5329
Bikes, parts, and repairs.

Eats and Drinks

Mile High Pies
617 Lincoln Avenue, Leadville. 970-879-2483
This small pizza-place hides about a block west of US-24. It has not been established if this is actually the best pizza in the world or if it just tastes that way after an epic ride.

Provin' Grounds Coffee & Bakery
508 Harrison Avenue (US-24), Leadville.
719-486-0797
A cozy atmosphere, great coffee, pastries, and a nice view of the mountains. What else could you need?

Bongo Billy's Coffees
409 E Main Street, Buena Vista. 719-395-4991
Locally roasted coffee and delicious muffins.

Amicas Pizza
136, E 2nd Street, Salida. 719-539-5219
This place makes pizza and serves its own microbrew beer.

Downtown Leadville by night.

Beautiful mountain views along Hagerman Pass - dirt road riding at its best.

(A) Colorado Trail - Camp Hale to Tennesse Pass ★★★★☆

(17 miles north of Leadville)

Technical Difficulty:	
Physical Difficulty:	**Moderate**
Distance:	13.8 miles
Time:	2 – 3 hours
Type:	Out-and-back
Surface:	Singletrack
Climbing/ Descending:	1,600'/300' (one-way)
Season:	Summer
Crowds:	Some
Dogs:	🐕

Classic Colorado riding through forests and meadows

Ride Description

This small slice of the Colorado Trail packs plenty of great riding and glorious views into just 7 miles (one-way). There are some sections of tough climbing that might require a bit of pushing, but most of the trail consists of incredible, smooth singletrack. This ride starts from Camp Hale, the training camp for the Tenth Mountain Division troops during World War Two.

From the end of this ride at Tennessee Pass, the Colorado Trail continues west for about 7 miles before reaching the Holy Cross Wilderness Area (no bikes allowed). For a longer ride, consider riding some or all of this section as an out-and-back.

Driving Directions

From Leadville, head north on US-24 for about a mile. Turn left on US-24 (as CO-91 goes straight) and go 14.6 miles. Turn right at a sign for "Camp Hale Memorial Campground" and follow the dirt road east, across the Eagle River, and go about 0.5 miles. At a T-intersection, turn right on FS-714, towards the East Fork Group Campground. Drive 1.6 miles and turn left into a trailhead for the Colorado Trail.

Riding Directions

A1 - 0.0 From the trailhead, ride west (back the way you came) along the dirt road.

A2 - 0.1 Turn left at the first intersection, following signs for the Colorado Trail.

A3 - 0.5 Bear left onto the Colorado Trail singletrack. *(Before you make the turn, check out the ruins of old Tenth Mountain Division buildings on the right.)*

A4 - 1.4 Cross a dirt road and continue on more wonderful singletrack!

A5 - 3.4 Cross US-24 and the Denver and Rio Grande Western Railroad tracks. Continue riding on the Colorado Trail.

A6 - 4.9 Turn left on an old dirt road. *(Make a mental note of this intersection; it's easy to miss as you are speeding back down the dirt road.)*

A7 - 6.9 Arrive at Tennessee Pass. Turn around and go back the way you came.

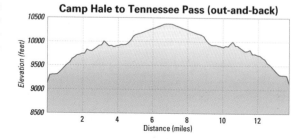

Camp Hale to Tennessee Pass (out-and-back)

(vertical label: Leadville & Salida)

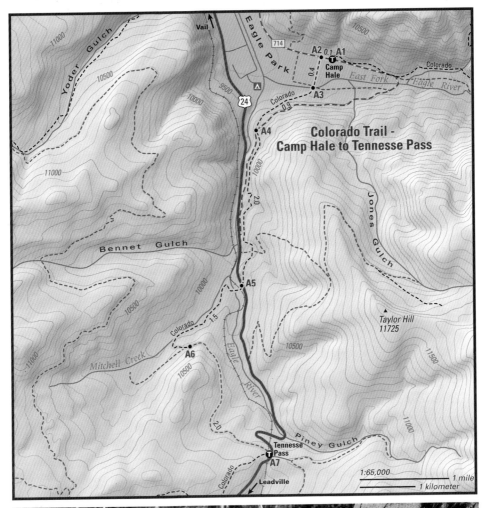

Colorado Trail -
Camp Hale to Tennesse Pass

The Colorado Trail offers excellent riding throughout the Arkansas Valley.

Ⓑ Hagerman Pass ★★★☆

(4 miles west of Leadville)

Technical Difficulty:	 ●
Physical Difficulty:	**Moderate**
Distance:	up to 22.4 miles
Time:	1.5 – 5 hours
Type:	Out-and-back
Surface:	Dirt road, paved road (optional)
Climbing/ Descending:	2,400'/300' (one-way from the dam)
Season:	Summer
Crowds:	Some
Dogs:	🐕

A dirt road up to the Continental Divide with some of the best views in the state

Ride Description

The views along Hagerman Pass Road are simply stunning. First it passes the picturesque Turquoise Lake, which looks like something out of a fairy tale. Next it climbs, providing views into the Mount Massive Wilderness to the south and the Holy Cross Wilderness to the north. Once at Hagerman Pass, the position is so impressive that it feels like you have a view of every mountain in Colorado.

A passenger car can drive most of the way to Hagerman Pass, so there are several options of where to park and start the ride. To maximize the time spent on the bicycle, start near the dam at Turquoise Lake. Other possible starting points are at mile 3.4, where the road turns to dirt, and at mile 7.0 where there are several large parking areas. Any car can reach mile 7.0, but a higher clearance vehicle is required after that.

Driving Directions

From Leadville, head west on 6th Street for 0.8 miles. Turn right onto County-4 and go for about a block. Bend left onto Turquoise Lake Road (remains County-4) and go 2.5 miles. Turn right to stay on County-4 as County-5 and County-48 go left. After 0.9 miles you will arrive at the dam at Turquoise Lake. Park just before the dam in a large pullout on the left or continue driving to one of the higher parking areas (see above).

Riding Directions

B1 - 0.0   From the parking area, ride across the dam and continue west on the paved road.

B2 - 3.4   At a Y-intersection, turn left on a dirt road (Hagerman Pass Road).

B3 - 7.0   Continue on Hagerman Pass Road as it makes a sharp right, passing several parking areas. *(This is a good parking area for the shorter version of the ride. Passenger cars can easily make it this far, but might have trouble venturing higher.)*

B4 - 8.1   Continue past a parking area on the right and the CO Midland Centennial Trail on the left (see Hagerman Tunnel Ride).

B5 - 10.0   Continue on Hagerman Pass Road as a spur to the Skinner Hut goes right.

B6 - 11.2   Arrive at Hagerman Pass. What a view!

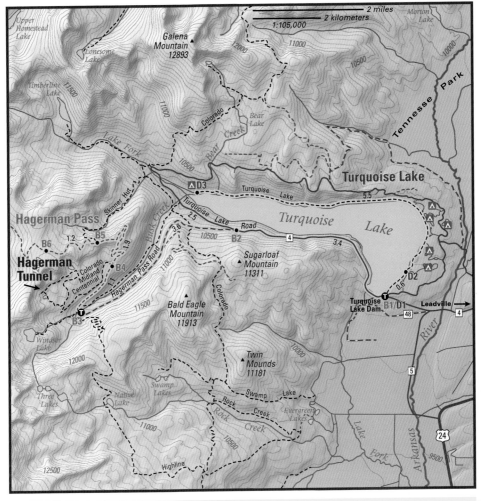

Ⓒ Hagerman Tunnel ★★★★★

◆ **Distance: 5.7 miles**

The Colorado Midland Railway was one of the first railroads to cross the Rockies. This ride follows sections of old railroad grade as it climbs to the huge, ice-filled Hagerman Tunnel that used to take the railroad beneath the Continental Divide. The singletrack is a mixed bag: some sections are delightful, but other parts are steep, loose, and poorly maintained.

From mile 8.1 of the Hagerman Pass ride description, start riding on the Colorado Midland Centennial Trail, which follows the old railroad grade. After 1.4 miles, turn right onto singletrack. Go about 0.2 miles and turn left at a T-intersection. When you arrive back at the old railroad grade, turn left and ride a few hundred feet to the tunnel. Check out the huge chucks of ice inside the tunnel! On the way back, make a loop by riding down the railroad grade for 0.8 miles and making a right on the singletrack. In less than one mile, you'll end up back at the T-intersection at mile 1.6. Turn left and ride back to the trailhead.

D Turquoise Lake ★★★★☆

(4 miles west of Leadville)

Technical Difficulty:	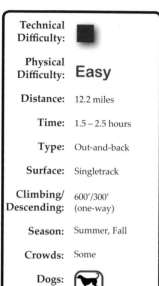
Physical Difficulty:	**Easy**
Distance:	12.2 miles
Time:	1.5 – 2.5 hours
Type:	Out-and-back
Surface:	Singletrack
Climbing/ Descending:	600'/300' (one-way)
Season:	Summer, Fall
Crowds:	Some
Dogs:	

Gentle singltrack along the shore of Turquoise Lake

Ride Description

This ride is guaranteed to delight! The singletrack is generally smooth, there is very little elevation gain, and the views are lovely. Turquoise Lake is a popular spot for camping, hiking, boating, and fishing. Consequently, the trail can be very crowded on summer afternoons. Some people ride a loop around the lake by connecting the singletrack on the north and east sides with the paved road on the south side. However, most prefer riding the singletrack as an out-and-back since it is much more fun than riding on the road.

Driving Directions

From Leadville, head west on 6th Street for 0.8 miles. Turn right onto County-4 and go for about a block. Bend left onto Turquoise Lake Road (remains County-4) and go 2.5 miles. Turn right to stay on County-4 as County-5 and County-48 go left. After 0.9 miles you will arrive at the dam at Turquoise Lake. Park just before the dam in a large pullout on the left.

Riding Directions - see map on previous page

D1 - 0.0 From the parking area near the dam, cross the road and find the sign for the Turquoise Lake Trail on the north side of the road (it's near the edge of the lake).

D2 - 0.6 Arrive at the boat launch. Ride across the paved parking lot and find the trail on the other side. Continue riding along the Turquoise Lake Trail, never straying more that 400 feet from the edge of the lake.

D3 - 6.1 Arrive at the May Queen Campground. Turn around and ride back. *(To complete a loop around the lake, follow the road out of the campground and turn left onto Turquoise Lake Road. Stay on the road as it wraps around the south side of the lake and arrive back at the parking area at the dam.)*

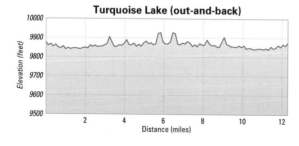

Leadville & Salida

(E) Twin Lakes ★★★☆☆

(17 miles south of Leadville)

Technical Difficulty:	
Physical Difficulty:	**Easy**
Distance:	9.2 miles
Time:	1 – 2 hours
Type:	Out-and-back
Surface:	Singletrack
Climbing/ Descending:	400'/300' (one-way)
Season:	Summer, Fall
Crowds:	Some
Dogs:	🐕

A nice flat trail with stunning views of Twin Lakes and of Mount Elbert

Ride Description

Who says that all the good trails are rocky and difficult? This trail, along the south side of the Twin Lakes Reservoir, offers lovely, smooth trail riding through aspens with views of Mount Elbert. In addition to a journey through space, this ride also features a trip back in time: the trail passes the beautifully restored 19th century buildings of the Interlaken Resort ghost town.

It is possible to continue the ride all the way around Twin Lakes using CO-82 and the Colorado Trail. Unfortunately, the trail from the end of this ride to CO-82 is difficult to follow and involves a large stream crossing now that the bridge has washed out. Those looking for more riding in the area should note that the section of the Colorado Trail that runs from the start of this ride to the South Elbert Trailhead is excellent and can be used to access the start of Ride F (see next page).

Driving Directions

From Leadville, drive south on US-24 for 15 miles. Turn right on CO-82 and go 0.8 miles. Turn left on County-25 (a dirt road). At the dam, turn left to stay on County-25. After about 0.5 miles, arrive at a small dirt parking lot with a sign for the Colorado Trail.

Riding Directions - see map on following page

E1 - 0.0   From the parking lot, follow the sign for the Colorado Trail and begin riding on singletrack. During the first few miles, two trails come off to the left, but just continue straight, staying as close to the lake as possible.

E2 - 2.1   Pass the historic Interlaken Resort.

E3 - 2.3   Continue straight, crossing singletrack.

E4 - 4.6   Arrive at a four-way junction where the option to go straight is overgrown. Turn around here.

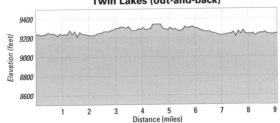

Twin Lakes (out-and-back)

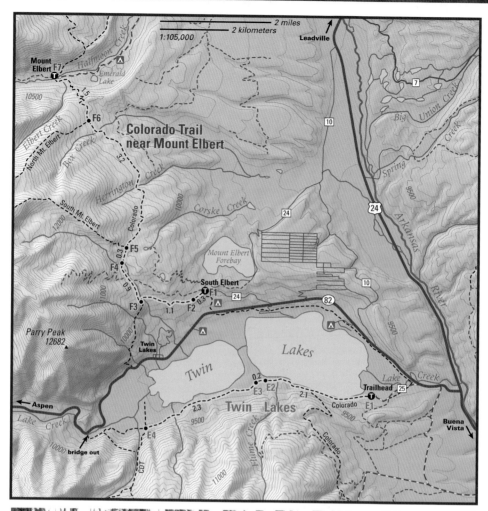

Admiring the view of Twin Lakes and Mt. Elbert from Twin Lakes Trail.

(F) Colorado Trail near Mount Elbert ★★★★★

(20 miles southwest of Leadville)

Technical Difficulty:	◆
Physical Difficulty:	**Strenuous**
Distance:	14.6 miles
Time:	2 – 4 hours
Type:	Out-and-back
Surface:	Singletrack
Climbing/ Descending:	1,900'/1,300' (one-way)
Season:	Summer, Fall
Crowds:	Some
Dogs:	🐕

More fantastic cruising on the Colorado Trail, featuring breathtaking aspens and well-crafted singletrack

Ride Description

Though both ends of this section of the Colorado Trail are guarded by steep climbs, the smooth singletrack in the middle is well worth the pain. Be sure to bring a camera since the views of the Twin Lakes Reservoir are stunning. Those looking for a shorter ride can do just the first part. Riders craving more miles after completing this ride can take the Colorado Trail south along the eastern end of Twin Lakes Reservoir. This ride can be started at either the north or the south end, but starting at the north end (Mt. Elbert parking area) involves a steep climb right out of the parking lot. It is much better to start at the southern end near Twin Lakes.

Driving Directions

From Leadville, head south on US-24 for about 14 miles (from Buena Vista, head north for about 20 miles). Turn right (west) on CO-82 towards Aspen and go 4.0 miles. Turn right on County-24 and go 1.3 miles and turn left into the South Elbert Trailhead.

Riding Directions

F1 - 0.0 From the South Elbert Trailhead, head west on smooth singletrack.

F2 - 0.3 Turn right on the Colorado Trail.

F3 - 1.4 Continue straight on the Colorado Trail as unmarked singletrack leading to the town of Twin Lakes goes left.

F4 - 2.3 Pass a small trailhead, cross a wooden bridge, and continue on the Colorado Trail. At a Y-intersection, turn left, following signs for the Colorado Trail and Mt Elbert.

F5 - 2.6 Continue straight on the Colorado Trail as the southern trail to the summit of Mount Elbert goes left. *(If you like suffering, go ahead and hike up Mount Elbert!)*

F6 - 5.8 Reach an intersection with the northern summit trail. *(From here, the trail descends steeply to the Mount Elbert Trailhead. If riding as an out-and back, consider turning around here.)*

F7 - 7.3 Arrive at the Mount Elbert Trailhead. Turn around and ride back to Twin Lakes!

Colorado Trail Near Mount Elbert (out-and-back)

Ⓖ Colorado Trail - Cottonwood to Princeton Hot Springs ★★★★☆

(9 miles west of Buena Vista)

Technical Difficulty:	
Physical Difficulty:	**Moderate**
Distance:	up to 19.8 miles
Time:	1 – 4 hours
Type:	Out-and-back
Surface:	Singletrack
Climbing/ Descending:	1,900'/1,800' (one-way)
Season:	Summer, Fall
Crowds:	Some
Dogs:	

Classic summer singletrack along the base of the mighty Sawatch Range

Ride Description

The Colorado Trail delights once again, this time offering a nice blend of smooth singletrack with some technical sections to keep things interesting. Though there are a few tough climbs, this segment of the Colorado Trail is generally rolling, with many fun descents. There is not much elevation difference between the northern and southern ends of this ride, but riding southbound is much more difficult, so it is best to get this over with first. This ride could be completed as a shuttle, but the singletrack is so good that it's worth riding twice.

Driving Directions

From Buena Vista, head west on Main Street (County-306) towards Cottonwood Pass. After 8.9 miles, turn right into the Avalanche Trailhead.

Riding Directions

G1 - 0.0 From the Avalanche Trailhead, start riding south on the Colorado Trail. Cross County-306 and continue on the Colorado Trail.

G2 - 1.6 Continue straight on the Colorado Trail as an umarked trail goes left.

G3 - 2.3 Cross a dirt road, pass through the South Cottonwood Trailhead and continue on the Colorado Trail.

G4 - 3.0 Cross another dirt road. Tackle some loose, steep climbing.

G5 - 6.5 Continue on the Colorado Trail as a small trail goes left to a viewpoint.

G6 - 9.9 Arrive at a dirt road (FS-322). Turn around and go back the way you came. *(Riders interested in taking a dip in the hot springs should bear left on FS-322 and arrive at Princeton Hot Springs in about 3 miles. Follow signs for the Colorado Trail.)*

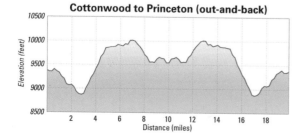

Cottonwood to Princeton (out-and-back)

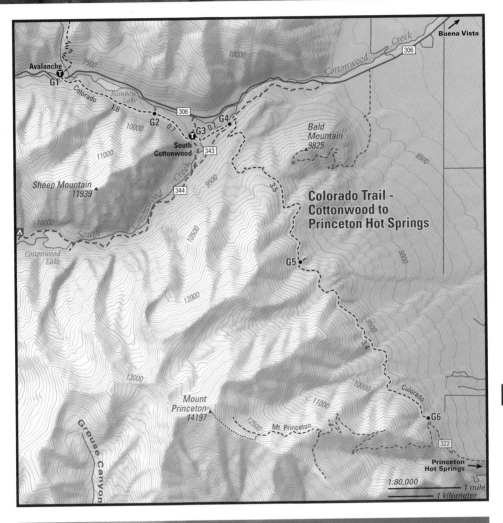

Colorado Trail -
Cottonwood to
Princeton Hot Springs

A glorious view from the Monarch Crest Trail after a tough climb up the Fooses Creek Trail.

(H) Salida Mountain Trails

(Starts from Downtown Salida)

Technical Difficulty:	● to ◆
Physical Difficulty:	**Easy** to **Strenuous**
Distance:	3 – 20 miles
Time:	1 – 4 hours
Type:	Loop
Surface:	Singletrack
Elevation (min/max):	7,000'/8,000'
Season:	Summer, Fall, Spring
Crowds:	Some
Dogs:	Trails may be crowded

Wonderful, winding singletrack in the hills above Salida

Ride Description

When summer thunderstorms or fall snow flurries shut down the high-country riding, savvy riders head straight for Salida. In addition to pizza and beer, downtown Salida offers easy access to excellent low-elevation riding. The Arkansas Hill Trail System is home to about 20 miles of singletrack of all difficulties. The trails are constructed as stacked loops, so it is possible to ride as much or as little as you like. Try a quick loop of Frontside, Li'l Rattler, Backbone, and Sand Dunes.

Driving Directions

The trailhead is located at the northeast end of F Street in downtown Salida. As you are driving into Salida on US-50, simply turn left on Oak Street (CO-291) and turn right on F Street. Cross the bridge over the Arkansas and park in the large dirt parking area.

Riding Directions

From the parking lot, head southeast along the railroad tracks for about 0.1 miles until you can turn left, cross the tracks, and turn left again. Find the Frontside Trail singletrack that runs behind a house.

A good loop is to climb Frontside to Li'l Rattler, and then connect to Backbone and Sand Dunes.

The trails are color-coded by difficulty on the map.

The trees are strange in Salida.

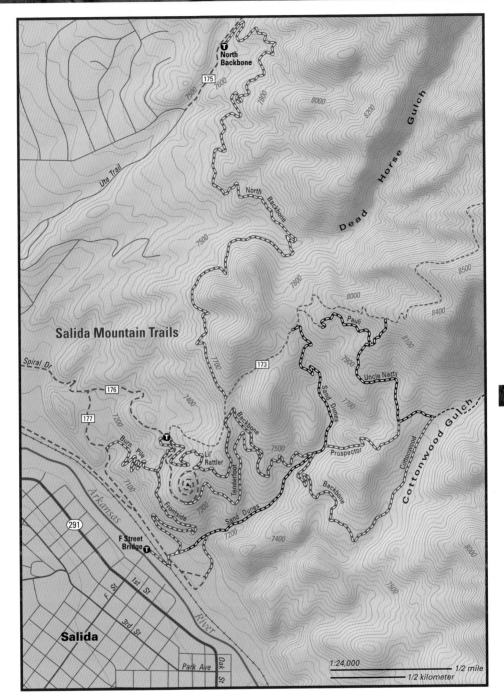

North
Backbone

175

Ute Trail

North Backbone

Dead Horse Gulch

Salida Mountain Trails

Spiral Dr

176

177

173

Pauli

Uncle Nazty

Sand Dunes

Prospector

Cottonwood Gulch

Burn Pile

Backbone

Lil' Rattler

Tenderfoot

Backbone

Frontside

Sand Dunes

291

F Street
Bridge

Arkansas

River

Salida

E. St.
1st St.
3rd St.

Park Ave

Oak St.

1:24,000

1/2 mile

1/2 kilometer

(I) Rainbow Trail - Bear Creek to Methodist Mountain ★★★★☆

(8 miles southeast of Salida)

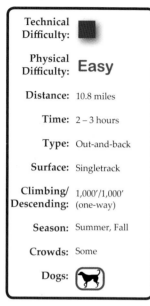

Technical Difficulty:	■
Physical Difficulty:	**Easy**
Distance:	10.8 miles
Time:	2 – 3 hours
Type:	Out-and-back
Surface:	Singletrack
Climbing/ Descending:	1,000'/1,000' (one-way)
Season:	Summer, Fall
Crowds:	Some
Dogs:	🐕

Great rolling singletrack without too much climbing

Ride Description

Ah, it's wonderful to be riding in the mountains on a smooth trail for a change! The Rainbow Trail offers beautiful views and solitude without the massive climbs and loose rock that generally accompany such alpine bliss. There are some hills, but they are generally mild and short. The hardest part of the ride may be getting to the trailhead! The last 2.3 miles of the dirt road are fairly rough and low-riding cars might not make it all of the way. But don't worry – it's easy to park lower down and ride the last section of the dirt road. In fact, many of the locals complete the Rainbow Trail as part of a loop from Salida, simply turning right on the dirt road at mile 5.4 and riding back to town.

Driving Directions

From Salida, head east on US-50 and go about 3 miles. Turn right on County-101 and follow this as it turns into County-49. After 3.2 miles you come to a dirt parking area just before a cattle guard. Park here if you have a very low-clearance vehicle. Otherwise, continue another 2.3 miles to the main trailhead.

Riding Directions

I1 - 0.0 From the Bear Creek Trailhead, start riding west on the Rainbow Trail (to the right as you are driving up the road). There are no intersections to worry about on this section of the Rainbow Trail, so just enjoy the rolling singletrack!

I2 - 5.4 Come to a dirt road and the Rainbow Trail Trailhead. Turn around and go back the way you came.

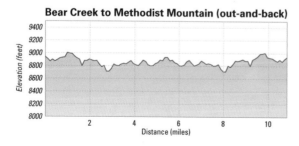

Bear Creek to Methodist Mountain (out-and-back)

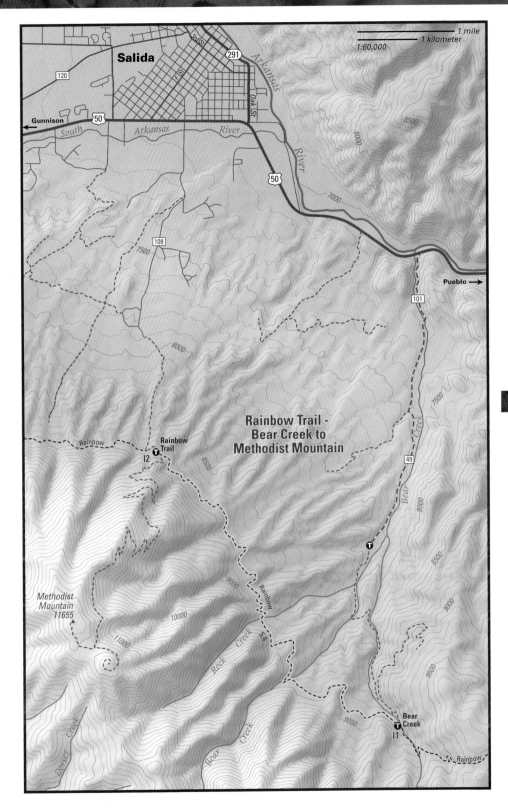

1 mile
1 kilometer
1:60,000

Salida

291

Arkansas

120

F St

3rd St

Oak St

River

50

Gunnison ←

South   Arkansas   River

50

8500

8000

7000

108

7500

Pueblo →

101

8000

**Rainbow Trail -
Bear Creek to
Methodist Mountain**

7500

Rainbow

**Rainbow
Trail**

I2

8500

Bear   Creek

49

8000

8500

9000

9000

Rainbow

9000

Methodist
Mountain
11655

10000

11000

Rock   Creek

Rainbow
Trail

8500

9000

9500

**Bear
Creek**

I1

Dorsey   Creek

Bear   Creek

9000

Rainbow

(J) Colorado Trail - Shavano to Chalk Cliffs ★★★★☆

(15 miles northwest of Salida)

Technical Difficulty:	◆◆
Physical Difficulty:	**Very Strenuous**
Distance:	up to 29 miles
Time:	4 – 6 hours
Type:	Out-and-back
Surface:	Singletrack
Climbing/ Descending:	2,700'/3,500' (one-way)
Season:	Summer
Crowds:	Few
Dogs:	

A very "adventurous" section of the Colorado Trail

Ride Description

The Colorado Trail has many moods: this is an angry one. This segment is not frequently ridden because it is guarded by a number of tough climbs and several very rocky sections. Nevertheless, those with sufficient tenacity will be treated to great views and sections of excellent riding. The riding directions describe this ride as an out-and-back, but setting up a shuttle is also highly recommended. Those looking for a longer ride can start the Colorado Trail where it crosses US-50.

Driving Directions

From Salida, head west on US-50 for 10.6 miles, following it past Poncha Springs. Turn right on County-240 and go 3.9 miles. Turn right into the Angel of Shavano Trailhead (a dirt parking area). There is a Forest Service campground just past the trailhead.

Riding Directions

J1 - 0.0   From the Angel of Shavano Trailhead, start riding northeast on the Colorado Trail.

J2 - 2.2   Continue straight on the Colorado Trail as a trail to Mount Shavano and Mount Tabeguache goes left.

J3 - 7.9   Continue on the Colorado Trail past an intersection with the Brown's Creek Trail. Keep going past the Wagon Loop Trail and Little Brown's Creek Trail.

J4 - 12.2   Cross a dirt road and continue on the Colorado Trail. *(Those riding this as an out-and-back should consider turning around here before descending the steep switchbacks to Princeton Hot Springs.)*

J5 - 14.5   Arrive at the Chalk Creek Trailhead.

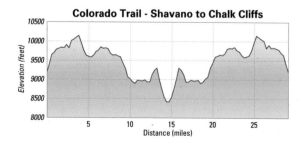

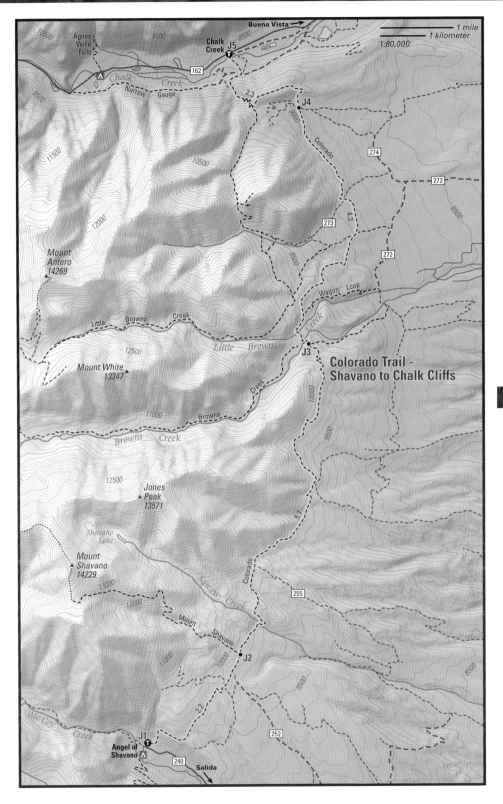

Buena Vista

Agnes
Vaille
Falls

Chalk
Creek   J5

162

Narrow   Gauge

Chalk   Creek

J4

Colorado

274

272

273   4.3

272

Mount
Antero
14269

Wagon   Loop

Creek

Little   Browns   Creek

Little   Browns

J3

**Colorado Trail -
Shavano to Chalk Cliffs**

Mount White
13347

Creek

Browns

Browns   Creek

Jones
Peak
13571

Shavano
Lake

Mount
Shavano
14229

Colorado

255

Squaw   Creek

Mount
Shavano

J2

252

McCoy   Creek

J1

Angel of
Shavano

240

Salida

1 mile
1 kilometer
1:80,000

Leadville & Salida

(K) Fooses–Green Loop ★★★★★

(15 miles W of Salida)

Technical Difficulty:	
Physical Difficulty:	**Very Strenuous**
Distance:	25.1 miles
Time:	4 – 8 hours
Type:	Loop
Surface:	Singletrack, paved road, dirt road
Climbing:	4,500'
Season:	Summer
Crowds:	Few
Dogs:	

Incredible singletrack, tough climbing, wild downhills

Ride Description

The Fooses–Green Loop is a great adventure through the woods and is much more difficult than the nearby Monarch Crest ride. Most riders will be walking the upper section of the Fooses Creek Trail, which is gentle at the start but soon becomes very steep and challenging. These efforts are rewarded with great riding on the Monarch Crest Trail, followed by an endless rocky downhill on the Green Creek Trail. An early start is recommended to avoid crowds on the Monarch Crest Trail and to outrun Colorado's frequent afternoon thunderstorms.

If ridden as a loop (as described here), the ride involves several miles of unpleasant riding along US-50. This could be avoided by leaving a car at the Green Creek Trailhead, but this option earns fewer "suffer points." Those fond of shuttling can drive to Monarch Pass, ride a few miles of the Monarch Crest Trail, and descend either the Fooses Creek or Green Creek Trails.

Driving Directions

From Salida, drive west on US-50 for 14.6 miles (9.6 miles from Poncha Springs). Turn left on County-225 and go 0.4 miles. Turn right to stay on County-225 and go 0.4 miles. Park at a small parking lot near Fooses Lake. If the parking here is full, there is additional parking (as well as some nice primitive campsites) further up the dirt road.

Riding Directions - see map on page 212

K1 - 0.0   From the parking lot, continue west on the dirt road.

K2 - 0.9   Bear left on the main road as another road goes right.

K3 - 2.0   Turn left on a dirt road, following a sign to the Fooses Creek Trailhead.

K4 - 2.1   Arrive at the Fooses Creek Trailhead and start riding on the Fooses Creek Trail. The trail starts easy and then becomes very steep.

K5 - 7.9   Reach the Monarch Crest Trail and turn left.

K6 - 9.6   At a sign, turn left onto the Green Creek Trail. Get ready for a long, fun downhill!

K7 - 16.4   Arrive at the Green Creek Trailhead. Turn left on the road (County-221).

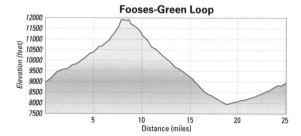

Leadville & Salida

K8 - 19.0   Go left on County-220.

K9 - 20.3   Turn left to stay on County-220.

K10 - 22.0   Go left onto US-50. If you drove from Salida, the rest of the ride should be familiar.

K11 - 24.3   Make a left on County-225.

K12 - 24.7   Turn right to stay on County-225.

K1 - 25.1   Arrive back at your car!

One of the occasional smooth sections of the Colorado Trail, from Shavano to Chalk Cliffs.

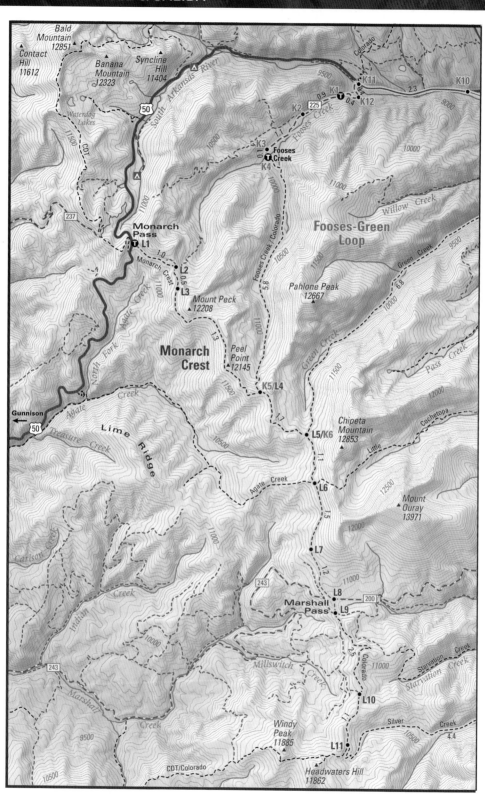

Bald
Mountain
12851

Contact
Hill
11612

Banana
Mountain
12323

Syncline
Hill
11404

South Arkansas River

9500

Colorado

K11

K10

2.3

50

K1

0.9

K2 225

0.4

K12

Waterdog
Lakes

11500

CDT

0.1

K3

Fooses
Creek

K4

Fooses Creek

1.1

9000

10000

11000

Willow Creek

237

Monarch
Pass
L1

1.0

Monarch Crest

L2

0.5

L3

Mount Peck
12208

Fooses-Green
Loop

Pahlone Peak
12667

Green Creek

9500

6.8

10000

1.3

Peel
Point
12145

**Monarch
Crest**

Green Creek

11500

Pass Creek

Gunnison

50

Agate

Creek

Lime
Ridge

K5/L4

1.7

L5/K6

Chipeta
Mountain
12853

12000

Cochetopa

Little

Agate Creek

10500

11000

L6

1.5

12500

Mount
Ouray
13971

12000

Carlson Creek

Creek

Indian

243

10000

L7

1.2

243

11000

Marshall
Pass

L8

200

L9

2.5

Colorado

11000

Starvation Creek

Millswitch Creek

Marshall

Creek

9500

L10

1.1

Silver

Creek

10500

4.4

Windy
Peak
11885

L11

CDT/Colorado

Headwaters Hill
11862

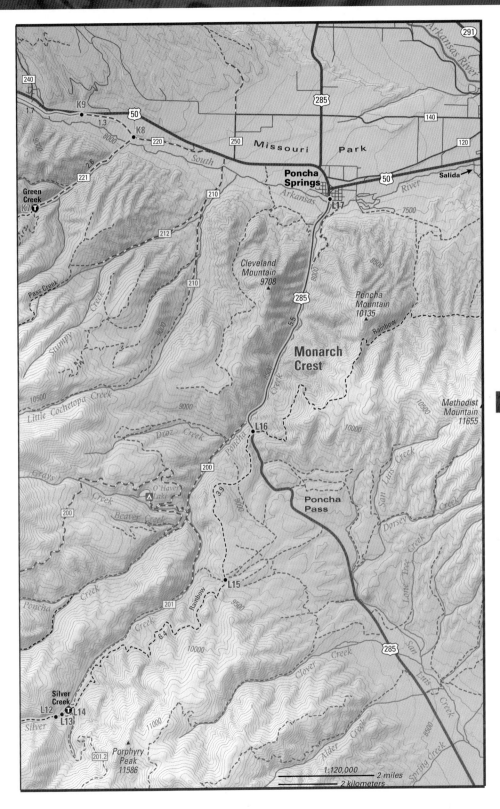

ⓁMonarch Crest ★★★★★

(20 miles west of Salida)

Technical Difficulty:	◆
Physical Difficulty:	**Moderate**
Distance:	34.7 miles
Time:	4 – 8 hours
Type:	Shuttle
Surface:	Singletrack, paved road
Climbing/ Descending:	3,000'/6,900' (with shuttle)
Season:	Summer
Crowds:	Some
Dogs:	🐕 *

Among the best rides in Colorado: mile after mile of high alpine riding with spectacular views

Ride Description

Darting through dense forests and soaring along an alpine ridge for miles, the Monarch Crest Trail captures everything great about Colorado mountain biking. There are long, smooth downhill sections where you can shift into the big ring and break the sound barrier. The trail starts at Monarch Pass (11,312') and ends at Poncha Springs (7,464'), losing almost 4,000 feet of elevation. But make no mistake; Monarch Crest is a tough ride. The sheer distance, combined with 3,000 feet of climbing, makes Monarch Crest a test-piece of physical endurance and an introduction to the realm of "epic rides."

The first section of the Monarch Crest Trail can be ridden as an out-and-back, but the full experience requires a car shuttle. It takes approximately 30 minutes to drive from Poncha Springs (the end of the ride) to Monarch Pass (the beginning). Riders can either leave a car in Poncha Springs and set up the shuttle themselves or pay about $20 per person and have High Valley Shuttles do the driving.

High Valley Bike Shuttle - **6250 US-285, Poncha Springs. 800-871-5145**
Based out of the Sinclair gas station, High Valley Bike Shuttle offers shuttle service for the Monarch Crest Trail and other trails in the area. It is located on the east side of US-285 just south of the junction with US-50.

* Dogs are allowed, but are not recommended due to the length of the ride as well as the sections of highway riding.

Driving Directions

From Salida, head west on US-50 and continue through Poncha Springs. Leave a car here for the shuttle and continue on to Monarch Pass, located 18 miles from Poncha Springs.

Riding Directions - see map on previous page

L1 - 0.0 From Monarch Pass, ride up the dirt road near the tram station. When you come to a sign for the Continental Divide Trail (CDT), turn right on the CDT/Monarch Crest Trail.

L2 - 1.0 Stay on the Monarch Crest Trail as Fooses Creek Road goes left.

L3 - 1.5 At a CDT signpost, make a right onto singletrack.

L4 - 5.0 Continue on the Monarch Crest Trail as the Fooses Creek Trail goes left.

L5 - 6.7 Go straight as the Green Creek Trail goes left.

L6 - 7.8 Continue on the Monarch Crest Trail past a junction with the Little Cochetopa Trail and the Agate Creek Trail.

L7 - 9.3 The trail becomes a dirt road.

L8 - 10.5 Arrive at Marshall Pass. Turn right and ride up the road.

L9 - 10.7 Turn left onto a dirt road, following signs for the Colorado Trail. Go 0.1 mile and arrive at a five-way intersection. Start riding on the Colorado Trail singletrack.

L10 - 13.2 Go left on doubletrack and climb a short-but-steep hill.

L11 - 14.3 Turn left on the Silver Creek Trail.

L12 - 18.7 The trail joins the (hopefully dry) streambed and soon becomes a road.

L13 - 18.8 Bear left as FS-201.2 (Toll Road Gulch Road) goes right.

L14 - 18.9 Arrive at the Silver Creek Trailhead. For the full experience, turn right and enjoy the excellent Rainbow Trail. *(If you are tired at this point, you can continue straight and ride the dirt road to US-285.)*

L15 - 25.3 Cross a dirt road and continue on the Rainbow Trail.

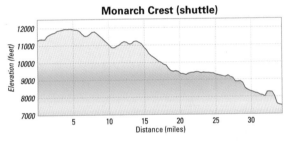

L16 - 29.2 Turn left on US-285 and follow this back to Poncha Springs.

L17 - 34.7 Arrive back at Poncha Springs, "Crossroads of the Rockies."

Leadville & Salida

Curt Stevens devours the deliciously smooth singletrack at 11,000 feet on the Monarch Crest Trail.

Ⓜ Canyon Creek ★★★★★

(40 miles west of Salida)

Technical Difficulty:	◆
Physical Difficulty:	**Insanely Strenuous**
Distance:	19.1 miles
Time:	3 – 6 hours
Type:	Loop
Surface:	Singletrack, dirt road
Climbing:	3,900'
Season:	Summer
Crowds:	Few
Dogs:	

Is the fantastic descent worth carrying your bike for an hour?

Ride Description

The Canyon Creek Trail will be a very popular ride when someone gets around to building a gondola to the top. The descent is excellent, with great scenery and fast singletrack. However, getting to the fun part is far from easy. Riders must first climb a steep dirt road, and then carry their bikes up a long steep section of rough singletrack. The steep section lasts for a mile, so you should expect to be pushing and carrying your bike for about one hour.

Driving Directions

From Salida, head west on US-50 for 30.7 miles. Turn right on County-888 and go 7.7 miles until you reach the Snowblind Campground. The ride starts here, but there isn't a good place to park at the Snowblind Campground unless you pay for a campsite. So, either camp at Snowblind, or continue up the road past Whitepine, find a place to park, and start riding from there.

Riding Directions

M1 - 0.0   From the Snowblind Campground, start riding up Tomichi Pass Road towards the town of Whitepine.

M2 - 0.9   Continue past the Whitepine Cemetery.

M3 - 2.7   Pass some primitive campsites (possible parking) on the left.

M4 - 7.2   Less than a mile before the road reaches Tomichi Pass, turn left on the Canyon Creek Trail. Most of the first mile of the trail will be hike-a-bike.

M5 - 8.4   Arrive at the high point of the ride (~12,600') and start the descent!

M6 - 9.4   Continue straight on the Canyon Creek Trail as the Horseshoe Trail goes left.

M7 - 13.7   At an outfitter's camp, turn left and cross the creek on a rickety bridge.

M8 - 15.4   Continue on the Canyon Creek Trail as the Waunita Trail goes right.

M9 - 16.8   Continue on the Canyon Creek Trail as the Horseshoe Trail goes left.

M10 - 18.2   Climb up some horrible, sandy switchbacks.

M1 - 19.1   Arrive back at the Snowblind Campground!

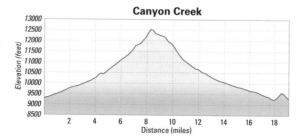

Canyon Creek

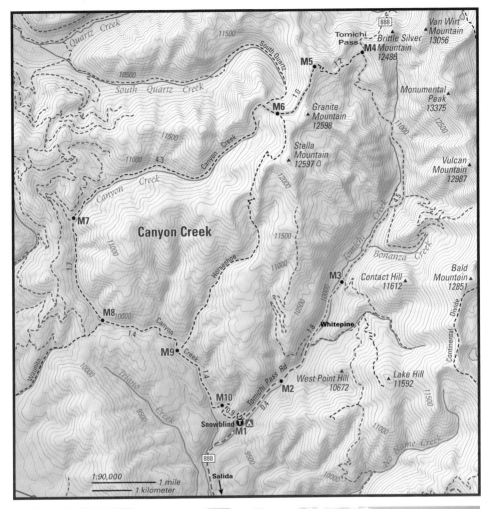

Finally done with the massive climb, the epic descent of the Canyon Creek Trail awaits.

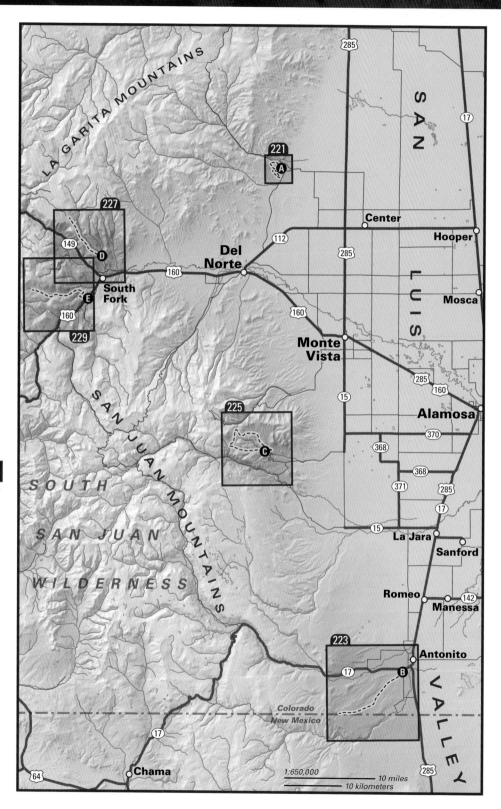

San Luis Valley

The mountain biking around the San Luis Valley can be summarized in one word: "wild." The riding here is wild both in the sense of wilderness and in the sense of wild-and-crazy, rocky, challenging mountain biking. You won't see many people riding mountain bikes in this part of Colorado, but you will find an abundance of rugged trails through some of the most beautiful terrain in the state.

There is a tremendous diversity of landscapes around the valley. The pancake-flat center of the valley is prime farmland and this region is famous for its potatoes and barley but not for its mountain biking. Along the foothills that form the valley there is gorgeous desert landscape with gentle trails. Penitente Canyon offers an appealing combination of smooth trails, technical rock features, and first-class rock climbing. Further west, in the higher mountains, the trails are rugged and it is common to see bear and elk. There are a lifetime of trails to explore around South Fork, Creede, and Wolf Creek. However, most of these trails are adventurous, poorly maintained, and rugged. The majestic Sangre de Cristo Mountains form the eastern edge of the San Luis Valley. Not much is said about mountain biking in the Sangres. It is possible that the trails are so good that mountain bikers who venture there never leave.

Accommodations

Many of the small towns in the San Luis Valley offer motel rooms, but the real gem of the area is the camping. This is one of the few regions in Colorado where it is possible to find developed campgrounds (with toilets and picnic tables) that are still completely free. Of course, there are plenty of pay campgrounds and an endless supply of primitive camping along dirt roads through the National Forests.

Bike Shops

Alpine Bike and Ski
28266 W US-160, South Fork. 719-873-2495
Located in a cute little red log cabin, this shop is one of the best within 100 miles. Offers bike, raft, and kayak rentals.

Kristi Mountain Sports
3223 Main Street, Alamosa. 719-589-9759
This large outdoor shop has you covered for biking, hiking, and skiing needs. Located on US-285 in the western outskirts of Alamosa.

Eats and Drinks

Coffee: Milagros Coffeehouse
629 Main Street, Alamosa. 719-589-9299
Coffee and internet.

San Luis Valley Brewing Company
631 Main Street, Alamosa. 719-587-BEER
This place brews its own beer and serves up sandwiches, pasta, and steaks.

Bliss Café
187 W. Silver Avenue, Crestone. 719-256-6400.
The most blissful food in the valley.

Penitente Canyon ★★★★★

(25 miles northwest of Monte Vista)

Technical Difficulty:	
Physical Difficulty:	**Easy**
Distance:	5.3 miles
Time:	About 1 hour
Type:	Loop
Surface:	Singletrack, dirt road
Climbing:	650'
Season:	Spring, Fall
Crowds:	Few
Dogs:	🐕

Several loops, many with fun rock features

Ride Description

Penitente Canyon has long been popular with rock climbers, offering short, but highly entertaining climbs. Who would have suspected that it would offer similarly short-but-sweet trails for mountain biking? Despite being packed into a small area, the trails at Penitente Canyon are varied: some of them feature smooth cruising through sagebrush, while others are loaded with rock features that can serve as drops and jumps. The landscape seems like it was designed for mountain biking, and there are many sections that offer both easy and expert options. There are additional trails at Penitente that are not described in this book. A pay campground is located near the trailhead, so consider spending the night.

Driving Directions

From Monte Vista, head north on US-285 for 17 miles. Turn left on County Road G and follow it (through a zig-zag) for 7 miles. At a Y-intersection, turn right on County-40G, and continue past several campsites, until you reach the main Penitente Canyon Trailhead.

Riding Directions

A1 - 0.0 From the trailhead, start riding south on the singletrack that begins near the big information sign.

A2 - 0.6 Arrive at the Loop B Trailhead, continue roughly straight on a dirt road signed for "Witches Canyon."

A3 - 0.9 Bear left on a dirt road as a road to Witches Canyon Trailhead goes right.

A4 - 1.2 Go right on faint, unmarked singletrack and enjoy a fast descent!

A5 - 1.8 The singletrack ends at a dirt road; turn right.

A6 - 2.1 Turn right, leave the road, and start riding on narrow singletrack.

A7 - 2.8 Reach a dirt road and turn right. Climb a short, steep hill and turn left on the dirt road, heading back the way you came.

A2 - 3.2 Arrive back at the Loop B Trailhead. Turn left and start riding on the A Trail.

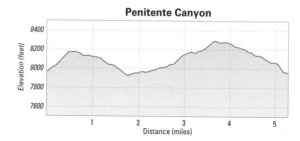

Penitente Canyon

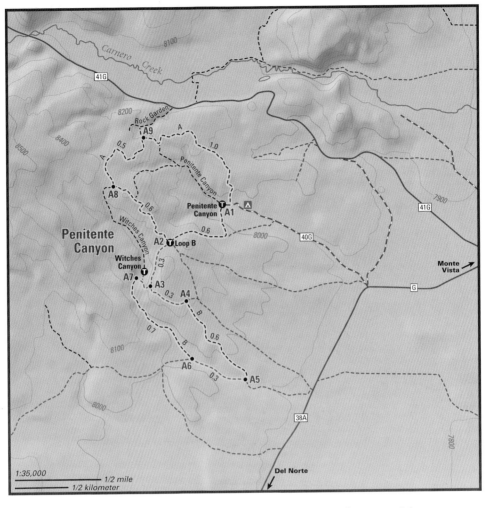

A8 - 3.8 Go right on the A Trail as the WC (Witches Canyon) Trail goes straight.

A9 - 4.3 Go right again on the A Trail as RG (Rock Garden) goes left.

A1 - 5.3 Arrive at a dirt road. Turn right and ride a short distance back to the trailhead.

Ⓑ Cumbres & Toltec Railroad ★★⯪☆☆

(30 miles south of Alamosa)

Technical Difficulty:	
Physical Difficulty:	**Easy**
Distance:	17.7 miles
Time:	3 – 4 hours
Type:	Out-and-back
Surface:	Dirt road
Climbing/ Descending:	900'/0' (one-way)
Season:	Spring, Fall
Crowds:	None
Dogs:	🐕

A gentle dirt road follows a historic railroad into the Land of Enchantment

Ride Description

Sometimes you don't want a crazy trail. Sometimes you just want a nice, wide trail without too many rocks where you and your special someone can ride side-by-side. This ride offers an opportunity to cruise on smooth trail and even takes you into New Mexico, the "Land of Enchantment." This old dirt road follows the historic Cumbres and Toltec Scenic Railroad. The road is technically open to vehicles, but it is in the middle of nowhere and doesn't lead to any destination, so it is unlikely that you will encounter any vehicles. There is little shade along this ride, so wait for a cool day and bring plenty of water.

While you are in the area, consider taking a ride on the Cumbres and Toltec Scenic Railroad, which runs from Antonito, CO to Chama, New Mexico. The route crosses over Cumbres Pass (10,020'), the highest point on a passenger railroad in the United States.

Driving Directions

From Alamosa, head southwest on US-285 for about 28.4 miles until you reach the small town of Antonito. Just past Antonito, make a sharp left to stay on US-285 and go about one block. Cross the railroad tracks and quickly turn right on County Road 12.5 and drive 1.2 miles. Turn right on County-E5 (County-11) and go 0.4 miles. The ride starts where this road crosses the tracks.

Riding Directions

B1 - 0.0 From the intersection of County-11 and the railroad tracks, start riding southwest on the dirt road that parallels the railroad tracks.

B2 - 5.2 Cross the railroad tracks and continue on the dirt road. Enjoy the desert scenery.

B3 - 8.8 Cross the railroad tracks again. You have entered New Mexico! Turn around and ride back the way you came.

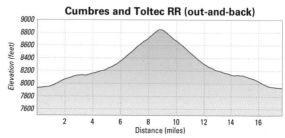

Cumbres and Toltec RR (out-and-back)

Elevation (feet) vs. Distance (miles)

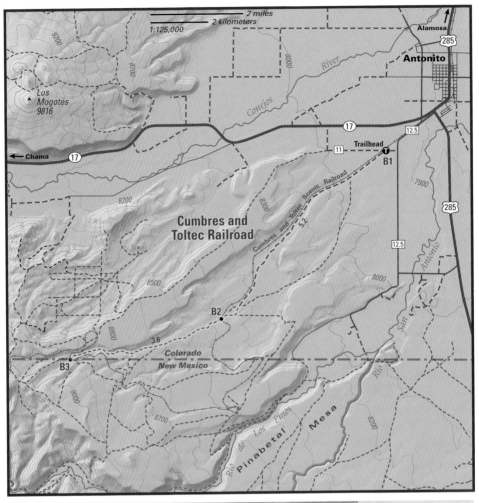

San Luise Valley

A great view of the Sangre de Cristo Mountains from the Cumbres & Toltec Trail.

Ⓒ Cat Creek ★★★★☆

(30 miles west of Alamosa)

Technical Difficulty:	◆
Physical Difficulty:	**Strenuous**
Distance:	13.2 miles
Time:	3 – 4 hours
Type:	Loop
Surface:	Dirt road, singletrack
Climbing:	2,100′
Season:	Summer, Fall
Crowds:	Few
Dogs:	

This hidden gem features a glorious descent along Cat Creek

Ride Description

Great singletrack, beautiful aspens, expansive views, and zero crowds make Cat Creek a fantastic ride. Sure, some of the trail is badly rutted and there are sections of very steep riding on dirt roads, but the descent along Cat Creek is legendary. It is possible to drive most of the way up the dirt road and set up a car shuttle, but riding the whole loop is recommended since the grade is generally mellow and the views are lovely.

There is great free camping at the Comstock Campground, located on County-28. It is possible to access this loop from the campground by riding up FS-703, intersecting the ride description at mile 6.4.

Driving Directions

From Alamosa, head southwest on US-285 for about 2.5 miles. Turn right on CO-370 and go 14.1 miles. Turn left on CO-15 and go 2.0 miles. Turn right on County-12 (turns into FS-250) and drive 7.0 miles. Turn right onto FS-271 and travel 4.3 miles. As the road makes a sharp right turn, look for a small sign for the Cat Creek Trail on the left. Park here at a small pullout.

Riding Directions

C1 - 0.0   From the Cat Creek Trailhead, continue up the dirt road (FS-271). Continue on FS-271 past several intersections with smaller roads.

C2 - 3.1   Go left on FS-271 as FS-236 goes right.

C3 - 6.4   Turn left on trail #703. (Turning right on 703 leads to the Comstock Campground.)

C4 - 7.8   Continue straight as unmarked singletrack comes in from the left.

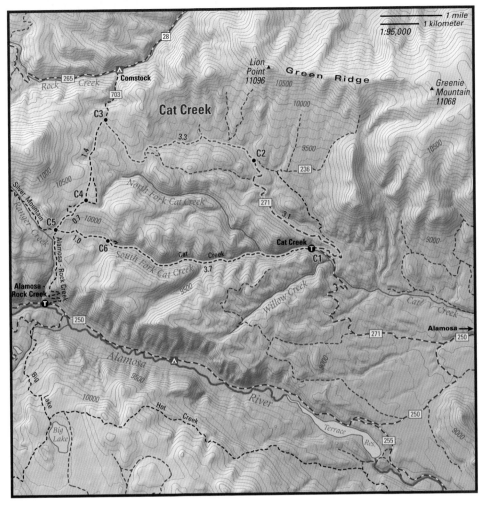

C5 - 8.5 Arrive at a four-way junction and turn left on Cat Creek Trail. The Cat Creek Trail is not marked, but there is a sign to the right that reads, "Trail construction by Mountain Trails Youth Ranch..."

C6 - 9.5 Come to an unmarked Y-intersection and turn right. (These trails re-join shortly.)

C1 - 13.2 Arrive back at the trailhead.

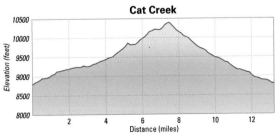

D Alder Bench ★★★★☆

(4 miles north of South Fork)

Technical Difficulty:	◆
Physical Difficulty:	**Very Strenuous**
Distance:	13.0 miles
Time:	1 – 5 hours
Type:	Out-and-back
Surface:	Singletrack
Climbing/ Descending:	2,500'/300' (one-way)
Season:	Summer, Fall
Crowds:	Few
Dogs:	

A tough start leads to excellent riding

Ride Description

Out on the Adler Bench Trail, men are real men, women are real women, and the bears are real bears. On this trail, the author came around a turn to find a large bear sitting right in the middle of the trail. Unlike most modern, civilized bears that run away immediately for fear of being shot, this bear sat right in the middle of the trail and refused to budge. The author eventually picked up his bike and hiked into the woods, making a large circle around the surly bear. And that was not all! A few minutes later he was again surprised by a huge herd of elk and then several moose!

The trail itself is equally wild: tough climbing, rutted sections, and loose rocks will challenge the best riders. However, those who aren't afraid of a little hike-a-bike will discover other sections that offer wonderful riding as well as great scenery near the top of the ride. The trail ends at a dirt road, and those with high-clearance vehicles might be able to shuttle to the top.

Driving Directions

From US-160 in South Fork, head northwest on CO-149 for 1.0 miles. Turn right on CO-15 (River Road) and go 1.2 miles. Turn left on FS-610 and drive 2.1 miles. The trailhead parking area is on the left, just past the historic "Guard Station," a small cabin that can be rented for approximately $50 per night from the National Forest Service.

Riding Directions

D1 - 0.0 From the trailhead, start riding on the signed Alder Bench Trail. Continue on the main trail past several faint, unmarked trails. Climb steep switchbacks up a hill.

D2 - 1.7 Continue straight, past a four-foot tall rock cairn with a sign sticking out of it. *(This sign indicates a faded trail that leads downhill to CO-149 near South Fork.)* Enjoy a few miles of mostly flat riding before the next challenging climb.

D3 - 5.5 Arrive at a Raven Park, a beautiful meadow that just begs you to stay for a picnic. This a good place to turn around. Otherwise, continue climbing!

D4 - 6.5 Arrive at a dirt road. Turn around and enjoy an awesome, technical descent.

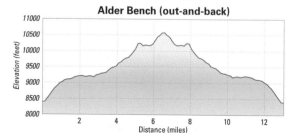

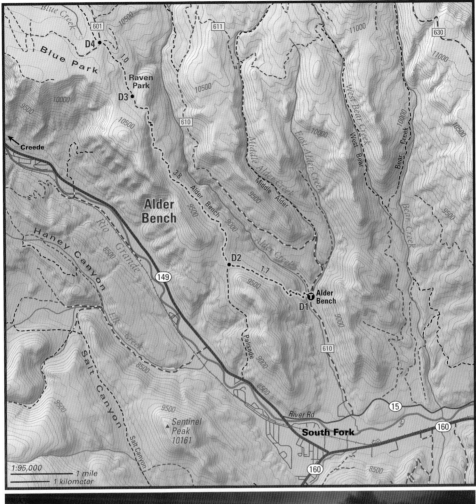

A beautiful sunset near South Fork.

(E) Trout Creek ★★★☆☆

(3 miles southwest of South Fork)

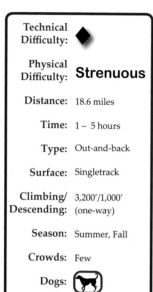

Technical Difficulty:	◆
Physical Difficulty:	**Strenuous**
Distance:	18.6 miles
Time:	1 – 5 hours
Type:	Out-and-back
Surface:	Singletrack
Climbing/ Descending:	3,200'/1,000' (one-way)
Season:	Summer, Fall
Crowds:	Few
Dogs:	🐕

The first few miles are moderate and fun. After that, the trail gets gnarly

Ride Description

Trout Creek is basically two trails in one. Riders looking for a nice, moderate ride, can complete the first four miles and turn around. There are still some steep hills involved, but it should be fun for the intermediate rider. Venturing past mile four is a true wilderness experience, featuring numerous creek crossings, rocky sections, steep hills, and, of course, beautiful forests and solitude.

Driving Directions

From the intersection with CO-149 in South Fork, head southwest on US-160 for 3.0 miles. The trail starts on the right side of the road in a large meadow next to a small sign, which is difficult to see from the road.

Riding Directions

E1 - 0.0 Start riding on the Trout Creek Trail (#831).

E2 - 3.9 Turn left on doubletrack.

E3 - 6.7 Arrive at a faint Y-intersection that is marked by a stick stuck in a pile of rocks. Go right on Trail #831 as trail #833 goes left.

E4 - 9.3 Eventually the trail becomes impossible to follow. The author turned around at this point, but with more tenacity, it should be possible to reach the ridge.

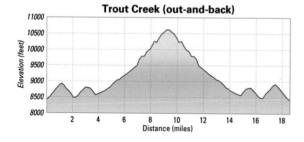

San Luis Valley

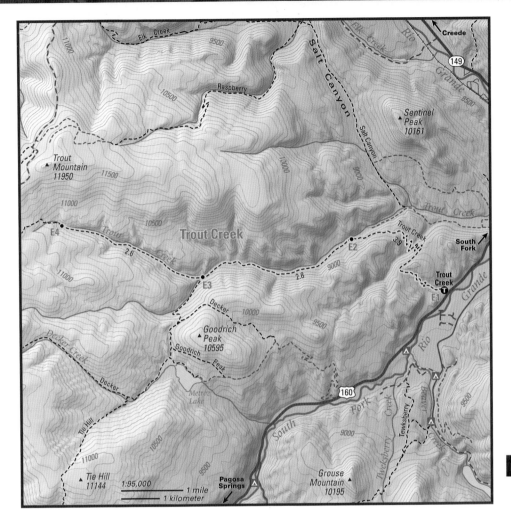

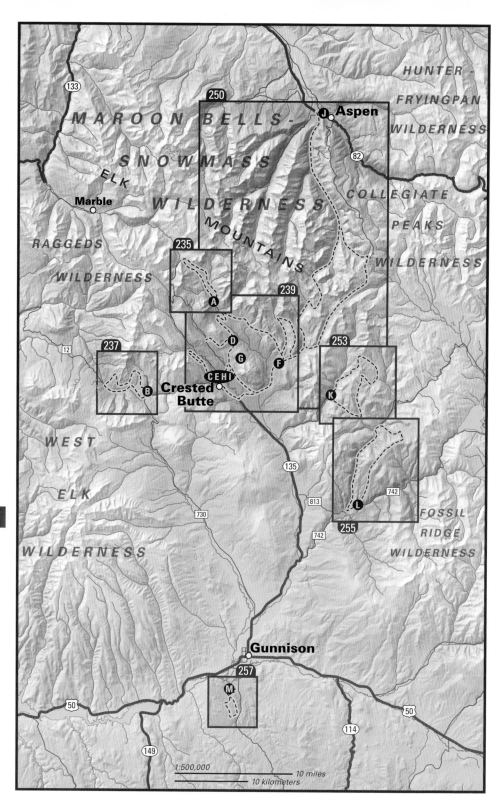

Crested Butte & Gunnison

Crested Butte is the birthplace of Colorado mountain biking: back in 1976 a few wild locals got the idea to ride their bikes over the insanely rugged Pearl Pass and into Aspen. Several decades later, Crested Butte is still a fabulous place to ride spectacular aspen-lined singletrack. Though there are some delightful easier rides near town – like the Lower Loop or Snodgrass Trail – most of the classic Crested Butte rides are tough, featuring long climbs and challenging descents.

Gunnison, located just over 30 minutes to the south, is at a lower elevation than Crested Butte, so many of the nearby trails remain dry even when Crested Butte is buried in snow. There are a number of good trails, but Hartman Rocks is by far the most popular option, offering dozens of miles of fantastic sandy singletrack with exciting "rock-rolling" over huge boulders.

Descending the 401 Trail.   photo: Fredrik Marmsater

Crested Butte & Gunnison

Accommodations

Crested Butte is a major skiing destination and offers an assortment of hotels, motels, and lodges. Likewise, Gunnison is a popular tourist stop along US-50 and boasts plentiful motel options that are generally cheaper than Crested Butte. There are many beautiful campgrounds near Crested Butte, but most require at least 15 minutes of driving from the town. Free camping abounds on many dirt roads outside of Crested Butte. Near Gunnison, Hartman Rocks offers little shade or shelter, but plenty of free camping spots (4WD helpful).

Bike Shops

The Alpineer
419 6th Street, Crested Butte. 970-349-5210
This climbing, hiking, and backpacking shop is also a great bike shop, offering gear, service, and rentals.

Tomichi Cycles
104 N. Main Street, Gunnison. 970-641-9069
Bikes, gear, and service. Offers well-priced rentals.

Rock N' Roll Sports
608 W. Tomichi Avenue, Gunnison. 970-641-9150
A cool shop run out of a tiny house. Also stocks climbing and skiing gear.

Dolly's Mountain Shuttle
dollysmountainshuttle.typepad.com 970-349-2620
Dolly's will take you to most of the trailheads near Crested Butte for about $15 per person (must have at least 4 people) or to Aspen (so you can ride back to Crested Butte!) for $60 per person (6 person minimum). They also offer rides to the local airports and can be your designated driver in the evening.

Eats and Drinks

Almost all of the restaurants and bars in Crested Butte are located along Elk Avenue (on the left when entering town from the south on CO-135). So, those hungry for dinner can just cruise down Elk Avenue and pick a restaurant. Similarly, in Gunnison, most of the restaurants and shops are located along North Main Street or Tomichi Avenue.

Paradise Cafe
303 Elk Avenue, Crested Butte. 970-349-6233
Great pancakes.

Buckaroo Beanery
601 6th Street, Crested Butte. 970-349-5252
Tasty coffee, internet, and a nice view of Mount Crested Butte. This is a good place to hang out on a rain-day.

The Bean Coffeehouse & Eatery
120 North Main Street, Gunnison. 970-641-2408
Located near the turn to Crested Butte, this is a convenient place to get a coffee or sandwich.

Downhill racing at Crested Butte Resort.   photo: Brandon Turman

The 401 ★★★★★

(8 miles north of Crested Butte)

Technical Difficulty:	
Physical Difficulty:	**Strenuous**
Distance:	13.5 miles
Time:	2 – 4 hours
Type:	Loop
Surface:	Singletrack, dirt road
Climbing:	2,200'
Season:	Summer, Fall
Crowds:	Some
Dogs:	

An enduring classic that epitomizes all things Crested Butte; incredible views and fast singletrack

Ride Description

The 401 is one of the best trails in Colorado and can serve as a great introduction to Crested Butte mountain biking since it is not nearly as long as many of the nearby classic rides. Despite being less than 14 miles long, it still features incredible views, aspen groves, and hillsides covered in wildflowers. This ride is not recommended for complete beginners, since some sections are narrow and perched on a steep hillside. However, riders who are confident on blue-square terrain will love this legendary trail. Consider riding to the trailhead from Crested Butte; it takes less than one hour.

Driving Directions

From Crested Butte, head north on 6th Street (CO-135). The road turns into Gothic Road, passes Mount Crested Butte and turns to dirt. When you have gone about 8.5 miles from downtown Crested Butte, and 0.4 miles past the Gothic Research Station, turn right into a dirt parking lot.

Riding Directions

A1 - 0.0   From the parking lot, ride northwest on FS-317 (Gothic Road, Schofield Pass Road) towards Schofield Pass.

A2 - 1.5   Pass a turnoff to the 403 Trail (the Washington Gulch Trail).

A3 - 2.0   Continue straight past the Rustler Gulch Trailhead on the right. You can park here if you wish to ride a shortened version of the 401.

A4 - 5.1   Arrive at Schofield Pass (10,707'). Turn right onto the 401 ("The Trailriders Trail"). The next mile is very steep and strenuous.

A5 - 6.5   Reach the high point of the ride and bear right, dropping down a hill. The next several miles are perched on a steep hillside – ride carefully!

A6 - 7.1   Negotiate a steep rock section.

A7 - 10.2   Turn right on a dirt road (County-317.3c). Go about 0.1 miles and turn left onto the 401 singletrack.

A8 - 11.4   Go left up an old dirt road and climb steeply. Go 0.3 miles and turn right onto singletrack.

A9 - 13.1   Come to the dirt parking lot (the Copper Creek Trailhead) and turn right down a dirt road (FS-317.3A).

A1 - 13.5   Arrive back at the parking lot near Gothic Road. Do another lap!

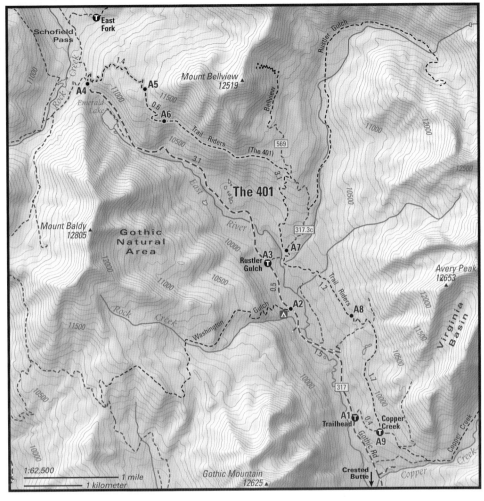

1:62,500

1 mile

1 kilometer

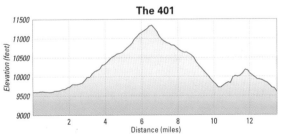

The 401

B Dyke Trail ★★★★½

(7 miles west of Crested Butte)

Technical Difficulty:	
Physical Difficulty:	**Strenuous**
Distance:	13.8 miles
Time:	3 – 5 hours
Type:	Loop
Surface:	Singletrack, dirt road
Climbing:	2,500'
Season:	Summer
Crowds:	Few
Dogs:	

Narrow singletrack through gigantic aspen groves

Ride Description

The Dyke Trail follows the same winning formula as other Crested Butte classics like The 401, Reno-Flag-Bear-Deadman, and Teocalli Ridge: ride a dirt road for several hours to access incredible singletrack that cruises through lush forests. The Dyke Trail is less travelled than the other classics and is a bit tougher. Numerous hills require most people to walk their bikes, and muddy sections of trail should be expected, even during dry periods. Riders who are up to the challenge won't be disappointed. The Dyke Trail features memorable sections of fast, tight singletrack through gigantic aspen groves. Making a loop involves a few miles of riding on Kebler Pass Road, but this can be avoided by leaving a car at Horse Ranch Park. The Dyke Trail can be quite muddy at times, so give it until July to dry out and don't ride it after a heavy rain.

Driving Directions

Drive into Crested Butte from the south (on CO-135), turn left on Whiterock Avenue (County-12, Kebler Pass Road), and go 6.8 miles. Turn right on FS-826 towards Lake Irwin and immediately park in a gravel parking area on the left.

Riding Directions

B1 - 0.0 Start riding uphill on FS-826 towards Lake Irwin. Bear left to stay on FS-826 as FS-826a goes right.

B2 - 2.5 Turn left at the entrance to the campground. Go left at every intersection as you pass through the campground.

B3 - 3.1 Come to a small trailhead and turn left on the Dyke Trail (#837).

B4 - 6.9 Turn left on Trail #833 towards Horse Ranch Park.

B5 - 8.1 Come to a small clearing. Turn left on doubletrack as the Dark Canyon Trail goes right.

B6 - 8.4 Arrive at Horse Ranch Park. Continue straight and head out towards the road. Turn left on County-12.

B1 - 13.8 Turn left on FS-826 and arrive back at the parking area.

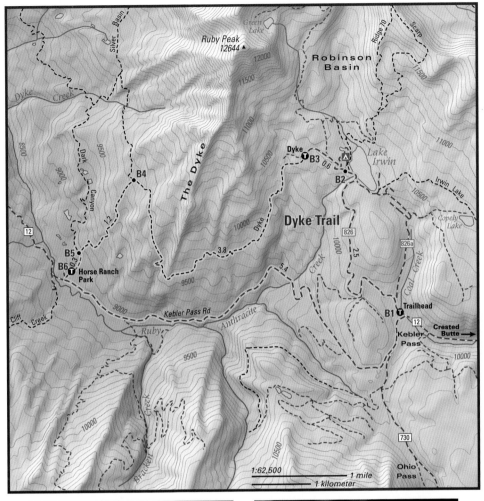

Perfect singletrack at the start of the Dyke Trail.

©Lower Loop ★★★★☆

(Starts from downtown Crested Butte)

Technical Difficulty:	
Physical Difficulty:	**Easy**
Distance:	8.8 miles
Time:	1 – 2 hours
Type:	Lollipop Loop
Surface:	Singletrack, paved road
Climbing:	650′
Season:	Summer, Fall
Crowds:	Crowded
Dogs:	Trail can be crowded

A delightful cruise — perfect for the novice rider

Ride Description

The Lower Loop is guaranteed to put a smile on any mountain biker's face. It's a great ride for those looking for entertaining singletrack through meadows and aspen groves, but wishing to avoid the tough technical challenges typical of Crested Butte trails. The trail is described below as starting from downtown Crested Butte, which involves some nice riding along the Woods Walk Trail. Lazier riders can drive to the Peanut Trailhead and start at mile 2.2, shortening the ride to only 3.4 miles.

Driving Directions

Start the ride from the intersection of CO-135 (6th Street) and Elk Avenue in downtown Crested Butte.

Riding Directions

C1 - 0.0 From the corner of 6th Street (CO-135) and Elk Avenue, begin riding north on 6th Street.

C2 - 0.3 Turn left on Butte Avenue.

C3 - 0.8 Where Butte Road turns into Peanut Lake Road (and turns to dirt) turn left onto unmarked singletrack (the Woods Walk Trail). At the next junction, turn right, staying close to Peanut Lake Road.

C4 - 1.2 Turn right to stay on the Woods Walk Trail as an unmarked trail goes left.

C5 - 2.2 Arrive at the Peanut Trailhead. Follow signs towards the Lower Loop Trail.

C6 - 2.4 Turn right onto the Lower Loop Trail.

C7 - 2.8 Come to the junction of Lower-Lower and Upper-Lower. Turn left onto Upper-Lower.

C8 - 4.3 Turn right (downhill) on Gunsight Pass Road.

C9 - 4.7 Turn right onto unmarked singletrack. After 200 feet, turn right again on the Lower-Lower Trail.

C7 - 6.0 Arrive back at the junction with Upper-Lower Trail. Bear left and head back to Crested Butte the way that you came.

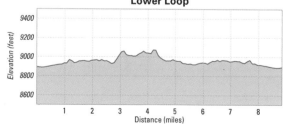

Lower Loop

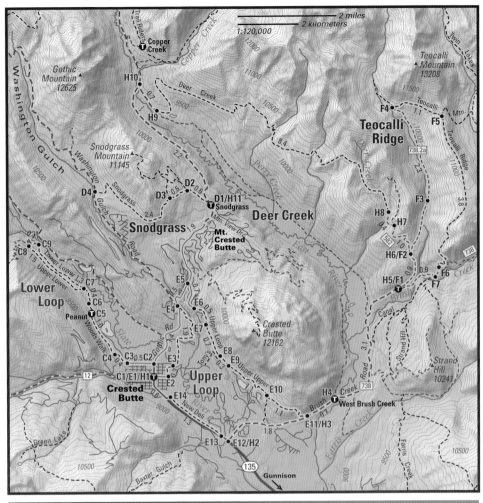

Descending the 401 Trail during the 2010 Crested Butte Classic.   photo: Fredrik Marmsater

D Snodgrass Trail ★★★★☆

(4 miles north of Crested Butte)

Technical Difficulty:	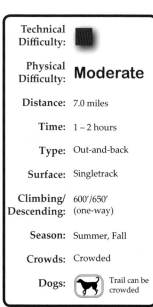
Physical Difficulty:	**Moderate**
Distance:	7.0 miles
Time:	1 – 2 hours
Type:	Out-and-back
Surface:	Singletrack
Climbing/ Descending:	600'/650' (one-way)
Season:	Summer, Fall
Crowds:	Crowded
Dogs:	Trail can be crowded

Great views of Mount Crested Butte on this short-but-sweet trail

Ride Description

Many of the classic trails around Crested Butte require that you ride uphill on a dirt road for several hours to enjoy great singletrack, but not the Snodgrass Trail! A quick 10-minute hill-climb brings riders to some of the best singletrack in Crested Butte. The singletrack is less than 3 miles long, but it is fun to ride in both directions. Additionally, the Snodgrass Trail can be linked with some of the trails at the ski resort to create a larger loop.

Most of the Snodgrass Trail is located on private property. Since the land is used for cattle grazing, the trail may be closed at any time. The trail is generally open from late-May until mid-August. A sign is located at the trailhead that indicates whether or not the trail is open.

Driving Directions

From the town of Crested Butte, drive north on 6th Street, which soon becomes Gothic Road. Take this for about 4 miles, past Mount Crested Butte, and park in a dirt pullout on the left just after you pass Mountain View Drive. Consider biking from Crested Butte: there is a bike path that starts near the school and takes you most of the way to the trailhead.

Riding Directions - see map on page 239

D1 - 0.0 From the parking area, climb over the turnstile and start riding on the Snodgrass Trail

D2 - 0.6 Cross another turnstile and turn left on the Snodgrass Trail singletrack.

D3 - 1.1 Bear left on the Snodgrass Trail as an unmarked trail goes right.

D4 - 3.5 Arrive at Washington Gulch Road. Turn around and go back the way you came. *(Alternatively, you can make a loop by turning left on Washington Gulch Road and taking this back to Gothic Road.)*

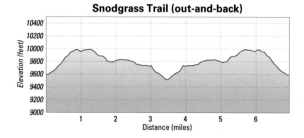

Snodgrass Trail (out-and-back)

Crested Butte & Gunnison

Spectacular wildflowers and steep climbing on the Teocalli
Mountain Trail.

(E) Upper Loop ★★★★☆

(Starts from downtown Crested Butte)

Technical Difficulty:	◆
Physical Difficulty:	**Moderate**
Distance:	11.3 miles
Time:	1.5 – 3 hours
Type:	Loop
Surface:	Singletrack, bike path, some road
Climbing:	1,200'
Season:	Summer, Fall
Crowds:	Some
Dogs:	Bike path can be crowded

A quick ride along the flank of Mount Crested Butte

Ride Description

The perfect Sunday ride! Start with a big breakfast in town, warm-up slowly with a cruise on the bike path, rock some great technical singletrack on the Upper Loop Trail, and then cruise back into town on the New Deli Trail. The Upper-Upper Loop gets progressively more difficult after the turn to Tony's Trail (mile 4.9). Luckily, there are easy bailout options at mile 4.9, mile 5.2, and mile 6.3. Needless to say, this trail has all of the wonderful views, colorful aspen groves, and stellar riding that we expect from Crested Butte, the mountain biker's paradise.

Driving Directions

Start the loop from the Chamber of Commerce in downtown Crested Butte at the intersection of CO-135 (6th Street) and Elk Avenue.

Riding Directions - see map on page 239

E1 - 0.0   Start riding east on Elk Avenue from the intersection of Elk and 6th Street.

E2 - 0.3   At the cattle-guard, turn left onto a gravel bike path.

E3 - 0.6   Pass a nice dirt-jumping park on the left and continue across the small bridge and onto a paved bike path.

E4 - 2.5   Turn right on Gothic Road.

E5 - 3.0   Turn right on Hunter Hill Road. In one block turn right again to stay on Hunter Hill Road.

E6 - 3.7   Come to a small dirt parking lot. Find the sign for the Upper Loop (Trail #435) and follow the singletrack.

E7 - 4.2   The trail forks, but rejoins in 0.15 miles. Go either way.

E8 - 4.9   Continue straight. Tony's Trail leads right and will quickly take you back to Crested Butte (no dogs allowed on this trail).

E9 - 5.2   Head left on the Upper-Upper Trail. (The Upper-Upper is significantly harder than the Upper Trail. If you turn right here you can connect with Country Club Drive and take this to CO-135, thus shortening the ride and avoiding the most difficult sections.)

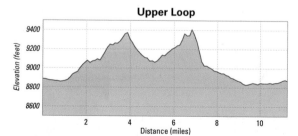

E10 - 6.3 Stay left on the Upper-Upper Trail. (The Whetstone Vista trail goes right and connects with Brush Creek Road.)

E11 - 7.4 Go right on Brush Creek Road.

E12 - 9.2 Turn right onto CO-135.

E13 - 9.4 Make a right on the New Deli Trail (aka "Jim Deli Trail") that parallels the highway.

E14 - 10.7 The Deli Trail ends behind the school. Wander west until it is possible to turn right onto 6th Street and ride back to the starting point.

Timmy Kughler just before the crux on the 401 Trail.   photo: Fredrik Marmsater

(F) Teocalli Ridge ★★★★☆

(7 miles northeast of Crested Butte)

Technical Difficulty:	◆◆
Physical Difficulty:	**Strenuous**
Distance:	10.4 miles
Time:	2 – 4 hours
Type:	Loop
Surface:	Singletrack, dirt road
Climbing:	2,300'
Season:	Summer, Fall
Crowds:	Some
Dogs:	🐕

A long climb on a dirt road brings you to one of the steepest, fastest descents in Crested Butte

Ride Description

At the water park, children face a difficult decision: they can choose the water slide that is really long but reasonably boring, or they can opt for the thrilling slide that drops straight down, but only lasts for two seconds. Riders who prefer the short-but-terrifying option will enjoy Teocalli Ridge. This ride gains 2,300 feet in about two hours of struggle on a dirt road, then loses all that elevation in two miles of crazy-fast singletrack. The riding isn't overly technical, but it is very steep and riders will need good bike handling skills to enjoy the descent.

Driving Directions

From Crested Butte, drive southeast on CO-135 for about 2 miles. Turn left on Brush Creek Road (County-738) and go 4.6 miles. Park at the intersection of FS-738.2a and FS-738. If there is no parking available here, drive a short distance down FS-738 for additional parking.

Riding Directions - see map on page 239

F1 - 0.0   Turn left and ride uphill on FS-738.2a (West Brush Creek Road).

F2 - 0.9   Turn right onto FS-557 (signed for Teocalli Ridge).

F3 - 2.0   Cross a stream. (This stream is often deep enough to require wading.)

F4 - 4.3   Turn right onto the Teocalli Mountain Trail (#554). Now it's time for some really steep climbing!

F5 - 5.4   Turn right on the Teocalli Ridge Trail (#557). Climb for awhile longer, and then fasten your seatbelt for a rip-roaring descent.

F6 - 9.2   Turn right on a dirt road.

F7 - 9.5   Turn right on Brush Creek Road.

F8 - 10.4   Arrive back at the intersection of FS-738 and FS-738.2a.

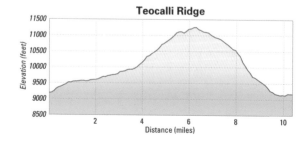

Teocalli Ridge

ⓖ Crested Butte Resort ★★★★☆

(3 miles north of Crested Butte)

Hours:	9:00 - 4:00, seven days a week. Late-June through Late-August
Price:	$25 * As of 2011
Vertical Relief:	860'

Description

What Crested Butte Resort lacks in quantity of trails, is made up for in quality. Avery, their main downhill course, is spectacular, with enough jumps, drops, and rock gardens to challenge expert riders. Ride carefully; there is an optional 20-foot drop waiting around a corner! Wood's Trail, their freeride trail, has a huge wall-ride and other exciting jumps and features. Unfortunately, this trail requires a long ride on a paved road to get back to the base of the chairlift. Cross-country riders will be impressed by Westside, Prospector, and Columbine, which all feature classic Crested Butte singletrack through aspens and meadows. Uphill riding is allowed on most of these trails, so strong riders can create some great loops without taking the chairlift. More trail construction was in progress as this book went to press, so it is possible that Crested Butte Resort could be a five-star downhilling destination within a few years.

Driving Directions

From Crested Butte, head north on 6th Street, which becomes Gothic Road, and go about 2.5 miles. Turn right on Treasury Road and park in the large ski resort parking area. Parking is free during the summer season.

Breaking the sound barrier during the Wildflower Rush race at Crested Butte Resort.   photo: Brandon Turman

Crested Butte & Gunnison

(H)Deer Creek Trail ★★★★★

(Starts in Crested Butte)

Technical Difficulty:	◆
Physical Difficulty:	**Strenuous**
Distance:	26.7 miles
Time:	4 – 6 hours
Type:	Loop
Surface:	Singletrack, dirt road, paved road
Climbing:	4,000'
Season:	Summer
Crowds:	Some
Dogs:	🐕 *

This odyssey circumnavigates Mount Crested Butte on scenic roads and spectacular singletrack

Ride Description

This isn't just a ride - it's an adventure! The views are among the best in the state and there are sections of legendary single-track. Unfortunately, it's not all peaches-and-cream: the loop climbs for miles on dirt roads, only to climb even more on the Deer Creek Trail. Nevertheless, riders who can tolerate the physical abuse will simply love this ride.

Riders can eliminate much of the paved road riding and add some great technical singletrack by starting at the top (north end) of the Upper Loop Trail. Ride this to Brush Creek Road, intersecting the main ride description at mile 4.0.

A car shuttle can be used to avoid the road-riding involved in the complete loop. This decreases the mileage, but it's difficult to avoid the climbing. It is best to leave a car in Downtown Crested Butte and drive to mile 7.8 of the ride description. Owners of high-clearance trucks might be able to drive all the way to the start of the singletrack at mile 10.1.

*Dogs are allowed, but the ride has a few sections along busy highways. Riders who want to bring dogs along should set up a car shuttle.

Driving Directions

Start at the visitor center in downtown Crested Butte. It is located at the corner of 6th Street (CO-135) and Elk Avenue.

Riding Directions - see map on page 239

H1 - 0.0 From the visitor center, head south on CO-135 for several miles. (As you leave downtown Crested Butte, it's possible to bear slightly left by the school and find a bike path that parallels CO-135.)

H2 - 2.1 Turn left on Brush Creek Road.

H3 - 4.0 Continue on Brush Creek Road as the Upper-Upper Trail goes left.

H4 - 4.7 Bear right to stay on Brush Creek Road (FS-738) as West Brush Creek Road goes left.

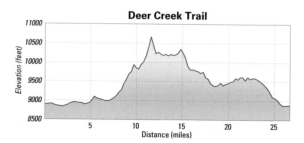

H5 - 7.8 Come to a Y-junction. Turn left on West Brush Creek Road, FS-738.2A. (The right fork goes to Pearl Pass Road, FS-738). There are a few places to park here and some additional parking a short distance down Pearl Pass Road.

H6 - 8.7 Go left on Deer Creek Road (sometimes signed FS-528, sometimes FS-582).

H7 - 9.7 Turn left on the Deer Creek Trail (still a dirt road).

H8 - 10.1 Start the Deer Creek Trail singletrack. It's beautiful, but the first few miles involve some tough climbing. Keep following signs for the Deer Creek Trail as you enjoy the scenery.

H9 - 18.5 Arrive at a dirt road. Turn right.

H10 - 19.2 Turn left on Gothic Road (a gravel road).

H11 - 22.4 Continue straight on Gothic Road as you pass the Snodgrass Trailhead. *(If you still have energy, ride the Snodgrass Trail and turn left on Washington Gulch Road.)*

H1 - 26.7 Gothic Road turns into 6th Street as you roll triumphantly back to the visitor center in Crested Butte.

Mount Crested Butte as seen from the Snodgrass Trail.

Crested Butte & Gunnison

Pearl Pass

(Starts in Crested Butte)

Technical Difficulty:	◆◆
Physical Difficulty:	**Insanely Strenuous**
Distance:	37.7 miles
Time:	5 – 10 hours
Type:	Shuttle
Surface:	Jeep road
Climbing/ Descending:	4,100'/3,900' (one-way)
Season:	Summer
Crowds:	Some
Dogs:	🐕

A massive epic from Crested Butte to Aspen

Ride Description

Pearl Pass and Taylor Pass are the two primary mountain biking routes from Crested Butte to Aspen. Taylor Pass is easier and involves more singletrack, but Pearl Pass has more historic charm. Many people trace the birth of Colorado mountain biking to the summer of 1976, when a group crazies from Crested Butte rode over Pearl Pass on heavy single speed "clunker" bikes. Even with a modern mountain bike, the ride over Pearl Pass is a huge undertaking. The route is long, rocky, and steep with several lengthy sections that are completely unrideable. It's not all suffering, though; the views are incredible and the route is generally easy to follow. Additionally, though the ride is quite exposed to the sun, there are frequent stream crossings to keep you cool, even on a hot day.

It is possible to drive the first 8 miles of this ride with a low-clearance vehicle, and much further with a truck or jeep. However, to be awarded points for the "Crested Butte to Aspen" ride, contestants must start in town – sorry, those are the rules. There are a number of ways to complete the ride, but the classic, and most historic, method is to start in Crested Butte, ride all the way to Aspen, spend the night in Aspen, and then drive or bike back to Crested Butte the next day. For a logistically simpler ride, just ride up to Pearl Pass and turn around. Alternatively, riders can make a giant 38-mile loop by riding over Pearl Pass, turning right on Express Creek Road, and riding back over Taylor Pass and Star Pass (see next ride).

Driving Directions

Start in downtown Crested Butte. A good place to park is at the visitor center at the corner of 6th Street (CO-135) and Elk Avenue. However, if you'd like to make the ride shorter, it is possible to drive to mile 8.0 in a low-clearance vehicle and significantly further in a high-clearance truck. To start this shorter option, head south from Crested Butte on CO-135 for 2.0 miles. Turn left on Brush Creek Road and go 5.6 miles. At a Y-intersection, turn right on FS-738 and park at a small grassy pullout on the right.

Riding Directions - see map on page 250

I1 - 0.0 From the visitor center, head south on 6th Avenue and continue along CO-135.

I2 - 2.1 Turn left on Brush Creek Road.

I3 - 8.0 Bear right to stay on Brush Creek Road (FS-738) as West Brush Creek Road goes left.

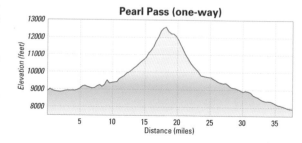

I4 - 8.7   Go left to stay on Brush Creek Road as a rough, unmarked road goes right.

I5 - 10.9   Turn left on Pearl Pass Road as FS-738.2b goes straight.

I6 - 14.0   Come to a Y-intersection: turn right to stay on Pearl Pass Road (FS-738)

I7 - 18.2   Arrive at Pearl Pass! Carefully ride down the steep, rocky road.

I8 - 21.1   Bear right on Upper Castle Creek Road as an unmarked road goes left.

I9 - 24.1   Turn left on Castle Creek Road towards Ashcroft. From here, follow a paved road all the way to Aspen.

I10 - 37.7 Turn right on CO-82 and arrive in Aspen!!

The author posing atop Pearl Pass.

Crested Butte & Gunnison

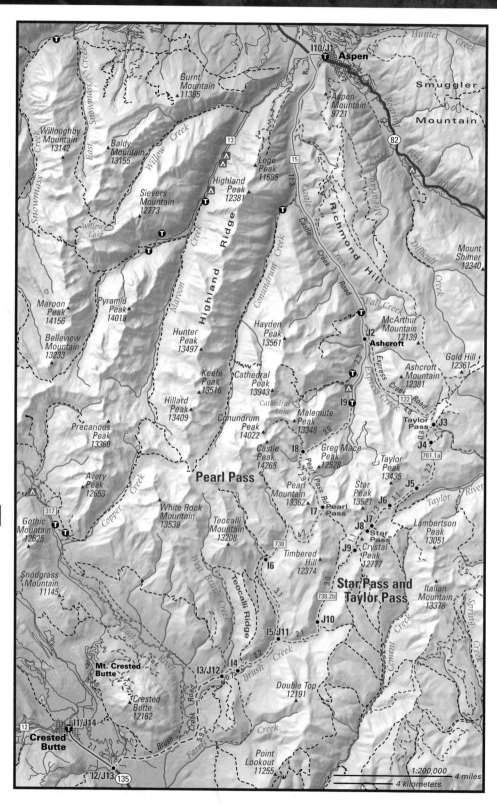

Hunter Creek

I10/J1
Aspen

Smuggler

Aspen
Mountain
9721

Mountain

82

Willoughby
Mountain
13142

Burnt
Mountain
11385

Baldy
Mountain
13155

13

Loge
Peak
11685

15

Richmond Hill

Mount
Shimer
12340

Sievers
Mountain
12773

Highland
Peak
12381

Highland Ridge

Castle Creek

Fall Creek

Maroon
Peak
14156

Pyramid
Peak
14018

Hunter
Peak
13497

Hayden
Peak
13561

McArthur
Mountain
12139

J2
Ashcroft

Gold Hill
12361

Belleview
Mountain
13233

Keefe
Peak
13516

Cathedral
Peak
13943

2.3

Ashcroft
Mountain
12381

Cathedral
Lake

Conundrum
Peak
14022

Malemute
Peak
13348

122

I9

Taylor
Pass

J3

Hillard
Peak
13409

3.0

0.8

J4

Precarious
Peak
13360

Castle
Peak
14265

I8

Greg Mace
Peak
12528

Taylor
Peak
13435

761.1a

J5

Avery
Peak
12653

White Rock
Mountain
13539

Pearl
Mountain
13362

2.9

Star
Peak
13521

J6

1.1

Taylor River

317

Pearl Pass

I7

Pearl
Pass

J7

Lambertson
Peak
13051

Gothic
Mountain
12625

Teocalli
Mountain
13208

4.2

738

Timbered
Hill
12374

J8

Star
Pass

J9

Crystal
Peak
12777

Snodgrass
Mountain
11145

I6

3.0

**Star Pass and
Taylor Pass**

Italian
Mountain
13378

Teocalli Ridge

3.1

738.2b

J10

I5/J11

2.1

Mt. Crested
Butte

I4

I3/J12

2.2

0.7

Brush Creek

Double Top
12191

12

*Crested
Butte
12162*

I1/J14

2.1

**Crested
Butte**

5.9

Point
Lookout
11255

I2/J13

135

Farris Creek

1:200,000   4 miles

4 kilometers

Ⓙ Star Pass and Taylor Pass ★★★★↙

Technical Difficulty: ◆

Physical Difficulty: **Very Strenuous**

Distance: 38.8 miles

Climbing/ Descending: 6,700'/5,700' (one-way)

The route over Star Pass and Taylor Pass is a very difficult ride, yet it is significantly easier than the ride over Pearl Pass. It may not have the same history as Pearl Pass, but it has significantly less loose rock (though it still has plenty) and involves much more singletrack riding. Since the road from Aspen to Taylor Pass is reasonably smooth, this is a better ride going from Aspen to Crested Butte, since riding in the opposite direction would involve climbing tough singletrack and descending the road. That said, both directions offer easier and better riding than the arduous Pearl Pass. The ride directions assume that you are starting on the Aspen side, but the route is straightforward to reverse.

Riding Directions

J1 - 0.0   From Aspen, head west on CO-128 and go about 0.5 miles. At the roundabout, turn left on Castle Creek Road.

J2 - 11.3   Turn left on Express Creek Road (County-15C). Go about 0.2 miles and turn right to stay on Express Creek Road (FS-122).

J3 - 16.1   Arrive at Taylor Pass! Turn right on an unmarked dirt road.

J4 - 16.9   Turn right onto Taylor Pass Divide Road (FS-761.1a).

J5 - 19.1   Bear right on Taylor Pass Divide Road (FS-761.1a) as Taylor Pass Divide Trail (#440) goes left.

J6 - 20.2   Turn left on East Brush Creek Trail (#400).

J7 - 21.5   Come to a Y-intersection and turn right on East Brush Creek Trail as Crystal Peak Trail goes left.

J8 - 21.7   Arrive at the top of Star Pass.

J9 - 22.8   Head right on East Brush Creek Trail as Doubletop Trail (#405) goes left.

J10 - 25.8   Come to a dirt road and bear right.

J11 - 27.9   Turn left onto Brush Creek Road.

J12 - 30.7   Turn left on Brush Creek Road as West Brush Creek Road goes right.

J13 - 37.6   Turn right on CO-135.

J14 - 38.8   Arrive in Crested Butte.

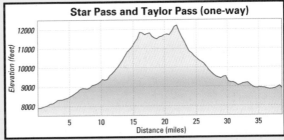

Star Pass and Taylor Pass (one-way)

Crested Butte & Gunnison

(K) Reno-Flag-Bear-Deadman ★★★★☆

(14 miles SE of Crested Butte)

Technical Difficulty:	◆
Physical Difficulty:	**Strenuous**
Distance:	19.4 miles
Time:	4 – 6 hours
Type:	Loop
Surface:	Singletrack, dirt road
Climbing:	3,800′
Season:	Summer
Crowds:	Some
Dogs:	

Silly name, seriously good singletrack

Ride Description

Reno–Flag–Bear–Deadman (named for the trails that compose the loop, in the order they are ridden) is a Crested Butte classic. A long climb up a dirt road leads to great singletrack riding through gorgeous meadows and forests. This trail is open to motorcycle use, so be prepared for some loose terrain and some motorbikes. Make sure your brakes are in good shape for the steep descent down Deadman Gulch Trail.

Driving Directions

From Crested Butte, take CO-135 south for 6.7 miles. Turn left on Cement Creek Road (FS-740) and drive 6.9 miles to the small Deadman's Gulch Trailhead on the right.

Riding Directions

K1 - 0.0   From the Deadman Trailhead, start riding up (north) FS-740 (Reno Divide Road).

K2 - 1.3   Stay on Reno Divide Road as the singletrack bends right. (Do not continue straight on the Cement Creek Trail.)

K3 - 1.7   Turn right on a dirt road (FS-759) and continue to climb.

K4 - 5.8   Arrive at Reno Divide (11,146′), a good spot for lunch. Find the sign for Flag Creek Trail (#422) and follow it downhill. Enjoy a great downhill section!

K5 - 8.7   Make a right on the Bear Creek Trail (#415) and cross a creek. Prepare for a long climb.

K6 - 11.1   Come to a four-way intersection and turn left on a dirt road.

K7 - 11.8   At a large junction, turn left on the Bear Creek Trail singletrack (trail #415).

K8 - 13.2   Pass through a barbed wire gate.

K9 - 15.0   Turn right on the Deadman Gulch Trail (#420).

K10 - 17.3 Continue straight on Deadman Gulch as Cement Mountain Trail (#553) goes left.

K11 - 17.5 Continue straight on Deadman Gulch Trail as Reno Ridge Trail (#607) goes right.

K1 - 19.4   Arrive back at the Deadman Trailhead.

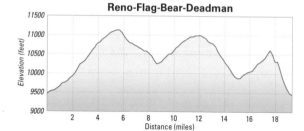

Reno-Flag-Bear-Deadman

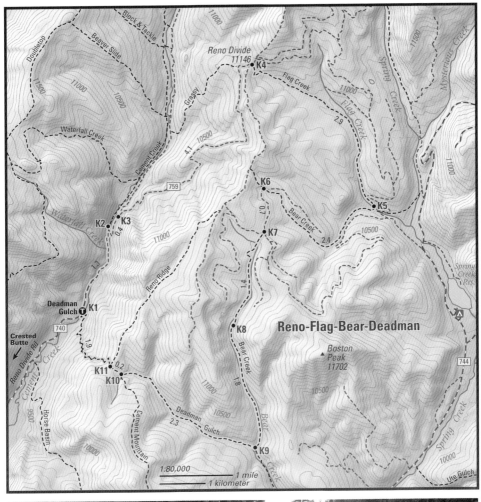

Curt Stevens splashes through a summer rainstorm on the Bear Creek Trail.

Ⓛ Doctor Park ★★★★★

(25 miles SE of Crested Butte)

Technical Difficulty:	◆
Physical Difficulty:	**Strenuous**
Distance:	21.1 miles
Time:	3.5 – 6 hours
Type:	Loop (shuttle possible)
Surface:	Singletrack, dirt road
Climbing:	3,500'
Season:	Summer
Crowds:	Few
Dogs:	

A few hours of climbing up dirt roads earns one of the best descents in Colorado

Ride Description

This ride begins with 12 miles of progressively steeper riding on washboarded dirt roads, but your efforts are rewarded with glorious singletrack. The riding on the Gunnison Spur of the Colorado Trail is mostly downhill, and it is phenomenal. The trail is generally smooth and fast, but there are some exciting technical sections as well. The climbing can be reduced considerably by leaving a car at the trailhead on County-742 and shuttling up Spring Creek Road until the stream crossing (mile 9.3).

Driving Directions

From Crested Butte, head southeast on CO-135 for 17.1 miles. Turn left on County-742 (Taylor River Road) and drive 7.5 miles to a parking area on the left. The parking area is about 0.5 miles after Spring Creek Road and just before the road bends right and crosses the Taylor River. (If you get to Onemile Campground or Rosy Lane Campground, you've gone a little too far.)

Riding Directions

L1 - 0.0 Begin riding west (back towards Crested Butte) on Taylor River Road (County-742).

L2 - 0.6 Turn right on Spring Creek Road (County-744).

L3 - 2.5 The road becomes gravel.

L4 - 9.3 Go right on FS 554 and cross the creek.

L5 - 10.2 Turn left on FS 550. (If you want to shorten the ride, turn right onto FS 554.)

L6 - 11.6 Head right onto Trail #550.1b

L7 - 12.3 Turn right onto the Gunnison Spur of the Colorado Trail (GSCT). This is where the fun begins!

L8 - 14.0 Turn right at a junction to stay on the GSCT as singletrack signed "No ATVs" goes left. This singletrack is a nice alternate route and rejoins the GSCT in about 2 miles.

L9 - 14.3 Turn left to stay on the GSCT.

L10 - 15.5 Continue straight as the "No ATV's" trail (see mile 14.0) joins on the left. Take a break here, have a snack, and get ready for 5 miles of nonstop downhill fun!

L11 - 20.5 The singletrack finally ends. Turn right on the dirt road.

L1 - 21.1 Go right on County-742 and arrive at your car!

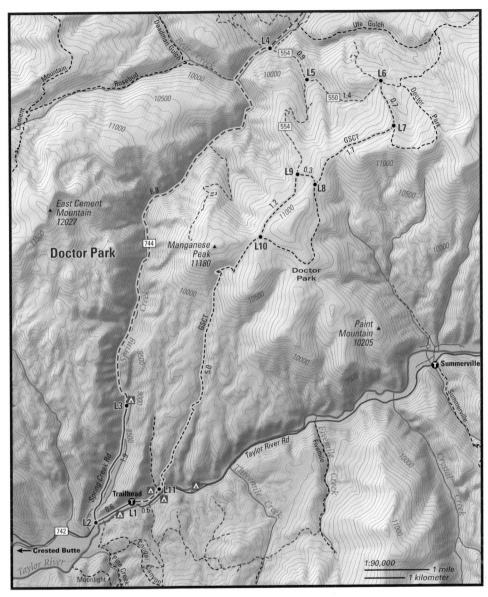

Doctor Park

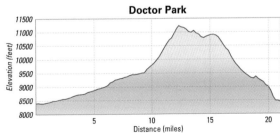

Ⓜ Hartman Rocks ★★★★☆

(4 miles southwest of Gunnison)

Technical Difficulty:	
Physical Difficulty:	**Moderate**
Distance:	8.9 miles
Time:	1.5 – 3 hours
Type:	Loop
Surface:	Singletrack
Climbing:	1,500′
Season:	Spring, Fall
Crowds:	Some
Dogs:	🐕

Great, smooth riding through the sagebrush with occasional rock-rolling

Ride Description

Gunnison is a town for all seasons! When it's hot, there's plenty of great riding in nearby Crested Butte. When the autumn snow begins to fly in the high country, the riding at Hartman Rocks is perfect. The sandy soil doesn't get too muddy and the lack of trees means that the trails dry quickly. When winter does finally set in, several of the roads are groomed for cross-country skiing. Most of the trails are technically easy, consisting of smooth singletrack without many long climbs. However, there are several more technical trails with huge rounded rock features. This suggested loop is just the tip of the iceberg of the riding possibilities at Hartman Rocks – go forth and explore!

Driving Directions

From Gunnison, head west on Tomichi Avenue (US-50) for about 1.5 miles. Turn left on County-38 and go 2.5 miles. Turn right into the Hartman Rocks parking area.

Riding Directions

M1 - 0.0 From the trailhead, negotiate a tangle of singletrack and start riding on Jack's Trail.

M2 - 0.8 Turn left on the dirt road.

M3 - 1.5 Make your second left onto another dirt road.

M4 - 1.7 Go right onto the Rocky Ridge Trail (#9).

M5 - 2.9 At a T-intersection, turn left. Ride down a short hill and find the start of Broken Shovel Trail.

M6 - 3.7 Cross a dirt road and continue straight onto Josho's Trail (#17).

M7 - 5.9 Continue straight across a dirt road onto The Rattlesnake Trail (#18).

M8 - 7.1 The singletrack ends at a dirt road. Make a left, go a short distance, and make another left on another dirt road.

M4 - 7.6 Turn right onto Beck's Trail (#7).

M9 - 8.0 Cross a dirt road and continue onto The Notch Trail (#2). Follow this back down to the trailhead.

M1 - 8.9 Arrive back at the trailhead.

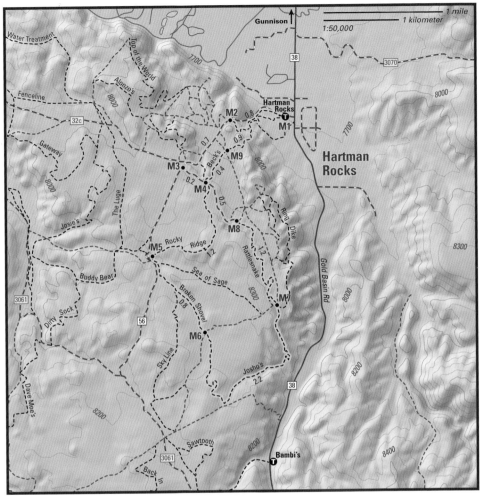

Gunnison

1 mile
1 kilometer
1:50,000

Water Treatment

Top of the World

7700

3070

8000

Alonzo's

Fenceline

8000

32c

Gateway

8000

The Luge

Josie's

Buddy Bear

3061

Dirty Sock

56

Dave Moe's

8200

Sawtooth

3061

Back In

M2 0.8

Hartman
Rocks

M1

0.7

M3 0.2

Back's

0.9

M9

0.4

M4

0.5

M8

0.1

Rocky

Ridge

M5

Sea of Sage

1.2

Broken Shovel

0.8

M6

Sky Line

Josho's

2.2

38

Bambi's

Ring Dike

Rattlesnake

1.2

8300

M7

8000

Gold Basin Rd

8200

8400

7700

8000

8300

Hartman
Rocks

8000

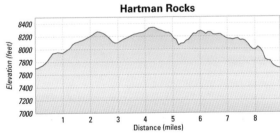

Hartman Rocks

Elevation (feet)

8400
8200
8000
7800
7600
7400
7200
7000

1 2 3 4 5 6 7 8

Distance (miles)

Fine desert scenery at Hartman Rocks.

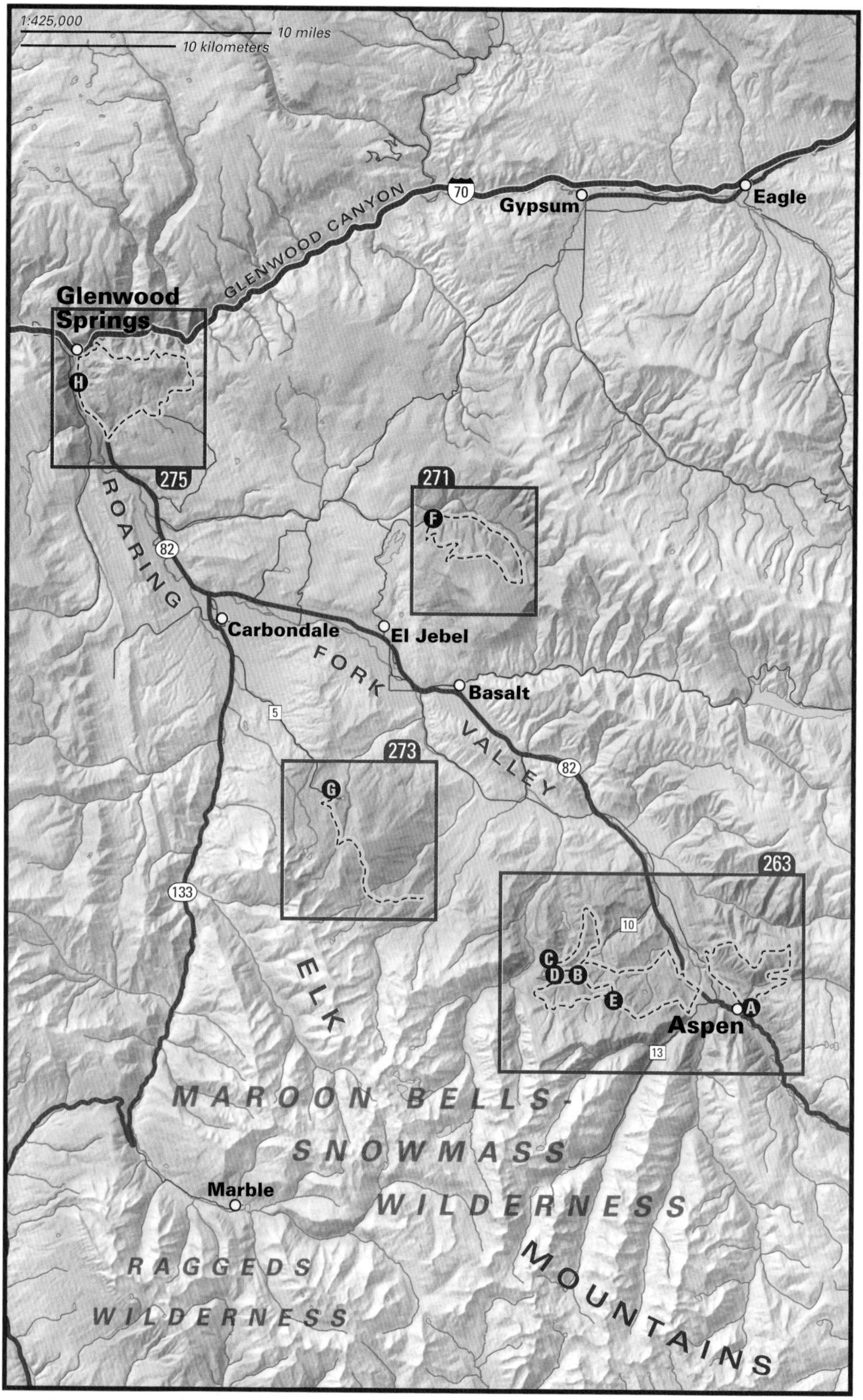
1:425,000
10 miles
10 kilometers
70
Gypsum
Eagle
GLENWOOD CANYON
Glenwood Springs
H
275
ROARING
82
271
F
Carbondale
El Jebel
FORK
Basalt
5
VALLEY
82
273
G
263
133
10
C
D
B
E
A
Aspen
13
ELK
MAROON BELLS-
SNOWMASS
WILDERNESS
Marble
MOUNTAINS
RAGGEDS
WILDERNESS

Aspen & the Roaring Fork Valley

"There he goes. One of God's own prototypes. A high-powered mutant of some kind never even considered for mass production. Too weird to live, and too rare to die."
– Hunter S. Thompson

Aspen has the reputation for being a playground for millionaires wearing fur coats and arriving in private jets. This might be true, but it's totally beside the point; Aspen and the rest of the Roaring Fork Valley are home to some of the best mountain biking in Colorado! Aspen, Snowmass, and Carbondale all boast excellent singletrack rides that start right from town. Snowmass has one of the best trail systems anywhere, with over 50 miles of great singletrack winding through the ski area and encircling the town.

As one might expect, the ski destinations of Aspen and Snowmass get a lot of snow, and it takes the hills a long time to melt out in the spring. The higher elevation trails often remain damp well into June. The northern end of the valley is lower in elevation, providing a longer riding season. Additionally, if it's raining in Aspen, the blissful desert riding near Grand Junction and Fruita is a quick drive west on Interstate-70.

Accommodations

Like most things in the Roaring Fork Valley, accommodation options are fabulously expensive near Aspen and become more affordable as you move "down valley" through Basalt, Carbondale, and Glenwood Springs. If you can afford to stay in Aspen or Snowmass, by all means do so; they are beautiful towns. Carbondale is small and charming and, being a little off the highway, is much more casual. Located next to I-70, Glenwood Springs offers an assortment of inexpensive motels and is home to one of the few hostels in Colorado.

There are many developed campgrounds in the Roaring Fork Valley, but they tend to fill up quickly on popular weekends. There are several campgrounds on Independence Pass Road near Aspen. Free camping options are limited around Aspen, but more plentiful around Basalt and Carbondale. Basalt Mountain (Ride F) offers some nice free camping spots.

Aspen

The Glenwood Springs Hostel
1021 Grand Avenue, Glenwood Springs.
970-945-8545   Located on CO-82, this cute hostel offers bunks for $16 per night.

Bike Shops

Many of the ski shops in Aspen and Snowmass convert into bike shops during the summer. There are several places to rent mountain bikes near the base of Snowmass Resort.

Mountain Sports Outlet
215 6th Street, Glenwood Springs. 970-945-5001
Huge stock of bikes, parts, and clothing. Rentals available.

Ajax Bike and Sport (two locations)
571 CO-133, Carbondale and
635 E. Hyman Avenue, Aspen. 970-963-0128
Large, full-service shops, with locations in both Aspen and Carbondale.

Eats and Drinks

Main Street Bakery and Café
201 East Main Street, Aspen. 970-925-6446
Great breakfast and lunch with prices that are somewhere closer to normal than most restaurants in Aspen. The community table is a great place to chat with the locals about your most recent Learjet purchase.

The Aspen Brewing Company
555 North Mill Street, Aspen. 970-920-2739
One of the few breweries in the Roaring Fork Valley, the Aspen Brewing Company offers delicious beer in a charming, no-frills taproom.

The Village Smithy Restaurant
26 South Third Street, Carbondale. 970-963-9990
The best place to get breakfast within 100 miles. Also serves lunch and (sometimes) dinner.

Hunter S. Thompson (1937—2005)

A great American author and creator of Gonzo Journalism, Hunter Thompson lived in the small hamlet of Woody Creek, just outside of Aspen, form the late 1960s until his death. The prototypical mountain-dwelling Colorado radical, he loved alcohol, drugs, guns, and hated authority. In 1970 he ran for sheriff of Pitkin County (the county containing Aspen, Snowmass, and Basalt), shaving his head so that he could refer to the republican candidate as "my long haired opponent." His platform included renaming Aspen "Fat City," replacing the streets with grass, and legalizing drugs. Though he carried the city of Aspen itself, he narrowly lost in the countywide election.

The Rio Grande Trail

Built on the old railroad bed on the Denver and Rio Grande Western Railroad, The Rio Grande Trail runs 42 miles from Aspen to Glenwood Springs. Most sections are paved and the rest are compacted gravel. It is open to hiking, biking, horse riding, and skateboarding. The Roaring Fork Transportation Authority (RFTA) runs buses that can carry bikes (for a $2 fee). So, those wishing to ride all the way from Aspen to Glenwood Springs can take the bus from Glenwood to Aspen and ride back down the valley on their bikes. In the winter, many sections of the trail are plowed for biking and some are groomed for cross-country skiing.

Aspen

Sunnyside Loop ★★★★★

(Starts in Aspen)

Technical Difficulty:	
Physical Difficulty:	**Strenuous**
Distance:	16.0 miles
Time:	4 – 6 hours
Type:	Loop
Surface:	Singletrack, dirt road, bike path
Climbing:	3,500'
Season:	Summer, Fall
Crowds:	Some
Dogs:	

A savage climb leads to excellent singletrack and mind-blowing views

"I hate to advocate drugs, alcohol, violence, or insanity to anyone, but they've always worked for me."

– Hunter S. Thompson

Ride Description

The Sunnyside Trail cuts across a steep hillside and provides views of all four ski-hills through a canopy of trembling aspen leaves. The Sunnyside Trail itself consists of great technical riding and is mostly downhill. Unfortunately, there is not an easy way to reach the top of Sunnyside Trail. This loop starts with a tough climb up Smuggler Mountain Road, drops into Hunter Valley on the delightful Iowa Shaft Trail, and then climbs another dirt road to the start of the Sunnyside Trail. By the time riders arrive back in Apsen, they will have completed over 3,500 vertical feet climbing – woah!

Driving Directions

From downtown Aspen, head east on CO-82. Turn left on Park Avenue and go about 0.2 miles. Turn right on Park Circle and go another 0.2 miles. As the road makes a broad left turn, park in the gravel pull-out on the left. There is additional parking a short distance up Smuggler Mountain Road.

Riding Directions - see map on page 263

A1 - 0.0 From the parking lot, ride up Smuggler Mountain Road.

A2 - 1.5 Go left on the Hunter Creek Cutoff (a dirt road).

A3 - 2.0 Go left again on Hunter Creek Cutoff as Smugglers Loop goes right.

A4 - 2.3 Bust right on the excellent Iowa Shaft singletack.

A5 - 3.3 Make a right on the Hunter Creek Trail. Go 0.1 miles, cross the creek at a bridge, and turn left on the Hunter Valley singletrack. Continue straight on Hunter Valley as numerous trails (including Sunnyside Plunge) intersect.

A6 - 4.3 Make a right and climb steeply on a dirt road (Hunter Creek Road).

A7 - 5.3 Continue on the road past the Sunnyside Plunge Trail.

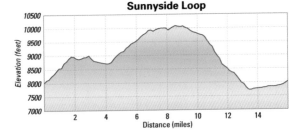

Sunnyside Loop

Elevation (feet) / Distance (miles)

A8 - 5.5   At a Y-intersection, turn left on Four Corners Rd as another dirt road goes right.

A9 - 6.5   Arrive at Four Corners. Turn left on the Sunnyside Trail (#1987). Go about 0.1 miles and turn left on the unmarked "Secret Trail."

A10 - 7.2   The Secret Trail ends at the Plunge Trail. Turn right on Plunge, ride a short distance, and then turn left on the Sunnyside Trail (an old dirt road).

A11 - 7.9   Turn left on the Sunnyside Trail as the Shadyside Trail goes right.

A12 - 10.4   Continue straight on Sunnyside as Shadyside rejoins from the right.

A13 - 13.4   Arrive at the paved Rio Grande Trail and turn left, following the bike path.

A14 - 15.4   Turn left at a sign for "Hunter Creek Trail," and immediately turn right onto Red Mountain Road. Continue straight onto Gibson Road, then onto Park Circle.

A1 - 16.0   Arrive back at the parking area.

Ⓑ Snowmass Resort ★★★★☆

Hours:	10:00 - 4:00, mid-June through early September
Price:	$34 full day (As of 2010)
Vertical Relief:	1,400'

"Some people will tell you that slow is good – but I'm here to tell you that fast is better. I've always believed this, in spite of the trouble it's caused me."

–Hunter S. Thompson

Description

Snowmass Resort has long been famous for its excellent cross-country trails, including the Government Trail (which runs from Snowmass to Aspen). Recently, Snowmass has decided to become a downhilling destination as well. In 2010, they switched their lift-served operation from a small chairlift on the west side of the mountain to the massive gondola on the east side and started building downhill trails complete with jumps and berms. In 2011, there were only a few true downhill trails, but Snowmass has plans to expand and it will be exciting to see what trails they build in the coming years.

Snowmass is an excellent vacation destination for the whole family. Without getting in the car, riders can take a quick loop on the Rim Trail, complete an epic ride to Aspen on the Government Trail, or strap on a full-face helmet and enjoy the lift-served terrain. Being a ski resort, Snowmass Village offers a good assortment of restaurants, bars, and shops. In the summer, mountain bikers can enjoy hotel rooms that are offered at a fraction of the price that skiers pay during the winter.

Driving Directions

(Follow directions for Ride D, The XC Racecourse Loop on page 266.)

Aspen

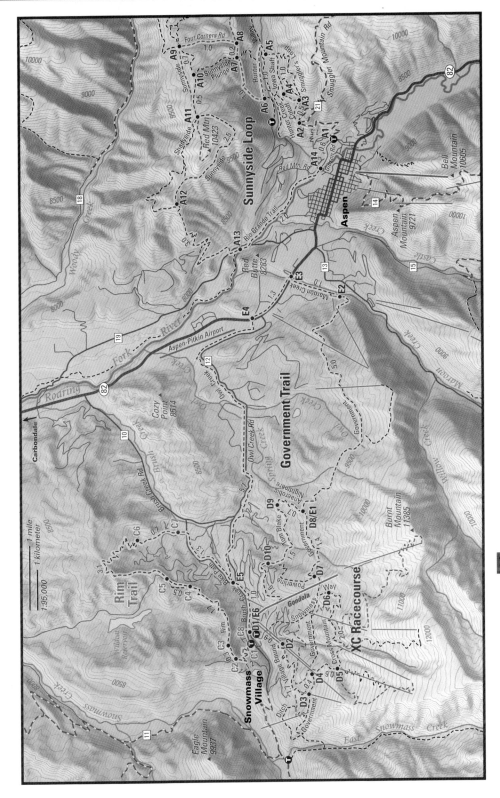

Aspen

Ⓒ The Rim Trail ★★★★★

(Starts in Snowmass)

Technical Difficulty:	
Physical Difficulty:	**Strenuous**
Distance:	10.3 miles
Time:	2 – 4 hours
Type:	Loop
Surface:	Singletrack, bike path
Climbing:	2,100'
Season:	Summer, Fall
Crowds:	Crowded
Dogs:	

Beautiful wildflowers, stunning views, and smooth winding singletrack

"When the going gets weird, the weird turn pro."
                                         –Hunter S. Thompson

Ride Description

The perfect afternoon ride, the Rim Trail serves up hearty portions of smooth singletrack, eye-popping wildflowers, and fast descents, then tops it all off with a convenient bike path that leads right back to the trailhead. The eastern half of the rim trail is *closed from October 30 through June 20* for elk calving, but the first half is open year-round. To ride just the first half, simply turn right on Sinclair Road at mile 3.2 and take this back to Brush Creek Road. This is also a good option for riders looking for a shorter and easier ride.

The directions below describe riding the Rim Trail by starting at the western end. This is a nice way to complete the ride because it involves some climbing at the beginning and some climbing on the bike path at the end. To get all of the climbing out of the way at the start of the ride, simply park at the Rec Center on Brush Creek Road and start the ride at mile 7.5

Driving Directions

This trail starts in Snowmass. As you are heading into Snowmass on Brush Creek Road, continue past the main parking lots and turn right on Divide Road. Go about 0.1 mile and park in the small pullout on the left.

Riding Directions - see map on page 263

C1 - 0.0 From the pullout, head down the road for 200 feet, then turn left on the Rim Trail.

C2 - 1.2 Come to an unmarked fork and go right.

C3 - 1.5 Bear left on the Rim Trail as an unmarked trail goes right.

C4 - 3.2 Stay right as a sign explains that the more difficult route goes left.

C5 - 3.7 Cross a paved road and find the Rim Trail on the other side. (This section is closed Oct 30 through June 20 for elk calving. If the closure is still in effect, either turn right on the road, or go back the way you came.)

C6 - 6.8 Arrive at the end of the Rim Trail and continue on the dirt road, which soon turns into a paved bike path.

C7 - 7.5   Continue on the bike path past by the Rec Center. Go under Brush Creek Road at an underpass, and then turn right on the Brush Creek Bike Path.

C8 - 9.9   The bike path crosses a bridge and enters a parking lot for an apartment complex. Turn right, ride through the parking lot, and turn left on Brush Creek Road. Turn right on Divide Road and quickly reach the trailhead parking.

Views of the Maroon Bells compete with stunning wildflowers on the Rim Trail.

(D) Snowmass Resort —
XC Racecourse Loop ★★★★★

(Starts in Snowmass)

Technical Difficulty:	
Physical Difficulty:	**Moderate**
Distance:	11.8 miles
Time:	2 – 3 hours
Type:	Loop
Surface:	Singletrack, a little dirt road
Climbing:	2,700′
Season:	Summer, Fall
Crowds:	Some
Dogs:	

Beautiful, well-maintained singletrack with plenty of options

"In a closed society where everybody's guilty, the only crime is getting caught. In a world of thieves, the only final sin is stupidity."
–Hunter S. Thompson

Ride Description

The XC-Racecourse Loop samples some of the best singletrack at Snowmass Resort and offers fantastic views of the valley and into the Maroon Bells Wilderness. The course has changed slightly over the past several years and will likely change again in the future with the planned trail construction at Snowmass. So, either follow these directions or pick up the current trail map at Snowmass Village and follow the highlighted race-course loop. The Government Trail is closed for elk calving from May 15 through June 20. Fortunately, this closure can be avoided by turning onto the Powerline trail at mile 6.3 and taking this down to the Tom Blake Trail.

Driving Directions

From CO-82, head west on Brush Creek Road, following the signs for Snowmass Ski Resort. Stay on Brush Creek Road through several intersections until you reach Snowmass Village. Continue past the main parking garage. When you reach the Village Mall, park in one of several parking lots on the left.

Riding Directions - see map on page 263

D1 - 0.0 From the parking in Village Mall, head to the top of the Sky Cab Gondola (the free gondola that runs from Snowmass Village to the Village Mall). Head uphill on the dirt road and turn right at the junction.

D2 - 0.9 Come to a T-intersection and turn right on a dirt road. In a few hundred feet, turn left on the Village Bound Trail and climb on smooth singletrack.

D3 - 2.6 Cross the Government Trail and continue on Village Bound.

D4 - 3.0 Arrive at a dirt road near a small bike patrol tent. Turn right onto the Cross Mountain Trail, which follows a combination of singletrack and dirt roads. Follow signs to stay on the Cross Mountain Trail.

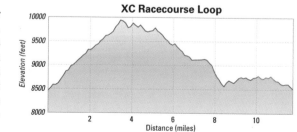

D5 - 3.6 Continue on the Cross Mountain Trail as you pass the Ullrhof Restaurant. There is a short section of dirt road, and then the Cross Mountain Trail becomes technical singletrack.

D6 - 5.6 Bear left on the Snowmass Way Trail. Go a few tenths of a mile, and turn right on the Government Trail. When this ends at a dirt road, turn left on the dirt road and ride a short distance to a small, flat clearing.

D7 - 6.3 Turn right on the Government Trail, passing through a gate. (This section of the Government Trail is closed for Elk Calving from May 15 through June 20.)

D8 - 7.7 Head left on the Anaerobic Nightmare Trail.

D9 - 8.4 Go left on the Tom Blake Trail.

D10 - 9.9 Continue onto the paved East Ridge Road. Make the first left (Faraway Road), go a few hundred feet, and turn right on the Ridge Section of the Tom Blake Trail. Eventually the Tom Blake Trail takes you back to the base of the gondola. Make your way west back to Village Mall.

At Snowmass Resort, narrow singletrack glides through meadows and aspen groves. Can life get any better?

Aspen

Government Trail ★★★★★

(Starts in Snowmass)

Technical Difficulty:	
Physical Difficulty:	**Strenuous**
Distance:	21.7 miles (loop)
Time:	2 – 6 hours
Type:	Loop or shuttle
Surface:	Singletrack, bike path
Climbing:	4,400' (for the loop)
Season:	Summer
Crowds:	Some
Dogs:	

Ride all the way from Snowmass to Aspen on singletrack!

"You better take care of me Lord, if you don't you're gonna have me on your hands."

–Hunter S. Thompson

Ride Description

The Government Trail links the Snowmass ski resort to the town of Aspen via many miles of legendary singletrack through forests and aspen groves. The Government Trail technically begins at the far west end of the Snowmass ski area, however, several sections of the western portion of the Government Trail are tough, loose, and not recommended. So, this version of the Government Trail begins with a sample of the excellent singletrack offered at Snowmass ski area before picking up the Government Trail at the eastern edge of the ski area.

The Government Trail is rocky and steep in places, so most people only ride from Snowmass to Aspen. Of course, you could set up a car shuttle by leaving a car in Aspen. However, there is also a bus that runs frequently between the two towns and can carry bikes. For the hardcore, there is a great bike path that runs all the way from Aspen to Snowmass. Though it gains a significant amount of elevation, the bike path is still a very enjoyable ride. The Government Trail is Closed May 15 through June 20 for elk calving.

Driving Directions

From CO-82, head west on Brush Creek Road, following the signs for Snowmass Ski Resort. Stay on Brush Creek Road through several intersections until you reach Snowmass Village. Continue past the main parking garage. Brush Creek Road makes a broad left turn and takes you to Village Mall, where there are several parking lots on the left.

Riding Directions - see map on page 263

Follow the ride directions for the XC Racecourse Loop (Ride D) until mile 7.7.

E1 - 7.7   Continue straight on the Government Trail as the Anaerobic Nightmare Trail goes left. Enjoy the excellent Government Trail singletrack all the way to Aspen.

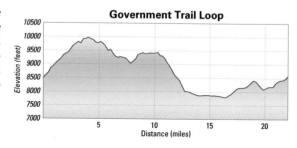

Aspen

E2 - 12.9 Arrive at a paved road in Aspen, turn left, and go about 0.1 miles. Come to a bridge and turn right on a dirt road, following signs for the Maroon Creek Trail. You quickly reach the Maroon Creek Trail, located directly under the middle of the bridge. Turn left on the Maroon Creek singletrack.

E3 - 13.9 As you are passing under another bridge, turn right on a dirt road. Make your first right onto a paved road that passes near a golf course. Turn right again onto the bike path that parallels CO-82.

E4 - 15.2 Turn left on the Owl Creek Trail bike path toward Snowmass Village.

E5 - 20.9 Continue straight onto the Brush Creek Bike Path.

E6 - 21.7 Arrive back in Snowmass Village. Make your way up to Village Mall.

Columbines, aspens, and the Government Trail singletrack.

(F) Basalt Mountain – Cattle Creek Trail ★★★★☆

(15 miles northeast of Carbondale)

Technical Difficulty:	◆
Physical Difficulty:	**Moderate**
Distance:	15.1 miles
Time:	3 – 6 hours
Type:	Loop
Surface:	Singletrack, dirt road
Climbing:	2,800'
Season:	Summer, Fall
Crowds:	Few
Dogs:	

A memorable descent on steep-and-narrow trail

"I have a theory that the truth is never told during the nine-to-five hours."

–Hunter S. Thompson

Ride Description

There are a number of options for mountain biking at Basalt Mountain. Many people just like to cruise up and down Basalt Mountain Road, but there is also plenty of exciting singletrack. This loop is one of the longer and more difficult rides on Basalt Mountain and the final descent on the Cattle Creek Trail features great riding on a narrow, technical trail through a dense forest. As one might expect, sections of the Basalt Mountain Trail are littered with bowling-ball size basalt rocks, so a full-suspension bike is helpful. Some sections of the trail stay muddy until late in the season, so it's prudent to give this ride until July to melt out.

Driving Directions

From Carbondale, head east on CO-82 for 7.2 miles. Turn left on El Jebel Road and continue as the road becomes Cattle Creek Road. About 7.5 miles from CO-82, arrive at a junction with Basalt Mountain Road. Park here at the large trailhead parking area.

Riding Directions

F1 - 0.0   From the parking area, start riding up Basalt Mountain Road.

F2 - 3.3   Continue on the dirt road as Mill Creek Trail goes left. (Mill Creek Trail leads down to Cattle Creek Road and can be used to make a much shorter, easier loop.)

F3 - 5.3   As you reach the top of a hill, turn left on a dirt road which soon passes around a gate and becomes Basalt Mountain Trail (#1911). The first mile is often very muddy, but the trail quickly improves.

F4 - 8.8   Go left on the Cattle Creek Trail as the Red Table Trail goes right. Hold onto your socks during a wild descent!

F5 - 12.4   The singletrack ends at a dirt road (Cattle Creek Road). Turn left.

F6 - 13.1   Continue straight on Cattle Creek Road as a dirt road goes right.

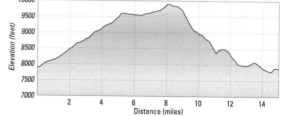

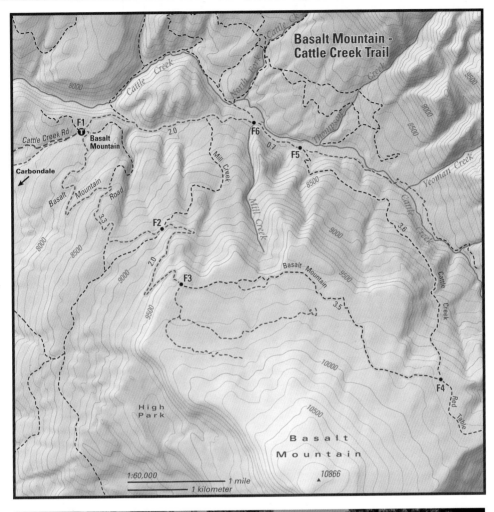

Basalt Mountain - Cattle Creek Trail

The Snowmass Bike Patrol inspects a newly built trail at Snowmass Resort.

G Hay Park ★★★★☆

(10 miles southeast of Carbondale)

Technical Difficulty:	
Physical Difficulty:	**Strenuous**
Distance:	up to 18.6 miles
Time:	2 – 6 hours
Type:	Out-and-back
Surface:	Singletrack
Climbing/ Descending:	1,700'/1,800' (one-way)
Season:	Summer
Crowds:	Few
Dogs:	

The first half is beautiful moderate riding, but then the trail gets tough

"On some nights I still believe that a car with the gas needle on empty can run about fifty more miles if you have the right music very loud on the radio."

–Hunter S. Thompson

Ride Description

Located away from the major destinations of Aspen and Snowmass, Hay Park is not a popular mountain bike ride. However, it offers excellent singletrack and beautiful views. The initial climb out of the parking lot is rocky and steep, but it is a small price to pay for the glorious riding that awaits at the top of the hill. Riders looking for a quick out-and-back can turn around when they come to the beautiful meadow at mile 4.4. Those looking for a tougher ride – complete with tricky stream crossings and some muddy sections – should continue all the way to the southern trailhead. It is possible to set up a car shuttle, but the full ride is also good as an out-and-back. Be sure to bring the camera on this ride, as the views are fantastic.

Driving Directions

From Carbondale, head south on CO-133 for 1.7 miles. Turn left on County-111 and go about 6 miles. The road turns to dirt and becomes Prince Creek Road (County-5). Turn right on County-6a (Dinkle Lake Road) and go 2.0 miles until you see the large Thomas Lakes Trailhead parking area on the left.

Riding Directions

G1 - 0.0 From the parking lot, cross the road and start riding on the Thomas Lakes Trail (#1958). Climb steeply on a wide trail.

G2 - 1.8 Turn left on the Hay Park Trail as the Thomas Lakes Trail goes right.

G3 - 4.4 Come to a fence with a barbed wire gate. Beyond this fence, the trail is more difficult and involves some big creek crossings. Turn around here or continue on.

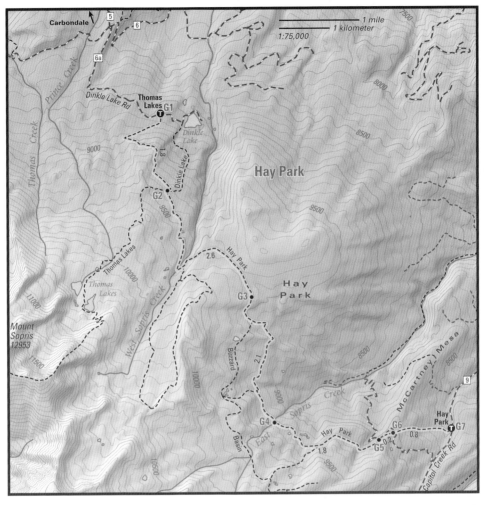

G4 - 6.5 Cross East Sopris Creek. This crossing is tricky and might not be possible in the early season.

G5 - 8.3 Turn right on a dirt road. Go about 0.1 miles and turn right onto the Hay Park Trail singletrack.

G6 - 8.5 Cross another dirt road. Most people will want to turn around at this point, since the trail descends steeply to the east trailhead.

G7 - 9.3 Come to the end of the trail. Turn around and go back the way you came.

(H) Scout Trail ★★★☆☆

(Starts in downtown Glenwood Springs)

Technical Difficulty:	◆
Physical Difficulty:	**Strenuous**
Distance:	17.9 miles
Time:	3 – 5 hours
Type:	Loop
Surface:	Singletrack, dirt road, paved road
Climbing:	2,600′
Season:	Summer, Fall
Crowds:	Few
Dogs:	Must be leashed on bike path

Exciting singletrack perched on a steep hillside

"The Edge... There is no honest way to explain it because the only people who really know where it is are the ones who have gone over."

–Hunter S. Thompson

Ride Description

The Scout Trail was created several hundred years ago by the Ute Indians as a path to the sacred Yampah hot springs, the same springs that now feed the pools at Glenwood Springs. The singletrack riding on the Scout Trail is great fun for the skilled rider who isn't bothered by riding on a steep hillside. The faint of heart should steer clear. This ride is best on a relatively cool day, as Red Canyon Road offers little shade. Lazy riders can leave a car in Glenwood Springs and shuttle to the parking lot at mile 7.3, eliminating most of the grueling climb.

Driving Directions

Start from the town of Glenwood Springs – Sayre Park offers parking and serves as a convenient starting point for this ride. To reach the park from I-70, take Exit 116 and head south on CO-82. After about one mile, turn left into Sayre Park, which is just past City Market.

Riding Directions

Note: Route finding is difficult. Several intersections are unmarked.

H1 - 0.0   From Sayre Park, ride south on CO-82.

H2 - 0.4   At 23rd Sreet, merge right onto the Rio Grande Trail bike path.

H3 - 2.7   At a "YIELD" sign on the bike path, turn left, carefully cross CO-82, and continue on Red Canyon Road (aka, Red Cañon Road).

H4 - 3.5   Continue straight on Red Canyon Road as another gravel road goes right.

H5 - 5.3   Go straight on Red Canyon Road as Kindall Road goes right.

H6 - 5.6   Turn left on County-120 and climb steeply.

H7 - 7.3   Turn right into a parking lot and bear right onto the Forest Hollow ATV Trail (FS-408).

H8 - 7.6   Continue straight on FS-408 (following the "trail" sign) as another dirt road goes left.

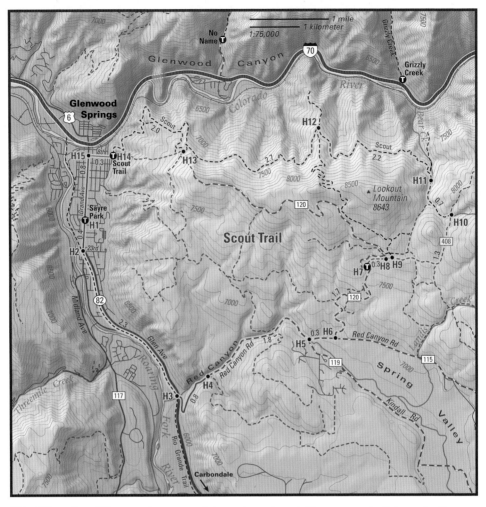

H9 - 7.7   At a T-intersection, turn right and go downhill on a rough dirt road. Cross a metal cattle guard within a few tenths of a mile.

H10 - 9.0   After coming down a long hill, and just before a really steep uphill, turn left on wide, unmarked singletrack.

H11 - 9.7   Turn left onto singletrack marked by a small sign that reads, "Glenwood Springs: 7." In 0.3 miles you'll pass under some high-voltage power lines.

H12 - 11.9   A brown sign reads: "Bear Creek 3, Glenwood Springs 5". Enjoy more terrifying downhill riding.

H13 - 14.6   At a small "Trail" sign, turn right and go downhill on singletrack.

H14 - 16.8   Arrive at the trailhead for the Scout Trail. Continue on the road for a few hundred feet and then turn right on 8th Street.

H15 - 17.1   Turn left on CO-82 (Grand Avenue).

H1 - 17.9   Arrive back at Sayre Park!

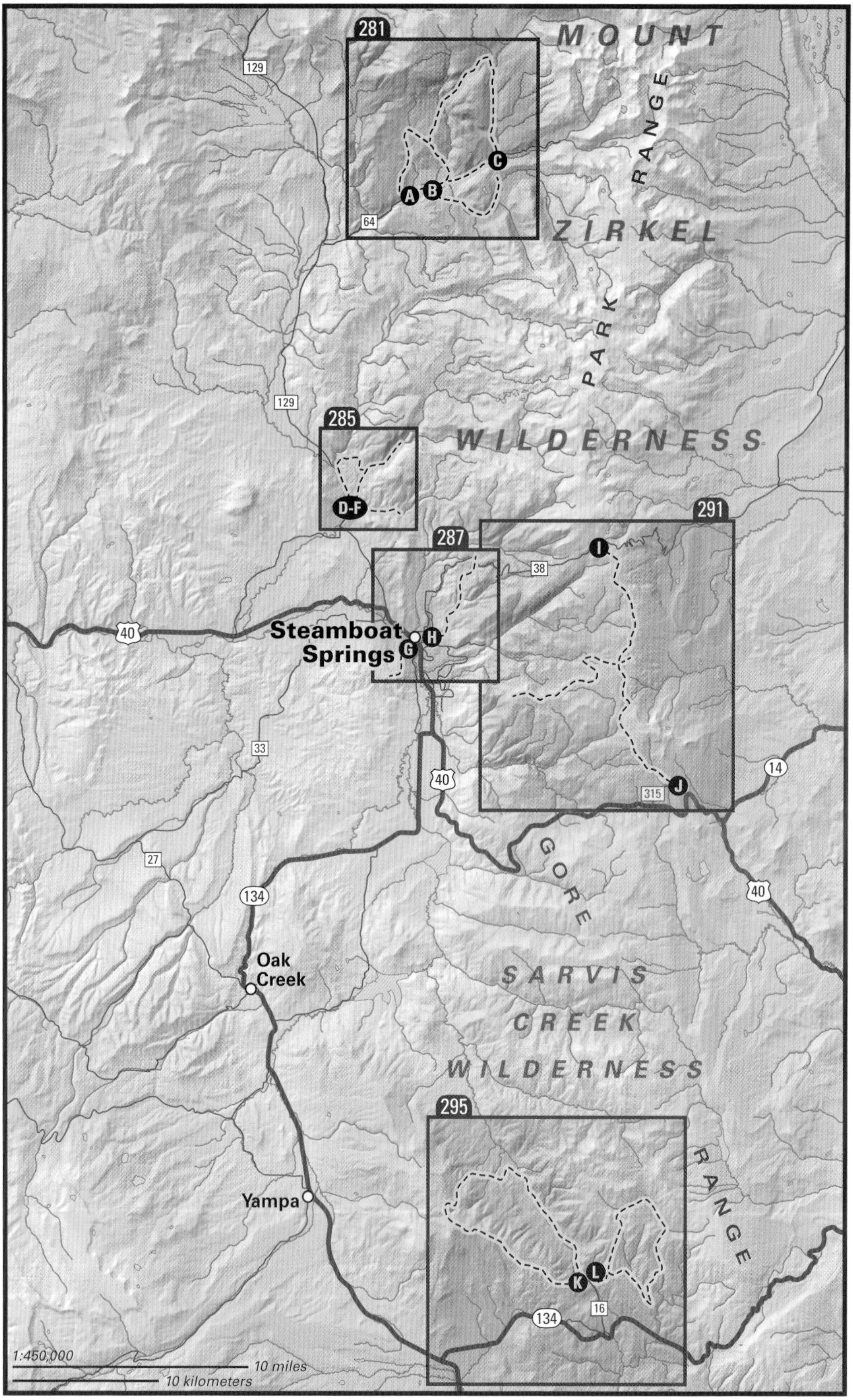
MOUNT ZIRKEL
PARK RANGE
WILDERNESS
281
285
287
291
295
A
B
C
D-F
G
H
I
J
K
L
129
64
38
40
33
27
134
14
315
16
Steamboat Springs
Oak Creek
Yampa
GORE
RANGE
SARVIS
CREEK
WILDERNESS
1:450,000
10 miles
10 kilometers

Steamboat Springs

Steamboat Springs was named for the sound of the bubbling hot springs that French settlers confused for the sound of a steamboat. The town is still a popular place for the foolish, especially those who ride skis, snowboards, and mountain bikes. Steamboat has a wide variety of trails, but it is paradise for those who love long alpine adventures through beautiful forests. The trails listed here are just the tip of the iceberg: there is a lifetime of singletrack hidden in the forests surrounding Steamboat.

Accommodations

Being a ski town, Steamboat has hotels and motels for most budgets. For the dirtbags, free, primitive camping also abounds. However, finding a campsite generally requires driving at least 20 minutes from downtown. There are primitive campsites near the northern Morrison Divide Trailhead (see ride K). The Seedhouse Road has a plethora of camping options (both primitive and pay-camping), with some of the best spots requiring a high clearance vehicle. There are also a few camping spots on the road up to Buffalo Pass.

Bike Shops

Steamboat Ski and Bike Kare
442 Lincoln Avenue. 970-879-9144
You can't miss this one: it's right on a busy corner along US-40.

Orange Peel Bike Service
1136 Yampa Street. 970-879-2957
Located in downtown Steamboat Springs on Yampa Street (one block SW of US-40), Orange Peel carries lots of the hip brands: Moots, Ellsworth, Kona, Pivot, Surly.

Eats and Drinks

Winona's
617 Lincoln Avenue. 970-879-2483
Excellent eggs benedict and cinnamon rolls larger than small children explain the crowds.

Mahogany Ridge Brewery and Grill
435 Lincoln Avenue. 970-879-3773
Upscale brew-pub with nice outdoor dining.

The Steaming Bean
635 Lincoln Avenue. 970-879-3393
Good coffee and free WiFi.

Creekside Cafe and Grill
131 11th Street. 970-879-4925
With about two-dozen versions of Eggs Benedict, Creekside is a great spot for a hardy pre-ride breakfast.

Backcountry Provisions
635 Lincoln Avenue (US-40). 970-879-3617
Delicious gourmet sandwiches.

Off the Beaten Path Bookstore
68 9th Street. 970-879-6830
Serves great coffee and a fine selection of books.

(A) Coulton Creek ★★☆☆☆

(24 miles north of Steamboat Springs)

Technical Difficulty:	◆
Physical Difficulty:	**Strenuous**
Distance:	9.1 miles
Time:	1.5 – 3 hours
Type:	Loop
Surface:	Singletrack, dirt road, paved road
Climbing:	1,200'
Season:	Summer
Crowds:	Few
Dogs:	

A fast downhill near the end doesn't make up for the horrible, loose climbing encountered at the beginning

Ride Description

The Coulton Creek Trail traverses some lovely landscape and could be a classic trail if it were not covered with loose sand, horse manure, and fallen trees. Though this trail was in bad condition when this book was written, it might be great in a few years. The final roller-coaster ride downhill on Trail #1177 is fantastic and could be ridden as an out-and-back, although this would involve some very steep climbing.

Driving Directions

From Steamboat, head northwest on US-40 for about 2 miles and turn right onto County-129 (Elk River Road). After 17.7 miles, turn right onto County-64 (Seedhouse Road). Drive on Seedhouse for 4.5 miles, then turn left onto FS-429, arriving at the Coulton Creek Trailhead in 0.2 miles.

Riding Directions - see map on page 281

A1 - 0.0 Take the Coulton Creek Trail (#1188) up a steep, loose hill that is littered with fallen trees. The trail crosses a few dirt roads; simply continue straight across them.

A2 - 3.8 Go right on the unmarked Cutover Trail (#1188.1a). It is the most well-worn trail.

A3 - 5.1 Turn right on Trail #1177 and rip down a sandy downhill section.

A4 - 5.5 Reach a spur trail to Himan Lake. Check out the lake if you want, or turn left and follow the main trail (#1177).

A5 - 6.2 Pass a green gate on the right and continue on the main trail. Cross a bridge and immediately turn right onto a dirt road (FS-430).

A6 - 7.3 Turn right on Seedhouse Rd (FS-400).

A7 - 9.0 Turn right onto the Coulton Creek Trailhead road (FS-429).

A1 - 9.1 Arrive back at the trailhead.

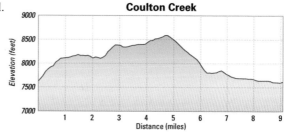

Ⓑ South Fork of the Elk ★★★★☆

(25 miles north of Steamboat Springs)

Technical Difficulty:	◼
Physical Difficulty:	**Moderate**
Distance:	9.8 miles
Time:	1.5 – 2.5 hours
Type:	Out-and-back
Surface:	Singletrack
Climbing/ Descending:	900'/200' (west to east)
Season:	Summer
Crowds:	Few
Dogs:	🐕

A fantastic cruise on great singletrack through fields, forests, and aspens, interrupted by a stream crossing and a few short, tough climbs

Ride Description

The South Fork of the Elk is one of the best moderate trails around Steamboat, but is fun for any rider. It is often ridden as a loop using Seedhouse Road, but it's better to simply ride the singletrack out and back. The stream crossing at 1.4 miles will probably require some wading, even late in the summer. In the spring and early summer the water could be quite high and riders may want to consider avoiding the stream crossing by starting the trail from the Burn Ridge Trailhead (the eastern end) and riding the trail out-and-back from the other end, stopping when they get to the stream.

Driving Directions

From Steamboat, head northwest on US-40 for about 2 miles and turn right onto County-129 (Elk River Road). After 17.7 miles, turn right onto County-64 (Seedhouse Road). Take Seedhouse Road for 5.5 miles and go right on FS-400. After about 0.2 miles, turn left into the large dirt parking area.

Riding Directions - see map on page 281

B1 - 0.0 From the South Fork Trailhead, start riding on the South Fork Trail (#1100.3a).

B2 - 1.4 Come to a stream and ford it! Only a few inches deep in August, it could be much more interesting during the early-summer run-off.

B3 - 2.9 Go left on the Swamp Creek Trail (#1100).

B4 - 4.9 Arrive at the Burn Ridge Trailhead. Turn around and ride back!

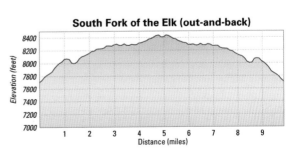

South Fork of the Elk (out-and-back)

Ⓒ Scott's Run ★★★★☆

(28 miles north of Steamboat Springs)

Technical Difficulty:	◆
Physical Difficulty:	**Strenuous**
Distance:	14.6 miles
Time:	2.5 – 4 hours
Type:	Loop
Surface:	Singletrack, dirt road
Climbing:	1,800′
Season:	Summer
Crowds:	Few
Dogs:	

Long and exciting, Scott's Run is the enduring Seedhouse Road classic

Ride Description

The Scott's Run Trail is a favorite Steamboat ride, consisting of everything from smooth singletrack to rugged descents. A forest fire has reduced many of the trees in this area to blackened sticks, giving the ride an eerie feel. In particular, the Diamond Run Trail is lines with standing dead trees and could rendered impassible if a windstorm blows the trees down. Inquire in town for current trail conditions.

Driving Directions

From Steamboat, head northwest on US-40 for about 2 miles and turn right onto County-129 (Elk River Road). After 17.7 miles, turn right onto County-64 (Seedhouse Road). Take Seedhouse Road for 8.6 miles and turn left into the North Fork Trailhead parking lot. There is only room for about five cars at this parking lot. If the lot is full, there is additional parking near FS-430 and Seedhouse Road.

Riding Directions

C1 - 0.0 Start riding on the Diamond Run Trail (#1189). This is a closed forest service road that has now become nice smooth singletrack.

C2 - 3.8 The Diamond Run Trail ends at a dirt road. Continue left, uphill on the dirt road (FS-431).

C3 - 4.7 Arrive at the Diamond Park Trailhead (a big dirt parking area). Continue left on the main road, which is now called FS-409.

C4 - 5.0 Just when it seems like you're going to have to climb a steep hill on the dirt road, turn left onto the Hinman Creek Trail (#1177). This trail is also called Scott's Run.

C5 - 10.0 Reach a junction with the cutover trail (#1188.1a), and continue straight on 1177. Rocket down steep, fun singletrack.

C6 - 10.4 Turn left to follow the main trail (#1177) as a spur trail to Hinman Lake goes right.

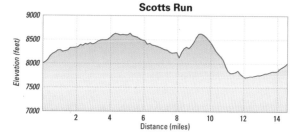

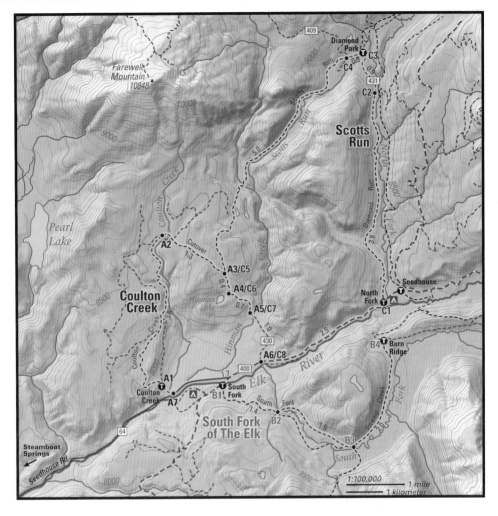

C7 - 11.1 Pass a green gate on the right and continue on the main trail. Cross a bridge over a creek and immediately turn right onto FS-430.

C8 - 12.1 Turn left on Seedhouse Road (FS-400) and follow this back to the trailhead.

C1 - 14.6 Arrive back at the car.

(D) Mad Creek ★★★☆☆

(7 miles north of Steamboat Springs)

Technical Difficulty:	
Physical Difficulty:	**Moderate**
Distance:	7.5 miles
Time:	1 – 2 hours
Type:	Out-and-back
Surface:	Wide trail, singletrack
Climbing/ Descending:	900'/200' (one-way)
Season:	Summer, Fall
Crowds:	Some
Dogs:	Watch for other off-leash dogs

A good workout on wide, often crowded trail, leads to the historic Mad Barn

Ride Description

The Mad Creek Trail can be ridden as an out-and-back on its own or as a great way to start the Red Dirt Trail. The climb is tough but not insanely steep. The downhill would be fantastic if it were not for a few problems: the abundance of people and dogs on the trail, the massive cliff on the side of the trail, and the many blind corners. This combination could send a careless cyclist plummeting into the canyon. So, ride carefully on the way down!

Driving Directions

From Steamboat, head northwest on US-40 for about 2 miles and turn right onto County-129 (Elk River Road). Turn right on County-129 (Elk River Road) and go 5.5 miles. Turn right into the Mad Creek Trailhead parking lot (a huge dirt lot right off the road).

Riding Directions - see map on page 285

D1 - 0.0 From the parking lot, find the well-signed start of trail #1100. Climb on wide singletrack.

D2 - 1.5 Reach a green gate and continue straight on the main trail.

D3 - 1.7 Come to a fork in the trail. Follow the left fork towards the Mad Barn.

D4 - 1.8 Reach the Mad Barn. The trail turns left, heads through an opening in the fence, and reaches a small sign, which reads, "Trail." Turn right. *(The left fork leads to the Red Dirt Trail, Ride E.)*

D5 - 3.7 After some nice singletrack through a lush forest, a wooden sign indicates that Trail #1100 (which continues up past Seedhouse Road!) enters a wilderness area and is closed to bikes. So, turn around and enjoy the downhill ride back to the parking area.

D1 - 7.5 Arrive back at the trailhead!

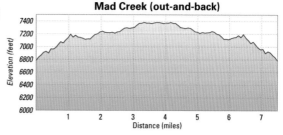

Mad Creek (out-and-back)

 Red Dirt Trail ★★★★☆

(7 miles north of Steamboat Springs)

Technical Difficulty:	◆
Physical Difficulty:	**Moderate**
Distance:	6.1 miles
Time:	1.5 – 2.5 hours
Type:	Loop
Surface:	Singletrack, wide trail
Climbing:	1,200'
Season:	Summer, Fall
Crowds:	Some
Dogs:	Watch out for cows

A quick ride with a wild downhill

Ride Description

This is one of the best short rides near Steamboat. The trail is consistently fun: never easy but not overly difficult. That said, there are numerous sections, both on the Mad Creek and Red Dirt Trails, that are on steep hillsides and riders should be cautious to avoid taking a tumble. To make the ride a bit longer, consider riding the upper section of the Mad Creek Trail before turning around and riding the Red Dirt section.

Driving Directions

Same as for Mad Creek (previous page).

Riding Directions - see map on page 285

This ride follows the Mad Creek Trail until mile 1.8

E1 - 0.0 From the parking lot, find the well-signed start of trail #1100. Climb on wide single-track.

E2 - 1.5 Reach a green gate and continue straight on the main trail.

E3 - 1.7 Come to a fork in the trail. Follow the left fork towards the Mad Barn.

E4 - 1.8 Reach the Mad Barn. The trail turns left, heads through an opening in the fence, and soon reaches a small sign, which reads, "Trail." Turn left onto the Saddle Trail (#1140).

E5 - 2.1 Turn right on the Saddle Trail (#1140) as the Swamp Park Trail (#1100) goes left.

E6 - 3.1 At a T-intersection with the Red Dirt Trail, turn left. (If you're feeling energetic, you can turn right and ride up the Red Dirt Trail for a while before turning around and cruising back down. You can go for about 4 miles that way before you hit the Wilderness Boundary.) This next section of trail is perched on the side of a steep hillside; be careful!

E7 - 4.9 Turn left on County-129 and ride back to the Mad Creek Trailhead.

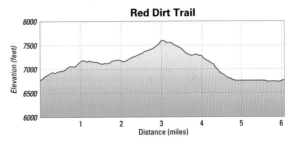

(F) Hot Springs Trail ★★☆☆☆

(7 miles north of Steamboat Springs)

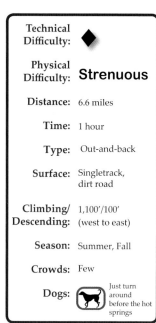

Technical Difficulty:	◆
Physical Difficulty:	**Strenuous**
Distance:	6.6 miles
Time:	1 hour
Type:	Out-and-back
Surface:	Singletrack, dirt road
Climbing/ Descending:	1,100'/100' (west to east)
Season:	Summer, Fall
Crowds:	Few
Dogs:	Just turn around before the hot springs

An exciting, technical trail that is disappointingly short, but does involve a swim in the hot springs

Ride Description

The Hot Springs Trail is a nice bit of technical singletrack that runs from Strawberry Hot Springs to Elk River Road. It would be a classic ride if it was longer than 2.6 miles. Here, the Hot Springs Trail is described as a simple out-and-back ride. However, the trail is more commonly used a "secret passage" to connect Strawberry Park road to Elk River Road and create a huge loop from Steamboat Springs. The trail is named for the Strawberry Hot Springs that are located at the eastern end of the trail. A dip in the steaming pools costs about 10 dollars, but beware: bathing suits are optional after sunset.

Driving Directions

(Same as for the previous ride, Red Dirt.) From downtown Steamboat (7th Street and US-40), head 1.7 miles west on US-40. Turn right on County-129 (Elk River Road) and go 5.5 miles. Turn right into the Mad Creek Trailhead parking lot (a huge dirt lot).

Riding Directions

F1 - 0.0   From the Mad Creek Trailhead, grab your swimsuit and ride towards Steamboat Springs on County-129.

F2 - 0.4   Turn left onto County-128, which is unsigned, but is the first major road on the left. Pass through two large gates.

F3 - 0.7   Turn right onto the (signed) Hot Springs Trail (#1169). County-128 can be used to access Mad Creek or Red Dirt and joins these rides near the Mad Barn.

F4 - 3.3   Arrive at the Hot Springs. Pay the entrance fee and soak for a while! Turn around and ride back to the Mad Creek Trailhead.

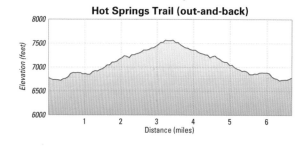

Hot Springs Trail (out-and-back)

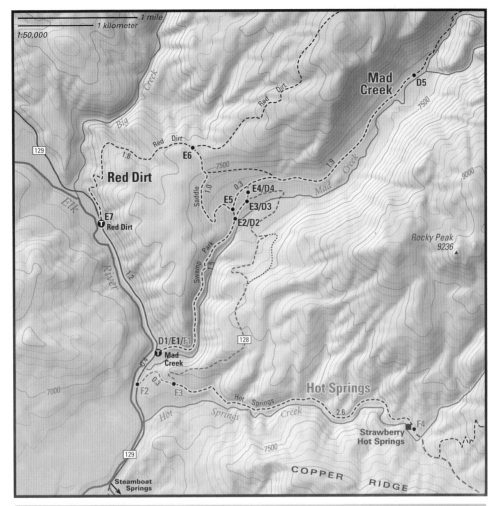

Laura Johnson blasts past the lush foliage on Emerald Mountain.

Ⓖ Emerald Mtn Loop ★★★☆☆

(Start from Steamboat Springs)

Technical Difficulty:	■
Physical Difficulty:	**Strenuous**
Distance:	4.8 miles
Time:	1 – 1.5 hours
Type:	Loop
Surface:	Dirt road, singletrack
Climbing:	1,100'
Season:	Summer, Fall
Crowds:	Some
Dogs:	6ft leash required

A tough grind on the way up with swooping switchbacks on the way down

Ride Description

Emerald Mountain, the hillside above the Howelsen Hill ski area, boasts glorious singletrack within walking distance of downtown Steamboat. There is a tremendous amount of riding up here, but the first rule of Emerald Mountain is that you don't talk about Emerald Mountain since much of the riding is on private property. This loop is on trails managed by the ski area, so it's not quite so secret and offers a taste of what Emerald Mountain has to offer.

Driving Directions

From downtown Steamboat Springs go southwest on 5th Street. Cross the Yampa River and turn right on Howelsen Parkway. Make the first left and wrap around the rodeo grounds on a small road. Park in the parking lot next to the stables.

Riding Directions

G1 - 0.0   Find the sign near the stables that has a map of all of the Howelsen Hill Trails. Check it out and then start riding up the dirt road following the green signed Emerald Meadows Trail. There are lots of turns and intersections, but just follow signs for the green trail. It's mostly a dirt road.

G2 - 2.2   Arrive at a nice overlook of Steamboat Springs. (The dirt road makes a sharp switchback here and continues steeply up to the top of Emerald Mountain in 0.7 miles: an awesome view if your legs can handle the challenge.) Admire the view and then descend on the Lupine Trail, which is signed in purple. The first 0.1 miles of the Lupine Trail are very technical and quite rocky, but it quickly eases to fun switchbacks. There are many intersections, but just keep following the purple signs.

G1 - 4.8   Arrive back at the stables.

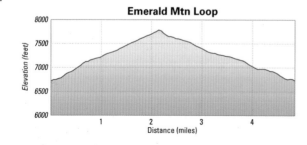

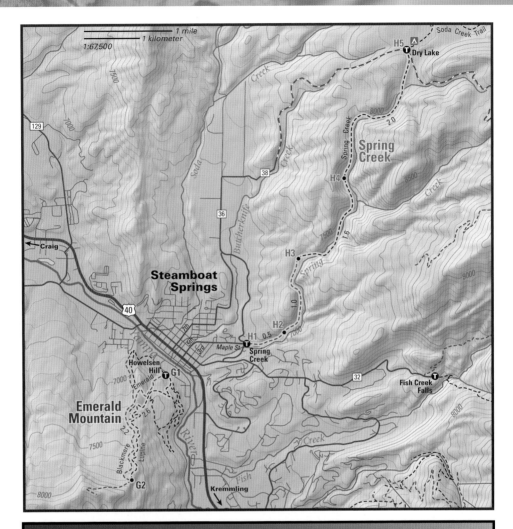

LINK-UPS

At first glance it appears that most of the rides in Steamboat are a little short for a strong rider looking for an all-day epic. However, many of the local rides can be linked together to create massive challenges. Here are a few examples:

BUFFALO PASS LOOP: Bike up Spring Creek Trail (Ride H), and turn right on Buffalo Pass Road. At Buffalo Pass, take the Wyoming Trail to the Fish Creek Trail (see Ride I). Take the Mountain View Trail to the top of the ski area, and then bomb down one of the ski area trails back to town (See Ride J). Yeah!

SCOTT'S RUN AND SOUTH FORK OF THE ELK: Riders who have not had enough after they hit the road on Scott's Run (Ride C) can turn right on Seedhouse Road and ride to the Start of the South Fork Trailhead. Then, they can follow the South Fork of the Elk trail (Ride B) back to towards the starting point of Scotts Run.

HOT SPRINGS, MAD CREEK, RED DIRT: These three trails are right next to each other; ride them all!

Dave Penny breezes over logs on the Emerald Mountain Trails   photo: Mitchell W. Sprinsky

Spring Creek ★★★☆☆

(Start from Steamboat Springs)

Technical Difficulty:	
Physical Difficulty:	**Moderate**
Distance:	10.2 miles
Time:	1.5 – 2 hours
Type:	Out-and-back
Surface:	Wide trail, dirt road
Climbing/ Descending:	1,800'/400' (one-way)
Season:	Summer; Fall
Crowds:	Crowded
Dogs:	Leash required

This celebration of smooth trail through the forest is frequently crowded with cyclists, hikers, and dog-walkers

Ride Description

The Spring Creek Trail begins with 1.5 miles of dirt road and then turns into smooth widetrack. Generally, the Spring Creek Trail is overrun with trail users, an unfortunate situation for the mountain biker with a need-for-speed. Try to ride this trail early in the morning to avoid the crowds.

Driving Directions

There is limited trailhead parking at Spring Creek, so consider parking downtown and riding to the trailhead; it is only about a mile away. From downtown Steamboat (7th Street and US-40), head southeast on US-40 for 0.3 miles. Turn left onto 3rd Street and go 0.3 miles. Turn right onto Maple Street and go about 0.4 miles until the road ends and park here.

Riding Directions - see map page 287

H1 - 0.0 Continue riding east along Maple Street as it turns to dirt.

H2 - 0.5 Come to a handicap parking area and stay on the left, following the road past a gate.

H3 - 1.5 Come to a large sign about the seasonal elk closure. About 100 feet after this sign, go right on the Spring Creek Trail singletrack.

H4 - 3.1 Climb "The Wall", a short, but heinously steep rocky section.

H5 - 5.1 Arrive at the end of the Spring Creek Trail. Turn around and head back. *(If you haven't had enough, the Soda Creek Trail continues on the other side of the road.)*

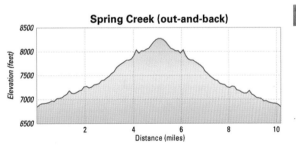

Spring Creek (out-and-back)

ⓘWyoming Trail from Buffalo Pass ★★★★☆

(13 miles east of Steamboat Springs)

Technical Difficulty:	
Physical Difficulty:	**Moderate**
Distance:	15.2 miles
Time:	3 – 4 hours
Type:	Out-and-back
Surface:	Wide trail and dirt road
Climbing/ Descending:	800'/500' (one-way)
Season:	Summer
Crowds:	Few
Dogs:	

A great romp through the woods on an ATV trail

Ride Description

Singletrack snobs might turn up their noses at this wide ATV trail, but they don't know what they are missing! This section of the Wyoming Trail provides fantastic, fast riding through the forest. Plenty of tree-roots keep things interesting and become insanely slippery in the rain. This trail can be ridden as a loop using a dirt road (FS-310), but the Wyoming Trail is so good that it's worth riding it both out and back. Keep in mind that the trail loses elevation as it heads south, so the way back is bound to be a little tougher. Those looking for an epic adventure should consider riding all the way to Rabbit Ears Pass (see Ride J).

Driving Directions

From downtown Steamboat (7th Street and US-40), head northeast on 7th Street for 0.4 miles. Turn right on Missouri and go 0.3 miles. Turn left on North Park Road and go 0.2 miles. Turn right on Strawberry Park Road, which becomes County-36. After 0.8 miles turn left to stay on County-36, and go another 0.8 miles. Turn right on County-38, drive 10.8 miles to Buffalo Pass, and park near the toilets. County-38 becomes progressively rockier and very low-clearance cars may not be able to make it all the way to Buffalo Pass. Consider parking and riding the last few miles to the pass.

Riding Directions

I1 - 0.0 Ride south on Divide Road (County-310) towards the horse trailer parking lot, which is just a few tenths of a mile down the road.

I2 - 0.2 At the horse trailer parking lot, find the small sign for the Continental Divide Trail (CDT, also called "Wyoming Trail" and "Trail #1101") that leaves from the south side of the parking lot. Climb a short, steep hill to gain the trail.

I3 - 7.3 Reach a four-way junction with the Fish Creek Trail and the Percy Lake Trail. Turn left and ride for a few minutes to Percy Lake.

I4 - 7.6 Arrive at Percy Lake, a lovely spot to have lunch. Turn around and ride back the way you came.

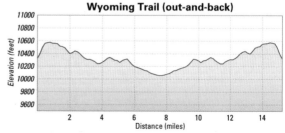

Steamboat Springs

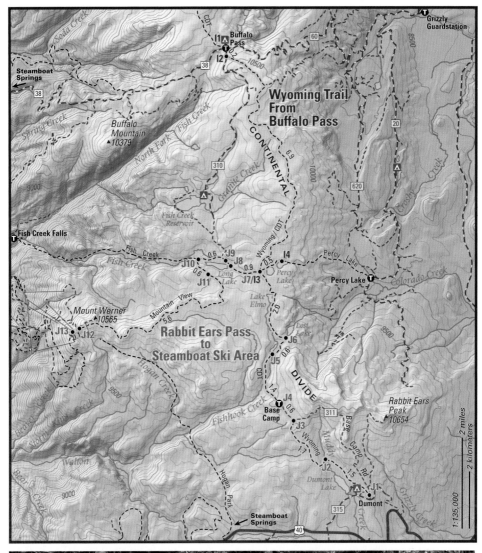

Buffalo
Pass
CDT
60
Steamboat
Springs
38
38
I1
I2
10.2
10500
10500
8500
Grizzly
Guardstation

**Wyoming Trail
From
Buffalo Pass**

Buffalo
Mountain
▲10379

Soda Creek
Spring Creek
North Fork Fish Creek
Fish Creek
Granite Creek
310
CONTINENTAL
6.9
10000
20
620
Crosby Creek
9000

Fish Creek
Reservoir

Fish Creek Falls

Fish Creek
Fish Creek
J10
J9
J8
0.6
0.5
0.9
J7/13
J11
0.6
Long
Lake
Percy Lake
I4
Percy
Lake
Percy Lake
Colorado Creek
Wyoming CDT

Mount Werner
▲10565
J13 J12
Mountain View
5.6
Lake
Elmo
2.0
Lost
Lake
J6
0.6
J5
9500

**Rabbit Ears Pass
to
Steamboat Ski Area**

Hogan Creek
Beaver Creek
Walton Creek
Bear Creek
9500
9000
Fishhook Creek
CDT
DIVIDE
1.4
J4
0.6
Base
Camp
J3
1.7
Wyoming
311
Base Camp Rd
Muddy
Rabbit Ears
Peak
10654
2 miles
2 kilometers
1:135,000

J2
1.5
Dumont
Lake
315
J1
Dumont
Hogan Park
Steamboat
Springs
40
Grizzly Creek

(J) Rabbit Ears Pass to Steamboat Ski Area ★★★★★

(22 miles east of Steamboat Springs)

Technical Difficulty:	
Physical Difficulty:	**Moderate**
Distance:	31.6 miles
Time:	4 – 7 hours
Type:	Out-and-back
Surface:	Singletrack
Climbing/ Descending:	2,300'/1,500' (one-way)
Season:	Summer
Crowds:	Few
Dogs:	🐕

A fantastic alpine journey with beautiful lakes, meadows, and forests

Ride Description

This ride is a rare gem: a long tour through the mountains that is both technically and physically moderate. Most high elevation trails in Colorado involve huge climbs and are much rockier. Though this ride is generally moderate, it is nevertheless a big outing, and to complete the whole thing will require sturdy legs and good planning. However, since this is an out-and-back, riders can always turn around when they get tired.

To make this ride shorter (and more fun!), leave a car at the Steamboat ski area and take one of the ski area trails back down to Steamboat after you reach the top of the ski area. Insanely fit riders could create a great link-up by combining this ride with The Wyoming Trail from Buffalo Pass (Ride I).

Driving Directions

From downtown Steamboat Springs (7th Street and US-40) drive 20.3 miles east on US-40. Turn left on FS-315 and drive 1.4 miles. Just past the campground, make a left and travel a short distance to the Dumont Trailhead, which is a dirt parking lot at the junction of Base Camp Road (FS-311) and Grizzly Creek Road (FS-291).

Riding Directions - see map on previous page

J1 - 0.0 From the Dumont Trailhead, start riding west on the signed Continental Divide Trail (CDT), which is also called the Wyoming Trail here. Follow signs as the trail winds through the campground, eventually merging onto an old road-grade.

J2 - 1.5 Cross a small creek and climb steeply.

J3 - 3.2 Turn left on an unsigned dirt road (Base Camp Road, FS-311) and take it to the Base Camp Trailhead.

J4 - 3.8 Reach the dirt parking at the Base Camp Trailhead. Find the sign on the right pointing toward the CDT (aka the Wyoming Trail or #1101).

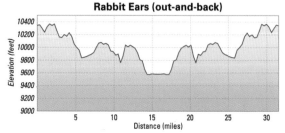

J5 - 5.2 Come to the beautiful Fishhook Lake and continue on the CDT. This is a good turn-around spot for those who are just out for a quick ride.

J6 - 5.8 Continue straight, towards Lake Elmo, as the Lost Lake Trail goes right.

J7 - 7.8 A large four-way junction. Go left on the Fish Creek Trail. *(Straight-ahead is the Wyoming Trail, which continues straight to Buffalo Pass.)*

J8 - 8.7 Behold beautiful Long Lake! Turn right and follow an old road that wraps around the lake.

J9 - 8.9 Continue straight on the road as a road to Fish Creek Reservoir goes right.

J10 - 9.5 Make a left on the Mountain View Trail (#1032).

J11 - 10.1 Bear right on the main trail as a side trail goes left towards Long Lake.

J12 - 15.7 Make a left on a dirt road and follow it towards the top of the Storm Peak ski lift.

J13 - 15.8 Arrive at the top of the Storm Peak lift at the Steamboat ski resort. Turn around and head back to Rabbit Ears Pass. *Or, if you've planned well and shuttled to the start, ride one of the fine trails at the ski area back to town.*

Admiring the view of Fishhook Lake.   photo: Mitchell W. Sprinksy

(K) Muddy Slide ★★★★★

(50 miles southeast of Steamboat Springs)

Technical Difficulty:	
Physical Difficulty:	**Strenuous**
Distance:	19.4 miles
Time:	3 – 5 hours
Type:	Loop
Surface:	Dirt road, ATV-track
Climbing:	3,200'
Season:	Summer
Crowds:	Few
Dogs:	Watch for hunters!

Several hours of dirt road riding earns great views of Muddy Slide and 15 minutes of downhill fun

Ride Description

The Muddy-Slide–Morrison-Divide Loop is one of those "classic rides" that involves way to much riding on dirt roads. Not only does the loop include many miles on FS-270 (maintained and open to vehicle traffic), but much of the Morrison Divide ATV "trail" consists of dirt roads of varying roughness. That being said, the downhill section shortly after the Muddy Slide Viewpoint is memorable: an exuberant downhill charge over rocks and slippery roots. Consider parking at the northern trailhead to get the bulk of the boring dirt road riding done first.

Driving Directions

From Steamboat Springs drive 4 miles southeast on US-40. Turn right on CO-131 and drive 35.6 miles. Just past a lonesome gas station, turn left on CO-134. Go 8.6 miles and then turn left on County-16. Turn right after 0.4 miles to stay on County-16. 2.8 miles from CO-134, and about 0.2 miles past the outhouse, turn left at the sign for the Morrison Divide Trailhead (Trail #1174).

Riding Directions

K1 - 0.0 From the Southern Morrison Divide Trailhead, find the signed start of the Morrison Divide Trail (#1174) and climb steeply on wide trail. The trail crosses several dirt roads in the first few miles, but in each case it is obvious where the trail continues on the other side.

K2 - 3.7 The trail becomes a dirt road. Turn left and follow the dirt road downhill.

K3 - 6.6 Merge onto another dirt road, continuing straight.

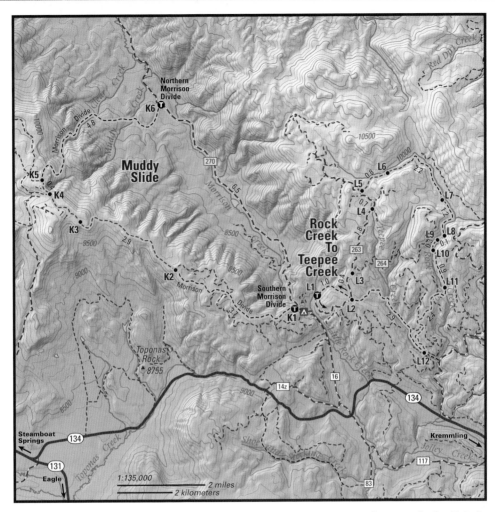

K4 - 7.7   Go around a green gate and continue straight. Soon you reach an overlook of Muddy Slide. A sign explains which soils are responsible for this geological anomaly.

K5 - 8.1   Go right on The Morrison Divide Trail (#1174) while the dirt road goes left. Try to maintain some semblance of control during this fantastic high-speed descent.

K6 - 12.9   Pass through a red gate and arrive at the Northern Morrison Divide Trailhead. (There are a number of undeveloped campsites here.) Turn right onto FS-270 (County-16) and take this back to the Southern Morrison Divide Trailhead.

Ⓛ Rock Creek to Teepee Creek Loop ★★★★☆

(51 miles southeast of Steamboat Springs)

Technical Difficulty:	
Physical Difficulty:	**Moderate**
Distance:	16.4 miles
Time:	2.5 – 4 hours
Type:	Loop (figure 8)
Surface:	Singletrack dirt road
Climbing:	2,300'
Season:	Summer
Crowds:	Few
Dogs:	🐕

A wonderful cruise on smooth singletrack and dirt roads

Ride Description

Though this loop involves several stream and swamp crossings, the excellent singletrack make it a marvelous ride. The initial climb on Teepee Creek Road is several miles long, but is actually reasonably enjoyable due to the smooth dirt road and moderate grade. The singletrack is generally pure bliss, swooping through the woods with only a few tough climbs. There are only two things that keep this ride from being the perfect woodland cruise: the many fordings of Rock Creek and nearby swamps, and the abundance of cows on some sections of the Rock Creek Trail. However, riders who accept in advance that they're going to end the ride with wet shoes and cow feces in their hair will love this ride.

Driving Directions

From Steamboat Springs drive 4 miles southeast on US-40. Turn right on CO-131 and drive 35.6 miles. Just past a lonesome gas station, turn left on CO-134. Go 8.6 miles and then turn left on County-16. Turn right after 0.4 miles to stay on County-16. After 2.4 miles from CO-134, just before you get to the outhouse, turn right onto Teepee Creek Road. Go about 0.5 miles and park in a small dirt pullout at a sharp right turn.

Riding Directions

L1 - 0.0 Start riding up Teepee Creek Road.

L2 - 0.4 You might not notice it, but here the road crosses Trail #1173. Continue straight on Teepee Creek Road.

L3 - 0.7 Go left of FS-263 as FS-264 goes right (as indicated by the post with the green arrow and little bicycle symbol).

L4 - 3.3 Go right on the main road as another road goes left.

L5 - 4.6 Go right on FS-272.

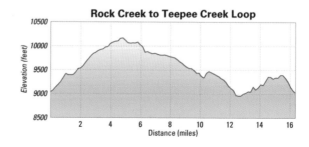

L6 - 5.4 Ride around a big red gate. The road soon turns into nice singletrack.

L7 - 7.6 Cross a swamp.

L8 - 8.8 Ford Rock Creek.

L9 - 8.9 Ford the creek again.

L10 - 9.2 Ford the creek again. I hope you have dry socks back in the car…

L11 - 10.1 Surprise! Ford the creek AGAIN. Soon the trail becomes a dirt road.

L12 - 12.5 Turn right on the Teepee Creek Trail (marked by a red arrow). (This turn is easy to miss. If you come to a "T" in the road, you've gone about 30 seconds too far.)

L2 - 15.4 Come to a campsite, cross Teepee Creek Road, and continue on the Teepee Creek Trail (#1173).

L1 - 16.4 Arrive back at the car!

Leisa Young goes into hyper-drive on the Spring Creek Trail.   photo: Paula Jo Jaconetta   www.naturallightimages.net

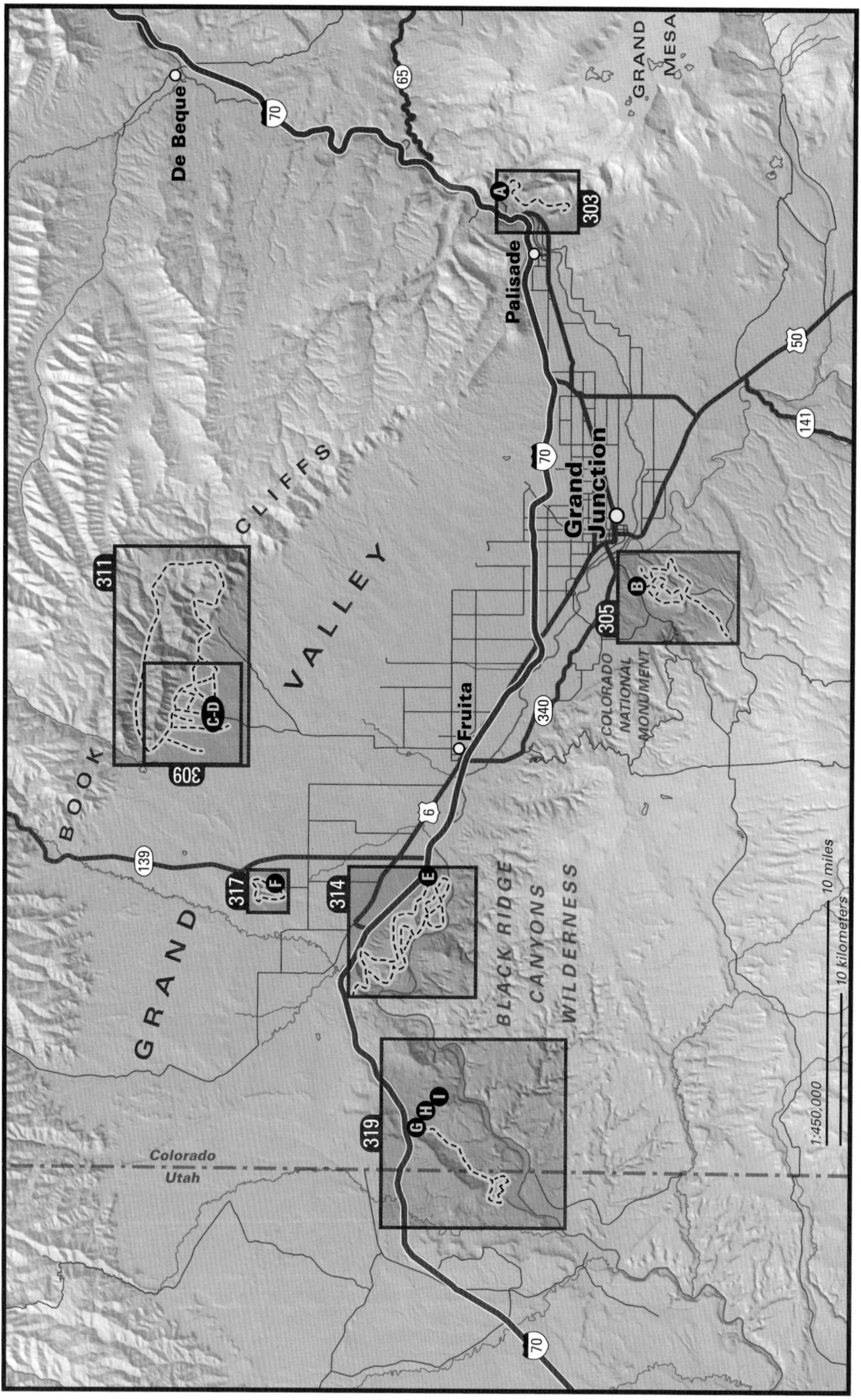
De Beque
70
65
GRAND MESA
A
303
Palisade
50
141
70
Grand Junction
BOOK CLIFFS
GRAND VALLEY
311
C–D
309
B
305
COLORADO NATIONAL MONUMENT
340
Fruita
6
139
F
317
E
314
BLACK RIDGE CANYONS WILDERNESS
G H I
319
Colorado
Utah
70
1:450,000
10 miles
10 kilometers

Grand Junction & Fruita

Traditionally, when people talked about the "classic Colorado mountain biking trails," they were referring to high elevation rides through the aspens near Crested Butte or Steamboat Springs. However, some of the best riding in the state is actually located in the desert! In the past decade, the trails around Grand Junction and Fruita have multiplied and now the area is one of the premier mountain biking destinations in the country.

Much of the riding around Grand Junction and Fruita can be broken into several riding areas, each consisting of a network of shorter trails that can be combined into longer rides. Each area has a different landscape and features a different style of riding. The Bookcliffs is Fruita's most famous area and offers silky-smooth singletrack, roller-coaster ridgelines, and sublime desert scenery. The trails at Kokopelli's are significantly rockier, with technical slickrock sections and million-dollar views of the Colorado River. Tabeguache is located just a few miles from Grand Junction and offers some of the best freeride trails in the state. Rabbit Valley sees fewer visitors than the other areas and boasts a vast network of remote motorcycle trails, which provide excellent riding.

Desert Etiquette: Stay On the Trail
As visitors will quickly discover, the desert is one of the most beautiful landscapes in Colorado. It is also one of the most fragile. Some might wonder why the sand doesn't just blow away in the wind, taking all of the plants along with it. The answer is that the soil is alive! A bunch of tiny organisms live in the top layer of the soil and form a "cryptobiotic crust." This crust is the skin of the desert, locking in moisture and allowing the plants to thrive.

Unfortunately, it is very easy for humans to destroy this crust and it can take decades for it to grow back. Tire tracks and footprints crush the microorganisms and the crust dies. If mountain bikers are not careful, they can quickly turn narrow trails into 15-foot wide swaths of destruction. Please do your part to keep the desert alive. First and foremost, stay on the trail. When encountering other riders, stop and let them pass instead of riding off-trail. While driving, stay on established roads.

Accommodations

Grand Junction is a town of about 60,000 people and offers numerous hotels and motels. In addition, camping in the desert is beautiful and often free. There are several pay-campgrounds in state parks in the region, with Highline State Park being especially popular (see ride "F", page 316). The Bookcliffs (aka 18-Road) area features a nice campground that has picnic tables and toilets. This camping fills up very quickly on weekends in the spring and fall. The Rabbit Valley area also has a small campground with toilets and picnic tables.

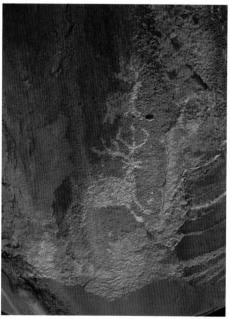

Ancient petroglyhps near the Palisade Rim Trail.

Bike Shops

Over the Edge Sports
202 E. Aspen Avenue, Fruita. 970-858-7220
These guys built the trails around Fruita and this is the place to go for everything: parts, service, rentals, maps, trail conditions, etc. They are located in downtown Fruita.

"The Bike Shop"
950 North Avenue, Unit #108, Grand Junction. 970-243-0807
Good service and plenty of sweet Niner and Cannondale demo bikes.

Ruby Canyon Cycles
301 Main Street, Grand Junction. 970-241-0141
Parts, service, rentals. Located right in downtown Grand Junction.

Eats and Drinks

Hot Tomato Pizza
124 N Mulberry Street, Fruita. 970-858-1117
The best place to eat in Fruita: great pizza, great beers.

Rockslide Brewery
401 Main Street, Grand Junction. 970-245-2111
Just another wonderful Colorado Brewpub!

Pablo's Pizza
319 Main Street, Grand Junction. 970-255-8879
Located in downtown Grand Junction, Pablo's serves up delicious pizza and a wide selection of beers.

Phil Marsh busts a move at the Lunch Loops

Palisade Rim ★★★☆☆

(15 miles east of Grand Junction)

Technical Difficulty:	◆
Physical Difficulty:	**Moderate**
Distance:	12.2 miles
Time:	2 – 3 hours
Type:	Out-and-back
Surface:	Singletrack, dirt road
Climbing/ Descending:	1,600'/1,100' (one way)
Season:	Spring, Fall
Crowds:	Few
Dogs:	🐕

Ride singletrack past petroglyphs to reach a beautiful cliff-top vista

Ride Description

Located right next to the town of Palisade, the Palisade Rim Trails are the perfect way to meet your daily bicycling quota while you are partaking in one of Palisade's famous celebrations of deliciousness: the Peach Festival in August and the Winefest in September. Some of these trails aren't very popular and can be a little hard to find. However, most of the trails are very well built and offer great technical riding. This route journeys all the way to the end of the trail system, arriving at a nice vista. The loop trails at mile 4.2 are excellent and many people just ride these and don't go all the way to the overlook. It is also possible to make a loop by taking the trail that connects from the loops near mile 4.2 down to US-6 and then riding roads back to the trailhead. This is a fun option, but the trail down to the road is very steep and loose (double diamond).

Driving Directions

From Grand Junction, head east on I-70. Take Exit 42 and head south on 37 3/10 Road (I know, the names are ridiculous). Turn left on G Road (8th St) and go 2.9 miles. Turn right on Rapid Creek Road and follow it for 1.5 miles until you come to a dirt trailhead on the left. Park here and ride up the road.

Riding Directions

A1 - 0.0 From the trailhead, continue riding up the dirt road.

A2 - 0.8 Shortly after you cross the creek, turn sharply right, go through a gate, and start riding on singletrack.

A3 - 2.4 Hop a barbed wire fence.

A4 - 2.8 Come to an old mining operation with several dilapidated corrugated-metal structures. Turn left on a dirt road. Continue on the road past some tempting singletrack options.

A5 - 3.9 The road ends at the bottom of a gully where it has been washed out. Scramble to the other side of the gully and push your bike up some singletrack until you can continue riding.

Palisade Rim (out-and-back)

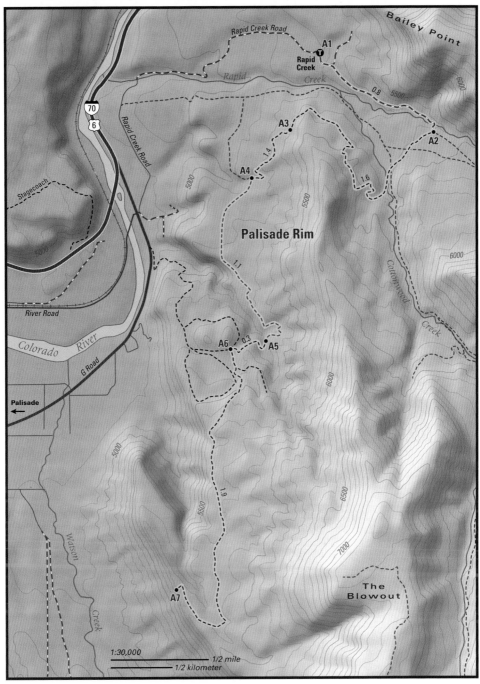

A6 - 4.2 Come to a four-way intersection and check out the petroglyphs on the right! Then turn left and climb up the steep hill. *(Turning right at this intersection takes you to the optional loops, which offer about a mile of excellent singletrack each.)*

A7 - 6.1 The trail ends at the top of some large cliffs. Enjoy lunch here at "the edge of the earth" and then ride back.

B Tabeguache ★★★★★
(aka The Lunch Loops)

(4 miles west of Grand Junction)

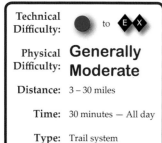

Technical Difficulty:	● to **E X**
Physical Difficulty:	**Generally Moderate**
Distance:	3 – 30 miles
Time:	30 minutes — All day
Type:	Trail system
Surface:	Singletrack
Season:	Spring, Fall
Crowds:	Crowded
Dogs:	Trails can be crowded

One of the best trail systems anywhere: everything from green circle cruising to gigantic drops and jumps

Ride Description

The Lunch Loops trail system is a vast mountain biking playground located just a few miles from downtown Grand Junction. Intermediate riders will enjoy riding the smooth trails located closer to the parking area, and the "dude bros" will appreciate several freeride trails that feature huge double jumps, 10-foot drops, and massive wall rides.

Almost all of the trails at Tabeguache are fun, so riders are advised to explore using the map. Few of the trails are easy, and most have at least a bit of black diamond riding. Descriptions of the major trails are provided below. Advanced riders simply must ride Holy Cross Trail – it is phenomenal.

Driving Directions

To reach the main trailhead on Monument Road, Take I-70 to Exit 26 and head southeast on US-6/US-50 for 4.8 miles. Turn right on W Grand Avenue (which quickly turns into Broadway) and go 0.8 miles. Make a left onto Monument Road and drive 1.6 miles. Turn left into the trailhead parking lot. Some trails, such as Free Lunch and the Ribbon Trail are better accessed from the trailhead on Little Park Road (see map).

Recommended Trails:

Holy Cross Trail - ◆◆ Distance: 2.3 miles
Lots of drops, jumps, and wall-rides make this one of the best black diamond challenge loops in the state. Holy Cross is a good introduction to the harder riding at Tabeguache, offering an assortment of small features. If Holy Cross seems too easy, try one of the "freeride" trails like Pucker Up or Free Lunch.

Eagle's Wing - ◆◆ Distance: 2.4 miles
You might need wings if you fall while riding this trail! Eagle's Wing features mega-steep riding along an exposed ridgeline. Fantastic!

Free Lunch - **E X** Distance: 1.1 miles
Hands-down the best freeride trail in the state (that isn't at a ski resort). Free Lunch consists of over a mile of well-constructed drops, jumps, and difficult rock-features. There are several designated "freeride areas" where riders with enough courage are free to ride off whatever they can find. (Obviously, don't ride off-trail except in these designated areas.)

Ribbon Trail - ◆ Distance: 3.0 miles
Pedal up Little Park Road for about one hour to reach the top of the Ribbon Trail on the right.

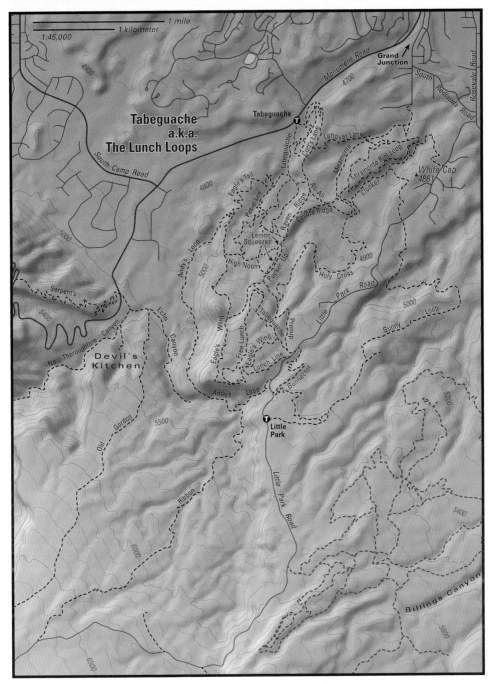

The way down features spectacular riding on massive slickrock slabs. Bring your camera (good views), a map (it's easy to get lost), and a snorkel (there is a flash flood risk).

Pucker Up - ◆◆ Distance: 0.3 & Lemon Squeezer - ◆◆ Distance: 0.3

These two trails are short-but-sweet freeride trails offering jumps, drops, and technical features. Lemon Squeezer offers some good technical challenges for the advanced rider. Pucker Up is totally insane and has sections of back-to-back double jumps and giant drops.

Curt Stevens soars along Eagles Tail Trail, Tabeguache Trailhead.

©The Bookcliffs ★★★★★
(aka 18 Road)

(11 miles north of Fruita)

Technical Difficulty:	to
Physical Difficulty:	**Moderate** to **Strenuous**
Distance:	2 – 40 miles
Time:	20 minutes — 12 hours
Type:	Trail system
Surface:	Singletrack, dirt road
Elevation (low/high):	5,000'/5,600'
Season:	Spring, Fall
Crowds:	Crowded
Dogs:	🐕

A paradise of buttery-smooth singletrack

Ride Description

Built by mountain bikers for mountain bikers, the trails at the Bookcliffs are a wonderful, unique experience. The singletrack here is narrow and curvy, providing a sense of flow unlike anywhere else. The trails range in difficulty from the mellow Prime Cut, to the steep-n'-wild Zippety Do Da. The trails are generally easy to follow, so take a look at the map and create the perfect ride based on how much time you have.

Driving Directions

From downtown Fruita, head east on Aspen Avenue. Turn left on Maple Street (which soon turns into 17 ½ Road) and go 3.6 miles. Turn right on N 3/10 Road and go 0.5 miles. Turn left on 18 Road and drive 7.1 miles until you reach the large dirt parking lot on the left (there is an outhouse here).

Recommended Trails:

Joe's Ridge - ■ Distance: 1.1 miles
A classic ride on an exposed ridge, Joe's serves as a good warm-up to the even scarier ridge riding found on Zippety Do Da. It is best ridden downhill.

Kessel Run - ■ Distance: 1.9 miles
Half bobsled course, half mountain bike trail, Kessel Run is the most fun you can have on a bike! Best ridden downhill.

Chutes and Ladders - Distance: 4.4 miles
This ride starts with some scary downhills (the chutes) and some loose uphills (the ladders), but soon turns into a fast slalom course through the desert. Downhill riding is recommended.

Prime Cut - ◉ Distance: 1.9 miles
The easiest trail at the Bookcliffs, Prime Cut is still a fun ride and is a fantastic way to reach the top of 18 Road and the start of Chutes and Ladders and Joe's Ridge. Uphill riding recommended.

Frontside - ◆ Distance: 3.4 miles
The Frontside Trail has a number of difficult climbs. It is used to reach the start of Joe's Ridge, Zippety Do Da, and the Edge Loop. Can be ridden in both directions.

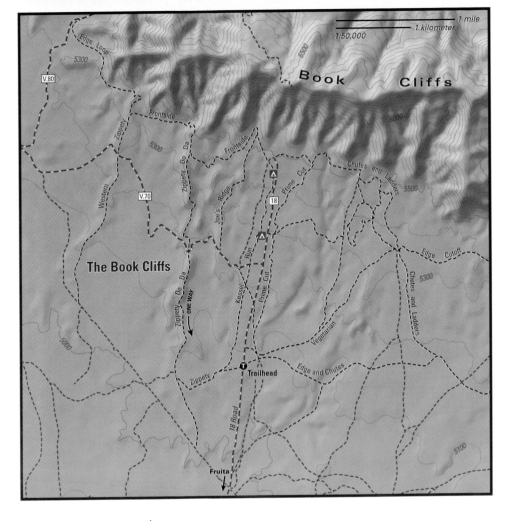

Zippety Do Da - ◆ Distance: 2.1 miles

The scariest trail at the Bookcliffs, Zippety Do Da involves incredibly steep downhill riding along an undulating ridge. An unforgettable experience, but only recommended for those who know how to get their butt way behind the saddle. Uphill riding is NOT allowed on Zippety Do Da. Downhill riding ONLY.

Western Zippety - ▨ Distance: 1.8 miles

This is a nice (but long) way to reach Frontside and Zippety Do Da as the climbing is reasonably gentle. Can be ridden both directions.

G. J. & Fruita

Ⓓ The Edge Loop ★★★★☆

(11 miles north of Fruita)

Technical Difficulty:	◆
Physical Difficulty:	**Strenuous**
Distance:	27.3 miles
Time:	5 – 9 hours
Type:	Loop
Surface:	Dirt roads, singletrack
Climbing:	3,800'
Season:	Fall
Crowds:	Few
Dogs:	Long ride on rough terrain

A massive adventure culminating with a memorable descent!

Ride Description

Featuring nearly 30 miles of riding and involving an exhilarating scramble down a cliff, The Edge Loop provides 100 percent of your recommended daily allowance of adventure. Though the Edge Loop involves significantly more riding on dirt roads than it does on singletrack, the loop is nonetheless fantastic, unique, and memorable.

The ride is not particularly well marked, so it is a good idea to bring a comprehensive map, a compass, and a GPS. Many of the signs along the dirt roads have small stickers on them reading "EDGE." These stickers are a nice reassurance that you're still on the correct dirt road. The Edge Loop, being at a higher elevation, is much cooler than the other trails at the Bookcliffs and can take much longer to dry after a rainstorm. If the other Bookcliffs trails are even slightly damp, the Edge Loop is likely to be very muddy.

Driving Directions

From downtown Fruita, head east on Aspen Avenue and turn left onto Maple Street (which soon turns into 17 ½ Road) and drive 3.6 miles. Make a right on N 3/10 Road and go 0.5 miles. Turn left on 18 Road and motor 7.1 miles until you see the large dirt parking lot on the left.

Riding Directions

D1 - 0.0 From the parking lot, start riding up 18 Road. *(For more singletrack, ride up Prime Cut and turn left when you arrive at Chutes and Ladders.)*

D2 - 1.8 At the end of 18 Road, turn left onto the campground road. In about 0.1 miles, turn right on the Frontside Trail. Continue on the Frontside Trail as Joe's Ridge goes left.

D3 - 3.1 Stay on Frontside as Zippety Do Da goes left.

D4 - 4.1 Continue straight on Frontside as Western Zippety goes left.

D5 - 5.4 The singletrack ends at a dirt road (Coal Gulch Rd). Go right, riding up the road.

D6 - 11.7 Stay on Coal Gulch Road as another dirt road goes left.

D7 - 13.3 Continue straight on Coal Gulch Road as another dirt road goes right.

D8 - 15.4 Arrive at a Y-junction near a natural gas compressor facility. Go left. In 0.2 miles, continue straight through a four-way junction.

D9 - 19.0 Turn right on the Edge Loop singletrack (marked by a small sign) as the old road continues straight.

The Edge Loop

Garfield Mesa

Ross Ridge

Cliffs

Book

Coal Gulch

Coal Gulch Road

Edge Loop

Edge Loop

Edge Cutoff

Chutes and Ladders

Chutes and Ladders

Prime Cut

Prime Cut

Joe's Ridge

Kessel Run

Frontside

Zippety Do Da

ONE WAY

Zippety

Western

Vegetarian

Edge and Chutes

Zippety

18 Road

Fruita

D8
D7
D6
D9
D10
D11
D12
D13
D14
D15
D1 Trailhead
D2
D3
D4
D5

2.1
3.6
1.6
1.7
1.4
2.0
1.0
0.9
1.1
5.3
1.3
1.0
1.3
1.8
1.8

7000
6500
7000
6500
6000
6000
5500
5500
5500
6000
6000
6000
5500
5000
6500
6500

21
V.80
16
V.80
V70

1 mile
1 kilometer
1:70,000
0.50

D10 - 20.7 Arrive at the top of "The Waterfall," a 30-foot cliff. Descend the cliff using a series of tattered ropes. The cliff can be avoided by taking the hike-a-bike trail to the right. This option is safer, but far less exciting.

D11 - 22.1 The singletrack crosses the wash several times. Be sure to follow the singletrack to the right as it leaves the wash for the final time.

D12 - 24.1 Turn left on a dirt road.

D13 - 25.1 Make a right on the Edge Loop singletrack. In about 0.3 miles, turn left on unmarked singletrack ("Edge and Chutes") as Chutes and Ladders goes right.

D14 - 26.0 Cross a road and continue on "Edge and Chutes" singletrack.

D15 - 27.1 Arrive at a confusing junction near a cow pond. Continue roughly straight and quickly reach the parking lot.

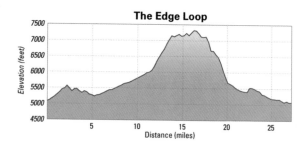

The Edge Loop

Riders almost to the singletrack on the Edge Loop.

Kokopelli's Trailhead ★★★★★

(5 miles west of Fruita)

Technical Difficulty:	● to ◆◆
Physical Difficulty:	**Easy** to **Strenuous**
Distance:	5 – 50 miles
Time:	1 – 10 hours
Type:	Riding Area
Surface:	Singletrack, dirt roads
Elevation: (high/low)	4,600'/5,400'
Season:	Spring, Fall
Crowds:	Some
Dogs:	

Rocky riding, stunning scenery

Ride Description

One of the crown jewels of Colorado mountain biking, the trail system at Kokopelli's is perched atop steep bluffs overlooking the Colorado River. The incredible views of the river and the spires of Colorado National Monument are only surpassed by the excellent riding. The various trails each have their own character and style, but the riding at Kokopelli's is generally rocky, technical, and fun. Most of the trails will require at least a little "hike-a-bike," and many of them have sections that are unnervingly close to massive cliffs. Most of the trails here are black diamond, but Rustler's Loop is one of the best beginner's rides in the state and Moore Fun is an amazing double-diamond challenge ride featuring non-stop technical fun.

Note: Many of the trails here are called "loop" when they are not in fact loops. This terminology dates back to a time when people commonly made the trails into loops by riding back to the parking lot on the frontage road. Currently, most riders make loops using the trails instead of the frontage road. However, the old names have stuck and we still call the trails "Mary's Loop", "Lion's Loop", and "Troy Built Loop" even though they aren't exactly loops.

Driving Directions

From I-70, take Exit 15 and head south on CO-139. Go a short distance and turn right at the T-intersection. Go a few hundred feet and turn left towards the Kokopelli's Trailhead sign. Arrive at the trailhead in about 0.5 miles.

Recommended Trails

The trails at Kokopelli's are well-signed and generally easy to follow. Riders should simply read the following ride descriptions and then use the map on page 314 to plan their own adventure.

Note: The distances listed are for the named trails only, not for a complete ride of that trail from the parking area. Most trails require riding another trail for several miles to get to the start.

Rustler's Loop - ● Distance: 3.4 miles

A fantastic beginner's ride, Rustler's is mostly smooth, but has enough tricky sections and short climbs to challenge the quick-learners. Novice riders will also appreciate the numerous signs that provide advice on trail etiquette and riding techniques. Follow the advice of the signs and ride the trail clockwise to avoid collisions on this popular trail.

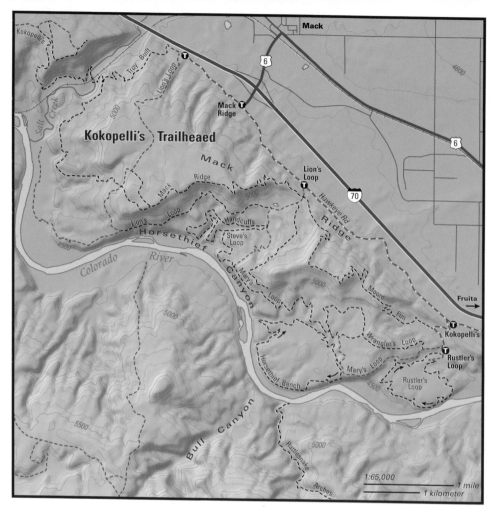

Moore Fun - ◆◆ Distance: 4.1 miles

A great challenge for the expert rider, Moore Fun serves up one technical section after another. No single section is too tough, but there are hundreds of black diamond and double diamond sections for riders to contend with. The trail is traditionally ridden east to west, but it is fun in both directions.

Mary's Loop - ■ Distance: 4.9 miles

Mary's Loop is a combination of wide jeep trail and singletrack with the occasional interesting technical section. It is mainly ridden to get to other trails like Horsetheif Bench and Steve's Loop.

Handcuffs - ■ Distance: 2.4mi and Steve's Loop - ■ Distance: 1.3mi

Steve's Loop and Handcuffs are fantastic short loops that come very close to giant cliffs. The riding is generally easy with a few short difficult sections but quite exhilarating!

Horsethief Bench - ◆ Distance: 3.8 miles

This trail is simply too much fun! After the giant rock staircase at the start (dismount!), the fast, sandy singletrack is punctuated with the occasional black-diamond section. Most people ride the loop clockwise.

Mack Ridge - ◆   Distance: 3.0 miles
Best ridden downhill (west to east), Mack offers good, technical singletrack.

Lion's Loop - ◆   Distance: 5.3 miles
The Lion's Loop has two distinct sections. The southern section (co-designated as the Koko-pelli's Trail) is mostly singletrack and is tough, rocky, and fun. The northern section, which climbs from the north end of Troy Built to Mack, is a slog up a really steep dirt road.

Troy Built - ◆   Distance: 3.8 miles
The Troy Built Trail is sweet, sometimes technical, singletrack. You can make this into a loop using the dirt road section of Lion's Loop, but Troy Built is even better as an out-and-back since the dirt road section of Lion's Loop is tough and monotonous.

Wrangler's - ■   Distance: 2.1 miles
Wrangler's has some nice sections of singletrack, but it also has a great deal of riding on old dirt roads. Wrangler's is steep, so ride up Mary's and come down Wrangler's.

Curt Stevens negotiates one of the many technical sections on the Holy Cross Trail, Tabeguache Trailhead.

(F) Highline Lake State Park ★★★☆☆

(12 miles northwest of Fruita)

Technical Difficulty:	●
Physical Difficulty:	**Moderate**
Distance:	6.6 mi
Time:	About 1 hour
Type:	Loop
Surface:	Singletrack
Climbing:	500'
Season:	Spring, Fall
Crowds:	Crowded
Dogs:	Must be leashed

Beautiful twisty singletrack on the shores of Highline Lake

Ride Description

This ride is so much fun that no one can resist completing a second lap. This loop follows the "18 Hour Trail" that serves as the racecourse for the 18 Hours of Fruita race that is held each spring. The singletrack is generally smooth and fast with only a few climbs and technical sections. The main challenge comes from the multitude of other trail users: bikers, hikers, horses, and fisherman. Try not to crash into any of them – they hate this. Highline Lake is a Colorado State Park, so visitors can expect to pay about $6 per car to get in the gate. For another $15 or so, they can enjoy a beautiful grassy campsite (reservations recommended).

Driving Directions

From Fruita or Grand Junction, head west on I-70. Take Exit 15 and head north on CO-139 (13 Road) for 5.0 miles. Turn left on Q Road and go 1.2 miles. Turn right on 11 8/10 Road and enter Highline Lake State Park. Pay the entrance fee and park near the visitor center.

Riding Directions

F1 - 0.0 From the parking area, ride west towards the lake and find the 18 Hour Trail near the toilets. Turn right on the trail, **riding counterclockwise** around the lake.

At each intersection, simply follow the "18 Hour Trail" markers around the lake – it's difficult to get lost. These additional instructions are provided only for the worryingly fastidious:

F2 - 0.8 Go left on the East Bluffs Loop as the Highline Lake Trail goes right.

F3 - 1.4 Head right on the 18 Hour Trail as the East Bluffs Loop goes straight. (If you go straight here, you can shorten the loop by about 1.0 mile.)

F4 - 2.4 Turn right, rejoining the East Bluffs Loop. At the next intersection, continue straight on the 18 Hour Loop as the Highline Lake Tail goes left.

F5 - 3.5 Turn left on the 18 Hour Trail.

F6 - 4.1 Continue straight on 18 Hour as Mack Mesa goes left.

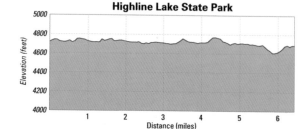

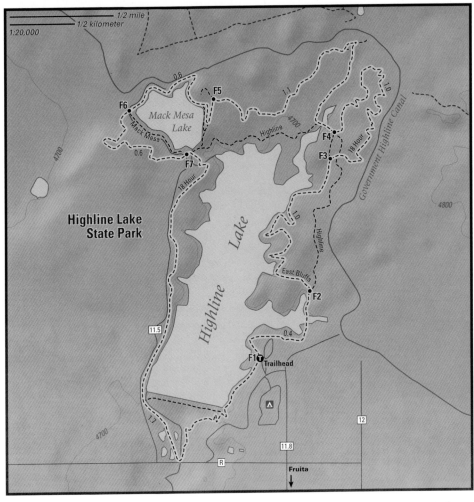

F7 - 4.7 After some fun bermed corners, cross a road and continue on the Highline Lake Trail. Follow signs for the 18 Hour Trail as it takes you around the west side of the lake and below the dam.

F1 - 6.4 Pass by the swim beach and arrive back at the parking area.

G Rabbit Valley - Western Rim ★★★★☆

(25 miles west of Grand Junction)

Technical Difficulty:	
Physical Difficulty:	**Moderate**
Distance:	15.9 miles
Time:	3 – 5 hours
Type:	Lollipop loop
Surface:	Singletrack, doubletrack
Climbing:	2,000′
Season:	Spring, Fall
Crowds:	Few
Dogs:	

Classic desert riding with plenty of adventure and solitude

Ride Description

Tired of the crowds at the Bookcliffs? Try Rabbit Valley! The trails are almost as excellent as those at the Bookcliffs, Tabeguache, or Kokopelli, but they are less crowded and offer nearly endless riding possibilities. Also, the solitude and views of the distant La Sal Mountains (near Moab) make Rabbit Valley a magical experience.

This book describes a few the most popular rides, but Rabbit Valley is also home to dozens of motorcycle trails and dirt roads that just beg riders to link them into huge epic rides. The Kokopelli's Trail passes through Rabbit Valley on its journey from Fruita to Moab.

The Western Rim is the classic ride at Rabbit Valley, and crosses the border to sample some incredible Utah singletrack. The month of May often provides nice temperatures and an abundance of wildflowers.

Driving Directions

From Grand Junction, head west on I-70, pass Fruita, and keep heading west. Take Exit 2 and head south on the dirt road. Quickly come to a huge dirt parking area – park here. (If camping, just start from the campground, which is about 1 mile down the road on the right.)

Riding Directions

G1 - 0.0 From the trailhead, start riding south on the dirt road. Continue on the main road through a few intersections.

G2 - 1.0 Turn right on the #2 Trail.

G3 - 2.3 Bear slightly right and merge onto well used dirt road (Kokopelli's Trail). (Another double track heads sharp right.)

G4 - 2.6 Shortly after the Mc-Donald Creek Trailhead, turn right onto the #2 Trail.

G5 - 3.5 The trail forks: the easy way goes right and the difficult way goes left; go right. The trails rejoin in less than a mile.

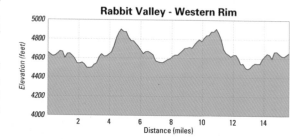

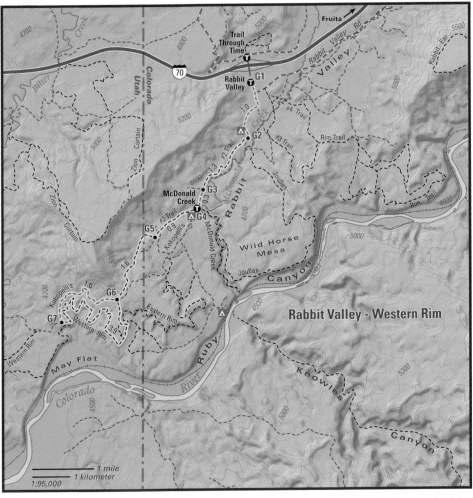

G6 - 5.1 Come to a large, flat junction. Turn right on the Kokopelli's Trail. (The end of the Western Rim Trail comes in on the left here.)

G7 - 6.7 Turn left on another dirt road. Head down a very steep hill and turn left on the Western Rim Trail singletrack. Enjoy the great riding and spectacular views! *(For a longer ride, continue straight on Kokopelli's for about 0.5 miles and turn left onto the Western Rim Trail.)*

G6 - 10.6 Climb a steep hill and arrive back at the flat junction. Find the #2 Trail and retrace the route back to the trailhead.

(H) 3–4 Loop ★★★⯪☆ ■ Distance: 5.4 miles

The 3–4 Loop features great singletrack riding, and it is located just a few minutes from the interstate, making it a convenient stop for riders cruising back from Moab. The loop is fun to ride in both directions, but clockwise is recommended.

From the main trailhead, ride south on the dirt road and make your first left onto a dirt road. Then, make your first right on another dirt road. Follow signs for Trail #4 and ride this until you can turn right onto Trail #3.

(I) The Rim Trail ★★☆☆☆ Distance: 7.7 miles

Don't confuse this trail with the Western Rim Trail when looking at maps. The Rim Trail can allegedly be fun, but it is actually a giant pit of sand. Legend has it that after a heavy rain, the sand hardens but this was not the experience of the author. This may be a great trail for dirt bikes, but it's really tough on a mountain bike. The Rim Trail starts at the intersection of Trails #3 and #4.

Tall-Tales around the campfire
The Top 10 Most Famous Rides in Colorado

10. Colorado Springs – Jones Park

9. Crested Butte – Reno-Flag-Bear-Deadman

8. Vail – Two Elk Trail

7. Fruita – Kokopelli's

6. Durango – Hermosa Creek

5. Summit County – Colorado Trail via Tiger Road

4. Denver – Kenosha to Georgia Pass

3. Crested Butte - The 401

2. Fruita – Bookcliffs

1. Salida – Monarch Crest

Curt Stevens bombs the steeps on Joe's Ridge Trail, The Bookcliffs.

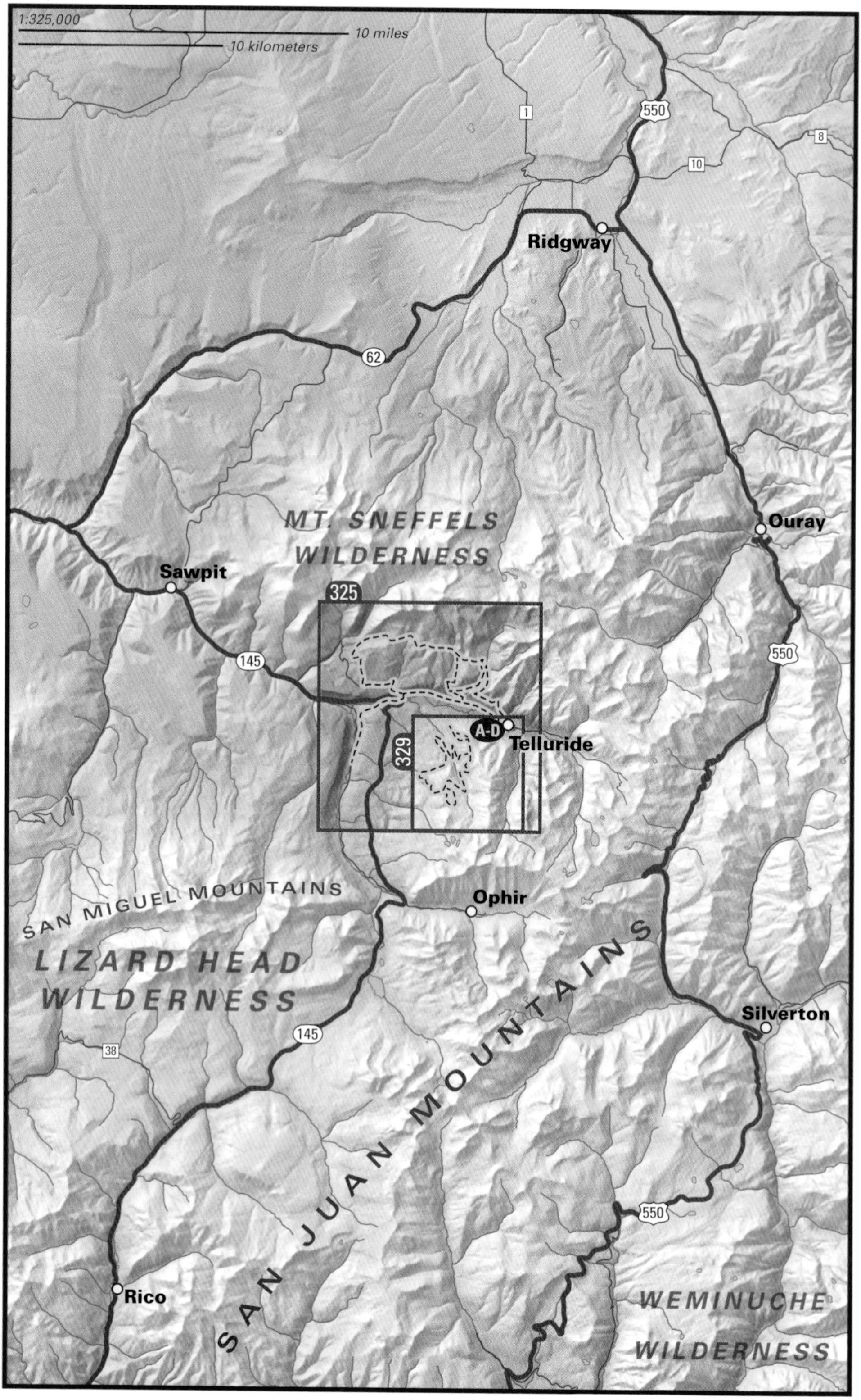

1:325,000

10 miles

10 kilometers

1

550

10

8

Ridgway

62

MT. SNEFFELS
WILDERNESS

325

Ouray

Sawpit

145

550

329

A-D Telluride

SAN MIGUEL MOUNTAINS

LIZARD HEAD
WILDERNESS

Ophir

SAN JUAN MOUNTAINS

Silverton

38

145

550

Rico

WEMINUCHE
WILDERNESS

Telluride

For residents of the Front Range, Telluride is one of the most remote places in the state. However, those willing to make the journey will discover a magical land of huge cliffs, lush forests, and incredible natural beauty. The mountain biking is excellent and riders can take advantage of the free gondola that carries people and bikes 2,000 vertical feet above the valley floor. Many of the trails start from town (or from the gondola), so riders staying in town can simply hop on their bikes and start riding.

Due to its location on the western side of the San Juan Mountains, Telluride receives plenty of precipitation. This is great for a ski town, but not ideal for a mountain biking destination. Thankfully, the trails hold up well in the rain, something that can't be said for most places in Colorado.

Telluride's historical roots are in mining. Billions of dollars in minerals (including tellurium, the town's namesake) have been mined from the hills surrounding the town. While Telluride has gentrified from the days when the main drag was populated by miners, horses, and saloons, the place still has lots of old-town charm. Despite the town's reputation as a vacation destination for movie stars and millionaires, it's still a fine place for the dirt-bag mountain biker to hang out.

Parking

Parking in Telluride can be frustrating, as spots near the main street (Colorado Avenue) cost 50 cents per hour and are limited to three hours. Also, parking on the neighborhood streets is free, but is generally limited to two hours. This is fine for getting lunch downtown, but worthless for the mountain biker who might be out for many hours. To solve this problem, park at a parking lot known as Carhenge. To reach it, turn right at the traffic circle (as you are driving into town) and head south on Mahoney Drive. Turn left on Pacific Avenue, go about a block, and turn right into Carhenge.

Accommodations

Telluride, being a ski town, offers an assortment of condos and hotels, with more accommodations available in Mountain Village. It has a reputation for being expensive. For those who don't want to shell out the cash for a bed, there is a campground just a few blocks east of downtown in the city park. If even this is too fancy, there is free camping near Alta Lakes and along Alta Lakes Road. Additionally, there are lots of dirt roads on National Forest land, where primitive camping is allowed.

Bike Shops

Paragon Ski and Sport
213 W Colorado Avenue and 236 S Oak Street. 970-728-4525
Sales, service, and rentals.

Eats and Drinks

The Steaming Bean
221 West Colorado Avenue. 970-369-5575
"The Bean" brews excellent coffee and is nice place to hang out on a rainy day.

Brown Dog Pizza
110 East Colorado Avenue. 970-728-8046
Sports bar and pizzeria on the main street. Good beers on tap.

Gondola Trails ★★★★½

(Starts in Telluride)

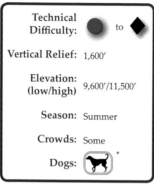

Technical Difficulty:	● to ◆
Vertical Relief:	1,600'
Elevation: (low/high)	9,600'/11,500'
Season:	Summer
Crowds:	Some
Dogs:	🐕 *

The free gondola provides access to the downhill bike park and several cross-country trails

Ride Description

The gondola in Telluride has two main advantages over other gondolas in Colorado. First, it runs from 7 a.m. until midnight. Second, it's totally free! This strange state of affairs exists because the gondola is mainly intended to transport people from the shopping in Telluride to the upscale condos in Mountain Village. On its way, it makes a stop at Station St. Sophia, which just so happens to be a great place to start a mountain bike ride. From there riders can enjoy some quick laps on the Bike Park trails that head down to Mountain Village, or ride cross country on the Prospect Trail or the Village Trail.

* Dogs are allowed on the Gondola, but are not allowed in the Bike Park.

Driving Directions

You can reach Station St. Sophia from either Telluride or Mountain Village. If you start in Telluride, your best bet is to park at the Carhenge lot, since it offers free day parking. From the traffic circle on the west side of town, head south on Mahoney Drive, turn left on Pacific Avenue, and turn right into Carhenge.

Recommended Rides

The Bike Park ★★★½ ■ through ◆◆ about 10 miles of trails

The bike park consists of three recently built trails that run from the top of the gondola at Station St. Sophia to the gondola station at Mountain Village, a vertical drop of about 1,000 feet. Obviously, such a bike park doesn't compare to the massive lift-served downhill biking operations in place at Winter Park, Sol Vista, and Keystone. However, what the Telluride bike park lacks in scale, it makes up for in quality. The black diamond trails are very challenging and all the trails are well-constructed and very entertaining. As prices for lift tickets at the major bike parks head towards 40 dollars per day, the free lift-served experience at Telluride can't be beat.

Village Trail ★★★½ ● 3.9 miles

A fantastic beginner's ride, the Village Trail meanders from the top of the gondola back down to the Village Parking gondola station. The singletrack ends at a road, but there are signs to guide you back to the gondola station in Mountain Village.

Map labels:
San, 9000, 9500, 10000, Telluride, Carhenge, Miguel, River, Station Mountain Village, Ridge, Gondola, Lift 1, Gondola, Station Telluride, Bear Creek, Station Village Parking, Gondola, 9500, Bike Park, Telluride, Lift 8, Station St. Sophia, Needle Rock 10656, Gondola Trails, Village, Coonskin, Lift 4, Lift 9, Bear Creek, 10000, Sheridan, Prospect, Lift 10, 11000, Lift 5, Lift 6, See Forever, Wasatch, 10500, Basin, Prospect, Creek, Prospect, Creek, Basin, Lift 13, Prospect Loop, Lift 14, Skunk Creek, 10500, 1 mile, 1 kilometer, Prospect Basin, Lift 12, East Fork, 12000, Boomerang Rd, Bald Mountain 11868, 11500, Gold Hill 12736, 11500, 12500, Turkey Creek, 1:42,500

Prospect Trail ★★★★☆ ◼ 8.9 miles

The Prospect Trail is a Telluride classic and features plenty of first-class singletrack through beautiful forests and meadows. It involves about 1,500 feet of climbing, but – thanks to the gondola – 2,500 feet of descending. At mile 3.5, riders have the choice of either the "Prospect Trail" or the "Prospect Loop." The Prospect Loop features better singletrack, but it is possible to shorten the ride by 1.5 miles by sticking to the Prospect Trail. The singletrack ends at a paved road and there is a series of small signs to guide riders back to Mountain Village. Those looking for a longer adventure can take the old Boomerang Road to the ghost town of Alta. For this option, look for the sign for Boomerang at mile 5.5.

Photo: Chris Nowak

Ⓑ Eider - Deep Loop ★★★★☆

(Starts in Telluride)

Technical Difficulty:	◆
Physical Difficulty:	**Strenuous**
Distance:	9.3 miles
Time:	2 – 3 hours
Type:	Lollipop Loop
Surface:	Singletrack, dirt road, bike path
Climbing:	2,200'
Season:	Summer
Crowds:	Some
Dogs:	*

A classic short-but-tough ride through lush forests

Ride Description

This loop can be ridden in both directions, but either way involves steep climbing and, most likely, a good deal of walking. The Eider-Deep Loop rewards its riders with some excellent singletrack through some of the most impressive aspen groves in the state.

* Dogs are required to be on a leash in Telluride. However, dog owners can simply drive to the start of the singletrack.

Driving Directions

Start from the Carhenge parking lot (see page 323).

Riding Directions

B1 - 0.0 Turn left out of Carhenge on Pacific Avenue. Make a right on Mahoney Drive, and go a few blocks. At the traffic circle, turn left and take the bike path that parallels CO-145.

B2 - 1.5 Just past the gas station, turn right onto an unmarked dirt road (Mill Creek Road).

B3 - 2.1 Pass the Eider Creek Trail on the left and continue on Mill Creek Road.

B4 - 3.0 Turn left on the Deep Creek Trail.

B5 - 3.7 Make another left on the Deep Creek Trail (towards Last Dollar Road).

B6 - 5.1 Continue on Deep Creek Trail as Sneffels Highline Trail goes right.

B7 - 5.6 Bust a left on the Eider Creek Trail.

B3 - 7.2 Turn right on Mill Creek Road and ride back to Telluride.

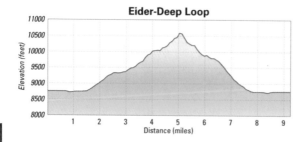

Ⓒ Western Deep Creek ★★★★☆   ◆ 17.1 miles

The Deep Creek Trail continues several miles west of the intersection with the Eider Creek Trail. The western section of the Deep Creek Trail offers great singletrack riding, but involves pushing your bike up a steep, loose hill for about 30 minutes. For those up to the challenge, this epic loop is very worthwhile.

C1 - 0.0   Start as for the Eider–Deep ride, but continue straight on the bike path at mile 1.5.

C2 - 3.2   Turn right on Last Dollar Road.

C3 - 5.0   Just before you get to the airport, turn right on Basque Boulevard and quickly make a left onto the Aldasoro singletrack. (This trail is nicknamed "Penelope's Cruise.")

C4 - 7.1   Turn right on the Deep Creek Trail. Enjoy a mile of flat riding before the horrible climbing starts. After the climb, enjoy some great singletrack.

C5 - 13.4   At a T-intersection, turn left towards the Jud Weibe Trail.

C6 - 15.4   At another T-intersection, go right on doubletrack and head down into Telluride.

C7 - 16.2   Arrive back in Telluride at the Jud Weibe Trailhead. Turn right and ride the city streets back to the Carhenge parking lot.

Lost in the aspens on the Eider Creek Trail

Telluride

(D) Galloping Goose ★★★☆☆

(Starts in Telluride)

Technical Difficulty:	
Physical Difficulty:	**Easy**
Distance:	13.6 miles
Time:	2 – 3 hours
Type:	Out-and-back
Surface:	Bike path, singletrack
Climbing/ Descending:	300'/900' (one-way)
Season:	Summer, Fall
Crowds:	Some
Dogs:	🚫

Gentle singletrack along a historical railroad grade

Ride Description

The Galloping Goose Trail is built upon the old railroad grade of the Rio Grande and Southern Railroad. The railroad took its name from a series of small, unintentionally-whimsical steam locomotives that ran along the tracks in the 1930s. These "geese" were created as a cost-saving measure for the railroad and were constructed by welding two delivery trucks together and swapping the usual wheels for steel train wheels.

This ride takes you for a leisurely cruise along the bike path west from Telluride and then connects to the Galloping Goose Trail. The trail begins as a wide gravel path and eventually narrows to excellent singletrack. The Galloping Goose Trail actually continues beyond the end of this ride, following the path of the old Rio Grande and Southern Railroad for many miles on a combination of dirt roads and trails.

Driving Directions

Start at the Carhenge parking area in Telluride (see page 323).

Riding Directions

D1 - 0.0 From the Carhenge parking lot, go left on Pacific Avenue. Make a right at Mahoney Drive and go a few blocks until you come to the traffic circle. Turn left at the traffic circle and ride west on the bike path that parallels Colorado Avenue (CO-145).

D2 - 3.5 Cross CO-145 near the Conoco gas station. The bike path usually connects directly to the Galloping Goose Trail, but a construction project may still be in progress that requires you to ride a short distance west on Society Drive and then turn right to access the Galloping Goose Trail.

D3 - 4.7 Continue straight on Galloping Goose as the Keystone Gorge Trail goes right. The Galloping Goose Trail soon turns from a wide path into narrow singletrack.

D4 - 6.8 Come to the end of the Galloping Goose singletrack. If you're having too much fun to stop here, turn left on the dirt road and ride as far as you like. Otherwise, turn around and go back the way you came.

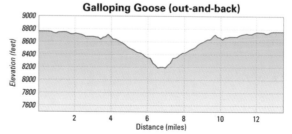

Iron
Mountain
12747

Campbell
Peak
13213

Dallas
Peak
13809

Mill Creek Basin

12500

11500

11000

Sneffels
Highline

9500

10500

Deep
Creek
4.3

12000

C4

Deep
Creek
2.1

Penelopes Cruise

Western Deep Creek

1.8

10000

B7

0.5

B6

.4

B5/C5

Eider
Deep

Eider
1.4

0.7

Mill Creek Rd

B4

C6

Jud Weibe

Telluride Regional Airport

C3 Last Dollar Rd

C2

9000

0.3

B3

0.6

0.9

Mill Creek

2.0

0.8 **C7**

145

Keystone
Gorge

1.2

D2

1.1

San

B2

Colorado Ave

1.5

Jud Weibe

T

Sunshine
Point
9321

D3

1.7

Meadows

Jurassic

Boomerang

San Miguel River

Miguel

Carhenge

T

Lift 1

B1/C1/D1

Telluride

T

Bear
Creek

River

**Galloping
Goose**

Gondola

Gondola

Ridge

Gondola

Lift 8

9500

2.1

Galloping Goose

Lift 4

Prospect

Village

Lift 9

Needle
Rock
10656

D4

9000

Vance

Creek

Lift 10

Prospect

**Gondola
Trails**

Lift 5

Lift 6

See

Bear
Creek

11000

11500

Wasatch

145

Turkey

10500

10000

Lift 13

Forever

Lift 14

Prospect

Basin

Gold
Hill
12736

Creek

9500

11000

Bald
Mountain
11868

Lift 12

Boomerang Rd

11500

12500

1:85,000

1 mile

1 kilometer

Taking the bike path into Telluride.

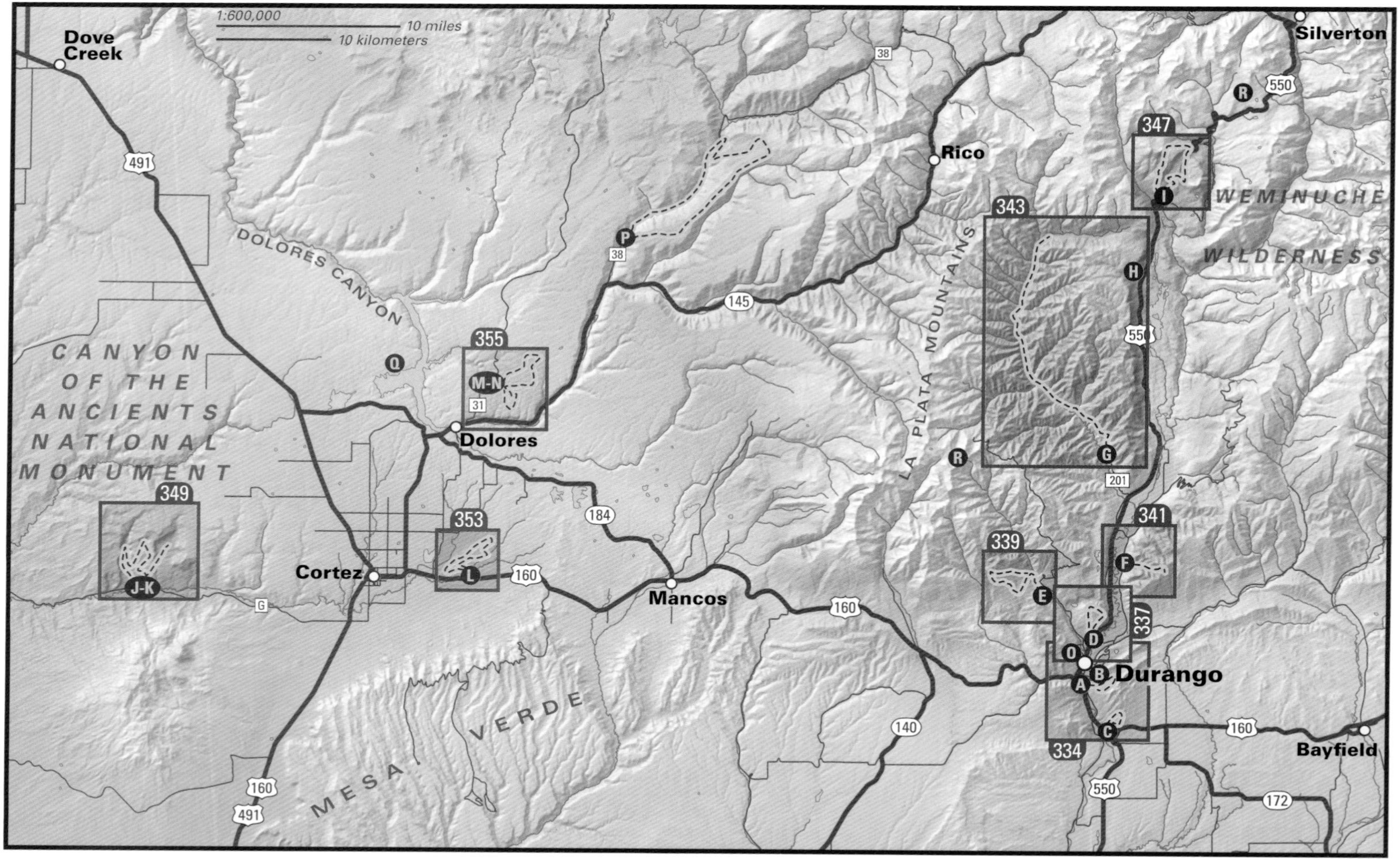
1:600,000
10 miles
10 kilometers
Dove Creek
Silverton
Rico
Dolores
Cortez
Mancos
Durango
Bayfield
DOLORES CANYON
CANYON OF THE ANCIENTS NATIONAL MONUMENT
LA PLATA MOUNTAINS
WEMINUCHE WILDERNESS
MESA VERDE
491
38
145
550
160
184
140
172
201
31
G
347
343
355
349
353
339
341
337
334
A
B
C
D
E
F
G
H
I
J-K
L
M-N
O
P
Q
R

Durango
& Cortez

The sheer amount of mountain biking in southwestern Colorado is stunning. Even more impressive is the variety of trials. For example, within one hour of Durango, riders can cruise on red-dirt trails through the desert, explore lush forests, or tackle the Colorado Trail at 12,000 feet.

There are trails for every season. Spring is the perfect time to ride the trails near Cortez before the temperatures climb. As soon as the snow melts in the summer, mountain bikers can savor the classic high-elevation trails like Engineer Mountain and the Colorado Trail. When temperatures dip in the fall, the rides near Durango – Horse Gulch and Telegraph – are in perfect condition. During the winter, most people go skiing. However, the die-hard mountain bikers make a short drive to Farmington, New Mexico, where the trails are frequently dry, even in the dead of winter.

Durango (population 15,000) hosted the first UCI Mountain Biking World Championships way back in 1990, and since then it has remained one of the best places in the world to ride a mountain bike. Though it seems to take forever to get to the southwest corner of the state from the Front Range, the riding is worth the journey. Arriving in Durango, visitors will find dozens of first-rate trails of all difficulties as well as a laid-back town with great places to grab coffee, pizza, or a gourmet meal. Most importantly, Durango is home to one of the best Breweries in Colorado: Ska Brewing.

Cortez (population 8,000) exists mainly as a gateway for tourists visiting Mesa Verde National Park and exploring the Four Corners region. The region features incredible red-rock desert scenery, complete with towering mountains in the background. Cortez gets very hot in the summer and gets some snow in the winter, so mountain bikers generally visit in the spring or fall.

Durango has its own small airport, offering many flights to and from Denver and Phoenix. Additionally, there are several good bike shops in town that rent bikes and various companies offering mountain biking shuttle-services as well as guided tours. Thus, Durango is a good place for those wishing to vacation without a car.

Durango

Accommodations

Durango is a college town (home to Fort Lewis College), and consequently has an abundance of hotel and motel options. As long as riders don't visit during graduation or a major bike race, finding a cheap room should be fairly easy. Likewise, Cortez, being a popular tourist stop, is also filled with motels marketed to the budget traveler.

Southwest Colorado is home to many nice campgrounds. However, it is a very popular place for the "RV crowd" during the summer, so many of the established campgrounds will fill up, even on the weekdays. To find free camping, visitors will have to drive a good distance from Durango and explore some of the dirt roads in the National Forest. Those who venture north of Cortez, past Dolores, will discover an abundance of free camping as well as a lifetime of largely unknown trails.

Bike Shops

Kokopelli Bike and Board
130 West Main Street, Cortez. 970-565-4408
The only bike shop in Cortez, Kokopelli offers a broad selection of bikes, parts, and skateboards. Great service and trail suggestions. Rental bikes available.

Mountain Bike Specialists
949 Main Avenue, Durango. 970-247-4066
Great selection of parts and skilled mechanics.

Papa Wheelies Bike Shop
1077 Main Avenue, Durango. 970-259-1975
This combination bike shop and bicycle messenger service specializes in eclectic bicycles and singlespeeds, but they are happy to service any bike.

Durango Cyclery
143 E. 13th Street, Durango. 970-247-0747
A small shop located half-a-block off Main St.

Hassle Free Sports
2615 Main Avenue, Durango. 800-835-3800
Bikes, service, and rentals available.

Second Avenue Sports
600 E. 2nd Avenue, Durango. 970-247-4511
Rentals and high-end demos available.

Hermosa Tours
www.hermosatours.net 877-ROLL-MTB
Offers a shuttle service to many trailheads in the Durango area: a great resource for shuttling those epic rides. They also offer multi-day guided tours.

Eats and Drinks

Downtown is packed with shops and great restaurants. So hungry mountain bikers shouldn't have any trouble finding delicious food and drink, but here are a few recommendations:

The Steaming Bean
915 Main Avenue, Durango. 970-385-7901
Great coffee and pastries. Wireless internet and computers.

Homeslice Pizza
441 E College Drive, Durango. 970-259-5551
Serves delicious pizza out of a converted house with a lovely patio in front.

Ska Brewing
225 Girard Street, Durango. 970-247-5792
Though it is now available throughout the state, the best place to enjoy a Ska beer is in Durango. Their Pinstripe Ale is the author's favorite, and their Modus Hoperandi is also fantastic. The brewery has a tasting room and offers free tours (call ahead). From Durango, head south on US-550 for about 2 miles and turn right on Girard St.

Steamworks Brewing Co
801 E. 2nd Avenue, Durango. 970-259-9200
Good beers and pub-food in the middle of downtown Durango.

Carver Brewing Co
1022 Main Avenue, Durango. 970-259-2545
Microbrewed beer and tasty food. Also serves breakfast.

Horse Gulch - Stacy's

(Starts in Durango)

Technical Difficulty:	
Physical Difficulty:	**Moderate**
Distance:	4.0 miles
Time:	1 hour
Type:	Lollipop Loop
Surface:	Singletrack, dirt road
Climbing:	600'
Season:	Spring, Summer, Fall
Crowds:	Some
Dogs:	Trails can be crowded

A small sample of the many miles of delightful singletrack found at Horse Gulch

Ride Description

There is a reason Durango has produced a disproportionate number of skilled mountain bikers: the town is surrounded by incredible singletrack. Horse Gulch is the crown jewel of the close-to-town riding, featuring a great combination of buttery-smooth singletrack and rocky, technical challenges. Most intersections have signs with maps, so this is a great place to wander around without getting too lost. The dirt at Horse Gulch is essentially dehydrated potter's clay, so any attempt to ride these trails when they are wet will result in the transformation of your bicycle into a giant ball of goop.

This loop of Telegraph Trail, Meadow Loop, and Stacy's Loop makes for a great, quick ride that is suitable for gung-ho beginners yet great fun for experienced riders as well. There are countless options to extend the ride. The local mountain biking club, Trails 2000, publishes up-to-date maps to these trails. They are available at local bike shops and on their webpage: Trails2000.org.

Driving Directions

The trailhead is located at the east end of 3rd St in the town of Durango. To reach the trailhead from Main Ave, head east until you reach 3rd Ave and turn right. Turn left on 3rd St and go for a few block until you reach the trailhead parking area at the end of the road.

Riding Directions - see map on the next page

A1 - 0.0 From the parking lot, head up the dirt road (Horse Gulch Rd).

A2 - 0.8 Turn right on the Telegraph Trail.

A3 - 1.4 Turn left on Meadow Loop.

A4 - 1.8 Turn right on Stacy's Loop.

A5 - 2.2 Continue straight on Stacy's Loop as Mike's Trail goes right.

A6 - 2.5 Continue roughly straight through two intersections, following signs for Meadow Loop.

A2 - 3.2 Arrive back at the Telegraph Trail. Head back to Horse Gulch Road and turn left.

A1 - 4.0 Arrive back at the trailhead!

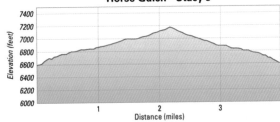

Horse Gulch - Stacy's

Durango

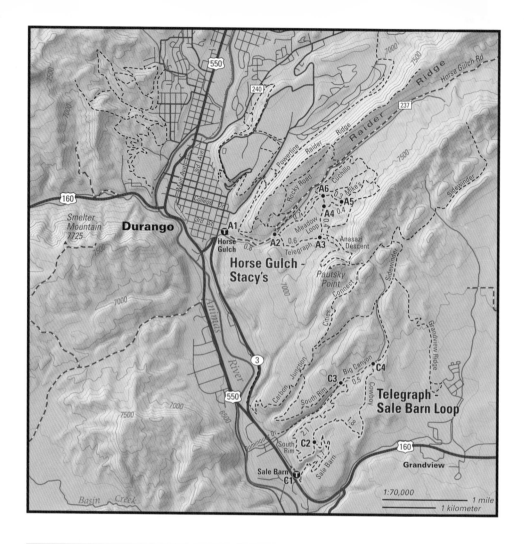

Ⓑ Raider Ridge ★★★★☆ ◆◆   Distance: 4.0 miles

Raider Ridge is a tough ride, featuring countless technical moves on an intimidating ridge. There are numerous connector trails that can be used to make loops out of various sections of the complete ridge trail, but riding the complete ridge as an out-and-back is a fantastic ride and is sure to challenge even the best riders.

Begin this ride the same way as Ride A, but continue past the turn to Telegraph Trail (mile 0.8). At mile 1.1, turn left on unmarked singletrack. The next section is a confusing mess of trails: continue uphill for less than a mile and you will soon reach the ridge. Turn right and follow the rocky ridge until you've had enough or until you reach the high point at mile 4.5.

ⓒTelegraph - Sale Barn Loop ★★★✦✦

(Located 3 miles south of Durango)

Technical Difficulty:	■
Physical Difficulty:	**Moderate**
Distance:	7.8 miles
Time:	1 – 1.5 hours
Type:	Lollipop loop
Surface:	Singletrack
Climbing:	1,000'
Season:	Spring, Summer, Fall
Crowds:	Some
Dogs:	🐕

A great singletrack loop near town with many options

Ride Description

The Telegraph Trails System is a collection of excellent single-track trails located just a few miles south of Durango. These trails can be linked with the trails at Horse Gulch by riding the Telegraph Trail over the hill. This suggested loop is just the tip of the iceberg. For the latest information on these trails, stop by a local bike shop and pick up one of the trail maps created by the local mountain biking group, Trails 2000. The Southern Telegraph Trails are often closed from December 1 to April 15 to protect deer and elk. The trails near Horse Gulch Road are not affected by this closure.

Driving Directions

From the junction of with US-160 and US-550 in Durango, head south on US-550 for 3.1 miles. Turn left on Dominquez Drive and turn immediately right to parallel US-550 on the frontage road and go 0.3 miles. Just before the frontage road merges into the highway, turn left on an unmarked dirt road that takes you to the trailhead parking area.

Riding Directions - see map on previous page

C1 - 0.0 Start riding on the Sale Barn Trail.

C2 - 1.7 At an unmarked Y-intersection, turn left on the South Rim Trail.

C3 - 3.8 Turn right on Big Canyon Trail and climb on an old dirt road.

C4 - 4.3 Turn right on the Cowboy Trail singletrack.

C2 - 6.1 Arrive back at the intersection with the Sale Barn Trail. Bear left and follow the Sale Barn Trail back to the trailhead.

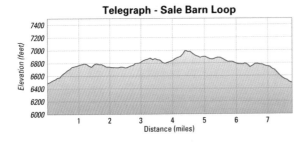

Telegraph - Sale Barn Loop

(D) Animas Mountain ★★★☆☆

(Starts in Durango)

Technical Difficulty:	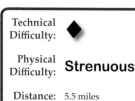 ◆
Physical Difficulty:	**Strenuous**
Distance:	5.5 miles
Time:	1 – 1.5 hours
Type:	Loop
Surface:	Singletrack, doubletrack
Climbing:	1,500′
Season:	Spring, Summer, Fall
Crowds:	Crowded
Dogs:	Trail can be crowded

Starting from town, Animas Mountain offers plenty of loose rock, exciting riding, and great views

Ride Description

This ride at Animas Mountain is deceiving: it seems like a leisurely five-mile loop in a city park, but turns out to be a strenuous battle on loose, rocky trails. However, the great views from the top of the mountain – down to the oxbows of the Animas River – are well worth the effort. The ride down is great fun for an advanced rider with a taste for rocky trails. The parking area at the trailhead is very small, so riders may want to park in town and ride to the trailhead.

Driving Directions

From downtown Durango, head north on US-550. Turn left onto 32nd Street. After three blocks, turn right onto 4th Street. As the road ends, turn right into a dirt parking lot. This parking area is in a quiet neighborhood, so keep your excitement to low volumes.

Riding Directions

D1 - 0.0 From the parking area, ride past the brown gate and up a dirt road.

D2 - 0.1 The trail forks; go left on the road. Note: there are many intersections in the next mile. Simply stay on the widest trail and head to the top of the mountain.

D3 - 2.3 Arrive at a glorious cliff-top vista, overlooking the Animas River. Head east along the edge of the mesa.

D4 - 3.1 Come to a Y-intersection and turn left, staying along the edge of the mesa. There are several braided trails that head down. Stay left (east).

D5 - 5.0 Turn left and ride down some technical switchbacks.

D2 - 5.4 Arrive back at the first Y-junction and turn left.

D1 - 5.5 Back at the parking area to face the dilemma: another lap or dinner at Steamworks?

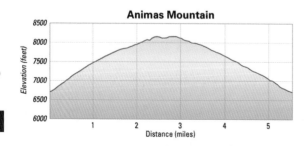

Animas Mountain

Durango

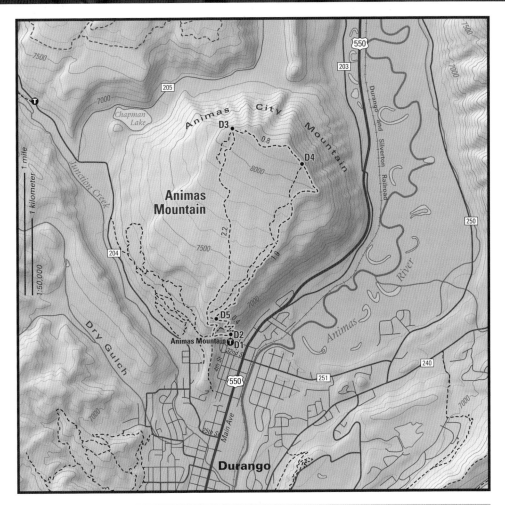

The author on the Engineer Mountain Trail.

(E) Colorado Trail–Dry Fork Loop ★★★★☆

(About 5 miles from Durango)

Technical Difficulty:	
Physical Difficulty:	**Strenuous**
Distance:	12.5 miles
Time:	2 – 3 hours
Type:	Lollipop loop
Surface:	Singletrack
Climbing:	2,200'
Season:	Summer, Fall
Crowds:	Crowded
Dogs:	Trail is often crowded

Lovely, varied trail riding with a nice vista

Ride Description

The Colorado Trail begins in Waterton Canyon, just outside of Denver, and winds through some of the most beautiful terrain in the world for about 470 miles. It finally ends here, at Junction Creek Road, just outside of Durango. This ride samples the last 5 miles of this epic trail.

This loop of the Colorado Trail with the Dry Fork Trail serves up hearty portions of steep climbing and fantastic downhilling. The initial climb up to Gudy's Rest is especially taxing, and those looking for a quick (5.6 mile) after-work ride often turn around here. Once on the Dry Fork Trail, prepare for a wonderful downhill section through the woods.

Driving Directions

From downtown Durango, drive north on US-550 and turn left on 25th Street, which becomes Junction Creek Road. Follow this for 4.6 miles until you reach the signed parking for the Colorado Trail on the right.

Riding Directions

E1 - 0.0 Cross the road and start riding on the signed Colorado Trail. Just after you pass the trail sign, go left at the fork.

E2 - 0.1 Pass a big sign containing information about the Colorado Trail.

E3 - 1.5 Turn left and ride across a bridge over Junction Creek.

E4 - 2.6 Come to Gudy's Rest: a wooden bench with an excellent view.

E5 - 2.8 Continue straight on the Colorado Trail as Hoffhein's Connection goes left.

E6 - 5.3 Turn left onto Dry Fork Trail and enjoy a great downhill!

E7 - 8.3 Turn left on the Hoffhein's Connection, and climb back up to the Colorado Trail.

E5 - 9.5 Turn right on the Colorado Trail and retrace your route back to the trailhead.

Colorado Trail and Dry Fork Loop

Durango

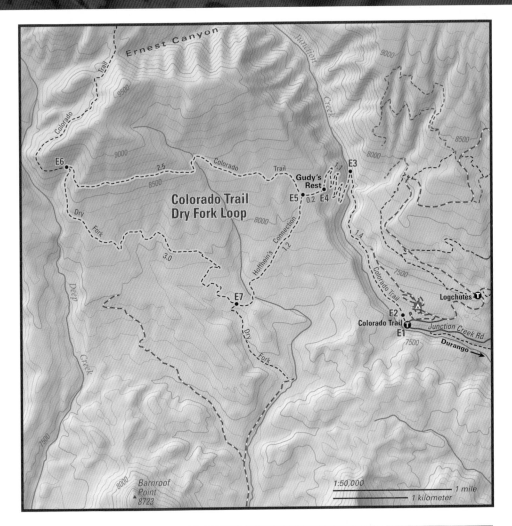

Ernest Canyon

Junction Creek

Colorado Trail

9000

9500

9000

8500

E6

2.5

Colorado

Trail

8500

Dry

Fork

**Colorado Trail
Dry Fork Loop**

8000

1.1

E3

8000

8500

9000

Gudy's
Rest

E5 0.2 E4

Hoffhein's Connection

1.2

7500

1.4

Colorado Trail

Logchutes

E7

3.0

Deep

Creek

Dry

Fork

E2

Colorado Trail

E1

Junction Creek Rd

7500

Durango →

7500

Barnroof
Point
8723

1:50,000

1 mile

1 kilometer

Laura Johnson lost in August wildflowers along Hermosa Creek. photo: Curtis Stevens

(F) Haflin Creek ★★★★★

(10 miles northeast of Durango)

Technical Difficulty:	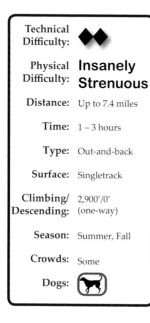 ◆◆
Physical Difficulty:	**Insanely Strenuous**
Distance:	Up to 7.4 miles
Time:	1 – 3 hours
Type:	Out-and-back
Surface:	Singletrack
Climbing/ Descending:	2,900'/0' (one-way)
Season:	Summer, Fall
Crowds:	Some
Dogs:	🐕

Steep, loose, technical and dangerous. Interested?

Ride Description

The Haflin Creek Trail is sustained double-diamond riding on steep slopes. It is included for the hot-shots who are bored by trails that don't constantly threaten to kill them. This trail is steep! Near the top, it drops about 1,200 vertical feet in one mile: a grade of 22-percent!

Previously, Halflin Creek was known as an amazing finish to a ride of the *Missionary Ridge Trail*. However, due to a large forest fire, the Missionary Ridge Trail is covered with about 500 downed trees (no exaggeration) and was virtually un-rideable as of 2009. Thus, it is best to access the downhill of the Haflin Creek Trail in an unpleasant way: by biking up the trail first. The upper section of the trail is littered with downed trees from the fire, so riders should simply go as high as they like before turning around. The ascent will require more walking than riding, so wear some comfortable shoes.

It may be possible to shuttle most of the way to the top using FS-071. Riders attempting this should budget extra time to find the start of the Haflin Creek Trail as the top of Missionary Ridge is a labyrinth of fallen trees.

Driving Directions

From Durango, head north on US-550 for 8 miles. Turn right on County-252 (Trimble Lane) and go one 1 mile until a T-intersection. Turn right onto County-250 and drive 1.2 miles until a small sign marks the Haflin Creek Trailhead on the left.

Riding Directions

F1 - 0.0 From the parking lot, ride uphill on the Haflin Creek Trail.

F2 - 3.7 Reach the Missionary Ridge Trail (if you make it this far). Turn around and attempt to survive the wild descent.

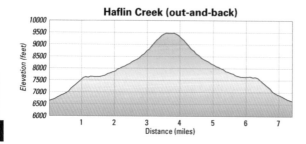

Haflin Creek (out-and-back)

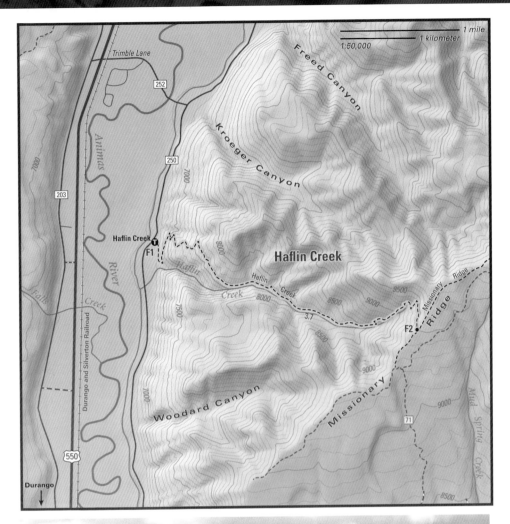

Beautiful wildflowers near Molas Pass.   photo: Dan Steuer

G Hermosa Creek

(South TH: 15 miles north of Durango. North TH: 35 miles north of Durango.)

Technical Difficulty:	
Physical Difficulty:	**Moderate**
Distance:	18.6 miles (shuttle)
Time:	2 – 4 hours (shuttle)
Type:	Shuttle/ Out-and-back
Surface:	Mostly singletrack, some dirt road
Climb/ Descend:	2,700 / 3,800 (riding north to south)
Season:	Summer, Fall
Crowds:	Few
Dogs:	

A classic Durango trail featuring plenty of singletrack cruising.

Ride Description

The Hermosa Creek Trail offers almost 20 miles of wonderful moderate riding on singletrack, widetrack, and dirt roads. The ride is traditionally completed by shuttling to the north trailhead and riding north-to-south, thus losing about 1,000 feet of elevation over the course of the ride. But be warned, there are still a lot of tough climbs even with the shuttle. The ride is even better as an out-and-back: start at the southern trailhead and ride as far as you like and then turn around. The ride is described as a 37-mile epic from the southern trailhead to the northern and back, but the intersection with the Salt Creek Trail (mile 12.2) also makes a good turnaround spot since this is where the singletrack turns into wide ATV trail.

Driving Directions

For the shuttle ride, leave a car at the South Trailhead and then bring bikes and riders to the North Trailhead. To ride the out-and-back, simply start at the South Trailhead.

South Trailhead: From Downtown Durango (junction of US-550 and Florida Road), drive 10.2 miles north on US-550. Turn left on County-201 and stay on it as it turns right and then left. Follow County-201 for about 4 miles until it ends at the South Hermosa Creek Trailhead.

North Trailhead: From the South Trailhead, head back to US-550. Turn left and drive north on US-550 for 15.8 miles. Turn left at the entrance to Durango Mountain Resort and follow signs for "Hermosa Park Road." Once on the Hermosa Park dirt road, there are several intersections; just follow signs for Hermosa Park Road. 8.5 miles after leaving US-550, turn left into the northern Hermosa Creek Trailhead.

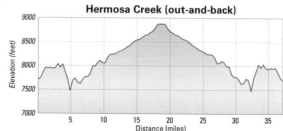

Durango

Riding Directions

These directions describe the out-and-back option. Those shuttling to the northern trailhead, must reverse these directions.

G1 - 0.0 From the Southern Hermosa Creek Trailhead, find the signed start of the Hermosa Creek Trail (#514). You will remain on the Hermosa Creek Trail for the entire ride.

G2 - 4.9 Continue straight on the Hermosa Creek Trail at the intersection with the Clear Creek Trail (#550).

G3 - 7.8 Continue straight at the intersection with the South Fork Trail (#549).

G4 - 12.2 Continue straight at the intersection with the Salt Creek Trail (#559). The trail becomes much wider (ATV accessible) from here on.

G5 - 12.9 Cross Hermosa Creek on a large wooden bridge.

G6 - 13.7 Continue straight at the intersection with the Big Bend Creek Trail (#519).

G7 - 15.6 Continue straight at the intersection with the Corral Draw Trail (#521).

G8 - 18.6 Arrive at the Upper Hermosa Creek TH. Turn around and go back!

Climbing up towards Engineer Mountain.

Durango Mountain Resort ★★★☆☆

Location:	25 miles north of Durango
Hours:	9:00 - 4:30, early June through mid-September
Price:	$15 (all day), $5 (single ride)
Vertical Relief:	1,000'
Dogs:	🚫

Description

Durango Mountain Resort (DMR) has not invested in elaborate downhill trails and fancy wooden features, which allows them to offer the cheapest mountain biking lift ticket in the state: five bucks for a single ride. Unfortunately, as of summer 2010, there were only two trails that run from the top of the lift to the bottom. The rest of the 50 miles of trails at the resort are loops that start and end at the top of the lift. Thus, the purpose of the lift is mainly to transport riders to the start of some rolling cross country trails and fire roads. Those looking for peaceful, well-signed trails will have a great time. Riders in search of lift-served descending should look elsewhere. The 1990 World Championship Course is a great ride, and buying a lift ticket lets you skip the boring uphill section and just ride the downhill section – five dollars well spent!

Driving Directions

From Durango, head north on US-550 for about 25 miles. DMR is on the left and is hard to miss due to the huge sign. Park in one of the numerous dirt parking lots near the lifts.

FEATURED RIDE

1990 WORLD'S COURSE ★★★★   Distance: 6.6 miles

This loop approximates the course that the competitors rode at the first UCI Mountain Bike World Championships back in 1990. The climb up to the top of the chairlift is mostly dirt roads, and is strenuous. However, once past the top of the chairlift, the ride back down is almost all singletrack and is very fun.

Find the start of the loop near the base of the summer chairlift. The route is very well signed, so simply follow the signs for the "1990 World's" course up to the top of the chairlift and back down. The resort is working to incorporate more singletrack into the loop, so the route will likely change slightly from year to year.

ⓘ Engineer Mountain ★★★★★

(30 miles north of Durango)

Technical Difficulty:	◆
Physical Difficulty:	**Moderate**
Distance:	12.7 miles
Time:	2.5 – 4 hours
Type:	Loop or shuttle
Surface:	Singletrack, paved road
Climbing:	3,000'
Season:	Summer, Fall
Crowds:	Few
Dogs:	🐕 *

One of the best singletrack descents in the state; short-but-sweet

Ride Description

In just eight miles of trail, this ride packs all of the best things about Colorado Mountain biking: glorious views, brilliant wildflowers, and, of course, incredible singletrack. When ridden as a loop, this ride involved about an hour of grinding up a busy highway. A better option is to bring two cars and shuttle from the lower trailhead to Coal Bank Pass and start the ride here. The shortens the ride to just 7.9 miles and reduces the climbing to 1,000 feet.

*Dogs will enjoy the singletrack, but the riding along US-550 would be dangerous. Use a car shuttle if the pooch wants to come along.

Driving Directions

From Durango, head north on US-550 for approximately 28 miles. Go past Durango Mountain Resort. Continue on the highway as it makes a big 180-degree right turn and a dirt road to Cascade Creek goes left. About 1 mile after this turn, make a left onto an unmarked dirt road. Arrive at a small grassy parking area in about 0.1 mile. (If you are shuttling, leave a car here and load the bikes and riders in the other car and follow the Riding Directions to Coal Bank Pass.)

Riding Directions

I1 - 0.0   Head back towards US-550.

I2 - 0.1   Turn left on US-550. Grind up the hill and try not to get run over by an RV.

I3 - 4.7   Arrive at the Coal Bank Pass parking area and toilets. Continue on US-550 for a few hundred feet and turn left on a gravel road, quickly arriving at a trailhead parking area. Turn right on the Pass Trail and climb steeply.

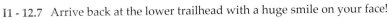

I4 - 7.3 At a three-way intersection, turn left on unmarked singletrack (the Engineer Mountain Trail). Get ready for a great downhill!

I1 - 12.7 Arrive back at the lower trailhead with a huge smile on your face!

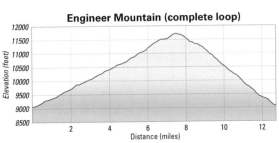

Engineer Mountain (complete loop)

(J) Canyon of the Ancients - East Rock Creek Trail ★★★★★

(15 miles west of Cortez)

Technical Difficulty:	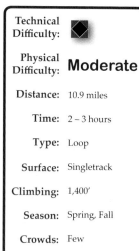
Physical Difficulty:	**Moderate**
Distance:	10.9 miles
Time:	2 – 3 hours
Type:	Loop
Surface:	Singletrack
Climbing:	1,400'
Season:	Spring, Fall
Crowds:	Few
Dogs:	🐕

Fantastic singletrack through a stunning desert landscape

Ride Description

The Canyon of the Ancients National Monument is named for the numerous ancient dwellings that are carved into the cliffs in this region. The Pueblo people had good taste in choosing a location to build their homes: this is one of the most beautiful places in Colorado. The cryptobiotic soil in the canyon is fragile and the ruins are obviously irreplaceable, so stay on signed trails and do not disturb any of the historical sites.

The East Rock Creek Trail is a ribbon of beautiful red-dirt singletrack snaking across a gorgeous desert landscape. The ride features plenty of cruising along beautiful, smooth trail but keeps things interesting with lots of rock features and a few slickrock sections. It's just like Moab, except the trail is narrow and there are few crowds. The ride can be shortened by ommitting the western Rock Canyon section, but some excellent technical riding will be missed.

Driving Directions

From Cortez, head southwest on US-160/US-491 for 2.6 miles. Turn right on County Road G and go 12.5 miles. Turn right into a slickrock parking area. There is a big, colorful sign for "Canyon of the Ancients National Monument."

Riding Directions

J1 - 0.0 Start riding straight uphill on the Sand Canyon Trail.

J2 - 0.3 Turn left on the signed East Rock Creek Trail.

J3 - 1.6 Turn right on singletrack as an old jeep road goes left.

J4 - 1.8 Continue straight as unmarked singletrack goes left.

J5 - 2.6 Bear left as a connector trail to Sand Canyon goes right.

J6 - 5.7 Turn right on the West Rock Canyon Trail (unsigned). (Continue straight to skip this section and shorten the ride.)

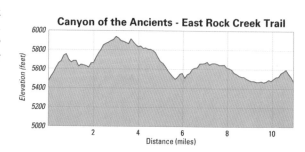

Canyon of the Ancients - East Rock Creek Trail

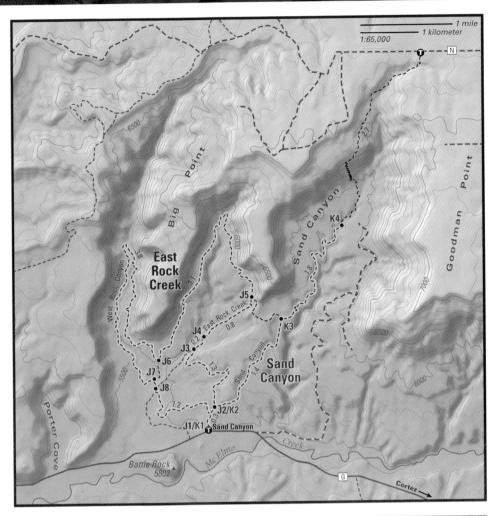

J7 - 9.5 Turn right onto the main East Rock Creek Trail.

J8 - 9.6 Arrive at an old road. Turn right and go about 100 feet. Turn left on a trail marked with a sign that reads, "Horses not recommended."

J2 - 10.8 Arrive at the intersection with the Sand Canyon Trail. Turn right and ride back to the trailhead.

(K) Sand Canyon Trail ★★★✫✫ ⬤ Distance: 7.0 miles

The Sand Canyon Trail is the main hiking and tourist trail in the Canyon of the Ancients National Monument. The trail is generally wide, but the riding is quite good. The trail can be crowded with sightseers, so be prepared to slow down. Also, budget some extra time to explore the spur trails and examine the cliff dwellings.

The complete Sand Canyon Trail is 6.4 miles long and runs from Road G to Road N. However, only the first 3.5 miles are recommended for mountain biking, as the upper section of is very technical and not nearly as enjoyable. That said, those who enjoy climbing technical boulder-strewn switchbacks, might really like this upper section.

Riding Directions

K1 - 0.0 From the trailhead, start riding straight uphill on the Sand Canyon Trail.

K2 - 0.3 At a wooden sign, turn right on the Sand Canyon Trail as the East Rock Creek Trail goes left. In the next few miles, numerous spur trails leave the main trail and lead to the ancient cliff-dwellings.

K3 - 1.7 Continue straight on the Sand Canyon Trail as a connector trail to East Rock Creek goes left.

K4 - 3.5 Come to a sign that reads, "The next mile is rocky and steep." Heed the warning and turn around (unless you are prepared for a heinous ascent).

Ancient cliff-dwellings at Canyon of the Ancients.

Next page: Dave Harris near Molas Pass, en route to Durango on the Colorado Trail.   photo: Scott Morris

(L) Phil's World ★★★★★

(3 miles east of Cortez)

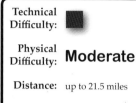

Technical Difficulty:	■
Physical Difficulty:	**Moderate**
Distance:	up to 21.5 miles
Time:	3 – 4 hours
Type:	Loop
Surface:	Singletrack
Climbing:	2,200′
Season:	Spring, Fall
Crowds:	Crowded
Dogs:	🐕 Crowded

A paradise of endless curvy singletrack

Ride Description

The riding at Phil's World is simply amazing. The winding singletrack is mellow enough for intermediate riders but great fun for experts as well. The clever arrangement of trails at Phil's World lets bikers ride for as long as they like. Riders that want the longest possible loop can simply make all the left turns. Riders who are looking for a short ride or get caught in a rainstorm can make a right turn and skip the optional loops. In order to ride Phil's World, bikers need to buy a membership with the local mountain biking club – it's some weird insurance thing. Day memberships are available at the trailhead for a few dollars. There are additional trails across the highway near the fairgrounds.

Driving Directions

From Cortez, head east on US-160 for about 2 miles until you see the fairgrounds and racetrack. Just past the gun club, make a left on a dirt road and go about 0.5 miles. Turn right into the large dirt parking lot that is probably filled with mountain bikers.

Riding Directions

(For the longest ride, make all left turns except for the "Stinky Cutoff" trail at mile 10.1.)

L1 - 0.0 From the parking lot, cross the road and find the large trailhead sign. Read the info, drop your paperwork and fee in the box, and take the left fork as indicated by the "Start" sign (the trails at Phil's World are designed to be ridden clockwise.)

L2 - 1.0 Go left on Coco Race.

L3 - 2.1 Go left on Lemonhead.

L4 - 5.6 Go left on Elbow (may not be signed).

L5 - 6.4 Go left on Abajo.

L6 - 6.9 Cross a dirt road and continue on Meditation.

L7 - 7.1 Turn left on Ledges. (Or skip this 4.7-mile loop by turning right and arriving at the end of the Ledges Loop in a few hundred feet.)

L8 - 10.1 Continue straight as Stinky Cutoff goes left. (The is the only right turn on the whole loop!)

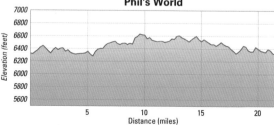

Phil's World

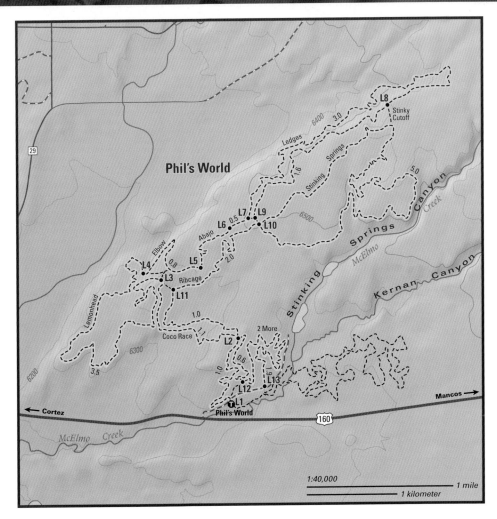

L9 - 11.7   Turn left on Ribcage.

L10 - 11.8   Turn left on Stinking Springs Loop and get ready to catch some air!

L10 - 16.8   Complete the Stinking Springs Loop and turn left on Ribcage.

L11 - 17.8   Continue left as More Ribs goes right.

L2 - 18.8   Turn left as Coco Race goes right.

L12 - 19.4   Turn left on "2 More." (If you're tired, turn right and arrive at the trailhead in about 0.2 miles).

L13 - 21.3   Turn right on the dirt road and ride back to the trailhead. (Should you desire even more riding, the singletrack continues on the other side of the road and takes you to the Trust Loop.)

(M) Boggy Draw - Boggy Loop ★★★☆☆

(15 miles northeast of Cortez)

Technical Difficulty:	
Physical Difficulty:	**Easy**
Distance:	8.4 miles
Time:	1.5 – 2.5 hours
Type:	Loop
Surface:	Singletrack
Climbing:	350′
Season:	Fall, Summer, Spring
Crowds:	Some
Dogs:	

Gentle singletrack though the forest with plenty of options for longer rides

Ride Description

When it's too hot to ride Phil's World and Sand Canyon, those looking for a nice loop ride near Cortez should head up into the hills to Boggy Draw. The singletrack here is generally smooth and fun, but can be muddy in the early season. The Boggy Loop Trail is the easiest loop in the Boggy Draw area, and riders searching for more challenge and more mileage can tackle the Bean Canyon Loop, Mavericks Loop (see next page), and the Italian Canyon Loop. By riding all of these loops, one could easily construct a great epic ride of about 25 miles.

Driving Directions

From Cortez, head east on Main Street until you near the edge of town. Turn left on CO-145 towards Dolores and go about 10 miles. As CO-145 passes through Dolores, turn left on 11th Street (County-31) and go 2.3 miles. Turn right on County Road W and go 1.0 miles to reach the trailhead parking.

Riding Directions

M1 - 0.0   From the trailhead, start riding north on the signed Boggy Draw Trail. Continue following the singletrack as it crosses several roads.

M2 - 0.7   Continue straight as an unmarked trail (the Bean Canyon Loop) goes left.

M3 - 1.7   Continue straight as Bean Canyon Loop comes in on the left.

M4 - 2.0   A tricky turn! Go right at an unmarked Y-junction. Note: there are several additional turns as the trail crosses old dirt roads, but they are well signed.

M5 - 7.8   Continue straight as Maverick's Trail goes left.

M6 - 8.2   Turn left on the gravel road (County Road W) and follow this for 0.2 miles back to the trailhead.

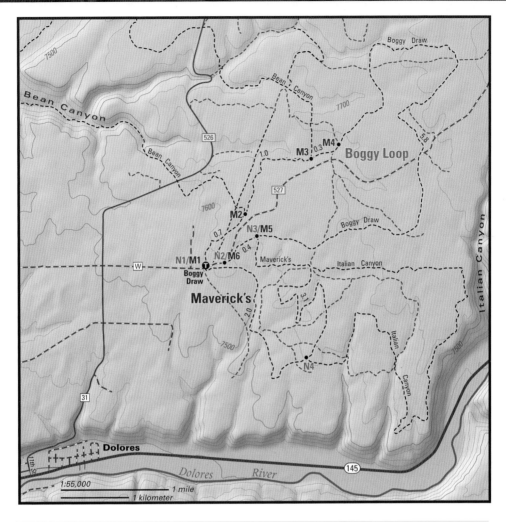

(N) Maverick's Trail ★★★⯪☆ ● Distance: 5.7 miles

Maverick's is a lovely meander through the woods and is similar to the Boggy Loop, but it is slightly more technical.

Riding Directions

N1 - 0.0 From the parking lot, continue east on County Road W.

N2 - 0.2 Turn right on the Boggy Draw singletrack.

N3 - 0.6 Turn right on the signed Maverick's Trail.

N4 - 3.7 Continue on Maverick's Trail as Italian Canyon Trail goes left.

N1 - 5.7 The singletrack ends at a dirt road. Make two quick right turns and arrive back at the parking lot in 200 ft.

Durango

BONUS RIDES

Durango

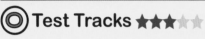 Test Tracks ★★★☆☆ to

"Test Tracks" is the name given to the trails located on the west side of Durango, right on the edge of town. There is some good riding tucked into these hills, with some trails meandering through the woods and others climbing steeply along ridges. The trails are not well signed, and there are many intersections. There are a dozen ways to access the Test Tracks: basically you just park somewhere in downtown Durango and head west, across the Animas River. There is trail access at the end of many streets in west Durango: Crestview, Montvivew, Layden, Valentine, and several others. These access points are on quiet residential streets, so don't use them as trailheads: the homeowners don't want to see you changing into your lycra shorts.

Cortez

 Stoner Mesa ★★☆☆☆   Distance: 26.9 miles

The Stoner Mesa Trail is a great piece of singletrack through aspen forests, and it is almost entirely downhill. Unfortunately, the land is home to large herds of cows, and not just any cows, but zombie-cows. While most cows tend to avoid mountain bikers, these zombie-cows try to chase anyone unfortunate enough to encounter them. To make matters worse, zombie-cows hate nice singletrack and make it their mission to turn it into a pit of mud. During August of 2010, the trail was nearly unrideable. However, in future years, it is possible that normal cows will displace the zombie-cows and the trail will become a cycling delight once more. Inquire about conditions at Kokopelli Bike and Board in Cortez, or at one of the many bike shops in Durango.

To reach the Stoner Mesa Trailhead from Cortez, head north on CO-145 and reach Dolores in about 10 miles. Continue about 12 miles past Dolores and turn left on County-38. After 3.4 miles, turn right into the Lower Stoner Mesa Trailhead and park here. From the trailhead, ride up County-38 for 8.1 miles. Turn right on Stoner Mesa road and ride 7.2 miles. Turn right on the Stoner Mesa Trail singletrack and follow this for 11.4 miles back to the trailhead.

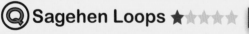 Sagehen Loops ★☆☆☆☆

Located about 15 miles north of Cortez on the shore of McPhee Reservoir, these once-popular trails have faded into a confusing network of cattle paths. In the spring of 2010, these trails were impossible to follow, but it's likely that some trail maintenance will make these trails great once again. To reach the Sagehen Loops from Cortez, head north on US-491 for about 10 miles, turn right on CO-184, left on County-25, and right on County Road X. Look for a small parking area on the left after about 1 mile.

Raindrops on roses and whiskers on kittens,
bright copper kettles and warm woolen mittens,
brown paper packages tied up with strings –
these are few of my

Favorite Rides

15. Colorado Springs – Falcon Trail

14. Pueblo – Pueblo Reservoir

13. Grand Junction – Tabeguache

12. Summit County – Keystone Gulch to Aqueduct Loop

11. Crested Butte – Doctor Park

10. Salida – Fooses–Green Loop

9. Crested Butte – Taylor Pass and Star Passes

8. Fruita – Rabbit Valley – Western Rim

7. Aspen – Snowmass – The Rim Trail

6. Telluride – Prospect Trail

5. Leadville – Colorado Trail near Mount Elbert

4. Summit County – The Copper Triangle

3. Cortez – Canyon of the Ancients – East Rock Creek

2. Denver – Buffalo Creek – The New Classic

1. Cortez – Phil's World

ⓇThe Colorado Trail ★★★★★

(10 miles southwest of Denver)

Technical Difficulty:	◆◆
Physical Difficulty:	**Insanely Strenuous**
Distance:	485 miles
Time:	1 – 2 weeks
Type:	Shuttle
Surface:	Singletrack, dirt road, paved road
Climbing/ Descending:	66,200'/66,700' (one-way)
Season:	Summer
Crowds:	Some
Dogs:	🚫 miles of highway riding

An epic adventure from Denver to Durango

Ride Description

The Colorado trail is a 485-mile long singletrack trail that stretches from Denver to Durango, and it can be a life-changing experience if you let it! The mountain bike version detours Wilderness Areas, where mechanized travel is off-limits, and can be done any number of ways: from weekend warrior-ing it a couple segments at a time, to a supported thru-ride with a vehicle, to bikepacking it unsupported in a single push. Because the wilderness detours pass through several towns where food resupply and motels abound, the Colorado Trail is particularly well suited for a bikepacking adventure of epic proportions. In fact, the route described here has been traversed solo and self-supported in an astonishing 4 days and 3 hours by Owen Murphy of Nederland in 2009.

With over 300 miles of singletrack – hardly any of which is flat – you will encounter nearly every style of riding imaginable: loads of swoopy fast trail, many rocky, rooty, technical climbs and descents, miles of pine-needle covered singletrack, some nearly unrideable talus, and a prodigious amount of hike-a-bike. The route averages over 10,000' in elevation, so you will also spend an immense amount of time at altitude. In fact, the section from Spring Creek Pass to Stony Pass road spends almost 30 consecutive miles above timberline! This piece of trail is a beautiful and amazing place to be on a gorgeous day, but it can also be extremely dangerous and scary if you are caught there in one of Colorado's notorious afternoon thunderstorms.

Riding Directions

The Colorado Trail begins in Denver at Waterton Canyon (see page 102). From Denver to Breckenridge, the trail is characterized by fast and buff singletrack, with the exception being the descent from Georgia Pass, which is rocky and rooty. After crossing CO-9 north of Breckenridge, the 12 miles leading to Copper Mountain are brutal and take second place in the bumpiest-and-rockiest category of the entire trail. A steep hike-a-bike is well rewarded by tremendous views, and a white-knuckle descent into Copper. More delicious singletrack, leads up to Searle Pass and some absolutely exquisite alpine meadow riding over to Kokomo Pass. From there, hold on for a fast and loose descent to Camp Hale followed by very enjoyable riding up to Tennessee Pass and on to Wurtz Ditch Road.

The route then detours through Leadville on dirt and paved roads, and regains the Colorado Trail at the Mount Massive trailhead. A steep (and sometimes crowded) climb on the Mt. Elbert trail leads to fast blasting through the aspens for many miles to Twin Lakes Reservoir and beyond to the next Wilder-

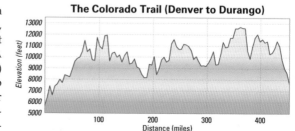

The Colorado Trail (Denver to Durango)

Durango

ness detour at Clear Creek Road. Easy pedaling through Buena Vista and up the pavement to the Avalanche trailhead ends abruptly with a fun technical descent and then some steep climbing and crazy-fast descending to Princeton Hot Springs. The trail beyond Chalk Creek is quintessential Collegiate Peak aspen groves and rounded granite mini-boulders, which have been affectionately dubbed "adult-heads" instead of "baby-heads."

After crossing US-50, the trail ascends gradually steepening roads and singletrack to a final gnarly hike-a-bike that joins the famous Monarch Crest trail on the Continental Divide. Once past Marshall Pass and onto Sargents Mesa, the trail really starts to feel isolated. Some of these sections easily take first place in the bumpy-rocky-bone-jarring-teeth-shattering category, and have even been described as "soul crushing." Fortunately, there is a lot of great forest riding interspersed throughout this area as well.

At Saguache Park road, the longest Wilderness detour is encountered and follows dirt roads for over 50 miles. At the pavement of CO-149, you will be tempted to descend into Lake City, but then you'd miss the Crown Jewel of the Colorado Trail: the Coney Summit and Cataract Ridge segments! These sections consist of incredible high-alpine riding and off-the-charts views in one of the most remote areas of Colorado. Start early, and pick a nice day. Even very strong riders can take upwards of 10 hours to complete the 40 miles from Spring Creek Pass into Silverton.

The route culminates with arguably the best continuous singletrack in the state as the route traverses the San Juan Mountains for over 75 miles from Silverton to Durango. Alpine ridges, wildflowers as far as you can see, gorgeous forested trail, and an insane descent from 12,000' to 7,000' – you'll still be smiling 20 years after riding this part of the Colorado Trail!

For the most part, the trail is very well marked, however, the Colorado Trail Foundation publishes a pocket-sized "Trailside Databook" that contains elevation profiles and mileages, as well as camping and water info that can be quite handy for any extended trip down the trail. While you're at it, donate some time or money to the Colorado Trail Foundation – without them, we wouldn't have this world class route to ride!

Hungry yet? Well, what are you waiting for?!

– *By Stefan Griebel*

Ride	Technical Difficulty	Physical Difficulty	Stars	Distance (miles)	Dogs	Location	Page Number
2 - FORT COLLINS							**20**
Bobcat Ridge	◆◆	Very Strenuous	4	9.7	🚫	15 mi SW of Ft Collins	22
Devil's Backbone	◈	Moderate	3.5	11.6	🚫	15 mi SW of Ft Collins	24
Blue Sky Trail	◉	Moderate	3	9.6	🚫	7 mi W of Ft Collins	26
Horsetooth Mtn Park	◈	Strenuous	3.5	9.2	🚫	8 mi W of Ft Collins	28
Lory State Park	◆	Strenuous	3.5	9.2	🚫	10 mi NW of Ft Collins	30
Foothills Trail	◆	Moderate	3.5	up to 11.0	🚫	3 mi W of Ft Collins	32
Youngs Gulch	◈	Moderate	3	9.4	🐕	20 mi NW of Ft Collins	34
Soapstone Prairie	◉	Moderate	3.5	21.6	🚫	30 mi N of Ft Collins	36
3 - BOULDER							**40**
S. Boulder Trails	◉	Moderate	2.5	up to 20.0	🐕	3 mi S of Boulder	44
Dirty Bismark	●	Easy	2	15.0	🚫	3 mi S of Boulder	46
E. Boulder Trail	●	Easy	1.5	12.0	🚫	5 mi E of Boulder	48
Foothills Trail	●	Easy	2	5.2	🐕	Starts in Boulder	50
Boulder Valley Ranch	○	Easy	2	up to 8.5	🐕	4 mi N of Boulder	52
Betasso Preserve	■	Moderate	3	3.1	🚫	6 mi W of Boulder	54
Switzerland Trail	●	Moderate	2	17.6	🐕	10 mi W of Boulder	56
Walker Ranch	◈	Strenuous	3.5	7.1	🚫	8 mi SW of Boulder	58
Heil Ranch	■	Moderate	2.5	9.3	🚫	10 mi N of Boulder	60
Picture Rock Trail	■	Moderate	3	10.0	🚫	1 mi SW of Lyons	63
Hall Ranch	◆	Strenuous	3.5	9.6	🚫	2 mi SW of Lyons	64
Antelope Trail	■	Moderate	3	7.6	🚫	1 mi NW of Lyons	65
Rabbit Mountain	■	Moderate	2	5.9	🚫	6 mi NE of Lyons	66
Ceran St Vrain	■	Moderate	3	6.1	🐕	20 mi N of Boulder	68

Ride	Technical Difficulty	Physical Difficulty	Stars	Distance (miles)	Dogs	Location	Page Number
West Magnolia	■	Easy	3.5	6.0	🐕	2 mi S of Nederland	70
East Magnolia	◆	Strenuous	4	11.1	🐕	2 mi S of Nederland	72
Mud Lake O.S.	●	Easy	2	2.1	🚫🐕	2 mi N of Nederland	73
Sourdough Trail	◆	Strenuous	3	11.4	🐕	7 mi N of Nederland	74
South St Vrain	◆	Very Strenuous	2.5	7.6	🐕	14 mi N of Nederland	76
4 - DENVER and GOLDEN							**78**
Golden Gate S.P.	◆	Strenuous	4	8.9	🐕	16 mi NW of Golden	80
White Ranch	◆	Very Strenuous	4	10.3	🚫🐕	3 mi NW of Golden	82
Centennial Cone	◉	Moderate	3.5	13.4	🚫🐕	14 mi W of Golden	84
Apex Park	◆	Moderate	3.5	5.5	🚫🐕	3 mi S of Golden	86
Chimney Gulch	◈	Strenuous	3	7.0	🚫🐕	1 mi W of Golden	88
Dakota Ridge	◆	Strenuous	3.5	6.1	🚫🐕	5 mi S of Golden	90
Green Mountain	◉	Moderate	2.5	6.9	🚫🐕	5 mi S of Golden	92
Mount Falcon	◈	Strenuous	3	9.2	🚫🐕	10 mi SW of Denver	94
Lair o' the Bear	■	Moderate	2	11.8	🐕	10 mi SW of Denver	96
Bergen Peak	◆	Strenuous	3	10.0	🚫🐕	15 mi W of Denver	98
Three Sisters Park	◈	Strenuous	3	7.1	🚫🐕	10 mi SW of Denver	100
Waterton Canyon	■	Moderate	3	17.3	🚫🐕	10 mi SW of Denver	102
Deer Creek	◈	Strenuous	3.5	7.3	🚫🐕	15 mi SW of Denver	104
Meyer Ranch	■	Moderate	2	4.0	🚫🐕	15 mi W of Denver	106
Buffalo Creek	■	Moderate	4.5	14.8	🐕	40 mi SW of Denver	108
The New Classic	■	Moderate	4.5	25.0	🐕	40 mi SW of Denver	110
CO Trail East	■	Moderate	4	up to 14.0	🐕	40 mi SW of Denver	110
Black Diamond Trail	◆◆	Very Strenuous	5	2.4	🐕	40 mi SW of Denver	110

Ride	Technical Difficulty	Physical Difficulty	Stars	Distance (miles)	Dogs	Location	Page Number
Kenosha to LCW	■	Moderate	4.5	13.6	🐕	50 mi SW of Denver	112
Kenosha Pass	◆	Strenuous	5	22.5	🐕	50 mi SW of Denver	114
Gold Dust Trail	◆	Moderate	4.5	9.0	🐕	70 mi SW of Denver	116

5 - COLORADO SPRINGS and PUEBLO — 118

Ride	Technical Difficulty	Physical Difficulty	Stars	Distance (miles)	Dogs	Location	Page Number
Falcon Trail	◉	Moderate	3.5	12.4	🚫🐕	15 mi N of CO Springs	120
Rampart Reservoir	◉	Easy	4	14.4	🐕	30 mi NW of CO Springs	122
Lovell Gulch	◉	Moderate	3	5.5	🐕	20 mi NW of CO Springs	124
Templeton Trail	◆◆	Strenuous	3.5	3.5	🐕	Starts in CO Springs	126
Garden of the Gods	◉	Easy	2	3.2	🚫🐕	5 mi NW of CO Springs	128
Barr Trail	◆◆	Insanely Strenuous	3	12.6	🚫🐕	7 mi W of CO Springs	130
Section 16	◆	Moderate	4	5.8	🚫🐕	4 mi W of CO Springs	132
Paul Intemann Trail	◆	Strenuous	3	1.7	🚫🐕	4 mi W of CO Springs	133
Captain Jack's	◼	Moderate	3.5	6.9	🐕	6 mi from CO Springs	135
Jones Park	◆	Strenuous	4	26.1	🐕	5 mi W of CO Springs	137
Pueblo Reservoir	● to ◆	Generally Moderate	5	up to 40.0	🐕	8 mi W of Pueblo	140

6 - WINTER PARK — 143

Ride	Technical Difficulty	Physical Difficulty	Stars	Distance (miles)	Dogs	Location	Page Number
Tipperary Creek	■	Moderate	4	13.2	🐕	5 mi NW of Winter Park	145
Creekside Loop	●	Easy	3.5	3.4	🐕	5 mi NW of Winter Park	146
Chainsaw-Flume	◉	Moderate	4	8.6	🐕	4 mi W of Winter Park	147
WTB Loop	■	Moderate	3	7.2	🐕	Starts in Winter Park	148
Idlewild Loop	■	Easy	3.5	9.3	🐕	Starts in Fraser	152
Strawberry	■	Moderate	3.5	13.8	🐕	10 mi N of Winter Park	154
Trestle Bike Park	● to ◆X	Easy to Strenuous	5	many	🚫🐕	Starts at Winter Park Resort	157
Sol Vista Resort	● to ◆X	Easy to Strenuous	5	many	🚫🐕	20 mi N of Winter Park	158

Ride	Technical Difficulty	Physical Difficulty	Stars	Distance (miles)	Dogs	Location	Page Number
7 - SUMMIT COUNTY and VAIL							**160**
Keystone Resort	● to ◆◆EX	Easy to Strenuous	4.5	many	🐕 (no)	6 mi SE of Dillon	163
Keystone Gulch	■	Moderate	5	17.5	🐕	Starts in Keystone	164
CO Trail - Tiger Rd	■	Moderate	4.5	23.8	🐕	4 mi N of Breckenridge	166
Peaks Trail	◆	Moderate	4	17.4	🐕	Starts in Frisco	168
Breck Resort	● to ◆◆	Easy to Strenuous	3	many	🐕 (no)	Starts in Breckenridge	170
Pioneer to Game	■	Moderate	3.5	6.6	🐕	Starts in Breckenridge	171
Flume Loop	◎	Moderate	4	6.0	🐕	1 mi N of Breckenridge	172
Bakers Tank	■	Easy	4	5.7	🐕	3 mi SE of Breckenridge	174
Tenmile Traverse	◆◆	Insanely Strenuous	4.5	24.4	🐕	4 mi N of Breckenridge	176
CO Trail to Searle	◆	Strenuous	4.5	15.8	🐕	Starts in Copper Mountain	178
Copper Rectangle	◆	Strenuous	5	32.8	🐕	Starts in Copper Mountain	180
Son of Middle	◆	Moderate	4	8.6	🐕	Starts in Vail	181
North Trail	■	Moderate	4	10.0	🐕 (no)	Starts in Vail	182
Cougar Ridge	◆	Moderate	4	13.6	🐕 (no)	Starts in Vail	184
Grand Traverse	■	Moderate	4	6.9	🐕 (no)	Starts in Vail	185
Whiskey Creek	◆	Strenuous	4	12.7	🐕	6 mi W of Vail	186
Vail Resort	● to ◆◆EX	Easy to Strenuous	3	many	🐕 (no)	Starts in Vail	187
Two Elk Trail	◆	Moderate	5	15.8	🐕	15 mi SE of Vail	188
8 - LEADVILLE and SALIDA							**191**
CO Trail - C. Hale	■	Moderate	4	13.8	🐕	17 mi N of Leadville	194
Hagerman Pass	◎	Moderate	3.5	up to 24.4	🐕	4 mi W of Leadville	196
Turquoise Lake	■	Easy	4	12.2	🐕	4 mi W of Leadville	198
Twin Lakes	◎	Easy	3	9.2	🐕	17 mi W of Leadville	199

Ride	Technical Difficulty	Physical Difficulty	Stars	Distance (miles)	Dogs	Location	Page Number
CO Trail - Mt Elbert	◆ (black diamond)	Strenuous	4.5	14.6	yes	20 mi SW of Leadville	201
CO Trail - Cttnwd	◆ (black diamond)	Moderate	4	19.8	yes	9 mi W of Buena Vista	202
Salida Mtn Trails	● to ◆ (Easy to difficult)	Easy to Strenuous	3.5	up to 20.0	yes	Starts in Downtown Salida	204
Rainbow Trail	■ (blue square)	Easy	4	10.8	yes	8 mi SE of Salida	206
CO Trail - Shavano	◆◆ (double black diamond)	Very Strenuous	4	up to 29.0	yes	15 mi NW of Salida	208
Fooses-Green Loop	◆ (black diamond)	Very Strenuous	5	25.1	yes	15 mi W of Salida	210
Monarch Crest	◆ (black diamond)	Moderate	5	34.7	yes	20 mi W of Salida	214
Canyon Creek	◆ (black diamond)	Insanely Strenuous	3.5	19.1	yes	40 mi W of Salida	216

9 - SAN LUIS VALLEY — 218

Ride	Technical Difficulty	Physical Difficulty	Stars	Distance (miles)	Dogs	Location	Page Number
Penitente Canyon	■ (blue square)	Easy	3.5	5.3	yes	25 mi NW of Monte Vista	220
Cumbres & Toltec	● (green circle)	Easy	2.5	17.7	yes	30 mi S of Alamosa	222
Cat Creek	◆ (black diamond)	Strenuous	4	13.2	yes	30 mi W of Alamosa	224
Alder Bench	◆ (black diamond)	Very Strenuous	4	up to 13.0	yes	4 mi N of South Fork	226
Trout Creek	◆ (black diamond)	Strenuous	3	up to 18.0	yes	3 mi SW of South Fork	228

10 - CRESTED BUTTE and GUNNISON — 230

Ride	Technical Difficulty	Physical Difficulty	Stars	Distance (miles)	Dogs	Location	Page Number
The 401	◆ (black diamond)	Strenuous	4.5	13.5	yes	8 mi N of Crested Butte	234
Dyke Trail	◆ (black diamond)	Strenuous	4.5	13.8	yes	7 mi W of Crested Butte	236
Lower Loop	● (green circle)	Easy	3.5	7.8	yes	Starts in Crested Butte	238
Snodgrass Trail	■ (blue square)	Moderate	4	7.0	yes	4 mi N of Crested Butte	240
Upper Loop	◆ (black diamond)	Moderate	4	11.3	yes	Starts in Crested Butte	242
Teocalli Ridge	◆◆ (double black diamond)	Strenuous	4	10.4	yes	7 mi NE of Crested Butte	244
C.B. Resort	● to ◆X (Easy to extreme)	Easy to Strenuous	4	many	no	3 mi N of Crested Butte	245
Deer Creek Trail	◆ (black diamond)	Strenuous	5	26.7	yes	Starts in Crested Butte	246
Pearl Pass	◆◆ (double black diamond)	Insanely Strenuous	4	37.7	yes	Starts in Crested Butte	248

Ride	Technical Difficulty	Physical Difficulty	Stars	Distance (miles)	Dogs	Location	Page Number
Star & Taylor Pass	◆	Insanely Strenuous	4.5	38.8	🐕	Starts in Aspen	251
Reno-Flag-Bear	◆	Strenuous	4	13.2	🐕	14 mi SE of Crested Butte	252
Doctor Park	◆	Strenuous	5	21.1	🐕	25 mi SE of Crested Butte	254
Hartman Rocks	■	Moderate	3.5	8.9	🐕	4 mi SW of Gunnison	256
11 - ASPEN and the ROARING FORK VALLEY							**259**
Sunnyside Loop	◆	Strenuous	4.5	16.0	🚫🐕	Starts in Aspen	261
Snowmass Resort	● to ◆	Easy to Strenuous	4	many	🚫🐕	Starts in Snowmass Village	262
Rim Trail	■	Strenuous	5	10.3	🚫🐕	Starts in Snowmass Village	264
Snowmass - XC	◆/■	Moderate	5	11.8	🚫🐕	Starts in Snowmass Village	266
Government Trail	◆	Strenuous	4.5	22.0	🚫🐕	Starts in Snowmass Village	268
Cattle Creek Trail	◆	Moderate	4	15.1	🐕	15 mi NE of Carbondale	270
Hay Park	◆/■	Strenuous	4	18.6	🐕	10 mi SE of Carbondale	272
Scout Trail	◆/■	Strenuous	3	17.9	🐕	Starts in Glenwood Springs	274
12 - STEAMBOAT SPRINGS							**276**
Coulton Creek	◆	Strenuous	2	9.1	🐕	24 mi N of Steamboat	278
S. Fork of the Elk	■	Moderate	4	9.8	🐕	25 mi N of Steamboat	279
Scott's Run	◆	Strenuous	4	14.6	🐕	28 mi N of Steamboat	280
Mad Creek	■	Moderate	3	7.5	🐕	7 mi of Steamboat	282
Red Dirt Trail	◆	Moderate	4	6.1	🐕	7 mi N of Steamboat	283
Hot Springs Trail	◆	Strenuous	2	6.6	🐕	7 mi N of Steamboat	284
Emerald Mtn	■	Strenuous	3	4.8	🚫🐕	Starts in Steamboat	286
Spring Creek	■	Moderate	3	10.2	🚫🐕	Starts in Steamboat	289
Wyoming Trail	■	Moderate	4	15.2	🐕	13 mi E of Steamboat	290
Rabbit Ears Pass	■	Moderate	5	31.6	🐕	22 mi E of Steamboat	292

Ride	Technical Difficulty	Physical Difficulty	Stars	Distance (miles)	Dogs	Location	Page Number
Muddy Slide	◆	Strenuous	2.5	19.4	🐕	50 mi SE of Steamboat	294
Rock Creek	■	Moderate	4	16.4	🐕	51 mi SE of Steamboat	296

13 - GRAND JUNCTION and FRUITA   298

Ride	Technical Difficulty	Physical Difficulty	Stars	Distance (miles)	Dogs	Location	Page Number
Palisade Rim	◆	Moderate	3	12.2	🐕	15 mi E of Grand Junction	302
Tabeguache	● to EX	Generally Moderate	5	up to 30.0	🐕	4 mi W of Grand Junction	304
The Bookcliffs	■ to ◆	Moderate to Strenuous	5	up to 40.0	🐕	11 mi N of Fruita	308
Edge Loop	◆	Strenuous	4	14.6	🐕	11 mi N of Fruita	310
Kokopelli's	● to ◆◆	Generally Strenuous	5	up to 50.0	🐕	15 mi W of Fruita	313
Highline Lake S.P.	◻	Moderate	3.5	6.6	🚫🐕	12 mi NW of Fruita	316
Western Rim	◆	Moderate	4	15.9	🐕	25 mi W of Grand Junction	318
3-4 Loop	■	Moderate	3.5	5.4	🐕	25 mi W of Grand Junction	320
The Rim Trail	◆	Very Strenuous	2	7.7	🐕	25 mi W of Grand Junction	320

14 - TELLURIDE   322

Ride	Technical Difficulty	Physical Difficulty	Stars	Distance (miles)	Dogs	Location	Page Number
Gondola Trails	● to ◆	Easy to Moderate	4.5	many	🐕	Starts in Telluride	324
Eider-Deep Loop	◆	Strenuous	4	9.3	🐕	Starts in Telluride	326
Galloping Goose	●	Easy	3	13.6	🚫🐕	Starts in Telluride	328

15 - DURANGO   330

Ride	Technical Difficulty	Physical Difficulty	Stars	Distance (miles)	Dogs	Location	Page Number
Horse Gulch	◻	Moderate	3	4.0	🐕	Starts in Durango	333
Raider Ridge	◆◆	Very Strenuous	4	4.0	🐕	Starts in Durango	334
Telegraph - Sale Barn	■	Moderate	3.5	7.8	🐕	3 mi S of Durango	335
Animas Mtn	◆	Strenuous	3	5.5	🐕	Starts in Durango	336
CO Trail - Dry Fork	◆	Strenuous	4	12.5	🐕	5 mi NW of Durango	338
Haflin Creek	◆◆	Insanely Strenuous	2	7.4	🐕	10 mi NE of Durango	340
Hermosa Creek	■	Moderate	4	18.6	🐕	15 mi N of Durango	342

Ride	Technical Difficulty	Physical Difficulty	Stars	Distance (miles)	Dogs	Location	Page Number
Durango Resort	● to ◆	Easy to Strenuous	3	many	(no dog)	25 mi N of Durango	345
Engineer Mtn	◆	Moderate	5	12.7	dog	30 mi N of Durango	346
Canyon of Ancients	◆	Moderate	5	10.9	dog	15 mi W of Cortez	348
Sand Canyon Trail	○	Moderate	3.5	7.0	dog	15 mi W of Cortez	350
Phil's World	■	Moderate	5	21.5	dog	3 mi E of Cortez	352
Boggy Draw	●	Easy	3.5	8.4	dog	15 mi NE of Cortez	354
Maverick's Trail	●	Easy	3.5	5.7	dog	15 mi NE of Cortez	355
Test Tracks	● to ◆	Easy to Strenuous	3	many	(no dog)	Starts in Durango	356
Stoner Mesa	◆	Moderate	2	26.9	dog	30 mi NE of Cortez	356
Sagehen Loops	■	Moderate	1	?	dog	15 mi N of Cortez	356
Colorado Trail	◆◆	Insanely Strenuous	5	485	(no dog)	10 mi SW of Denver	358

About the Author

Dan Hickstein has been crashing bicycles since he was a small child. When he's not riding trails, he enjoys rock climbing, skiing, hiking, and science research. In preparation for writing guidebooks, he earned a Bachelor's degree in chemistry from Pomona College and a Masters in physics from the University of Cambridge. He is currently a Ph.D. student at the University of Colorado at Boulder where he is developing new and novel methods for attaching lasers to sharks.

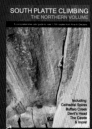